The Rowell Family of New England and Their English Origins 1560–1900

Descendants
of
Thomas Rowell
1594–1662

William Haslet Jones

HERITAGE BOOKS
2019

HERITAGE BOOKS

AN IMPRINT OF HERITAGE BOOKS, INC.

Books, CDs, and more—Worldwide

For our listing of thousands of titles see our website
at
www.HeritageBooks.com

Published 2019 by
HERITAGE BOOKS, INC.
Publishing Division
5810 Ruatan Street
Berwyn Heights, Md. 20740

Heritage Books by the author:

CD: *Genealogies, Volume 6: The William Haslet Jones Collection*

*Philip Towle, Hampton, New Hampshire: His English Origins
and Some American Descendants*

*The Rowell Family of New England and Their English Origins, 1560–1900:
Descendants of Thomas Rowell 1594–1662*

Vital Statistics of Chichester, New Hampshire, 1742–1927

Vital Statistics of Epsom, New Hampshire, 1727–1927

Vital Statistics of Seabrook, New Hampshire, 1768–1903

William Tilton: His English Origins and Some American Descendants

*Winkley Family: The English Origin of Captain Samuel Winkley
and Some New England Descendants*

International Standard Book Numbers
Paperbound: 978-0-7884-0421-4
Clothbound: 978-0-7884-8943-3

ROWELL FAMILY

TABLE OF CONTENTS

ROWELL FAMILY

TABLE OF CONTENTS, CONT.

INTRODUCTION

The English origin of the Rowell Family was
first published, by the author, in the New
England Historic Genealogical Register in April
1984 [v.138, p. 128-9] The home of THOMAS ROWELL
and his son VALENTINE ROWELL, original
proprietors of Salisbury, Mass., was traced to
Atherstone, County Warwickshire, England.
Additional research since then has added to what
was first reported.

PART 1 presents the ROWELL family and related
HAMPTON family genealogical findings in County
Warwickshire, England from 1560 to 1700. Parish
registers, probate court records and Manorial
rolls are presented.

The earliest Rowell identified was **VALENTINE
ROWELL** father of the immigrant. Where he was
born is unknown. Perhaps he came from adjacent
County Leicestershire. Rowell entries in the
Mancetter parish register start with the
marriage of Valentine Rowell to Margaret Hampton
in 1591 and continue up to 1700.

The name of ROWELL is quite ancient. Several
entries as early as the 14th century are found.
The earliest being 1309. Since half of all
English surnames are taken from localities, it
would be logical to search for a village named
Rowell. A small village named ROWELL or ROEL, as
spelled today, exists in County Gloucestershire.
It is thought to be the origin of the name.

PART 2 presents the ROWELL family records in New
England from 1638 to 1900. It is a summation of
information taken from all known sources on the
Rowell family. This pioneer family has been
researched by a number of authors over the last
100 years. The tireless effort by those earlier
Rowell Family researchers is gratefully
acknowledged and appreciated by the author.

The Rowell Family information comes primarily
from the following sources:

Proposed Rowell Genealogy, by George P. Rowell, Stamford, Conn. (1919); A Register of Rowells, by Melvin Rowell, Northwoods Narrows, N.H., (1956); 2nd Edition, (1957) and Supplement to the Register of Rowells, Concord, N.H. (1959); Biographical Sketch of Samuel Rowell, by Roland Rowell, Manchester, N.H. (1898); A Genealogy of the Rowell & Allied Families, by Henry K, Kilburn, (1898) and the Thomas Rowell Family Assoc. Records, (1975). Many other sources were examined, include the Morman I.G.I., vital records of numerous New England towns, Revolutionary War papers, Pension records, and private manuscripts at New England libraries.

At least two apparently unrelated Rowell families appear in New England records. One was ENOS ROWELL [b. c1750] of Piermont, N.H. The other was THOMAS ROWELL [b. c1650] of Hartford, Conn. What information was found on these two families is summarized in the APPENDIX.

In North and South Carolina a large ROWELL group appears before the Revolutionary War. This family was studied by the author. Their use of such common names as Valentine, Thomas, etc. would seem to indicate a probable connection with the ROWELLS of New England. See APPENDIX.

Regretfully quite a number of ROWELL names were found that could not be associated with any of the early known families. Some times the name of POWELL and ROWELL were used interchangeably, which added to the confusion. Female marriages were difficult to connect up with their parents. This was especially true in records in Maine.

Quite likely there are errors and omissions in some of the sources used to compile this book. The author has made every attempt possible to cross check and to verify all names and dates. But some information could not be fully verified. While in some cases names were spelled

INTRODUCTION Cont.

more than one way. All variations in names and
dates that I found have been included.

   This book is dedicated to my Great Grandmother
ANN BRAY ROWELL of Epsom, N.H. the wife of
DANIEL T. YEATON. [Ref. #2007]

                        William Haslet Jones
                        Villa Park, Illinois

MAP OF ENGLAND

Liverpool

Atherstone

Mancetter

Coventry

Roel

London

Bristol

Location of the parish of Mancetter,
County Warwickshire, and Roel County
Gloucestershire, England.

PART 1

ROWELL FAMILY – ENGLAND

1560 – 1700

ROWELL FAMILY - ENGLAND

The name of **THOMAS ROWELL** and his son **VALENTINE ROWELL** are found among the original proprietors of Salisbury, Mass. in 1638. During a visit to England in 1982, I was able to locate their English home. It was the village of Atherstone, County Warwickshire. Atherstone is approximately ten miles north of the city of Coventry, England. It sits astride the old Roman road known as Watling Street. Atherstone is in the parish of Mancetter. The parish registers go back to 1563, but are quite incomplete during the early years. Several pages are missing at the beginning of the 17th century.

ROWELL FAMILY

1. **VALENTINE ROWELL.** Atherstone. He was born about 1565 - 1570, probably in County Warwickshire, England. He was buried at Mancetter on 13 Sept. 1613. He married at Mancetter, 12 Jan. 1591/2 **ELIZABETH HAMPTON**. She was probably the daughter of **JOHN and ELIZABETH HAMPTON** of Atherstone. **JOHN HAMPTON** was a baker there. See HAMPTON FAMILY section for further information on her ancestral line.

ELIZABETH, the wife of **VALENTINE ROWELL**, was the mother of seven known children. She was buried at Atherstone on 14 February 1647/8. At the time of **VALENTINE ROWELL**'s death his estate was valued at £23..9..6. Apparently he left no will, but a court record of the administration of his estate survives as does the inventory of his property. A translation of the Latin text of the court record follows. The original of both documents is at the Lichfield Record Office, Lichfield, England. See the APPENDIX for copy of the originals.

At the Lichfield Court the 20th day of October in the year 1613 Amen. Administration of the estate of Valentine Rowell deceased, who lived in Atherston. Elizabeth his widow was given the sworn oath, etc.

- 1 -

ROWELL FAMILY - ENGLAND

A trust was established to provide for the children, Thomas Rowell, William Rowell, Alice Rowell, Elizabeth Rowell, Francis Rowell and Anne Rowell, created to pay at full age to the descendants of the deceased, Administration of the estate, until further notice, is by Elizabeth his widow, Descendants' payments to be withheld till full age, etc.

Children baptized at Mancetter, Warwickshire:

  i. - son - , b. probably Oct/Nov. 1592, buried 4 Nov. 1592.

2. ii. **THOMAS**, bp 27 Mar. 1594, d. 8 May 1662 at Andover, Mass., md. 1st 12 Oct. 1615 **MARGARET MILNER,** 7 children, md 2nd 5 Oct. 1650/1 **MARGARET (FOWLER) OSGOOD,** 1 child.

3. iii. **WILLIAM**, bp 8 June 1597, md. _____. 3 children.

  iv. **ALICE**, alive 1613.

  v. **ELIZABETH**, bp 29 Sept. 1605, md. 29 Aug. 1629 **WILLIAM HALL**

  vi. **FRANCES**, bp 12 April 1608, md. 1 Mar. 1646 **THOMAS CARTER?**

  vii. **ANNE**, bp 18 April 1613, buried 29 Aug. 1624.

The inventory of the Estate of **VALENTINE ROWELL** was taken 20 Oct. 1613 by John Roz, William Grewe, Francis Power and Thomas Hamton.

An inventory of all the goods of Valyntyne Rowell of Atherstone, late deceased taken by John Roz, Francis Power, Thomas Hamton, Will'm Grewe

In the Hall
1 table and frame and 2 forms, 3 chairs,
    1 cupboard, 2 shelves, 1 cradle - - - - - - - - 13s.4d.
19 pieces of pewter, 3 salt sellers, 3 candlesticks 13s.4d.
1 brass pot, 4 kettles, 1 posnet - - - - - - - - - 23s.4d.
2 benches, 2 pails, 1 churn, 1 stean, 1 piggin,
    1 can, 1 dozen of trenchers, 6 dishes, 1 meal,
    with other implements - - - - - - - - - - - - 4s.
1 andiron, fire shovel and tongs, the pot hangells,
    a pair of bellows - - - - - - - - - - - - - - 2s.

ROWELL FAMILY - ENGLAND

1 painted cloth, 1 brooch, 1 board cloth, 8 reeves
of onions with all other implements - - - - - -   2s.6d.

In the spence
1 kimmel, 1 barrel, 1 loom, 1 frying pan, 1 meal
sieve with other implements - - - - - - - - - -   5s

In the parlor
2 bed steads, 2 covers, 3 boxes, 1 shelf, 2 pillows,
1 twilly, 3 coverlets, 1 wool bed, 1 bolster -   30s.
For his apparel - - - - - - - - - - - - - - - -   30s.
6 pair of sheets, 1 board cloth, 2 pollow beres,
2 twillies - - - - - - - - - - - - - - - - -   20s.
3 painted cloths, 1 crock with cheeses in it, 1
pot of butter, and all other implements - - - -   13s.4d.

In the chamber
2 bed steads, 2 painted cloths, 6 fleeces of wool   8s.
hay and corn - - - - - - - - - - - - - - - - -   50s.
3 pitchforks, 2 bills, a little wheel, with all
other omplements - - - - - - - - - - - - - -   3s.
In the shop
His tools - - - - - - - - - - - - - - - - - -   20s.
1 new cart wheel, a clove stock with other
implements - - - - - - - - - - - - - - - - -   8s.

In the workhouse
All his timber - - - - - - - - - - - - - - - - £5.
1 cow, 1 calf - - - - - - - - - - - - - - - -   50s.
14 sheep - - - - - - - - - - - - - - - - - - -   30s.
1 grindstone, 1 scythe, and hemp, with other
implements - - - - - - - - - - - - - - - -   5s.
1 store pig - - - - - - - - - - - - - - - - -   3s.4d.

A total his debts owing him
Catell of Atherstone - - - - - - - - - - - - -   22s.
                        Sum is   £23.9s.6d.

John [] Roz
William Grewe   Thomas Hamton   20 October 1613
Francis Power

2. THOMAS ROWELL [VALENTINE 1] Atherstone. He
was baptized at Mancetter, Warwickshire on 17
March 1594/5. He married at Mancetter 12 Oct.

1615 **MARGARET MILNER**, who remained in England.
About 1638 he emigrated to New England with his
son **VALENTINE** and settled at Salisbury, Mass.,
where he received land grants in 1640, 1641 and
1642. He and his son **VALENTINE** took the oath of
fidelity there in 1642. **THOMAS** died at Andover,
Mass. on 8 May 1662 intestate. See PART 2 for
his life in New England.

Children born in England:

     i. **ALICE**, bp 27 Feb. 1619/20, md. 7 Oct.
        1641 **WILLIAM LAKIN**.
    ii. **SARAH**, bp 25 April 1621, md. 16 July
        1654 **JOHN BARTON**, feltmaker.
   iii. **VALENTINE**, bp 22 June 1622, d. 17 May
        1662 at Salisbury, Mass., md. 14
        Nov. 1643 **JOANNA PINDER** See PART 2.
4. iv. **THOMAS**, bp 1 Aug. 1624, md. **FRANCES**
        _____.

     v. **WILLIAM**, bp 30 April 1629, buried 13
        April 1659 aged 28 years, if not his
        cousin.
5. vi. **JOSEPH**, bp 26 Dec. 1630, md. July 1650
        ELIZABETH PEMMINGTON.
   vii. **SAMUEL**, bp 29 Dec. 1636.

3. **WILLIAM ROWELL** [VALENTINE 1] Atherstone. He
was baptized 8 June 1597. His wifes name is
unknown. He was probably the **WILLIAM ROWELL** who
died 8 May 1671. He was named in the Warwick
Hearth Rolls at Atherstone in 1664 and 1665.

Children: i. **SARAH**, bp 28 July 1633, buried 25
         July 1635.
     ii. **JOHN**, buried 8 Aug. 1642.
    iii. **WILLIAM**, bp 6 Apr. 1629, d. 13
         April 1659, aged 28 years.

4. **THOMAS ROWELL** [VALENTINE 1] Atherstone. He
was baptized 1 Aug. 1624. Probably the THOMAS
who died 20 Dec. 1695. He married **FRANCES** _____.
She was probably the **FRANCES** buried 6 May 1673.

ROWELL FAMILY - ENGLAND

He was named in the Warwick hearth Rolls in 1664, 1665 and 1671 at Atherstone.

Children: i. **MARGARET**, b. 24 Nov., bp 10 Dec. 1654, d.y.
ii. **MARGARET**, b. 9 July, bp 19 July 1657.
6. iii. **THOMAS**, bp __ Feb. 1651, d. 1699.
iv. **VALENTINE**, bp 11 Nov. 1660.
v. **FRANCES**, bp 3 Dec. 1663, bur. 6 May 1673?

5. **JOSEPH ROWELL [THOMAS 2]** Atherstone. He was baptized 26 Dec. 1630. He married July 1650 **ELIZABETH PEMMINGTON**.

Children: i. **JOSEPH**, bp 5 Aug. 1653.
ii. **SARA**, b 6 Oct., bp 1 Nov. 1655, bur. 10 Apr. 1657.
iii. **REPENTANCE**, bastard child, bp 19 Sep. 1658.

6. **THOMAS ROWELL [THOMAS 4]** Atherstone. He was baptized __ Feb. 1651. He was buried 6 March 1699/1700 at Mancetter. He married **SARAH** ____. Perhaps he married second 10 June 1690 **MARY HOLLYOACK** by Banns. His will dated 21 Mar. 1699/1700. His will names wife **SARA**. Estate value was £42..17..8.

Children: i. **SARAH**, bp 14 Oct. 1683.
ii. **MARY**, bp 20 Feb. 1689

HAMPTON FAMILY - ENGLAND

1. **JOHN HAMPTON** Atherstone, Warwickshire. Baker. He was buried on 21 Aug. 1591 at Mancetter. His wife **ELIZABETH** was buried there on 28 Mar. 1588. He was named **JOHNES HAMPTON**, baker in a 1584 Atherstone Manorial Record [Warwick Record Office, Ref. MR13, Roll 41] Based upon parish register entries, Lichfield wills, etc. the following children of JOHN HAMPTON are identified.

HAMPTON FAMILY - ENGLAND

Children: i. **HENRY**, bur. 1 Jan. 1637/8, wife **MARGARET** bur. 21 Feb. 1625/6. Had: **ALICE**, bp 10 April 1597 md. **VALENTINE JACKSON** 6 Nov. 1625; **WILLIAM** bp 27 Dec. 1599.

2.   ii. **ELIZABETH**, b. abt 1572, md, 12 Jan. 1591/2 **VALENTINE ROWELL**.

iii. **AGNES**, md. 28 Oct. 1592 **NICHOLAS HARDING**.

iv. **THOMAS**, bur. 21 Jan. 1650, wife **BARBARA** bur. 3 Nov. 1639. Had: **FRANCES**, bur. 21 Jan. 1601; **JOHN** bp 21 Mar. 1604; **WILLIAM** bp 1 June 1608, md. **MARY** _____, Had: **WILLIAM** bp 6 May 1640; **BARBARA**, bp 23 Aug. 1612 and **RICHARD** bp 26 June 1614, bur. 20 Aug 1641

v. **WILLIAM**, d.s.p. Baker at Atherstone. Buried 16 April 1610. Estate Admin. 21 April 1610. [Lichfield Record office, 1610 folio 1121]

vi. **JAMES**, bp 23 Sep. 1578.

2. **ELIZABETH HAMPTON [JOHN 1]** Atherstone. She was born there probably about 1572. She married at Mancetter, 12 Jan. 1591/2 **VALENTINE ROWELL**. She was buried 14 Feb. 1647/8. She was the mother of seven children. See **ROWELL** section for list of her children.

NOTE:
A second **JOHN HAMPTON** resided at Atherstone. He died in 1593 and left a will [PCC, 63 Nevell] His daughter-in-law **LUCY HAMPTON** left a will in 1600 [PCC, 51 Wallops] Using information found in those two wills, we can sort out the Hampton's found in the parish register. Those that belong to **JOHN HAMPTON** the bakers family can be identified with certainty.

ROWELL ENTRIES PARISH REGISTER

Mancetter, Warwickshire Parish Register.
Warwick Record office. Ref. PR130/1, PR130/2
and PR130/3. (1563 - 1750)

1591/2 Jan. 12	md.	Valentyne Rowell - Elizabeth Hampton.
1592 Nov. 4	bur	VA: Rowells son ye buried.
1594 Mar. 17	bp.	THO: Rowell, sonne of Valentine Rowell.
1596/7 Jan. 8	bp.	Wm Rowell, sonne of Valentine Rowell.
1605 Sep. 29	bp.	Elizabeth Rowell, dau. of Valentine Rowell.
1608 Apr. 12	bp.	ffrancis Rowell, dau. of Valentine Rowell.
1613 Apr. 18	bp.	Anne, dau. of Valentine Rowell.
1613 Sep. 13	bur.	Volantine Rowell.
1615 Oct. 12	md.	Thomas Rowell - Margaret Milner.
1617 May 24	bp.	Marye Rowle, dau. of Edward.
1619/20 Feb. 27	bp	Alice Rowell, dau. of Thomas Rowell.
1621 Apr. 25	bp.	Sarah Rowell, dau. of Thomas Rowell.
1622 June 22	bp.	Valentine Rowell, son of Thomas Rowell.
1624 Aug. 1	bp.	Thomas Rowell, son of Thomas Rowell.
1624 Aug. 29	bur.	Anne, dau. of Valentine Rowell.
1629/30 Feb. 8	md.	Elizabeth Rowell - William Hall.
1630 Dec. 26	bp.	Joseph Rowell, son of William Rowell and Anne his wife.
1633 July 28	bp.	Sarah, dau. of William Rowell & Anne.
1635 July 5	bur.	Sarah, dau. of William Rowell.
1636 Dec. 6	bp.	Samuell Rowell, son of William Rowell and Anne his wife.
1641 Oct. 7	md.	Alice Rowell - William Lakin

ROWELL ENTRIES PARISH REGISTER

1642 Aug. 8   bur. John Rowell, son of William Rowell.

1646 Dec. 6   bp. _____ Rowell, dau. of Thomas Rowell and Jane his wife.

1646/7 Mar. 1   md. ffrancis Rowwill - Thomas Carter

1647 Feb. 14   bur. Elizabeth Rowell, widow.

1650 July __   md. Joseph Rowell - Elizabeth Pemmington.

1651 Feb.   bp. Thomas son of Thomas Rowell & Frances.

1653 Aug. __   bp. Joseph Rowell, son of Joseph & Elizabeth his wife.

1654 July 16   md. Sara Rowell, spinster - John Barton, feltmaker by banns

1654 Dec. 10   bp. Margaret, dau. of Thomas Rowell & Frances, born 24 Nov.

1655 Nov. 1   bp. Sara, dau. of Joseph Rowell & Elizabeth, born 1 Nov.

1657 April 10   bur. Sara Rowell, dau. of Joseph Rowell.

1657 July 9   bp. Margaret Rowell, dau. of Thos. & Frances Rowell born 9 July

1658 Sep. 19   bp. Repentance, bastard child of Elizabeth Rowell.

1659 Apr. 13   bur. William Rowlie, 28 yrs.

1660 Nov. 11   bp. Valentine, son of Thomas Rowell & Frances.

1663 Dec. 3   bp. ffrancis, son of Thomas Rowell.

1671 May 8   bur. William Rowell of Atherstone

1673 May 6   bur. ffrancie Rowel.

1683 Oct. 14   bp. Sarah, dau. of Thomas Rowell & Sarah.

1689/90 Feb. 20   bp Mary, dau. of Thomas Rowell & Sarah.

1690 June 10   md. Thomas Rowell - Mary Hollyoack by Banns

1695 May 6   bur. ffrancis Rowell.

1699/1700 Mar. 6   bur. Thomas Rowell of Atherstone.

ROWELL ENTRIES PARISH REGISTER

1699/1700 Mar.21 Thomas Rowell will at
Atherstone. Named wife
SARA. Value of estate
£42..17..8.

No later Rowell entries found in parish
register. P/R read up to 1750.

ROWELL RECORDS PARISHES ADJACENT TO MANCETTER

1556 June 27   Anne Rowle md. George Smith at
                Barford.
1556   Robert Rowell, Will at
                Barleston. (missing)
1574 May 10   Thomas Rowle md. Elizabeth
                Milles at Walston.
1602 May 29   Roger Rowell, will at Overseal
                proved. Names dau. Joane,
                Joyce & Isabell, sons Lawrence
                & William. Wife mentioned but
                not named. [Liec. Record
                Office folio 32, 1602]
1606/7 Jan. 25 Johana, wife of William Rowell
                buried at Overseal.
1607 Aug. 20   Joshua, son of William Rowell
                bpt at Overseal.
1613 Sep. 5   Elizabeth, dau. William Rowell
                bpt at Stretton.
1622 Feb. 28   Emy, dau. of William Rowell bpt.
                at Stretton.
1629 Apr. 12   William son of Joseph Rowell bpt
                at Nether-Seal.
1629 May 9   William son of Joseph Rowell
                buried at Nether-Seal
1637 July 2   Mayrie Roowell md Richard Ward
                at Witherley.
1650 Apr. 21   Mary, dau. of Richard Rowell bpt
                at Grendon.
1650 Nov. 5   Thomas Rowell md. Joyce Hodges
                at Grendon.
1664   Widow Rowell, hearth tax at
                Atherstone.

EARLY ROWELL ENTRIES

The name of Rowell can be traced back to 1309 in County Gloucestershire, England and to 1332 in County Warwickshire. Since half of all English surnames are taken from localities, we might speculate that the name of Rowell is related to a village. A small village named Rowell, or ROEL as spelled today exists in County Gloucestershire. It is located 7-1/2 miles ENE of the city of Cheltonham.

Early Findings:

1309   John de Rowell was ordained as a minister by Bishop of Llandoff at the parish of Circencester, Co. Gloucestershire.
[Source: Dugdale Society Publ. v. 15]

1332   Henry Rowell, taxed 1s 8d at Tachbroke Episcopi, Hundred of Kineton, Co. Warwickshire.

Peter le Rowel, taxed 8d at Farnaburgh, Hundred of Kineton, Co. Warwickshire.

[Source: 6Edw3, Warwick Subsidy Roll E179-192/5, PRO.]

1377   Ricardo Rowell at Tachbrok, Co. Warwickshire.
[Source: Assize Roll #975, Sessions of the Peace, v.16.]

APPENDIX   ROWELL — ENGLAND

Latin Text of Court Record of administration
of the estate of Valentine Rowell 1613. Source
Lichfield Record office, Lichfield, England.

Apud Lich xx^mo die Octobris Anno dni 1613
Comissa fuit admistracio bonorum Valentini
Rowell vixit de Atherston defunct Elizabethe
ejus Relict in forma juris jurat etc
Comissa etiam fuit twice Thomo Rowell
William Rowell Alicie Rowell Elizabethe Rowell
Francisce Rowell et Anne Rowell liberorum
naliam dict defunct in minori eoru etate
existen unacu admistracione bonorum et
porcon ad eos spectan apsfate Elizabethe
ejus Relict duran eoru minore etate etc

Death entry of Valentine Rowell in the
Mancetter Parish Register for 13 Sep. 1613.

August, 1613

x Volantine Rowell was buried Septembar 1613
the xiiij day
Margarett Griffin was Buried the xxviij day

Parish entries. Marriage of Valentine Rowell
and Elizabeth Hampton 1591/2.

Baptism of Thomas Rowell, son of Valentine
Rowell 1594.

Marriage of Thomas Rowell and Margaret Milner
1615.

APPENDIX ROWELL - ENGLAND

Original text of the Inventory of the Estate of Valentine Rowell of Atherstone 1613. Note: numbers were written using Roman numerals, at that time. Source: Lichfield Record Office.

Inventory continued.

ATHERSTONE, COUNTY WARWICKSHIRE

ATHERSTONE comprises the northern part of the old ecclesiastical parish of Mancetter. The parish of Mancetter is in the north-east section of Warwickshire on the border of Leicestershire.

Atherstone dates back at least 900 years to the time of William the Conquerer. In 1246 King Henry III granted to the Abbey of Bec Herloiun, in Normandy a weekly market and a yearly fair. In 1573 when Valentine Rowell was born there were two mills, one being a windmill. The village comprised a single row of houses built along each side of Watling Street [Roman Road] At the rear of each house was a long rectangular garden. The market place and chapel were on the north side of the main street and behind them was the manor house with its gardens.

In 1628 the number of poor at Atherstone was reported to be: "extra ordinary great." [Wars. Co. Rec. i, 63; cf 209] This may give us a clue as to why the Rowell's left for America.

Source: Victorian Hist. of Warw, v.4, p 116-130.

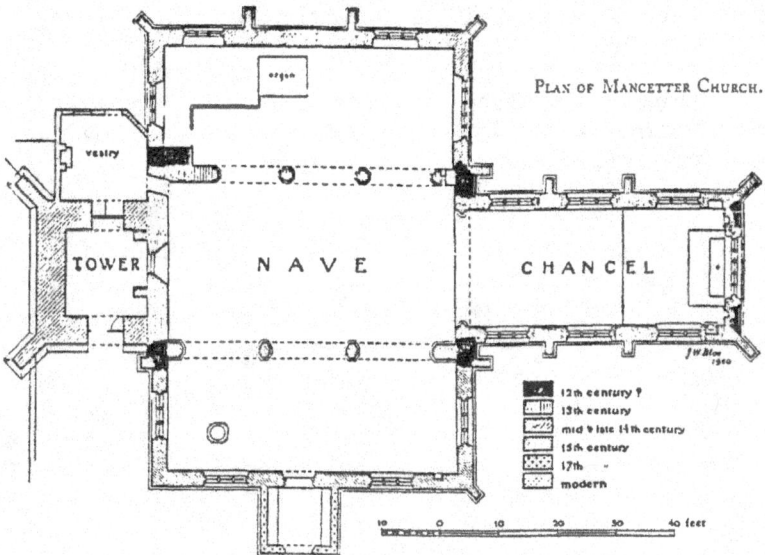

PLAN OF MANCETTER CHURCH.

organ

vestry

TOWER   N A V E   C H A N C E L

J W Blow
1940

12th century ?
13th century
mid & late 14th century
15th century
17th "
modern

10   0   10   20   30   40 feet

BIBLIOGRAPHY

1. NEHGR v.138, p.128-9.

2. Parish Register, Mancetter County Warwick, England. Adjacent parish registers. Warwick Record office, Warwick, England.

3. Parish Register, Overseal, Co. Leicester, England. Adjacent parish registers. Leicester Record Office, Leicester, England.

4. Wills and Administrations, Lichfield Record office, Lichfield, England.

5. PCC Wills, Public Record Office, London, England.

6. Manorial Records of Atherstone. Ref. MR-9 Warwick Record Office, Warwick, England.

7. Manor Rolls of Atherstone. Ref. MR-13 (40 Court Rolls) Warwick Record office, Warwick, England.

8. Hearth Tax Returns for County Warwick, v.1, 1664, 1665 & 1672.

9. Victorian History of Warwickshire, v.4, pg 116-130.

10. Threlfall, John B., Fifty Great Migration Colonies to New England, Madison, (1990) pp. 331-342.

PART 1   INDEX ENGLISH NAMES

PART 2

ROWELL FAMILY - NEW ENGLAND
1638 - 1900

ROWELL FAMILY - NEW ENGLAND
1st Generation

1. **THOMAS ROWELL** [Valentine] He was baptized 17 March 1594/5 at Mancetter, Warwickshire. He left his wife and family and emigrated to New England with his son VALENTINE in 1638. See PART 1 for English record. He settled at Salisbury, Mass. Where he received land in 1640, 1641 and 1642. In a December 1641 Civil case William Holdred sued Thomas Rowell [v.1, p.38] He took the oath of fidelity in 1646 before Lt. Pike. In September 1648 Sam. Winsley sued Thomas Rowell and Richard Currier [v.1, p. 150] In 1648/9 Thomas Rowell was fined for being in John Bourne's house during the "ordinance of a lecture day" [i.e. drinking on Sunday in an unlicensed place] In April 1649, being legally disabled, he was freed from all military training, he to pay 3 shillings yearly to the company of Salisbury. April 1649, ordered that Thomas Rowell of Salisbury, having used all proper means to fetch over his wife from old England, and she disenabled by sickness to come at present, shall not be constrained to go over to her at once, only he is to use what means he possibly can to get her over. [v.1, p. 166]

In June 1649, Robert Lemon charged him with defamation but then defaulted on the case. [v.1, p.171] He was a commoner and was taxed in 1650 in Salisbury for 6s 8d.

His wife in England died and he married second 5 Oct. 1650 **Mrs. Margaret (Fowler) Osgood**, daughter of **Philip and Mary (Winsley) Fowler**. She married first at Marlborough, Co. Wiltshire, England, 28 June 1636 **Christopher Osgood** who died in 1650. She married third before 1670 **Thomas Coleman** of Newbury and Nantucket.

At the time of his marriage to Margaret Osgood, the following antenuptial agreement was drawn up.

- 19 -

"Know all men by these Prsents Yt I Thomas Rowell
of Salisbury doe hereby covenant & make this agreemt
Concerning Margaret Ossgoods the widdow of Christopher
Ossgoods of Ipswich whome god willing I intend to make
my Lawfull wife & now being in perfect health sense &
memory Doe bind my self To the prmisses Following:
Videlizt: As I take her to be my loving wife
I firstly take her issue being tow sonnes & two
daughters to be my one to endeavor to bring them up as
a Father ought to doe: & Furthermorell bind myselfe
that the said Margaret Shall quietly owne & possesse
the halfe of my Estate which I shall be possessed with
all, when it shall please god to change my life
deliver the part or portion of goods which I shall
have with her paying to the said issue their several
portions Mentioned in there Fathers will acoording to
the appointed times out of the said estate which I
shall enjoy with her. In witness whereof I have here
Set my hand the 24th of February 1650
                        The Marke [of Thomas Rowell"
In the Presense of Philip ffowler P marke
                        Essex County Probate

Thomas Rowell moved to Ipswich in 1652. In
November 1653 he was sued by the Town of Ipswich
for not finishing a prison house. [v.1, p.319]
In 1654 he moved to Andover as the following
deeds indicate:

"These witnesse that I the said Tho: Rowell of Ipswich
Carpenter hath sold to the said Richard Ormsbie of
Salisbury a Comonage which did belong to ye
said houselott that did belong to the Lott he Sould to
William Allin:

Witness William Brown   Thomas X Rowell
Vallentine X Rowell Old Norfolk County Deeds, 1:100

"I Thomas Rowell of Andover ... Carpenter for ...
fourteen pounds ... sell unto Lieut Robert Pike of
Salisbury ... All my farme in ... Salisbury, 5 Apr.
1654" Witnesses: John Eaton, Robert Lord   "I Margery
Rowell doe give my Consent to my husbands bargin"
Recorded in Essex County Deeds, 9:271, in 1694

- 20 -

ROWELL FAMILY - NEW ENGLAND
1st Generation

In the court held Sept. 1654 Thomas Rowell was fined for taking tobacco out of doors and near a house. His wife was admonished for cruelty. [v.1, p.365]

In Sept. 1656 Thomas Rowell, in behalf of his step-daughter Abigail Osgood, sued Frances Leach for having slandered her by saying she was with child. The charge was withdrawn. Sept. 1659 Article of Agreement between Thomas Rowell and Alex. Knight and Robert Collings, all of Ipswich - lease of a farm. [v.2, p.177]

Thomas Rowell died at Andover, Mass. on 8 May 1662 intestate. Administration of his estate was granted to Margarey Rowell his widow, and an inventory of £123..3..0 was brought in. According to a contract before the marriage the widow was to have half the estate, and the court ordered £29..10..0 to be paid to Jacob Rowell, his son, to his grandchildren the children of his son Valentine Rowell £7, that is 40s to the eldest son and 20s to each of the other five children. Jacob Rowell to receive his portion at the age of 21 years and the widow was to have liberty to pay the £7 to the grandchildren. [v.2, p.442-3]

The inventory was taken 16 July 1662 by John Osgood, Richard Barber and John Lovejoy.

(Essex County Probate 1:395, as printed)
Inventory taken July 16, 1662 by John Osgood, Richard Barker and John Lovejoy.

	£	s	d
the house and barn and shop - - - - - - - - - - - -	24.		
a parcel of land by the house, fenced and sowed - -	40.		
3 acres of land near the house unfenced - - - - - -	3.		
meadow ground -	12.		
2 Oxen £14, 2 Cows £10 - - - - - - - - - - - - - - -	24.		
a mare £8, 2 calves £1, 4 sheep, 3 lambs £2.1 - - -	11.	1.	
7 swine £5.10, 3 stookes of bees £1.10 - - - - - -	7.		
6 bushels wheat, 4 bushels Indian corn - - - - - - -	2.	2.	
1 feather bed and bolster and 2 pillows and rug - -	6.		

- 21 -

```
1 flock bed and bolster and rug, 2 blankets  - - - -    3.
3 pair of sheets £1.10s, 3 pair of pillowbiers 10s -    2.
wearing apparel - - - - - - - - - - - - - - - - - - -   2.10.
1 cupboard 10s, 3 chests £1, 1 box 5s. - - - - - - -    1.15.
3 iron pots, 1 posent, 1 skillet - - - - - - - - - -    1. 4
1 brass kettle, 1 skimmer, 1 brass mortar - - - - - -   1.
pewter, 2 platters, 1 basin, 1 chamber pot - - - - -     6.
2 beer bowls, 2 saucers, 1 porringer, 1 candlestick -    3.
1 smoothing iron, 1 lamp - - - - - - - - - - - - - -     5.
1 warming pan, 1 frying pan, 1 spit - - - - - - - - -    5.
fire pan, tongs, tramell and chafin dish - - - - - - -   6.
carpenters tools - - - - - - - - - - - - - - - - - - - 1. 6.
3 gowns £1.10s, 1 sword and belt 7s - - - - - - - - - -1.17
1 mattock, 1 pick, 2 axes, 3 wedges, 4 beetle rings     14.
1 chain, 1 coulter, 1 yoke, 1 plow, 1 sled - - - - - -   15.
2 spinning wheels, 4 chairs, 4 cushions - - - - - - -    10.
wooden vessels, 2 barrels, 1 keller, 2 powdering tubs    8.
1 tub with trays, pails, sieves and other old vessels   10.
earthen vessels, 2 pair of cards, 2 sickles - - - - -    6.
Debts due to him: Mr. Dane - - - - - - - - - - - - - -  3.17. 6.
                  John Lovejoy owes - - - - - - - - - 3.00. 2.
                  Steven Osgood - - - - - - - - - - -   7. 6.
                  George Abbott, Senior - - - - - - -   2. 6.
                  Robert Collins of Ipswich           5.
                  William Avery, Ipswich             11.
                  Robert Kensman, Ipswich             2. 6.
                  Total                        156.10. 2.
```

```
Debts he owes: Mr. Horen              £19.12. 3.
               Mr. John Geedney          11.
               Phillip Whorten, Bosten  3.
               Samuel Williams, Salem   1.
               Mr. Robert Payne         1.10.
               Mr. John Appleton        1.
               John Whipple             1.
               Will Buckley            14.
        Total - - - - - - - - - - - - £28. 7. 3.
```

Allowed in Ipswich court Sept. 30, 1662
Since this inventory was made there is lost three swine and a sheep.
In debts appears about twenty shillings.

Income £156.10s. 2d.; debts £28. 7s. 3d.; cattle dead £5.; take
out her estate £50; remain £73; her half £36.10s; remain £36.10s.;
to her child £25.10s.; to his 6 grandchildren, the eldest £2, ye
rest £1. 7s.

ROWELL FAMILY - NEW ENGLAND
1st Generation

Additional inventory of the estate of Tho. Rowell brought in
June 28, 1681 by his son Jacob Rowell and to whom administrat.

Children, born in New England by 2nd wife:

3. JACOB, b. probably May 1656,
m.1, 29 April 1690 **MARY
YOUNGLOVE**, m.2, 21 Sep. 1691
ELIZABETH WARDELL/WARDWELL.

See PART 1 for children born in England.

SECOND GENERATION

2. **VALENTINE ROWELL [THOMAS 1]** He was born 22
June 1622 at Atherstone, England. He emigrated
with his father to Salisbury, Mass. He was
there by 14 Nov. 1643, when he married **JOANNA
PINDER**. She was born 1621, the daughter of **HENRY
& MARY (ROGERS) PINDER** of Cambridge, who came to
the colony when 14 years old in 1635, in the
ship "Susan and Ellen."

He took the oath of fidelity in 1646 at
Salisbury before Lt. Pike, was townsman and was
taxed in Salisbury 4s 6d in 1650. Occ.
carpenter. He received land in Amesbury in 1654
and 1662. There are a number of old Norfolk
County deed records starting in 1647 with his
name. [deeds 1:110, 119, 127, 138, 142, 145,
146]

23 October 1647 - Tho: Bradbury of Salisbury, planter,conveyed
to Valentine Rowell, 6 acres of meadow, formerly Mr. John
Hodges, bounded by Thomas Dumer and Anthony Colby. Witnesses:
Sam. Winsley, Tho. Rowell, Ackn. in Ct. 10:2:1660

12 April 1654 - Daniel Ladd of Haverhill conveyed to Valentine
Rowell of Salisbury 4 acres of planting land with commonage at
Salisbury-old-town, bounded by John Clough, Willi. Allin,
swamp and highway. Witnesses: Richard Littlehale, Roger
Lanckton.

ROWELL FAMILY - NEW ENGLAND
2nd Generation

April 1661 - Valentine Rowell of Salisbury, planter, for pine boards, conveyed to William Osgood of Salisbury, millwright, a right of commanage in Salisbury I bought of Daniel Lad.

4 April 1662 - Valentine Rowell of Salisbury, carpenter, conveyed to Henry Blesdale of Salisbury, tailor, one half of ye upper end of my lot of upland on west side of Pawwaus river in Salisbury, bounded by Edward Goe, Phillip Challis, etc. ... Witnesses: Tho: Bradbury, Samuel Hall. Acknowledged, wife Joanna released dower, in court at Salisbury 8 Apr. 1662

5 April 1661 - Richard Currier of Salisbury, planter, conveyed to Valentine Rowell of Salisbury, planter, 2 acres of upland in Salisbury, on west side of Pawwaus river, bounded by John Weed, John Bayly, deceased and highway.

5 April 1661 - John Bayly of Nuberie, husbandman, for the deed that follows, conveyed to Valentine Rowell of Salisbury, planter, 3 acres of meadow in Salisbury, bounded by Richard Currier, town creek and a little creek running up by Vinson's rocks.

5 April 1661 - Valentine Rowell of Salisbury, planter, for the above deed, conveyed to John Bayly of Nuberie, husbandman, 6 acres of meadow in Salisbury, bounded by Tho: Dumer (now of said Bayly) and Anthony Colby towards ye ferry.

12 April 1661 - Thomas Barnard of ye newtown of Salisbury, for £5.15s conveyed to William Barnes, Richard Currier and Valentine Rowell, inhabitants of the same town, in behalf of ye new town, 10 acres of upland in said new town late in the possession of Isaac Buswell, near the mill, Witnesses: Wymond Bradbury, Samuel Hall. The above grantees conveyed the said land to Joseph Peasley same day.

5 March 1661/2 - Valentine Rowell of Salisbury, planter, conveyed to John Clough of Salisbury, house carpenter, 4 acres of planting land in Salisbury, bounded by Willi Allin, highway to mill, grantee, etc. Witnesses: Tho: Bradbury, Jane Bradbury Acknowledged in court by grantor and his wife Joanna.

9 April 1662 - Valentine Rowell exchanged my lot of sweepage, bounded by Mr. Winsley and goodman Dickison, at ye beath, with Jarret Haddon for William Huntington's lot of Higgledee

ROWELL FAMILY - NEW ENGLAND
2nd Generation

pigledee meadow at fox island, bounded by Valentine Rowell and
Phillip Challis. Witnesses: Anthony Somerby, John Bayly,
Acknowledged by grantor, his wife releasing dower, in court at
Salisbury 8 April 1662.

Valentine Rowell died 17 May 1662, just 38
days after making his last deed. On 14 October
1662 administration of his estate was granted to
his widow JOANE. Lt. Challis and Richard Currier
were ordered to make distribution of his estate
to the widow and children, she to have half of
it.

Joanne remarried on 18 September 1670 to
WILLIAM SARGENT, and married third, 26 October
1676 at Amesbury, RICHARD CURRIER.

In 1725 the estate of Valentine Rowell was
still unsettled. PHILIP ROWELL was appointed
administrator of the estate of his grandfather.
He gave bond 12 Feb. 1725.

Children, born at Salisbury, Mass.
4. THOMAS, b 7 Sep. 1644, d. 1684, md. 8
Sep. 1670 SARAH BARNES.
5. JOHN, b. 1645-6, d. 12 Sep. 1649.
6. PHILIP, b. 8 March 1647/8, killed 7
July 1690 by Indians, md. 5 Jan.
1670/1 SARAH MORELL.(MORRILL)
7. MARY, b. 31 Jan. 1649/50, md. 18 Sep.
1673 THOMAS FREAME [FRAME] 6
children.
8. SARAH, b. 16 Nov. 1651, alive 1716,
md. 26 Oct. 1676 THOMAS HARVEY.
9. HANNAH, b. Jan. 1653, d. 9 Aug. 1707,
m.1 16 Sept. 1674 THOMAS COLBY,
m.2, about 1691 HENRY BLAISDELL.
10. JOHN, b. 15 Nov. 1655, d. 18 Feb.
1655/6.
11. ELIZABETH, b. 10 Aug. 1657.
12. MARGARITE, b. 8 Sep. 1659.

Note: Some sources claim a son SOLOMAN born
about 1650.

Sept. 1662 the children of Valentine Rowell split £7 from Thomas Rowell administration. 40s to the eldest son and 20s each to the other 5 children. [v.2, p.442-3]

3. **JACOB ROWELL [THOMAS 1]** He was born May 1656 at Ipswich, Mass. He married first 26 April 1690 **MARY YOUNGLOVE** d/o **SAMUEL & SARAH (KINSMAN) YOUNGLOVE**. She was born 17 Mar. 1667 and died 15 May 1691 in child birth. He married second, 21 Sep. 1691 **ELIZABETH WARDWELL** d/o **ELIHU & ELIZABETH (WADE) WARDELL**. She was born 15 Dec. 1666. Occ. "joiner." Reside at Elizabeth, N.J. in 1674. Back in Ipswich, Mass. by 1690. He died 18 Feb. 1700/1 at Ipswich. Children born at Ipswich, Mass.

Children: by 1st Wife;
       13. **BENONI**, b. April 1691.
by 2nd Wife;
       14. **ELIHU/ELLHU**, b. 29 Nov. 1693 at
           Ipswich.
       15. **ELIZABETH**, b. 3 Nov. 1695
       16. **MARY**, b. 25 June 1698.
       17. **JOHN**, b. 12 Oct. 1700.

On 29 March 1692 he was convicted of paternity of widow Gumage's child, order to pay her 20s, plus 2s 6d per week.

An additional inventory of the Estate of Thomas Rowell, who dyed in 1662 was taken by: Dudley Bradstreet and Thomas Chandler amounted to £182. Returned by Jacob Rowell 28:4:81.

The additional inventory which was filed was:

100 acres of upland in the great division in Andover . .£100
25 acres of upland on the Indian Plain being the 3rd div. 30
Meadow on ye west side of Shawshin River in 4 parcels . . 30
5 acres of meadow which was ye last division of meadow . 15
7 acres & ½ of upland, which was ye swamp division . . . 7
                           Total   £182

Nov. 1673, Jacob Rowell for being instrumental in said
Satters breaking prison and running away with him, was
sentence whyiped but upon interceson of
friends, the sentence resulted in a fine. [v.5, p.249]

Mar. 1674, Jacob Rowell chose George Norton for his guardian
and the court allowed it. [v.5, p.291]

Dec. 1676, George Norton, guardian of Jacob Rowell was
granted power to take into his hands said Rowell's estate
which was ordered to him 30:7:1662 at Ipswich Court. [v.6,
p.223]

A petition of JACOB ROWELL only son of the
deceased THOMAS ROWELL dated 26th of June 1681
mentioned that his father died in 1662 and that
he the petitioner was very young, and that his
mother returned a false inventory omitting the
things mentioned in his inventory amounting to
£182: his mothers name is Margery and that she
had administration of the estate granted her. He
wishes that order to be revoked, he is the only
child. Allowed & Admin. granted to sd Jacob
Rowell.

Source: Essex Inst. Hist. Coll., 3:66 and
Probate Records of Essex Co., Mass.

THIRD GENERATION

4. THOMAS ROWELL [VALENTINE 2] He was born 7
Sep. 1644 at Salisbury and died 1684 at
Amesbury, Mass. He married 8 Sep. 1670 SARAH
BARNES, d/o WILLIAM & RACHEL (LORD) BARNES of
Amesbury. She born 1651 at Salisbury, Mass. She
married second in 1685 JOHN HARVEY, s/o WILLIAM
& MARTHA (CAPP) HARVEY. His will is dated 6 May
1684 and was proved 30 Sep. 1684. The inventory
was taken 20 June 1684. She died 17 April 1720
at Amesbury.

He received "children's land" in 1659, "township" in 1660; meeting house seat in 1667; oath of alligence in 1677; signed Petition in 1680.

Children: 20. MARY, b. 5 Feb. 1671/2, md. 21 Nov. 1688 THOMAS COLBY Jr.
21. VALENTINE, b. 5 Aug. 1674, d, 1 Feb. 1726/7, md. HANNAH SARGENT.
22. JOANNA, b. abt. 1676, md. 1688 TITUS WELLS.
23. PHILIP, b. abt. 1678, md. 20 Jan. 1703/4, SARAH DAVIS.
24. SARAH, b. abt. 1680, d. 2 Jan. 1728/9, md. 9 Dec. 1710 DANIEL HOYT.

Thomas Rowell aged about 23 yrs deposed April 1668 that coming from the launching of a vessel where Thomas Sargent was, then went into Goodman Hadden's lot etc. [v.4, p.26]

5. JOHN ROWELL [VALENTINE 2] He was born June 1645/6 and died 12 September 1649.

6. PHILIP ROWELL [VALENTINE 2] Amesbury. He was born 8 Mar. 1647/8 and was killed by Indians 7 July 1690. Occ. shipwright, innkeeper, and mail carrier Newburyport to Portsmouth. He married 5 Jan. 1670 SARAH MORRILL, d/o ABRAHAN & SARAH (CLEMENTS) MORRILL. She born 14 Oct. 1650 at Salisbury, Mass. and died 11 Sep. 1731 at Amesbury. She married second 31 July 1695 ONESIPHEROUS PAGE. She married third 29 May 1708 DANIEL MERRILL. Res. Amesbury.

Children: 25. JACOB, b. 19 Jan, 1671/2, d. 18 Dec. 1745, md. 1 Dec. 1693, HANNAH BARNARD.
26. SARAH, b. 3 Mar. 1673/4, md. 6 Apr. 1693 SAMUEL GOULD.
27. THOMAS, b. 1 Apr. 1676, living 1713, md. DOROTHY KNIGHT.

28. **ABRAHAM**, b. 1678, md. 2 Dec.
    1701 **MARY WARDWELL**.
29. **JOHN**, b. 1683, d. 1 Feb. 1736,
    md. 2 Mar. 1714/5 **ELIZABETH
    COLBY**.
30. **JOB**, b. 1685, bp 30 Apr. 1699,
    md. 7 Apr. 1705 **BETHIA BROWN**,
    will 4 May 1736.
31. **HEPZIBAH**, b. 26 Mar. 1687/8, d.
    6 Oct. 1688.
32. **JUDITH**, b. 21 Nov. 1689, md. 5
    May 1715 **JOHN GILL**.
33. **AARON**, b. 21 Nov. 1689.

Sep. 1683, Philip Rowell of Amesbury, license
to sell drink until next March. [v.9, p.100]

March 1685, Philip Rowell constable of
Amesbury. [v.9, p.335 & 455]

September 1685, Essex Court. Mr. Thomas Madget
of Salisbury informed the Court that Philip
Rowell of Amesbury had left his wife with 7
children and had fled from authority contrary to
bond given for appearance to answer a charge
against him relating to the wife of George Carr
of Amesbury, who had also fled, Court order
Sarah, wife of said Rowell, have full power as
an administrix to collect any debts due his
estate, etc. for her support, and also confirmed
her in his place, as a keeper of a house of
public entertainment until the next court.
[March} [v.9, p.528]

September 1685 Philip Rowell of Amesbury was
bound for appearance to answer complaint for
offense keeping company of Mrs. An(n) Car(r) of
Amesbury. [v.9, p.538]

March 1686, Lic. renewed Sarah Rowell of
Amesbury.

Philip Rowell of Amesbury, who was Constable in 1684 having fallen into a transgession and not collecting his rates, but having fled the country, etc. [v.9, p.576]

Bond dated 26 March 1686 of Sarah Rowell of Amesbury against Samuel Colby of Amesbury for selling cider which had been greatly to her damage, as she could prove by these witnesses: John Which; Geo. Weed; Jarvis Ring; Thos. Fouller Jr. - petition of Samuel Colby that there had been a license granted to the widow Rowell to keep a house of public entertainment in Amesbury. [v.9, p.600]

7. **MARY ROWELL [VALENTINE 2]** She was born 31 Jan. 1649/50 at Amesbury, Mass. She married 18 Sep. 1673 **THOMAS FREAME.** He born 1639.

Children: i. **ELIZABETH,** b. 1 Jan. 1673/4, md. 15 Jan. 1693/4 **SAMUEL GEORGE.** 6 children.
ii. **MARY,** b. 2 Mar. 1674/5, m.1, 2 Dec. 1702 **JOHN COLBY,** m.2, **EDWARD LATIMORE.** 5 children.
iii. **HANNAH,** b. 12 Jan. 1676/7, m.1, 16 Mar. 1695 **JOHN HARTSHORN** Jr, m.2, **WILLIAM SMITH.** 11 ch.
iv. **SARAH,** b. c1678, d. c1752, md. 26 Jan. 1698 **JOHN CHALLIS.**
v. **SUSANNA,** b. abt. 1680, md. 6 Mar. 1699 **CALEB NORTON.** 1 ch.
vi. **THOMAS,** b. abt. 1684, d. 30 Aug. 1686.
vii. **JOHN,** b. c1685.
viii. **JAMES,** b. c1687.

8. **SARAH ROWELL [VALENTINE 2]** She was born 16 Nov. 1651 at Salisbury, Mass. She married 26 Oct. 1676 **THOMAS HARVEY, s/o WILLIAM & MARTHA (CAPP) HARVEY.** He born 16 Aug. 1652 and died 1716. She living 1716. Res. Amesbury, Mass.

Children: i. **MARY,** md. 15 May 1707 **JOSEPH BUSWELL.**

ROWELL FAMILY - NEW ENGLAND
3rd Generation

   ii. ELIZABETH, md. 8 Dec. 1710
      THEOPHILUS COLBY.
  iii. HANNAH, md. 8 Mar. 1721/2
      WILLIAM CURRIER.
   iv. WILLIAM, b. 9 Mar. 1687/8, d. 8
      Jan. 1689/90.
    v. WILLIAM, b. 15 Jan. 1689/90, d.
      14 Oct. 1714, md. ABIGAIL
      MARTIN.
   vi. THOMAS, b. 14 Feb. 1691/2, d.y.

9. HANNAH ROWELL [VALENTINE 2] She was born Jan.
1653 at Salisbury, Mass. She married first 16
Sep 1674 THOMAS COLBY, s/o ANTHONY & SUSANNA
(WITHERBRIDGE) COLBY. He born 8 Mar. 1650. She
married second about 1691 HENRY BLAISDELL at
Salisbury. She died 9 Aug. 1707.

Children: i. THOMAS, 1 July 1675, d. 4 June
        1741, md. Mrs. FRANCES COLBY.
        11 children.
      ii. HANNAH, b. 1677, md. JOHN
        TEWSKESBURY. 9 children.
     iii. ISAAC, b. c1679, adm. 1733, md.
        5 Dec. 1701 HANNAH H.
        GETCHELL. 5 children.
     iv. ABRAHAM, b. 1681, living
        1700.
      v. JACOB, b. 13 Apr. 1688, md.
        HANNAH HUNT, m.2? ELIZABETH
        ELLIOT.

10. JOHN ROWELL [VALENTINE 2] He was born 15
Nov. 1655 and died 18 Feb. 1655/6.

11. ELIZABETH ROWELL [VALENTINE 2] She was born
10 Aug. 1657. Either she or her sister MARGARITE
died before her father in 1662.

12. MARGARITE ROWELL [VALENTINE 2] She was born
8 Sep. 1659.

13. BENONI ROWELL [JACOB 3] He was born April
1691 at Ipswich, Mass. and died 1759/60. He

married **SARAH** _____. All children baptized 7
July 1728 at Haverhill, Mass. Occ. farmer and
trader. April 1739 sold boards for Salem Meeting
House. Named on ministerial rate in 1754. Res.
Salem 1734.

Children: 35. **BENONI** Jr, b. 1715, bp 7 July
1728, md. 28 Sep. 1742 **MARY
YOUNG.**
36. **JOSIAH,** b. 1717, bp 7 July 1728,
md. 1 May 1740 **HANNAH DAVIS.**
37. **MARY,** bp 7 July 1728.
38. **SAMUEL,** b. 1720, bp 7 July 1728,
d. 1760, md. 18 Aug. 1745
DEBORAH MORGAN.
39. **SARAH,** b. 1709, bp 7 July 1728,
md. 1751 **PETER JOHNSON.**

14. **ELIHU ROWELL [JACOB 3]** He was born 29 Nov.
1693 at Ipswich, Mass. living at Topsfield,
Mass. in 1728.

15. **ELIZABETH ROWELL [JACOB 3]** She was born 3
Nov. 1695 at Ipswich, Mass. Perhaps married
JOSEPH LEMMON at Ipswich 5 Mar. 1719.

16. **MARY ROWELL [JACOB 3]** She was born 25 June
1698 at Ipswich, Mass. Perhaps married **JOSEPH
HINES** 7 Mar. 1718 at Boston, Mass.

17. **JOHN ROWELL [JACOB 3]** He was born 12 Oct.
1700 at Ipswich, Mass. Had wife **ELIZA** _____.
Possibly moved to Berwick, Maine? If so had
following:

Children: 40. **JOHN,** bp 7 Nov. 1730, md.
MARY BEDEL.
41. **MARY,** bp 7 Nov. 1730, or 17
Aug. 1733.
42. **ELIZABETH,** bp 7 Nov. 1730.
43. **JACOB,** bp 8 Dec. 1732, d.
Sep. 1831, m.1, 6 Aug. 1772
HANNAH CARLTON, m.2, 17
July 1793 **LUCY (CUSHING)**

VINING. 27 children.
44. MOSES, bp 17 Apr. 1735, or 8
Dec. 1734.

FOURTH GENERATION

20. MARY ROWELL [THOMAS 4] She was born 5 Feb.
1671/2 at Amesbury, Mass. She married 21 Nov.
1688 THOMAS COLBY Jr. s/o JOHN & FRANCES (HOYT)
COLBY of Amesbury. He born 1667 at Salisbury.

Children: i. THEOPHILUIS, b. 22 Nov. 1689, d.
c1724, md. 8 Dec. 1710
ELIZABETH HARVEY.
ii. JUDITH, b. 23 Apr. 1690.
iii. DORITY, b. 9 June 1694, d. after
1737, md. 29 Jan. 1711/2
SAMUEL FOOT.
iv. ELIAS, b. 19 Apr. 1696, d. after
1737, md. 4 Nov. 1714 HANNAH
PRESSEY.
v. TIMOTHY, b. 19 Apr. 1698, d.
after 1737, md. 4 July 1718
HANNAH HEATH.
vi. MARY, b. 17 Nov. 1702.
vii. THOMAS, b. 23 Apr. 1706, d.
after 1742.

21. VALENTINE ROWELL [THOMAS 4] He was eldest
son , born 5 Aug. 1674 at Salisbury, Mass. and
died 1 Feb. 1726/7 at Amesbury. He married 1702
HANNAH SARGENT, d/o THOMAS & RACHEL (BARNES)
SARGENT of Amesbury. She was born 28 July 1685
and died 1738. Administration of his estate was
27 Feb. 1726/7 and the inventory taken 7 Mar.
1726/7.

Children: 50. THOMAS, b. 9 Feb. 1702/3, d. 21
Sep. 1790, md. 21 Apr. 1725
ABIGAIL STEVENS.
51. WILLIAM, b. 5 Sep. 1705, md. 5
Jan. 1731/2 ELIZABETH CHALLIS.
52. JOSEPH, b. 17 Dec. 1710, died
young.

53. HANNAH, b. 13 July 1713, d.
1738, md. 9 Aug. 1736 JONATHAN
CARLTON, at Plaiston, N.H..
54. ANNA, b. 15 Nov. 1718, d. 1746
unmd.
55. JOSEPH, b. 2 Sep. 1724, d. 23
June 1762, md. 26 Nov. 1747
ELIZABETH ROWELL. (#107)

22. JOANNA ROWELL [THOMAS 4] She was born about
1678. She married 1698 TITUS WELLS, s/o Rev.
THOMAS & MARY (PERKINS) WELLS. He born 14 Mar.
1675 at Amesbury.

Children: i. SARAH, b. 30 July 1698, md.
JONATHAN FERREN. 14 ch.
ii. THOMAS, b. 4 Mar. 1699, m.1,
SARAH HADLEY, m.2, MARY
SARGENT.
iii. MARY, b. 11 Mar. 1702, md.
CUTTING FAVOR.
iv. TIMOTHY, b. 16 Apr. 1704, md.
MARY PILLSBURY.
v. HANNAH, b. 5 Feb. 1705, twin.
vi. TITUS, b. 5 Feb. 1705, m.1, MARY
SAWYER, m.2, ABIGAIL BLAISDELL.
vii. PHILEMON, b. 3 Sep. 1708, md.
RUTH AYERS.
viii. JACOB, b. 29 Aug. 1710, md. RUTH
SARGENT.
ix. PHILIP, b. 7 Apr. 1713.
x. ELISABETH, b. 11 Mar. 1716, md.
JOSEPH DAVIS.
xi. ABIGAIL, b. 18 Dec. 1718.

23. PHILIP ROWELL [THOMAS 4] He was born c1678
at Salisbury. He married 20 Jan. 1703/4 SARAH
DAVIS, d/o JOHN & SARAH (CARTER) DAVIS of
Amesbury, Mass. She born 1682. Occ. husbandman.
Res. at Amesbury and Salisbury, Mass.

Children: 56. MARY, b. 21 Nov. 1704, md. 11
Apr. 1728 JOSEPH CHALLIS.

57. SARAH, b. 4 Oct. 1705, md. 1
    Jan. 1735 EDMUND SAWYER.
58. VALENTINE, b. 25 Nov. 1708.
59. JACOB, b. 14 Sep. 1710, md. 20
    Dec. 1733 DOROTHY STOW.
60. PHILIP, b. 13 Dec. 1713, md. 16
    Oct. 1736 ANN WOOD.
61. JUDITH, b. 25 Apr. 1716.
62. MERIAM, b. 5 Oct. 1718, md. 22
    Apr. 1741 TIMOTHY WHITTIER.
63. DOROTHY, b. 20 Jan. 1720/1, md.
    8 Apr. 1741 JOHN BLAISDELL.
64. ALICE (ALLIS), b. 22 June 1723,
    md. 25 Apr. 1744 JOSEPH COUCH.
65. RACHEL, b. 20 Jan. 1725/6, md.
    26 Apr. 1750 or 16 Dec. 1751
    EDWARD/EDMUND MORSE.
66. ICHABOD, b. 2 Nov. 1729, md. 5
    June 1755 SARAH TUCKER.

24. SARAH ROWELL [THOMAS 4] She was born about
1680 and died 2 Jan. 1728/9. She married 9 Dec.
1710 DANIEL HOYT, s/o JOHN & ELIZABETH (CHALLIS)
HOYT. He born 2 Mar. 1690. He married second 24
July 1729 ELIZABETH BAXTER, widow of NICHOLAS
BAXTER.

Children: i. MARY, b. 14 May 1712, md. 4 Oct.
                1737 ROBERT MULLICKIM.
            ii. RUBEN, b. 31 Oct. 1713, md. 27
                Feb. 1734/5 HANNAH
                BAXTER/BEARTER.
           iii. JETHRO, b. 1716.
            iv. ELIFELET, b. 28 Oct. 1716, d. 30
                Jan. 1720/1.
             v. LYDIA HOYT, b. 15 Mar. 1718, md.
                _____ TUCKER.
            vi. JOHN DEACON, b. 20 Dec. 1720, d.
                c1795, m.1, 4 Nov. 1745
                MERRIEM CURRIER, m.2, Widow
                MARY KELLER MOULTON.
           vii. ELIPHELET HOYT, b. 2 June 1723,
                md. 1 Aug. 1746 MARY PEASLEE.

ROWELL FAMILY - NEW ENGLAND
4th Generation

   viii. **SARAH**, b. 25 Aug. 1725, md. 6
        Feb. 1746 **ENOCH SARGENT**.

25. **JACOB ROWELL** [PHILIP 6] He was born 19 Jan.
1671/2 at Salisbury, Mass. and died 18 Aug.
1747. He married 1 Dec. 1693 **HANNAH**, d/o **THOMAS
& SARAH (PEASLEE) BARNARD**. She born 15 Apr. 1671
and died 26 Apr. 1731 at Salisbury. Called
"snowshoe man" in 1708. In 1730 had lot #2. Many
N.H. deeds several with son Philip. His will is
dated 28 Mar. 1741, proved 21 Sep. 1747. No wife
mention in will. Res. Amesbury, Mass.

Children: 67. **PHILIP**, b. 28 Mar. 1695, d. 18
              Apr. 1770, md. 10 Oct. 1719
              ELIZABETH PURRINGTON
          68. **RUTH**, b. 27 Nov. 1696, d. 24
              Dec. 1696.
          69. **SARAH**, b. 7 Aug. 1697, liv.
              1741, md. 19 Aug. 1719
              STEPHEN SAWYER. 10 ch.
          70. **MOSES**, b. 29 Nov. 1699, d. 20
              Jan. 1733, md. 28 Nov. 1723
              JEMIMA CHANDLER.
          71. **AARON**, b. 29 Nov. 1701, m.1, 19
              Nov. 1726 **RUTH PEARINGTON**,
              m.2, 18 Feb. 1735 **MARY
              CHALLIS**.
          72. **MIRIAM A.**, b. 3 Dec. 1703, d.
              prob. before 1741.
          73. **DANIEL**, b. 25 Nov. 1705, d.
              1778, md. 14 Mar. 1728/9 **ANNE
              CURRIER**.
          74. **SUSANNA**, b. 2 Oct. 1707, md. 28
              Nov. 1727 **NATHANIEL CHANDLER**.
              6 children.
          75. **GIDEON**, b. 17 Sep. 1709, d. by
              1785, md. 27 Jan. 1731/2
              ELEANOR MORRILL.

26. **SARAH ROWELL** [PHILIP 6] She was born 3 Mar.
1673/4. She married 6 April 1693 **SAMUEL**, s/o
NATHANIEL & ELIZABETH (PUTNAM) GOULD. He born 3
Mar. 1673.

Children: i. DAMARAS, b. 13 Sep. 1694, d. 1
Sep. 1782, md. 19 Jan. 1713/4
DANIEL LANCASTER. 12 ch.
ii. NATHAN, b. 20 Apr. 1696, d. 1747
md. 27 Apr. 1720 HANNAH
STEVENS.
iii. SAMUEL, b. 4 Aug. 1698, md. 17
Oct. 1719 LYDIA DOW. 1 son.
iv. JOSEPH, b. 1 July 1700, d. 1752,
md. 2 June 1726 ABIGAIL HOYT.
v. JUDAH, b. 25 Dec, 1701, md. 25
Dec. 1722 BENJAMIN QUIMBY. 2
children.
vi. HANNAH, b. 8 Nov. 1703, md. 10
Jan. 1722/3 JOSEPH FRENCH. 1
son.
vii. ELISABETH, b. 28 Oct. 1705, md.
30 Jan. 1724/5 EBENEZER
FRENCH.
viii. ELIHU/ELISHA, b. 22 Jan. 1707,
d. 1751, md. 20 Oct. 1729
MARTHA RING.
ix. SARAH, b. 14 May 1710, d. 1773,
md. 28 May 1730 DANIEL FRENCH.
9 children.
x. PHILIP, b. 3 Feb. 1711, d. 1778,
md HANNAH _____.

27. THOMAS ROWELL [PHILIP 6] He was born 1
April 1676, living 1713. Possibly the THOMAS
ROWELL at Boston who married 18 June 1702
DOROTHY KNIGHT. Children born at Boston.

Children: 76. THOMAS, b. 9 Feb. 1702/3.
77. DOROTHY, b. 22 July 1704, md. 21
Jan. 1719 ABRAM WHITE.
78. SAMUEL, b. 19 May 1705, md. 30
Aug. 1733 ELIZABETH ADAMS.
79. SARAH, b. 26 Feb. 1706.
80. HANNAH, b. 25 Apr. 1709.
81. HANNAH, b. 28 July 1711, md. 5
June 1729 JOHN COVERLY.
82. REBECCA, b. 15 July 1714.

83. **MARY**, b. c1715?, md. 26 May 1731
JONATHAN FISK at Boston.

28. **ABRAHAM ROWELL [PHILIP 6]** He was born in
1678 at Amesbury, Mass. and bp. 30 Aug. 1699. He
died possibly at Nottingham, N.H. in 1745. He
married 2 Dec. 1701 **MARY WARDELL** [or WARDWELL]
of Ipswich. She born 1677. Removed to
Nottingham, N.H. about 1712. One of the
original proprietors in 1722. Granted lot #43 on
Winter Street in 1730. April 1733 had lot 6 & 9,
Range 1, 100 acres each, just south of
Pawtuckawat Mt. Children born at Newbury, Mass.
except RICE. He was born at Nottingham, N.H.

Children: 85. **HEPZIBAH**, b. 21 Oct. 1702, md.
22 Dec. 1727 **WILLIAM HOOKLY**.
86. **MARY**, b. 17 Oct. 1704.
87. **ABRAHAM**, b. 16 Sep. 1706.
88. **SARAH**, b. 29 Aug. 1708.
89. **JACOB**, b. 17 Apr. 1710, soldier
on 1744 Cape Breton Expedition
90. **RICE**, b. 1714, d. 1754, md.
SARAH _____.

29. **JOHN ROWELL [PHILIP 6]** He was born in 1683
at Amesbury, Mass. and bapt. 30 April 1699 at
Salisbury. He died 1 Feb. 1736 at Kingston, N.H.
He married 2 March 1714/5 **ELIZABETH COLBY**, d/o
SAMUEL & DOROTHY (AMBROSE) COLBY. She was born 7
Dec. 1694 in Amesbury. Alive 1741. In 1729 they
moved to Chester, N.H. lot #114. Occ. joiner.
Estate 22 Feb. 1737/8 [4:14]

Children: 91. **ENOCH**, b. 1716, d. 19 Nov. 1776,
md. **MIRIAM** _____.
92. **JUDITH**, b. abt 1718, md. 19 Nov.
1744 **TIMOTHY SAUNDERS**.
93. **BENONI**, b. 1720-3, d.y.
94. **JOHN**, b. 22 Oct. 1729, d. 12
Oct. 1760, md. 1749 **ELIZABETH
PARSON**.

95. HANNAH/SARAH, b. 1724, md. 1744
    JOHN/JONATHAN SANDERS.
96. JUDITH, b. 1726.
97. ELIPHELET, b. 22 Oct. 1729, m.1,
    25 Dec. 1748 SARAH KING, m.2,
    MEHITABLE BAKER.
98. ABENDIGO, bp 25 July 1731, d.y.
99. ELIZABETH, b. 1736, d. 7 Mar.
    1808, md. 1756 JONATHAN
    ELKINS, 9 children.

30. JOB ROWELL [PHILIP 6] He was born in 19
Jan. 1671 and bapt. 30 April 1699 at Salisbury,
Mass. He married 7 Aug. 1705 BETHIA(H) BROWN,
d/o ABRAHAM & ELIZABETH (SHEPHARD) BROWN. She
born July 1684 at Salisbury. Occ. weaver.
Soldier 1703 at Salisbury. His will dated 4 May
1736, proved 21 May 1736. Res.at Salisbury.

Children: 100. JEMIMA, b. 18 Sep. 1705, d.
               1774, md. 30 Jan. 1728/9
               JOSHUA BLAKE.
          101. KEZIAH, b. 14 Feb. 1707, md. 12
               Sep. 1728 ORLANDO COLBY. 8 ch
          102. ELIJAH, b. 6 Jan. 1710, d.
               1774, md. 11 June 1733 JANE
               GREENFIELD. Named in N.H.
               Court Cases 1743 & 1760.
          103. JOHN, b. 23 Sep. 1713, d. 1757,
               md. 17 Jan. 1736/7 SARAH
               CHANDLER.
          104. JOB, b. 20 June 1716, d. 1772,
               md. 13 Dec. 1739 MERIBAH
               WEED.
          105. THOMAS, b. 1 Mar. 1718/9, d. 24
               Mar. 1745, m.1, 11 Nov. 1737
               SARAH CHANDLER, m.2, SARAH
               MORRILL.
          106. SARAH, b. 23 July 1722, md. 1
               Jan. 1735/6 EDMUND SAWYER.
          107. ELIZABETH, b. 27 Aug. 1725, d.
               23 June 1762, md. 26 Nov.
               1747 JOSEPH ROWELL. (#55)

31. HEPZIBAH ROWELL [PHILIP 6] She was born 21 Nov. 1687. She died 6 Oct. 1688.

32. JUDITH ROWELL [PHILIP 6] She was born 21 Nov. 1689 at Amesbury, Mass. She married 5 May 1715 **JOHN GILL**. Res. at Salisbury, Mass.

Children: i. SAMUEL, b. 22 Dec. 1716.
          ii. JOHN, b. 1 May 1720.

34. ELIZABETH ROWELL [PHILIP 6] She was born 8 Dec. 1695. Nothing further known.

35. BENONI ROWELL Jr.[BENONI 13] He was born 1715 and bapt. 7 July 1728 at Haverhill, Mass. He died about 1798 at Salem, N.H. He married 28 Sep. 1742 **MARY YOUNG** at Salem, Mass. d/o **ISREAL YOUNG**. She born 1725 at Amesbury. She alive July 1820. His will dated 6 Apr. 1798, inv. 15 Aug. 1798, $153.92 and 18 Dec. 1799, $113.11, Son **ISREAL** and Widow exectors. [v.32, pg. 469] Occ. yeoman and farmer. He bought land in Methuen 20 July 1742 [65:120] Sold land in Salem 1757 & 1759 [55:342, 67:391] Soldier 1746 and 1758. Signed Assoc. Test 1776. 1790 Census at Salem. Res. Salem, N.H.

Children: 111. ASA, b. 4 June 1743, md. HITTY
               SESSIONS.
           112. PHILIP S., bp 1745, md. 1776
               DORCUS REDINGTON.
           113. JACOB, b. 1 Mar. 1747, d. 14
               Aug. 1835, md. 21 May 1780
               MEHITABLE CLEMENT.
           114. MARY, b. c1750, liv. 1837, md.
               1774 WILLIAM DUTY.
           115. ISREAL, b. 24 July 1753, md. 22
               Nov. 1781 MARY YOUNG.
           116. LEMUEL, b. 1755, d. 29 Mar.
               1808, md. 2 Jan. 1780 SARAH
               HOOKER.

117. JAMES, b. 3 June 1763, liv.
     1826, m.1. 6 July 1800 POLLY
     McNEAL, m.2, 2 Apr. 1820
     ELSEA COLIMER.
118. PHEBE, b. c1764.
119. HANNAH, b. c1766, d. 1826, md.
     _____ MONTGOMERY. 4 children.
120. SIMON, b. 26 May 1768?

36. JOSIAH ROWELL [BENONI 13] He was born 1717
and bapt. 7 July 1728 at Haverhill, Mass. He
married 1 May 1740 HANNAH DAVIS of Haverhill.
Will of JOHN DAVIS of Hampstead, 15 Nov. 1756
gave 5 shillings to daughter HANNAH ROWELL
[v.20, p.101] He signed the Assoc. Test 1776 at
Salem, N.H. Res. Methuen, Mass. 1741, later at
Salem, N.H.

Children: 122. PHILIP, b. 1745.
          123. JOSIAH Jr., b. c1747, m.1,
               JUDITH _____, m.2, Mrs.
               ABIGAIL DUSTIN.
          124. JACOB, b. c1748.
          125. WILLIAM, b. c1749, d. Mar.
               1844, md. 6 June 1776
               HANNAH DUTY.

37. MARY ROWELL [BENONI 13] She was bapt. 7
July 1728 at Haverhill, Mass. Nothing further
known.

38. SAMUEL ROWELL [BENONI 13] He was born 1720
and bapt. 7 July 1728 at Haverhill, Mass. He
died intestate in 1760 at Salem, N.H. He
married 18 Aug. 1745 DEBORAH MORGAN. Admin.
estate granted to DEBORAH 1 Dec. 1760 at
Portsmouth [v.21, p. 543] Inv. 6 Apr. 1761 £916
[22:137]. She married second JONATHAN CORLISS.
Estate papers mention 2 daughters under age 7
years, but not named.

ROWELL FAMILY - NEW ENGLAND
4th Generation

39. SARAH ROWELL [BENONI 13] She was born 1709
and bapt. 7 July 1728 at Haverhill, Mass. She
married PETER JOHNSON.

40. JOHN ROWELL [JOHN 17] He married MARY
BEDEL. Res. Bath, N.H.

Children: 129. JACOB, b. 1 Sep. 1774, md.
                19 Feb. 1795 SARAH BELKNAP.

43. JACOB ROWELL [JOHN 17] He was bapt. 8 Dec.
1730 at Berwick, Maine and died Sept. 1831 at
Belfast, Maine. He married 1st. 6 Aug. 1772 at
Woolwich, HANNAH CARLTON and married 2nd 17
Jan. 1793 Mrs. LUCY (CUSHING) VINING.

Children by 1st Wife:
            130. JONATHAN, b. c1771, d. 6 Mar.
                 1861, md. 6 Feb. 1806 CLAUDIA
                 SHAW.
            131. JESSE, b. 2 Jan. 1777, d. 4
                 June 1850, m.1, FANNY JONES,
                 m.2, 12 July 1812 SUSANNAH
                 LINSCOTT.
            132. JAMES, m.1, June 1810 SUSAN
                 LITTLEFORD, m.2, _____.
by 2nd Wife:
            133. RUFUS VINEY, b. 9 Sep. 1793, d.
                 5 Sep. 1867, md. EDA BACON.
            134. NANCY (or MARY), b. 22 Feb.
                 1795, md. 16 Feb. 1817
                 FRANCIS CHAPMAN.
            135. LUCINDA, b. 24 Feb. 1797, md.
                 13 Nov. 1825 JOSEPH WOODMAN.
            136. HENRY, b. 10 May 1799, md. 15
                 Apr. or 23 May 1819 SARAH
                 SILVESTER.
            137. JULIA, b. 7 Oct. 1802, md. 5
                 Mar. 1823 JOHNSON S. HOWARD.
            138. HARRIET, b. 31 Dec. 1806, twin.
            139. HOAK or HOOKER, b. 31 Dec. 1806
                 twin.

ROWELL FAMILY - NEW ENGLAND

FIFTH GENERATION

50. **THOMAS ROWELL** [VALENTINE 21] He was born 9
Feb. 1702/3 at Amesbury, Mass. and died 21 Sep.
1790 ae 87 years. He married 21 April 1725
ABIGAIL STEVENS, d/o ROGER & SARAH (NICHOLAS)
STEVENS at Kingston, N.H. She born 17 July 1706
and died 30 April 1786, ae 80 years. N.H. deed
[31:493] sold land in Amesbury 8 Mar. 1743 to
Thomas Challis and [78:138] sold to William
Rowell 5 July 1757. Occ. Innkeeper at Amesbury
in 1737. Ensign, Deacon of West Parish 2nd
church. Public Service in Rev. War.

Children: 150. **VALENTINE**, b. 3 Jan. 1727/8, d.
                3 July 1736.
           151. **LOIS**, b. 16 Sep. 1729, d. 10
                Mar. 1817, md. 22 Nov. 1750
                SAMUEL GREENLEAF. 5 children.
           152. **EUNICE**, b. 1 Mar. 1731/2, md.
                24 Apr. 1753 **BENJAMIN
                KINGSBURY** at Newbury, Mass.
           153. **ABIGAIL**, b. 1 Nov. 1733, d. 5
                Jan. 1737, 4 yrs.
           154. **PHINEAS**, b. 21 Dec. 1735, d. 27
                Dec. 1736.
           155. **VALENTINE**, b. 27 Dec. 1738, d.
                3 July 1746, 9 yrs.
           156. **ABIGAIL**, b. 19 Dec. 1742, d. 11
                Jan. 1754.
           157. **MARY**, b. 25 Aug. 1745, d. 18
                Oct. 1840, md. 7 Jan. 1769
                WILLIAM COFFIN LITTLE.
           158. **ANNA**, b. 11 May 1748, d. 14
                Sep. 1827, m.1, **ELIPHALET
                HOYT**, m.2, **STEPHEN CLEMENTS**,
                m.3, **SETH KENDRICK**.

51. **WILLIAM ROWELL** [VALENTINE 21] He was born 5
Sep. 1705 at Amesbury, Mass. and died 1785. He
married first 5 Jan. 1731/2 at Amesbury
ELIZABETH CHALLIS, d/o **WILLIAM & MARGARET**
(FOWLER) CHALLIS of Amesbury. She born 25 Jan.
1701/2, died 24 May 1756. He married second Mrs.
HANNAH (SARGENT) ROGERS. He was a weaver at

weaver at Amesbury. Removed to Newtown, N.H. in 1765. His will dated 28 Aug. 1779, proved 29 Mar. 1785. [v.28, pg. 192] Inv. f388..4..8. Had 41 acres with buildings. Son WILLIAM executor. Children named in will. Bought land in Amesbury from Thomas Rowell 5 July 1757 [78:138] Had 4 deeds at Newton, N.H. He may have married third SARAH DAY.

Children: 159. CHRISTOPHER, b. 29 Oct. 1732, bp 5 Nov. 1732, d. 1812, md. 28 Oct. 1756 RUTH MORSE.

160. JACOB, bp 23 Dec. 1733, md. 6 Sep. 1759 ANNE CURRIER.

161. WILLIAM, bp 8 Feb. 1735/6, md. 10 Oct. 1765 HANNAH MORSE.

162. ANNE, bp 28 May 1738, md. 16 Nov. 1759 WILLIAM CALIF.

163. HANNAH, bp 28 Aug. 1740, md. ABNER ROGERS.

164. ELIZABETH, bp 20 Oct. 1742, md. _____ CARLTON.

165. SARAH, b. 1 July, bp 13 Sep. 1744, md. 22 Oct. 1766 ABNER SARGENT at Salem, Mass., 10 children.

166. LOUIS (LOIS), b. 7 Apr. 1750, d. 23 Jan. 1754.

by 3rd wife:

167. HANNAH ROGERS, b. 21 Aug. 1762.

168. HANNAH MORSE, b. 10 Oct. 1765.

55. JOSEPH ROWELL [VALENTINE 21] He was born 2 Sep. 1724 and died 23 June 1762. He married 26 Nov. 1747 ELIZABETH ROWELL, (#107) d/o JOB & BETHIA (BROWN) ROWELL. She born 27 Aug. 1725 and died 23 June 1762. He married second 1 Mar. 1763 OLIVE COFFIN at Newbury, Mass.. Did he die in 1762, or did he m.2, in 1763?

Children: 170. HANNAH, b. 26 Aug. 1748.

ROWELL FAMILY - NEW ENGLAND
5th Generation

171. THOMAS, b. 3 Apr. 1750, d. 12
      Dec. 1816, md. 10 Oct. 1778
      HANNAH BECKET.
172. JOSEPH, b. 27 Mar. 1752.
173. JOSEPH, b. 2 Dec. 1754.
174. ELISABETH, b. 23 July 1757, d.
      16 Aug. 1760.
175. VALENTINE, b. 19 Aug. 1760.
by 2nd wife:
176. ELIZABETH, b. 17 June 1764, d.>
      1824, md. JAMES PURINGTON.

58. VALENTINE ROWELL [PHILIP 23] He was born 25
Nov. 1708 at Salisbury, Mass.

59. JACOB ROWELL [PHILIP 23] He was born 14
Sep. 1710 at Salisbury, Mass. He married 20 Dec.
1732/3 DOROTHY STRAW, d/o WILLIAM & LYDIA
(PURRINGTON) STRAW. [STOW]

Children: 180. WILLIAM, b. 11 Sep. 1740, d. 27
                Sep. 1816, md. 5 Mar. 1763
                MARY BROWN.
           181. DOROTHY, b. 10 Nov. 1734.
           182. DANIEL, b. 10 May 1739.

60. PHILIP ROWELL [PHILIP 23] He was born 13
Dec. 1713. He married 16 Oct. 1736 ANN WOOD.

66. ICHABOD ROWELL [PHILIP 23] He was born 20
Nov. 1729. He married 5 June 1755 SARA TUCKER.
Will of JOSEPH TUCKER of New Ipswich, 2 Jan.
1769 gave to daughter SARAH ROWELL £4. He sold
land in Kingston, N.H. in 1757 and 1760 [51:416
& 61:162]

Children: 189. MOSES, b. Sep. 1774, d. 26
                Aug. 1848, md. 9 Oct. 1797
                PHOEBE EATON.
           190. RICHARD, b. c1775, md. 1798
                SUSANNA HEARD/HEALD.

67. PHILIP ROWELL [JACOB 25] He was born 28
Mar. 1695 at Amesbury and died 18 Apr. 1780,
aged 85 yrs. His will dated 10 Aug. 1765. He
married 10/17 Oct. 1719 ELIZABETH PURRINGTON,
d/o JAMES & ELIZABETH PURRINGTON of Salisbury.
She born 8 Dec. 1695 and died 5 Aug. 1765, aged
70 years at Amesbury, Mass. Many N.H. deeds.
Bought from Jacob Rowell of Amesbury land in
Nottingham 6 Feb. 1730/1. [30:110] Got share of
saw mill in Kingston in estate of Moses Rowell
30 Sep. 1737.

Children: 200. JACOB, b. 27 Jan. 1720, d. 7
              Feb. 1721.
           201. MIRIAM, b. 23 Mar. 1722, d. 22
              July 1752, md. 4 Nov. 1742
              EBENEZER SARGENT, s/o
              EBENEZER & ANN SARGENT.
           202. JACOB, b. 12 Apr. 1724, d. 29
              Sep. 1813, md. 22 Jan. 1761
              ANNA BUXTON.
           203. SARAH, b. 8 Jan. 1726, md. 24
              May 1748 MOSES WADLEIGH, 1
              child.
           204. LYDIA, b. 2 June 1728, md. 5
              Apr. 1753 EZEKIEL JONES, s/o
              JOHN & SUSANNA JONES.
           205. MARY, b. 23 Jan. 1729/30, d.
              26 May 1768, md. 5 Feb. 1761
              PELEG CHALLIS.
           206. HANNAH, b. 7 July 1732, d. 26
              July 1736.
           207. MOSES, b. 25 Jan. 1733/4, d. 8
              Aug. 1800, m.1, 26 Nov. 1761
              HANNAH PEASLEE, m.2, 23 Feb.
              1774 MARY COLLINS.
           208. RUTH, b. 27 Nov. 1735, d. 4
              Dec. 1735.

70. MOSES ROWELL [JACOB 25] He was born 29 Nov.
1699 at Amesbury and died 20 Jan. 1733 by a
cave-in at Kingston, N.H. He married 28 Nov.
1723 JEMIMA CHANDLER at Amesbury, Mass. She

married second Oct. 1737 **JACOB BROWN.** She born
18 Oct. 1788. His will is dated 1733 at
Kingston. Several N.H. deeds. He and Jacob
Rowell bought a saw mill in Kingston 10 Nov.
1776 [19:274] Jemima named Admin. of estate 22
May 1733 [13:253]. Inv. was £189.11.6. She sold
share in saw mill to Philip Rowell of Salisbury.
[23:109]

Children: 210. **HANNAH,** b. 16 Mar. 1724/5.
             211. **SARAH,** bp. 19 Nov. 1725.
             212. **PHEBE,** bp. 19 Nov. 1725.
             213. **SUSANNAH,** bp. 19 Nov. 1725.
             214. **JEMIMA,** b. 17 Jan. 1732/3.

71. **AARON ROWELL** [JACOB 25] He was born 29 Nov.
1701 at Amesbury and died 1768/9. He married
first 19 Jan. 1726/7 **RUTH PURRINGTON,** d/o **JAMES
& LYDIA (MASSEY) PURRINGTON** of Salisbury. She
born 14 Apr. 1708. He married second 18 Feb.
1735 **MARY CHALLIS,** d/o **THOMAS & MARY (COLBY)
CHALLIS.** She born 20 Jan. 1707/8. His will dated
3 Feb. 1769, proved 8 May 1769 at Sandown, N.H.
Will names widow and children. Son WILLIAM named
executor. Inv. 13 May 1769. Had 50 acres and
buildings in Sandown. £150. 13 acres woodland
£18. Total inv. £252..11..0. [v.5, p.200]
Quaker.

Children by 1st Wife:
             215. **JAMES** , b. 22 Jan. 1727/8, d.
                  by 1769 unmd?
             216. **HANNAH,** b. 11 Oct. 1730, liv.
                  1769, md. 7 Mar. 1754
                  BENJAMIN OSGOOD. 7 children.
2nd Wife: 217. **THOMAS,** b. 21 Apr. 1737, d. 27
                  1816, m.1, **MARY _____,** m.2,
                  SARAH KENT.
             218. **AARON Jr.,** b. 1 Dec. 1738, md.
                  3 Nov. 1759 **HANNAH LOWELL,**
                  m.2, **MIRIAM _____.**
             220. **RUTH,** b. 13 Feb. 1742, md. 12
                  Nov. 1767 **THOMAS WELLS** at
                  Hampstead, N.H.

221. **WILLIAM**, b. 19 June 1745, md.
     1762 **Mrs. HANNAH ROGERS**.
222. **MARY**, b. 6 Jan. 1747, d. 3 Apr.
     1801. md. 12 Nov. 1766 **SAMUEL
     CURRIER**. 7 children.
223. **ELIZABETH**, b. 8 May 1751.
224. **PHILIP**, b. 2 Oct. 1755, m.1, 7
     Oct. 1779 **HANNAH WILLIAMS**,
     m.2, 28 Jan. 1792 **ANN
     JOHNSON**.

73. **DANIEL ROWELL [JACOB 25]** He was born 25
Nov. 1705 at Amesbury and died 1778/9 at
Kingston, N.H. He married 14 Mar. 1728 **ANNE
CURRIER**, d/o **JOHN & JUDITH (STEVENS) CURRIER**.
She born 3 Mar. 1708/9 and died 1750. Signed
Assoc. Test 1776. Estate admin. 25 May 1778 to
son JOSEPH. [v.24, p.219] Inv. 25 Mar. 1778 P.P.
£319..19..6, 80 acres with buildings £800..0..0.
Res. East Kingston and Weare, N.H.

Children: 225. **JUDA/JUDITH**, b. 8 Oct. 1733,
              bp 23 Oct. 1743, md. 3 June
              1755 **STEPHEN LONG**.
          226. **JACOB**, b. 1 Oct. 1735, d. 1812,
              md. 8 Aug. 1760 **ABIGAIL
              PRESCOTT**.
          227. **HANNAH**, b. 24 Dec. 1737, d.
              1798, md **STEPHEN LONG**.
          228. **MIRIAM**, b. 24 Aug. 1739, bp 23
              Oct. 1743, md. **JOSEPH JEWELL**.
          230. **RHODA**, bp 23 Oct. 1743, Will 4
              Sep. 1815, unmd.
          231. **NANCY/NANNY**, b. 8 July 1744, bp
              15 July 1744, d.y.
          232. **DANIEL M.**, bp 1 Dec. 1745, d.
              Nov. 1831, m.1, 24 Nov.1768
              JUDITH FRENCH.
          233. **JONATHAN**, b. 8 Oct. 1732, bp 23
              Oct. 1743, d.y.
          234. **MARY**, bp 24 Dec. 1749.
          235. **ELIZABETH**, bp 29 Apr. 1750, d.
              6 Apr. 1797, md. **ADONIJEH
              FELLOWS**, 4 children.

236. MOSES, bp 15 Oct. 1752, d. 3
Feb. 1841, md. 1802 Mrs.
BETSY (BROWN) FOLSOM.

75. GIDEON ROWELL [JACOB 25] He was born 17
Sep. 1709 at Amesbury, Mass. and died by 1785.
He married 27 Jan. 1731 at Salisbury ELINOR
MORRILL, d/o DANIEL & HANNAH (STEVENS) MORRILL.
She born 27 Jan. 1710/11. He bought land in
Chester, N.H. 19 Mar. 1752. [61:1400] Res.
Amesbury, Mass.

Children: 242. BENJAMIN, bp 20 Aug. 1736, unmd
1785. Candia, N.H.
243. HANNAH, bp 19 Nov. 1738.
244. MERIAM, bp 7 Nov. 1740, living
1785.
245. SARAH, bp 10 Aug. 1749, living
1785.
246. MARY, bp 10 July 1752.
247. SAMUEL, b. c1754, d. 1815
unmd., Rev. War Soldier.

76. THOMAS ROWELL [THOMAS 27] He was born 9
Feb. 1702/3 at Boston, Mass.

78. SAMUEL ROWELL [THOMAS 27] He was born 19
May 1705 at Boston, Mass. He married there 30
Aug. 1733 ELIZABETH ADAMS.

87. ABRAHAM ROWELL [ABRAHAM 28] He was born 16
Sep. 1706 at Newbury, Mass. He sold land in
Nottingham, N.H. 10 Mar. 1728/9. [19:375]

90. RICE ROWELL [ABRAHAM 28] He was born 1714
at Nottingham, N.H. and died there in 1754. He
married SARAH _____. His will dated 14 Feb. 1754
and proved 22 Nov. 1754. Wife named Admin.
[v.19, p.157] Oldest sons ABRAHAM and RICE
divided land and mill equally. Other children
rec'd £20 each. Son RICE named guardian of
NEHEMIAH, age 14 yrs. Wife SARAH and children
named in will. He bought from Abraham Rowell
land in Nottingham, N. H. in 1736 [29:131] Res.
Nottingham, N.H.

Children: 260. **ABRAHAM**, c1733.
261. **RICE**, 1734, d. 1809, md. 1760 **ELIZABETH HARVEY**.
262. **JOHN**, c1735.
263. **MARY**,
264. **JUDITH** , possibly md. 6 Mar. 1764 **SAMUEL FISKE**.
265. **SARAH** , bp 24 July 1748.
267. **NEHEMIAH**, b. 1752, d. 1779, md. **ELIZABETH** _____.
268. **ELIZABETH**, md. 12 Feb. 1776 **JAMES MUCHMORE** at Portsmouth.
269. **WILLIAM**, b. 1755, d. 1811, md. 13 Dec. 1781 **RUTH MATTHEWS**.

91. **ENOCH ROWELL [JOHN 29]** He was born in 1716 at Amesbury and died 19 Nov. 1776 at Ticonderoga. He married **MIRIAM** _____. She died 12 Dec. 1812 at Candia, N.H. His will 24 Mar. 1776 [Exeter #4390]. Estate - widow Admin. 21 Dec. 1776. Names all children. [v.23, p.442] Inv. £150, 24 Mar. 1776. Division of 33 acres of real estate 23 July 1781. As heir of John P. Rowell, he sold land in Chester, N.H. to Enoch Colby. Res. Candia, N.H.

Children: 270. **ELIZABETH**, b. 12 April 1750, d. 13 July 1752.
271. **JOHN**, b. 13 April 1752, d. 14 Nov. 1752.
272. **MERIAM**, b. 30 Sep. 1753, md. 17 Oct. 1774 **Gen'l JOHN CAMMET**.
273. **ENOCH**, b. 3 July 1756, d. 2 Aug. 1840, md. 8 Sep. 1778 **RACHEL WORTHEN**.
274. **MARY**, b. 29 Jan. 1763 at Chester, md. **HENRY GOTHAM**. 11 children.
275. **DANIEL**, b. 3 Sep. 1765.
276. **ELEPHELET**, b. 8 June 1768, d. 3 July 1801, md. **ABIGAIL SMITH**.
277. **JUDITH**, d. 20 Dec. 1781.

94. **JOHN ROWELL [JOHN 29]** He was born 22 Oct.

1729 at Chester, N.H. and died 12 Oct. 1760 at
Charleston, N.H. He married in 1749 **ELIZABETH
PARSON** at Chester. Enlisted 24 Apr. 1755, Col.
Joseph Blanchard Reg't expedition against Crown
Point. Service ended 23 July 1755. Was soldier
in French and Indian War, Col. Haviland's
expedition against Canada, 10 Mar. 1760. He
became ill and died in service.

Children: 285. **MOSES**, b. 1748 at Chester.
            286. **BENJAMIN**, b. 1750.
            287. **PATIENCE**, b. 1752, md. 8 Oct.
                 1768 **PHILIP HAZELTINE** at
                 Haverhill, Mass.
            288. **SAMUEL**, b. 1754, d. 11 June
                 1830, md. 27 Nov. 1777 **SARAH
                 DUSTIN**.
            289. **JOSEPHINE**, b. 1756, md, a
                 BOWLES ?
            290. **SARAH**, b. 1758, md. a **NEWELL** ?

97. **ELIPHELET ROWELL** [JOHN 29] He was born 22
Oct. 1729 at Amesbury, Mass. and died at
Windham, Conn. 1801. He married first 26 Dec.
1751 **SARAH KING** at Sutton. He married second 14
June 1795 **MEHITABLE BAKER** at Charleston, Mass.
He served in the Rev. War as a private from
Mass. He sold land in Chester, N.H. 12 Dec. 1748
[38:136]

Children: 294. **ELIPHELET**, b. c1753, d. 1815,
                 md. **EUNICE PARKS**.
            295. **PETER**, b. 13 Aug. 1758, md. 10
                 Oct. 1782 **BETTEY MARSH**.
            296. **SARAH**, b. 10 Apr. 1762, md. 17
                 Feb. 1785 **JOHN SALTER**.
            297. **LUCY**, b. 9 Apr. 1768.
            298. **ELI**, b. 7 Oct. 1774, md. 5 Oct.
                 1797 **LOIS HAYDON**.

98. **ABENDAGO ROWELL** [JOHN 29] He was born in
1731. Nothing further known.

ROWELL FAMILY - NEW ENGLAND
5th Generation

102. **ELIJAH ROWELL JOB 30]** He was born 6 Jan. 1710 and died 1774. He married 11 June 1733 **JANE GREENFIELD** at South Hampton, N.H. She died after 1777. Some sources call him **ALIGO**. Will names widow **JANE** and son **NATHANIEL** as executor. Estate inv. £ 97..9..1. 4 acres with house and barn 24 Jan. 1775. [v.24, p.123] Res. So. Hampton.

Children: 305. **MEHITABEL**, b. 27 Oct. 1734.
            306. **MARY**, b. 13 Aug. 1736, d. 9
                 Dec. 1744.
            307. **JOB**, b. 4 Oct. 1738, md. 22
                 Oct. 1761 **PRISCILLA EMERSON**.
            308. **ELIJAH**, b. 2 Mar. 1741.
            309. **NATHANIEL**, b. 22 Sep. 1744, md.
                 8 Oct. 1764 **JUDITH MORSE**.
            310. **THOMAS**, b. 20 Feb. 1748.
            311. **JOHN**, b. 3 Dec. 1750, d. 14
                 June 1822, md. 10 Aug. 1770
                 ANNE CURRIER, m.2 **DOLLY
                 LEAVITT**.
            312. **MOLLY**, b. 9 July 1754, md. 16
                 Dec. 1776 **TIMOTHY HUNTINGTON**.
            313. **BETTY**, b. 31 May 1757, md. 7
                 July 1782 **EZEKIEL FLANDERS**.

103. **JOHN ROWELL [JOB 30]** He was born 23 Sep. 1713 at Salisbury, Mass. and died 1757 at Epping, N.H. He married 17 Jan. 1737 **SARAH (CHANDLER) RUSSELL**. The widow of **JOHN RUSSELL** by whom she had 7 children. She born 10 Mar. 1693. Occ. Joiner. His estate Inv. 20 Jan. 1758, £ 3869..2..0., had 36 acres. Admin. of estate granted to widow **SARAH** 26 Oct. 1757. [v.20, p. 329, 428] Bought land in Exeter 11 June 1738 [23:500] Res. Epping at Red Oak Hill.

Children: 315. **JOHN**, b. 15 Nov. 1737, md. 1760
                 HANNAH WINSLOW.
            316. **SARAH**, md. **JAMES RUNDLETT**.

104. **JOB ROWELL Jr.[JOB 30]** He was born 20 June 1716 at Salisbury and died 1772. He married 13 Dec. 1739 **MERIBAL WEED** at Hampstead, N.H. She

born c1718 and died 3 April 1791 at Strafford, Vt. At Goffstown in 1760. Occ. farmer. His will dated 13 Aug. 1767, proved 29 June 1772. Wife named. Son DAVID received 6 shillings, son JONATHAN lands in Goffstown. Inv. £162..12..0. [v.21, p.61] JOHN McCURDY app. guardian of JONATHAN ROWELL minor 14 yrs. Many land deeds in Exeter, N.H. 23 July 1765 he sold land in Goffstown to son David.

Children: 320. **DAVID**, b. 25 Nov. 1742, d. 30
                 Mar. 1820, md. 2 Apr. 1766
                 Mrs. SARAH (CHENEY) REMICK.
            321. **MAREY**, b. 21 Aug. 1744, d. 2
                 Nov. 1749.
            322. **JONATHAN**, b. 11 Oct. 1753 at
                 Salisbury, m.1, 27 Feb. 1776
                 MEHITABEL WELLS, m.2, 1787
                 HANNAH NEWMAN.

105. **THOMAS ROWELL [JOB 30]** He was born 1 Mar. 1718 and bapt. 24 Mar. 1743 at South Hampton, N.H. and died there 24 Mar. 1745. He married first 11 Nov. 1737 **SARAH CHANDLER** at South Hampton, N.H. He married second 1742 **SARAH MORRILL**, d/o **JACOB & ELIZABETH (STEVENS) MORRILL** of Salisbury, Mass. She born 22 June 1722 and died 19 Mar. 1788. Land grant 1735 at Hopkinton. ANDREW MORRILL named guardian of son ABRAHAM 8 April 1755. Children by 2nd wife.

Children: 323. **ABRAHAM**, b. 3 Dec. 1743, bp 14
                 Apr. 1745. d. 1815, md. 5
                 Apr. 1764 **ELIZABETH EASTMAN.**
            324. **ELIZABETH**, b. 16 Mar. 1744/5,
                 bp 14 Apr. 1745, d. Nov.
                 1748.

109. **JAMES ROWELL [AARON 33]** He was born 22 Jan. 1727 at Amesbury, Mass.

ROWELL FAMILY - NEW ENGLAND
5th Generation

111. ASA ROWELL [BENONI 35] He was born 4 June
1743 at Salem, N.H. He married about 1767
HITTY/MEHITABLE SESSIONS. She born 19 Aug. 1744
at Salem. Rev. War service. He bought 10 ac. in
Salem, N.H. 29 Mar. 1774 [59:138]

Children: 325. SIMEON, b. 26 May 1768, d. 26
Aug. 1772.
326. AMOS, b. 12 May 1770, d. 21
Nov. 1770.
327. DOLLY, b. 22 Sep. 1771.
328. HITTY, b. 14 Oct. 1773.
329. ASA, b. 12 June 1775.
330. BENJAMIN, b. 28 Mar. 1777, d.
12 Apr. 1813 at Thetford, Vt.
331. STEPHEN, b. 8 Mar. 1779, d. 13
Feb. 1855, md. HANNAH HOUSE.
332. LOIS, b. 2 July 1781, md. PETER
WELLS.
333. DARIUS T., b. 10 June 1783, d.
13 Feb. 1855, md. 29 Dec. 1812
POLLY MORAY at W. Fairlee, Vt.

112. PHILIP S. ROWELL [BENONI 35] He was born
about 1745 at Salem, N.H., bapt. 5 May 1745 and
died 1826 at Allentown, N.H. He married about
1776 at Tolland, Conn. DORCUS REDINGTON,
possible d/o DANIEL & HANNAH (HAYES) REDINGTON.
She born 1756 and died 15 Dec. 1798 at Salem,
age 42 yrs. 1790 census at Salem, N.H. Possibly
married 2nd at Allentown, N.H. ?

Children: 335. ISREAL, b. 4 Dec. 1776.
336. DANIEL, b. 24 May 1779, md.
1799 MEHITABLE SMITH.
337. HEZEKIAH, b. 27 Apr. 1781, d.
22 July 1852, md. 21 Dec.
1809 SARAH HASKELL.
338. JOSEPH, b. 22 Mar. 1783, d.y.
339. DORCUS, b. 25 Apr. 1785, d. 28
Jan. 1868, md. 11 Feb. 1811
BENJAMIN WHEELER at
Allentown, 2 children.

- 54 -

ROWELL FAMILY - NEW ENGLAND
5th Generation

340. JOSEPH, b. 7 May 1787, d. 7
    Jan. 1870, md. 1812 ANN
    BARTLETT.
341. JOHN REDINGTON, b. 24 July
    1790, d. 18 Mar. 1870, m.1,
    DORCUS WHEELER, m.2 20 Dec.
    1817 RHODA G. HARRISON.
342. SARAH, b. 13 Sep. 1793.

113. JACOB ROWELL [BENONI 35] He was born 1
Mar. 1747 at Salem, N.H. and died 14 Aug. 1835,
age 88 at Salem, N.H. He married 21 May 1780 at
Salem MEHITABLE CLEMENTS. She died 2 Mar. 1846,
age 84 years. He was named in the will of his
brother ISREAL on 7 Feb. 1826. Children born at
Hill, N.H.

Children: 345. SALLY, b. 5 Mar. 1790.
           346. BETTY, b. 25 Feb. 1792.
           347. SAMUEL, b. 24 May 1798.

115. ISREAL ROWELL [BENONI 35] He was born 24
July 1753. He married 22 Nov. 1781 MARY YOUNG.
Served in Rev. War for 3 years, 2nd N.H. Reg't,
Col. Geo. Ried's Company. Discharged April 1780.
Had pension #S45125. Says no children. Inventory
$109.17. In 1820 resident of Salem, N.H. age 68.
His will dated 7 Feb. 1826, proved 15 June 1831.
Wife MARY named with his brothers and sister.
JONATHAN MASSEY exec. [v.53, p.313] 1790 Census
[1-2-1] and 1800 Census [11001/3001].

116. LEMUEL ROWELL [BENONI 35] He was born 1755
at Salem, N.H. and died 29 Mar. 1808 at Croyden,
N.H. He married 2 Jan. 1780 at West Hartford,
Conn. SARAH HOOKER. She born 8 June 1758 and
died 17 May 1844 He married second MARY
SEVERENCE of Salem, N.H. Served 8 yrs Rev. War,
N.H. & Conn. 1790 census at Salem, N.H. and on
tax roll 1799-1808 at Croyton, N.H.

Children: by 1st Wife:
           350. LEMUEL, b. 1781, d. 18 Feb.
           1850.

ROWELL FAMILY - NEW ENGLAND
5th Generation

by 2nd Wife:
      351. **EDMUND RANDOLPH**, b. 1783, d.
         1827, md. 9 July 1823
         JOANNA N. COCHRAN.
      352. **CHARLES**, b. 1785, d. 11 Jan.
         1867, md. 9 Feb. 1809
         MARY (POLLY) DAVIS.
      353. **SHERBURNE B.**, b. 1788, d. 1859,
         md. **ANNA WITHERSPOON.**
      354. **NANCY**, md. **JONATHAN MERRILL.**
      355. **LOIS**,
      356. **MARTHA WHEELER**, b. 7 May 1794,
         d. 6 Feb. 1862 Illinois, md.
         1820 in N.H. **COMFORT ELLIOTT.**
      357. **MARY**, md. _____ **PERKINS.**
      358. **CLARISSE**, md. 4 July 1825 **JOHN HAZELTINE.**
      359. **LYDIA**,

117. **JAMES ROWELL** [BENONI 35] He was born 3 June 1763 at Salem, N.H. Living 1866. He married first 6 July 1800 **POLLY McNEAL.** He married second 2 Apr. 1820 **ELSA COLIMER** at Vershire, Vt. She born 1778. Occ. farmer. Named in 1810 Census in Vt. He enlisted March 1776, Col. Stark Reg't N.H. line. Wounded at Fort Montgomery 1776. Captured by British at Ticondaroga. Prisoner 3 months. Fought at battles of Monmouth and White Plains. Received pension #S41,101. Res. Vershire, Vt. Named in will of brother ISREAL 7 Feb. 1826.

Children: 361. **ELSEA**, b. 1802, md. _____ **McCALLEN.**
      362. **MARY/POLLY**, b. 1806, md. **Mr. ORDWAY.**
      363. **ELIZABETH**, b. 1810.

123. **JOSIAH ROWELL Jr.** [JOSIAH 36] He was born 1747 at Salem, N.H. and died 7 May 1823. He married first about 1766 **JUDITH _____**. He married second 14 Nov. 1792 **Mrs. ABIGAIL DUSTIN**

DUSTON of Hookset. Res. Hooksett in 1824. Son
PETER C. named executor of his estate 30 May
1823. Widow decline appointment. [v.30, p.278]
Inv. $846.61.

Children by 1st Wife:
      365. PHEOBE, b. 13 Nov. 1767, md. 31
          Mar. 1798 SAMUEL MARBLE.
      366. DAVID, b. 25 Aug. 1769, d.
          1834, md. 1794 MARY BROWN,
          m.2, 1809 DOLLY LOVERING.
      367. AMOS, b. 30 Sep. 1773, d. 1836,
          md. 12 July 1795 DOLLY
          GRIFFIN.
      368. RICHARD, b. 13 Jan. 1770, d. 12
          Nov. 1846 md. MARY CORLISS.
      369. JONATHAN, b. 14 Apr. 1781, d.
          18 Dec. 1833, md. 6 Mar. 1806
          LIVINIA ROWELL (#378).
by 2nd Wife:
      370. PETER CLEMENTS, b. 12 Jan.
          1794, md. 18 Aug. 1814 SUSAN
          EASTMAN of Pembroke, N.H.

125. WILLIAM ROWELL [JOSIAH 36]   He was born
c1749 and died 30 Mar. 1844. He married 6 June
1776 HANNAH DUTY, d/o MOSES & MARY (PALMER) DUTY
of Windham, N.H.   She died 3 March 1837 at
Derry, N.H. Rev. War service Pvt. N.H. Calib,
Sarah and John S. not named in will. Res. Salem,
N.H.

Children: 375. SARAH, b. 4 July 1777, md. 16
          Mar. 1796 BENJAMIN DUSTIN.
      376. MOSES DUTY, b. 5 Oct. 1778, d.
          16 Nov. 1857, md. 17 Jan.
          1808 LUCY ANN ADAMS.
      377. JOHN SULLIVAN, b. 1779, d.
          drowned Hudson River c1824
          md. MARGARET ALBERTSON.
      378. LIVINIA, b. 1782, d. 1 July
          1877, md. 6 Mar. 1806
          JONATHAN ROWELL (#369).

ROWELL FAMILY - NEW ENGLAND
5th Generation

379. JAMES, md. 12 Apr. 1821 REBECCA
     CHASE.
380. ELSIE, md. JOSIAH HOBART.
381. CALEB, md. MARY G. HUBBARD or
     HOBART.
382. MARY, md. JOHN SNELL.
383. ISAIAH, b. 1792, d. 25 June
     1847, md. SARAH ____. no
     children.
384. GEORGE WASHINGTON, b. 16 Oct.
     1794, md. 13 May 1818 RUTH
     CARTER.
385. HIRAM,

129. JACOB ROWELL [JOHN 40] He was born 1 Sep.
1774 at Bath, N.H. He married 19 Feb. 1795 at
Bath SARAH BALKNAP. Res. Bath, N.H.

Children: 400. JOHN, b. 30 Apr. 1797
           401. MARY, b. 4 Apr. 1801.
           402. JACOB, b. 4 June 1803, d.y..
           403. SUSANNAH, b. 5 June 1805.
           404. SALLY, b/d. 1811.
           405. MOODY, b. 10 Mar. 1810.
           406. SIMON,

130. JONATHAN ROWELL [JACOB 43] He was born
about 1771 and died 6 March 1861. He married 6
Feb. 1806 at Woodside CLAUDIA SHAW. She born
1786. Res. Montville, Maine.

Children: 410. MARY, b. 15 Feb. 1807.
           411. ESTHER (ANN), b. 3 Apr. 1809,
                md. 4 June 1834 JOHN ANNIS.
                7 children.
           412. DANIEL MERRILL, b. 28 June
                1811, m.1, 12 Aug. 1835
                HANNAH C. VOSS, m.2, 2 Feb.
                1878 Mrs. HANNAH F. VOSS.
           413. JESSE SHAW, b. 15 Oct. 1813,
                md. 8 or 25 Dec. 1836 HANNAH
                B. WRIGHT.
           414. WILLIAM, b. 28 Apr. 1816.
           415. PHEBE, b. 20 Aug. 1818.

131. JESSE ROWELL [JACOB 43] He was born 2 Jan.
1777 at Waldoboro, Me. and died 4 June 1850
(grave stone). Buried at Jefferson Village
Cemetary. He married 1st FANNY JONES. She born
11 Feb. 1785. He married 2nd, 12 July 1816
SUSANNAH LINSCOTT. She born c1791 and died 9 May
1865. Justice of Peace and Selectman. Res.
Jefferson, Maine. 1850 Census with son David.

Children by 1st Wife:
    416. ELIZA, b. 25 Apr. 1803.
    417. ALDEN, b. 23 Dec. 1804.
    418. FANNY, b. 17 July 1806, d. 25
        Sep. 1811.
    419. OLIVE, b. 28 Apr. 1808.
    420. MARY ANN, b. 22 Aug. 1809.
    421. GEORGE J., b. 26 Mar. 1811, d.
        22 May 1811.
    422. JANE, b. 8 May 1813.
    423. ARLETTE/ARALETTE H., b. 14 Sep.
        1815, md. 8 June 1839 LUTHER
        BIXBY Jr. at Boston.
by 2nd Wife:
    424. NANCY, b. 31 Aug. 1817, d. 15
        Nov. 1854, md. JOSIAH WINSLOW
        s/o JOHN & CHARLOTTE (CLARK)
        WINSLOW.
    425. HANNAH, b. 7 Oct. 1819, md.
        MERRIT DAMON.
    426. SARAH ANN, b. Aug. 1821, md. ?
        26 July 1840 IRA L. DELANO.
    427. DAVID, b. 17 Apr. 1823, d. 20
        Mar. 1890, md. 7 Dec. 1845
        MARY JANE KENNEDY, Served in
        Civil War, 21st Me. Reg't.
    428. PARIS, Rev., b. 31 Oct. 1825,
        d. 14 May 1894, md. 21 Sep.
        1855 ALMIRA P. HODGKINS.
    429. JESSE C., b. 18 Feb. 1831.

132. JAMES ROWELL [JACOB 43] He married first
June 1810 SUSAN LITTLEFORD at Frankfort, Maine.
She born 1789 in Maine alive 1850 census. He

married 2nd _____. Came from Montville. 1850
census at Frankfort, Me. Reportedly had 23
children.

Children: 430. **LORENZO DOW**, b. 4 Oct. 1811, d.
                  27 Mar. 1899, md. 7 Jan. 1837
                  Mrs. SUSAN HICKS FREEMAN at
                  Frankfort, Me.
             431. **DAVID**, b. 6 Sep. 1812, unmd.
             432. **ANDREW JACKSON**, b. 23 Feb.
                  1815, Lost at sea.
             433. **JAMES HARVEY**, b. 11 Feb. 1817,
                  d. 1884, m.1, **SARAH J.**
                  CHANERY/KENNEY, m.2, **MARY E.**
                  CLARK.
             434. **HARRIET**, b. 25 Apr. 1819, d.
                  c1839, unmd.
             435. **BENJAMIN FRANKLIN**, b. c1820,
                  md. 9 Mar. 1840 **SARAH BEAN**.
             436. **SUSAN**, d. c1900, m.1, **JOSEPH**
                  FOSTER, 3 ch. m.2, **Mr.**
                  DAYLEY.
             437. **AARON HOLBROOK**, b. 1828, d. 18
                  Nov. 1901, md. **MARY TAPLAY**.

133. RUFUS VINEY ROWELL [JACOB 43] He was born 9
Sep. 1793 Jefferson, Me. and died 5 Sep. 1867 at
Jefferson, Maine. He married **EDA BACON**, d/o
JABEZ & MARY (HILL) BACON. She born 19 April
1800. He is buried at Jamica Plain, Mass. Res.
Jefferson, Maine.

Children: 440. **SARAH B.**, b. 3 Mar. 1819.
             441. **WILLIAM H.**, b. 1 Jan. 1822.
             442. **SUSAN**, b. 10 Mar. 1824.
             443. **OLIVER PERRY**, b. 7 Sep. 1826,
                  md. **GEORGIANN P. BURCH**.
             444. **ANN SMITH**, b. 8 Dec. 1829.
             445. **SUSAN ANN**, b. 23 Feb. 1838.
             446. **ALBERT S/H.**, b. 13 Jan. 1834.

136. HENRY ROWELL [JACOB 43] He was born 10 May
1799. He married 23 May 1819 **SARAH/SALLY**
SILVESTER d/o **EBENEZER SILVESTER** of Freedom,

ROWELL FAMILY - NEW ENGLAND
5th Generation

Maine. She born 1798 and died 18 Feb. 1860 [62
yrs]. He married 2nd, 1 May 1861 **LARANE YOUNG.**
She died 4 March 1870 [71 yrs] Occ. farmer. 1850
census at Montville, Me.

Children: 449. **SARAH ANN**, b. c1824, d. 6 June
1839.
450. **JOHN W.**, b. 1830, md. ? 1860
LUCINDA FRANCES ROWELL,
(1834-1906), seaman.
451. **GEORGE F.**, b. 1834.
452. **JULIA L.**, b. 1836.
453. **CHARLES H.**, b. 1840, md. 19
Oct. 1864 Mrs. **SARAH A.D.**
ROWELL, m.2, ?? 9 Apr. 1885
IDA B. SANBORN.
454. **MERRILL**, b. 1838

SIXTH GENERATION

159. **CHRISTOPHER ROWELL [WILLIAM 51]** He was born 29 Oct. 1732 at Amesbury, Mass. and died 4 April 1812 at West Concord, N.H. He married 28 Oct. 1756 **RUTH MORSE**, d/o **BENJAMIN & MARGARET (BARTLETT) MORSE** of Amesbury. She was born 30 Aug, 1736 at Amesbury and died 1801 at West Concord. They resided at Amesbury until 1752, then removed to Newton, N.H., then Hampstead, N.H. in 1778, West Concord by 1782. They lived on a farm at north end of Penacock Lake. Occ. shoemaker. Had leather business at St. John's, Canada 1756-66. In 1764 he was Ensign in 9th Co. of 7th Reg't of foot. Had public service during Rev. War. Family was ordered out of Concord, N.H. 18 April 1780. They had come from Hampstead. [N.H. Court Case] Bought land in Newton 6 May 1761 [70:173] Sold land in Newton to Jacob Rowell 17 Oct. 1761 [87:321] Bought house and land in Newton 26 Dec. 1761 [78:175] Sold house and land to William Rowell 22 May 1765 [78:129]

Children: 500. **ELIZABETH**, b. 13 May 1759 at Newton, N.H., bp 6 Nov. 1759, d. 19 Jan. 1836, unmd.
           501. **RUTH**, b. 11 Aug. 1761, bp 16 Aug. 1761, d. 22 Sep. 1847, md. 25 Feb. 1814 **JOHN ICHABOD COLBY.**
           502. **CHRISTOPHER**, bp 16 Aug. 1761 at Kingston, N.H.
           503. **MOSES**, b. 11 June 1764, d. 14 Nov. 1846, m.1, **ELLICE CURRIER**, m.2, 7 Mar. 1799 **NANCY LEAVITT**, Rev. War Service.
           504. **THOMAS**, b. 13 Sep. 1767, d. 30 Sep. 1846, md. 1794 **LYDIA WILLIAMS.**

ROWELL FAMILY - NEW ENGLAND
6th Generation

505. CHRISTOPHER, b. 22 Aug. 1769,
     d. 1847, md. 27 Oct. 1798
     LYDIA ABBOTT.
506. JOHN, b. 27 Apr. 1772, d. 1796,
     unmd.
507. MICAJAH, b. 6 May 1774, d, 21
     July 1847, md. 1804 ELIZABETH
     SAVAGE.
508. HANNAH, b. 11 April 1776 at
     Hampstead, N.H., d. 1 Jan.
     1826 at Hartford, Vt. md. 4
     Dec. 1825 EDWARD BOSWORTH.

160. JACOB ROWELL [WILLIAM 51] He was born 23
Dec. 1733 at Amesbury, Mass. and died 1823 at
Salisbury, Mass. and buried at Frankfort, Me. He
married 6 Sep. 1759 ANNE CURRIER, d/o JONATHAN &
ANNE (CHALLIS) CURRIER. She born 6 April 1739 at
Amesbury, Mass. His will dated May 1805, proved
20 Mar. 1815 [v42, p. 270] Will names wife and
children. Inventory was $2,135.74. Res. Newton,
N.H.

Children: 510. LOIS, b. 14 Oct. 1758, md. 15
                Nov. 1782 DANIEL HOYT.
                Father's will gives her
                married name as KIMBALL.
           511. ANNE, b. 21 Nov. 1761, md.
                ANDREW WHITTIER.
           512. VALENTINE, b. 1 Nov. 1763.
           513. STEPHEN, b. c1764, md. PHEBE
                LITTLEFIELD.
           514. ELIZABETH, b. 27 May 1765, md.
                27 Mar. 1787 JOHN PILLSBURY.
           515. LYDIA, b. 31 July 1767.
           517. HANNAH, b. 11 May 1769, md. 4
                Dec. 1792 JOSEPH HOYT.
           518. MOLLY, b. 24 June 1771, d. 28
                Oct. 1832, md. 17 Feb. 1789
                THOMAS CURRIER at S. Hampton.
                7 children.
           519. JACOB, b. 5 June 1773, md. RUTH
                CURRIER.
           520. JUDITH, b. 28 Mar. 1775.

ROWELL FAMILY - NEW ENGLAND
6th Generation

    521. JONATHAN, b. 28 Jan. 1778.
    522. JUDITH, b. 15 Feb. 1779.

161. WILLIAM ROWELL [WILLIAM 51] He was born 8
Feb. 1735/6 at Amesbury, Mass. He married 10
Oct. 1765 HANNAH MORSE, d/o BENJAMIN & MARGARET
(BARTLETT) MORSE at Amesbury. Res. Newton, N.H.

Children: 523. JOSEPH, b. 15 Mar. 1767, d. 14
                 Nov. 1742, md. 15 Feb. 1803
                 HANNAH CHASE.
           524. SARAH, b. 22 Jan. 1769.
           525. WILLIAM, b. 10 Oct. 1770, d.
                 Feb. 1823, md. 31 Dec. 1806
                 ELIZABETH TEWKSBURY.
           526, HANNAH, b. 5 Oct. 1772.
           527. JOSHUA, b. 6 July 1774, md.
                 SARAH PEASLEE.
           528. ELIZABETH, b. 14 Apr. 1776.
           529. BENJAMIN, b. 8 Apr. 1778, m.1,
                 PHEBE (RHODA?) HOYT, m.2,
                 RUTH _____ .
           530. ANNE, b. 14 Aug. 1780.
           531. SIMMONS, b. 20 Jan. 1783.

171. THOMAS ROWELL [JOSEPH 55] He was born 3
April 1748/1750 at Newton, N.H. and died 12 Dec.
1816. He married 10 Oct. 1778 at Salem, Mass.
HANNAH BECKET, d/o WILLIAM & MAY (MURREY)
BECKET. Res. Salem, N.H.

Children: 535. THOMAS, possibly d. 29 Jan.
                 1831 at Salem.
           536. WILLIAM, md. 15 Feb. 1806
                 REBECCA CLOUTMAN.
           537. JOSEPH,
           538. HANNAH or BETSY, b. 22 June
                 1788, d. 24 June 1816, md. 28
                 July 1805 THOMAS SHATSWELL. 2
                 children.
           539. ELIZABETH,
           540. JAMES, bp 9 Jan. 1791.
           541. JONATHAN, bp 2 June 1793, d. 27
                 Mar. 1815.

ROWELL FAMILY - NEW ENGLAND
6th Generation

542. SAMUEL, bp 3 Apr. 1796.
543. JOHN, bp 20 Oct. 1802.

180. **WILLIAM ROWELL [JACOB 59]** He was born 11
Sep. 1740 at Amesbury, Mass. and died 27 Sep.
1816 at Parkersburg, W. Va. He married first 5
Mar. 1763 **MARY BROWN**, d/o **SAMUEL BROWN**. She born
1744 and died 1816. He married second **HANNAH
SARGENT**, d/o **JEREMIAH SARGENT**. Rev. War service.
Brevet Major, N.H. Militia. Received land grant
of 300 acres for military service, 21 July 1789,
BLWT-300-Capt.

Children: 544. ELIZABETH, b. 3 Jan. 1762.
           545. DANIEL, b. 1765, d. 1847, md.
                1788 **NANCY NEAL**.
           546. GEORGE, b. 1 Aug. 1770.
           547. JAMES, b. 29 Nov. 1772,
                possibly md. 6 July 1800
                POLLY MERRILL at Salem.
           548. SALLY, b. 22 Feb. 1778, md.
                JOHN REED, or md. 23 Sep.
                1804 **JAMES REED**.

189. **MOSES ROWELL [ICHABOD 66]** He was born Sep.
1774 and died 26 Aug. 1848 at Bath, N.H. He
married 9 Oct. 1797 **PHOEBE EATON** at Landoff. She
died 24 Sep. 1826. He married 2nd 14 April 1831
HANNAH MARTIN of Landolf, Me. Res. Bath, N.H.

Children: 550. **EBENEZER EATON**, b. 2 Jan. 1798.
                [Possibly the Ebenezer at
                Bath Poor Farm in 1850
                census]
           551. **MOSES Jr.**, b. 4 July 1800, d. 2
                Feb. 1849, md. 15 Feb. 1827
                ABIGAIL BANFIELD or **HANNAH
                MERRILL MARTIN**.
           552. JESSE, b. 25 Aug. 1807, d. 1870
                in Wisc., md. **MARY BATTEN**.
           553. ELIZA ELLEN, b. 7 June 1810,
                md. **GEORGE BANFIELD** at
                Corinth, Vt.

- 65 -

ROWELL FAMILY - NEW ENGLAND
6th Generation

554. **WILLIAM**, b. 28 Apr. 1812.

190. **RICHARD ROWELL** [ICHABOD 66] He was born
about 1775. He married 1798 **SUSANNA HEALD**. She
born about 1773 at Temple, N.H. Res. N.Y.

Children: 555. **IRA**, b. 1803, d. 1895, md. 1827
MARIA LUCY FORD.
556. **PHINEAS ASHLEY**, b. 1807, d.
1875, md. c1849 **ELIZABETH
SHEPARD**.

202. **JACOB ROWELL** [PHILIP 67] He was born 12
Apr. 1724 at Salisbury, Mass. and died 29 Sep.
1813. He married 22 Jan. 1761 at Salem, Mass.
ANNA BUXTON, d/o **JAMES BUXTON** of Amesbury. She
born 25 Feb. 1732 and died 9 Nov. 1822. Rev. War
service.

Children: 561. **PHILIP**, b. 6 Sep. 1762, d. 8
June 1838, md. 22 Nov. 1792
ANNA JOHNSON.
562. **ABIGAIL**, b. 14 June 1764, md.
25 Nov. or 25 Jan. 1790
EDWARD SOUTHWICK.
563. **JAMES**, b. 15 May 1766, d. 7
Sep. 1774, drowned.
564. **JOHN**, b. 16 Feb. 1768, d. 14
June 1823.
565. **ELIZABETH**, b. 10 Jan. 1770, d.
10 July 1799, md. 25 Jan.
1790/1 **JAMES PURRINGTON**.
566. **JACOB**, b. 30 Oct. 1771, d. 6
Feb. 1853, md. 22 Nov. 1804
ABIGAIL JONES.
567. **ANNA**, b. 25 Mar. 1774, d. 8
Feb. 1823.
568. **JAMES**, b. 28 Sep. July 1776, d.
16 June 1826, md. 4 July 1800
PHEBE JARVIS.

207. **MOSES ROWELL** [PHILIP 67] He was born 25
Jan. 1733/4 at Salisbury and died 8 Aug. 1800 at

ROWELL FAMILY - NEW ENGLAND
6th Generation

Amesbury, Mass. He married 1st 26 Nov. 1761 at
Salisbury **HANNAH PEASLEE**, d/o **JOSEPH & MARTHA
(HOAG) PEASLEE.** She born 19 Nov. 1740 and died
14 June 1773. He married second 23 Feb.
1774 **MARY COLLINS**, d/o **TRISTRAM & JUDITH
COLLINS.** She born 11 July 1745. Rev. War
service.

Children: by 1st Wife:
569. **ELIZABETH**, b. 18 May 1763, d. 8
Apr. 1804, md. 2 Dec. 1784
ELIJAH HUNTINGTON. 1 child.
570. **stillborn**, b. 5 May 1765.
571. **JOSEPH**, b. 2 Aug. 1766, md. 30
July 1796 **MARY COLBY.**
2nd Wife: 572. **MARK**, b. 22 Feb. 1776, md. 18
Feb. 1805 **LYDIA WORTHAM.**
573. **JUDITH**, b. 25 Aug. 1777, d.
infancy.
574. **LYDIA**, b. 26 May 1779, d. 25
Oct. 1840.
575. **MOSES**, b. 20 Apr. 1783, d. 5
Aug. 1784.

217. **THOMAS ROWELL [AARON 71]** He was born 21
April or 27 Aug. 1737 and died 27 Aug. 1816 at
Bradford, Vermont. He married first **MARY** _____.
She born 1732 and died 1817. He married 2nd 6
Sep. 1770 **SARAH KENT** at Hampstead, N.H. Served
in Rev. War. 1st Lt. 13th Reg't. N.H. Militia
1776. Rhode Island Exp. 1778. Perform public
service in Rev. War, N.H. Repr. State Assembly
at Exeter 1779. Res. Warner, N.H.

Children: 580. **AARON**, b. 1770, d. 1846, md.
5 Sep. 1795 **POLLY PUTNEY.**
581. **LEVI**,
582. **MARY**,
583. **MARGERY**,

218. **AARON ROWELL Jr.[AARON 71]** He was born 1
Dec. 1738. He married 3 Nov. 1759 **HANNAH LOWELL**
at Amesbury, Mass. She born c1738. He married
2nd **MIRIAM** _____. He bought land and buildings

in Sandown 24 Sep. 1760 [70:553] and sold land
in Kingston 3 Nov. 1760 [89:82] Res. Hopkinton,
N.H.

Children: 585. **AARON**, bp 15 Mar. 1767.
            586. **JOHN**, bp 15 Mar. 1767.
            587. **MOSES**, bp 15 Mar. 1767.
            588. **ELIJAH**, bp 8 May 1768, md. 10
                 Nov. 1792 **OLIVE POND**.
            589. **AMOS**, bp 17 May 1772.
            590. **MOSES**, bp 22 Mar. 1774, md. 24
                 June 1798 **SALLY FREELAND**,
                 m.2, **RUTH BROWN**.

221. **WILLIAM ROWELL [AARON 71]** He was born 19
June 1745 and died 31 May 1807 age 62 years at
Haverhill, N.H. He married 1762 Mrs. **HANNAH
ROGERS**. Rev. War soldier. Signed Assoc. Test
1776. Res. Sandown, N.H.

224. **PHILIP ROWELL [AARON 71]** He was born 2
Oct. 1755. He married first 7 Oct. 1779 **HANNAH
WILLIAMS**. He married 2nd 28 Jan. 1792 **ANN
JOHNSON** at Salisbury, Mass. His will 3 May 1783,
proved 25 June 1783.

Children: 595. **AVON**, b. 15 Oct. 1780.
            596. **JACOB**, b. 28 Sep. 1793.
            597. **LYDIA**, b. 15 May 1795.

226. **JACOB ROWELL [DANIEL 73]** He was born 1
Oct. 1735 at East Kingston, N.H. and died 1812
at Littleton, N.H. He married 8 Aug. 1760
ABIGAIL PRESCOTT. She died 1840 age 100 years at
East Kingston, N.H. His will dated 7 Mar. 1807,
proved 1 July 1812. [v.40, p.168] Names wife and
children. Son PHILIP named executor. Inv.
$3,339.17. He had a gristmill and saw mill at
the falls. Sgt. Rev. War.

Children: 599. **MOSES**, b. c1761.
            600. **PHILIP**, b. c1763.
            601. **JONATHAN**, b. 1765.

602. **HANNAH**, b. c1767.
603. **ANNA**, b. c1769, md. **JOHN THOMPSON**.
604. **JUDITH**, b. c1771.
605. **ELIZABETH** or **ELIZA R**, b. c1773, md. 6 Apr. 1797 **DANIEL SANBORN**.
606. **ABIGAIL**, b. c1775, d. 6 Feb. 1866, age 88 yrs. md. **JOHN SANBORN**.
607. **SARAH**, b. c1777, md. 28 Jan. 1813 **BENJAMIN WADLEIGH**.
608. **MIRIAM**, b. 1779.

232. **DANIEL M. ROWELL** [DANIEL 73] He was born 9 April 1745 and bp. 1 Dec. following at East Kingston, N.H.. He died Nov. 1831 at Littleton, N.H. He married 1st 24 Nov. 1768 **JUDITH FRENCH**, d/o **JOSHUA & SARAH (CARR) FRENCH**. She born 8 Apr. 1747 and died c1796. He married 2nd _____ **WISER**. Lt. in Rev. War. At Bunker Hill, Bennington, Saratoga, etc.   Moved 1789 to Starke. First town clerk at Perry in 1795. 1820 moved to Haverhill and 1824 to Littleton, N.H.

Children: by 1st Wife;
609. **EDWARD**, b. 24 May 1769, d. c1825, md 24 Apr. 1794 **ABIGAIL SMITH**.
610. **JONATHAN**, b. 14 May 1771, d. 31 Oct. 1863, md. 4 Mar. 1799 **SALLY HOSKINS**.
611. **SARAH H.**, b. 26 May 1773, md. 24 May 1791 **TRUEWORTHY DUDLEY**, 10 children.
612. **DANIEL Jr.**, b. 5 Sep. 1776, d. 25 June 1843, md. 31 Aug. 1799 **MEHITABLE SMITH**.
613. **JUDITH**, b. 1 Sep. 1777, d. 18 Jan. 1844, md. 9 Apr. 1797 **EDMUND COLE**. 4 children.
614. **JANET (MIRIAM?)**, b. 13 Oct. 1781, d. 20 May 1849, md. 6 Oct. 1799 **CLIFFORD COLE**.

615. **JOSHUA**, b. 1784, d. 15 Apr.
1812, md. 27 Nov. 1808 **POLLY
JACKSON**.
616. **RICHARD F.**, b. 1788, md. 22
Aug. 1826 **MELINDA MILLER**.
617. **PERCY/PIERCY**, b. 20 Jan. 1790,
d.y.
618. **LYDIA**, b. 20 June 1792, d. 15
June 1863, md. 1 Dec. 1814
ABIJAH POTTER Jr. 5 ch.
619. **ANN/ANNIE**, b. 8 Dec. 1794, d.
30 Aug. 1858, md. 1820
ALEXANDER WENTWORTH.

236. **MOSES ROWELL [DANIEL 73]** He was born 15
Oct. 1752 at Kingston, N.H. and died 3 Feb.
1841. He married 1802 **Mrs. BETSY (BROWN) FOLSOM**.
Res. Gilmonton, N.H. Possibly had son **SAMUEL**
born Dec. 1777. See #998.

260. **ABRAHAM ROWELL [RICE 90]** He was born about
1733 at Nottingham, N.H. Probably married about
1738. Wife's name unknown. 1790 Census lists
wife and 1 son. Rev. War soldier. 1776 Private
from Nottingham. Cont. Army, N.Y., Lt. Rhode
Island Exp. in 1778. Pension Roll 3 Mar. 1831,
age 71 yrs at Grafton, N.H. Age 73 in 1832.

261. **RICE ROWELL [RICE 90]** He was born in 1734
at Nottingham, N.H. and died there in 1809. He
married 1760 **ELIZABETH HARVEY**. Occ. farmer.
Signed Assoc. Test in 1776. Grand jury Oct.
1782, taxed $8.25 in 1806, had 8 acres. Estate 6
May 1809 Dolly Rowell Admin., York, Me. Res.
Nottingham, N.H.

Children: 620. **ABRAHAM**, b. 1761, md. **BETSEY**
_____.
621. **- SON -**, name unknown.
622. **SARAH**, b. 7 Apr. 1765, d. 28
July 1849.

623. BETSY, b. 7 Apr. 1767, d.
     c1799, md. 1798 MOSES M.
     WATSON.
624. JANE, d. c1799, md. 1793
     NATHANIEL MARTIN (MARSTON?)
625. LOVE, md. 12 Jan. 1797 JOSEPH
     GILMAN.
626. POLLY, b. 12 May 1778.
627. RICE RICHARDSON, b. 1782, d.
     1840, md. SARAH SPINNEY.
628. NANCY, md. 1803 WILLIAM PAGE of
     Deerfield.
629. FANNY, m.1, 1795 DANIEL MARTIN,
     m.2, _____ TEEG.
630. GRACE, md. 1802 DANIEL LADD,
     m.2, _____ NORCROSS.

267. NEHEMIAH ROWELL [RICE 90] He was born
about 1752 at Nottingham, N.H. and died 1779 at
Portsmouth, N.H. His widow ELIZABETH married
second 9 July 1786 THOMAS MOSES. She died 11
Dec. 1792, age 41 yrs. Inv. taken 17 Feb.
1780. P.P. and ½ small building used as a shop.
£3559..6..0. [v.25, p.330] Rev. War service.

Children: 631. JOHN, bp 1774, d. 1844.
            632. ELIZABETH, bp 11 Aug. 1776.
            633. SALLY, b. 17 Feb. 1778, md.
            May 1795 BENJAMIN MOSES.

269. WILLIAM ROWELL [RICE 90] He was born in
1755 at Nottingham, N.H. and died 30 Sep. 1811
at South Thomaston, Me. He married 19 Dec. 1784
Mrs. RUTH (MATTHEWS) TENANT, widow of JOSHUA
TENANT at Georgetown, Me. d/o COLL & CATHERINE
(CAMPBELL) MATTHEWS. She born 4 Sep. 1753 at
Plainfield, Conn, died 1832. Rev. War service.
Capt. Henry Dearborn Co. at Bunker Hill. Occ.
sawmill. Res. Salem, N.H., removed to Thomaston,
Me.

Children: 635. BETSEY, b. 4 Sep. 1782, d. 13
            Jan. 1854, md. 21 Jan. 1799
            WILLIAM RUSS. 11 children.

636. **WILLIAM**, d. drowned age 3 yrs.
637. **RICE**, b. 27 Apr. 1789, d. 11
     Apr. 1863, m.1, 8 Feb. 1816
     SALLY DUNNING, m.2, 30 Dec.
     1839 **Mrs. EUNICE DAVIS**, m.3,
     1856 **Mrs. SALLY ALLY.**
638. **JOHN**, d.y.
639. **RUTH**, b. 1792, d. 4 Jan. 1853,
     md. 23 Feb. 1817 **BRIGGS
     BUTLER.**
640. **MARY**, b. 1794, d. 4 July 1842,
     md. 9 Jan. 1817 **ROBERT
     DUNNING.**

273. **ENOCH ROWELL [ENOCH 91]** He was born 3 July
1756 at Chester, N.H. and died 2 Aug. 1840 at
Plainfield, N.H.. He married 8 Sep. 1778 at
Candia, N.H. **RACHEL WORTHAM**, d/o **JACOB & MARY
WORTHAM**, by Rev. David Jewell. She born about
1759 and died 1 Dec. 1844. Adm. 15 Jan. 1845. He
served as Sgt. in Rev. War, Mass, Capt. Thos.
Coggswell Co., Col. Baldwins Reg't Cont. Line.
Occ. farmer. Wife received pension #W-16392.
Inv. in pension application was $382.14 in 1840.
Res. Plainfield, Sullivan County, N.H.

Children: 642. **ENOCH**, b. 18 Mar. 1779, d. 9
           Sep. 1839, md. 1 Mar. 1804
           BETSEY HODGES.
       643. **MARY/POLLY**, twin b. 11 Oct.
           1780, d. 21 July 1871, md.
           JOHN FAIRMAN. No children.
       644. **WILLIAM**, twin b. 11 Oct. 1780,
           d. 17 Dec. 1782.
       645. **JUDITH**, b. 24 Feb. 1784, d.
           June 1872, md. 14 Mar. 1805
           HORACE FISHER.
       646. **DANIEL**, b. 23 June 1786, d. 16
           Oct. 1848, md. 17 July 1811
           MERCY JOHNSON.
       647. **WILLIAM**, b. 23 Jan. 1791, d. 1
           Aug. 1871, md. 22 Mar. 1818,
           SALLY LEAVITT.

648. **JACOB**, b. 25 Jan. 1792, d. 25
Sep. 1866, md. **POLLY CURRIER.**
649. **SAMUEL**, b. 10 July 1793, d. 7
July 1850, md. 2 Mar. 1825
MARY MOORE.
650. infant,
651. **ELIPHALET**, b. 28 Feb. 1796, d.
11 May 1875, md. **SALLY TRUE.**
652. **CONVERSE**, b. 20 May 1798, d. 11
Nov. 1889, md. 25 Mar. 1825
ORPHAR CHAMBERLIN.
653. **RACHEL**, b. 20 Jan. 1801, d. 26
Apr. 1883, md. **WILLIAM
CADMAN.**
654. **SARAH**, b. 17 Sep. 1803, d. 20
Nov. 1865, md. 19 Feb. 1830
HIRAM MOORE.

276. **ELIPHELET ROWELL [ENOCH 91]** He was born 8
June 1768 at Candia, N.H. Killed by tree 3 July
1801. Widow Admin. 18 Sep. 1801. He married
ABIGAIL SMITH, d/o **ELISHA & SUSANNA (WING)
SMITH.** She born 6 Dec. 1771 at Harwick, Mass.
Res. Livermore, Me. Yeoman.

Children: 658. **ABIJAH/ELIJAH**, b. 1795, d.
1895, md. **SOPHIA WARREN.**
659. **MIRIAM**, b. c1797.
660. **BEULAH**, b. c1799.
661. **ABIGAIL**, b. c1801.

288. **SAMUEL ROWELL [JOHN 94]** He was born the
latter part of 1754 on the farm at Chester, N.H.
He enlisted in Capt. Henry Dearborn Co. of Col.
Starks Reg't for Rev. War. Fought at Bunker
Hill. in Aug. 1775 he was member of Dearborn's
Co. under Col. Benedict Arnold in expedition
against Quebec. Became ill, returned. Received
£10 for five months service. Enlisted again 29
Nov. 1775 Capt. Titcombs Co., Col. Poor's Reg't
Sent to northern Continental Army under Brig.
General Sullivan in New York. He signed the
Assoc. Test in April 1776. Enlisted again.

Battles at White plains, N.Y. and Trenton, N.J. on 20 July 1777 enlisted again. Expedition of General Stark against Boygoyne. Battle of Bennington, Vt. Enlisted again. Served 6 years total. Granted Rev. War pension in 1818. He married 27 Nov. 1777 at Weare, N.H. **SARAH DUSTIN**, d/o **PAUL & BETTY DUSTIN**. She born 15 April 1758 at Chester and died 27 Aug. 1842 at Barnet, Vt. Methodist. He died 11 June 1830. Buried at Martin's Ferry, N.H. Res. at Weare, N.H. Moved 1795 to Chester. Family orderd out of Chester 18 Nov. 1794 [N.H. Court Case]

Children: 663. **SAMUEL**, b. 8 Oct. 1778, d. 28 Dec. 1871, md. 29 Oct. 1805 **MARY ATWOOD**.

664. **BETSY**, b. 4 Aug. 1780, d. 2 Jan. 1869, md. Jan. 1797 **SOMERS GOODELL**. m.2, 1850 Rev. **LEWIS FISHER**.

665. **DUSTIN**, b. 1782-3, d. 1 July 1866, md. 1808 **JANE GORDON**.

666. **LYDIA**, b. 7 Mar. 1785, d. 29 Oct. 1874, md. 1810 **JONATHAN JENKINS**.

667. **SARAH**, b. 1787/8, d. 10 June 1855, md. 1820 **AARON SARGENT**.

668. **MARY**, b. 5 Dec. 1791, d. 24 June 1857, md. 27 Dec. 1814 Rev. **JOHN LORD**.

669. **JAMES COLWELL**, b. 27 Nov. 1793, d. 7 June 1857, md. 24 Apr. 1817 **OLIVE A. WIGGINS**.

670. **JOHN PAGE**, b. 15 Oct. 1796, d. 20 Mar. 1875, md. 10 May 1820 **BETSY EMERSON**.

294. **ELIPHELET ROWELL** [ELIPHELET 97]. He was born about 1753 and bp. 5 Jan. 1777 at Salem, N.H. He died 1815. He married **EUNICE PARKS**. Named in 1790 census [1-3-2] and 1810 census

ROWELL FAMILY - NEW ENGLAND
6th Generation

[33201/11101] Inventory of his estate taken 15
Jan. 1816, $2,041.84. Had 159 acres at Bow, N.H.
Had saw mill. Widow **EUNICE** appt. executrix.
JOSEPH ROWELL of Croydon appt guardian of minor
son **AMOS** 27 Sep. 1817.

Children: 680. **JOHN**, b. 15 July 1778.
           681. **JOSEPH**, b. 13 Apr. 1780, d.y.
           682. **ELIPHELET**, b. 3 Feb. 1782, md.
                poss. 11 Mar. 1800 **SALLY**
                EMORY.
           683. **JOSEPH**, b. 13 Oct. 1784.
           684. **JAMES**, b. 3 Feb. 1787, d.y.
           685. **FANNY**, b. 20 Nov. 1789.
           686. **JAMES**, b. 26 Apr. 1795, md. 12
                Apr. 1821? **REBECCA P. CLARK**
                at Hampstead.
           687. **AMOS**, b. 7 Jan. 1797/8, d. 5
                Nov. 1867, md. 7 Apr. 1822
                ELIZABETH (BETSY) CHASE.
           688. **EUPHANA**, b. 25 Sep. 1800, md.
                23 Aug. 1821 **JOHN CHANDLER**.

295. **PETER ROWELL [ELIPHELET 97]** He was born 13
Aug. 1758 at Sutton and died 6 April 1819 at
Chenango, N.Y. He married 10 Oct. 1782
BETSY/BETTEY MARSH at Sutton. Served in Rev.
War. Fifer in Mass. Militia. 1790 Census Salem,
N.Y.

Children: 690. **STRATTON**, b. 1791, d. 1878,
                md. **OLIVE BURTCH**.
           691. **PERLEY MARSH**, b. 15 Sep. 1793,
                md. 24 Sep. 1818 **PAMELIA**
                JOHNSON.

298. **ELI ROWELL [ELIPHELET 97]** He was born 7
Oct. 1774 at Sutton, N.H. He married 5 Oct.
1797 **LOIS HAYDON** at Sutton, N.H.

307. **JOB ROWELL [ELIJAH 102]** He was born 4 Oct.
1738 at Salisbury, or Weare. He married 22 Oct.
1761 **PRISCELLA EMERSON**, d/o **ROBERT & SARAH**

ROWELL FAMILY - NEW ENGLAND
6th Generation

EMERSON at Hampstead. Owner and builder of Rowell mill. Home east of pond. Wife sold inheritance 8 Dec. 1760 to Caleb Emerson land in Hampstead [115:196] Ordered out of Plaiston 29 Mar. 1762 [N.H. Court Case] He was an Innkeeper at Goffstown 1764. Rev. War service. Res. Hampstead, N.H.

Children: 701. **BETTY**, b. 9 Feb. 1762, md. 7 July 1782 **EZEKIEL FLANDERS**.
702. **JONATHAN**, b. 1 Aug. 1763, md. 15 Sep. 1784 **OLIVE TUXBURY**. Rev. War pension.
703. **MOSES**, b. 11 June 1765, m.1, **ABIGAIL WARNER**, m.2, 10 Sep. 1799 **BETSY MANN**.
704. **ABIGAIL**, b. 16 June 1767, md. 21 Mar. 1790 **JOHN J. ATKINS**.
705. **ELIJAH**, b. 9 April 1769, d. 26 July 1847, md. **SARAH WHITTIER**.
706. **AARON**, b. 19 Nov. 1771, md. 18 Nov. 1802 **EUNICE BLOOD**.
707. **SARAH**, b. 17 Dec. 1774.
708. **JOB Jr.**, b. 15 Mar. 1778.
709. **ROBERT EMERSON**, b. 3 Aug. 1779, d. 17 June 1859, md. 25 Mar. 1800 **HANNAH WHITTIER**.
710. **MARY**, b. 15 Jan. 1783.

308. **ELIJAH ROWELL [ELIJAH 102]** He was born 2 Mar. 1741 at Salisbury, Mass. He married **SUSANNAH** _____. Res. Salem, Mass.

Children: 711. **MOLLEY**, b. 21 Sep. 1764.
712. **RHODA**, b. 3 Apr. 1769.
713. **ANNE**, b. 11 Mar. 1771.

309. **NATHANIEL ROWELL [ELIJAH 102]** He was born 22 Sep. 1744 at So. Hampton and died intestate in 1823 at Hopkinton, N.H. He married 8 Oct. 1764 **JUDITH MORSE** at South Hampton, N.H. MOSES appt. adm. of estate 29 Aug. 1823. [v.3, p.3] No widow mentioned. Inventory returned July 1827,

ROWELL FAMILY - NEW ENGLAND
6th Generation

$1,247.14. Bought 7 acres land 7 June 1768
[107:185] Res. So. Hampton and Hopkinton, N.H.

Children: 715. ABEL, b. 22 Dec. 1765, bp 8
                Nov. 1766, md. 19 July 1789
                SUSANNAH KIMBALL.
           716. MOSES, b. 1767, d.y.
           717. BETTY, b. 29 June 1768, md. 17
                Nov. 1794 JOHN TUCKER.
           718. MARTHA, b. 21 May 1771, bp 7
                July 1771, md. 16 Oct. 1797
                ENOCH PUTNEY.
           719. MOSES, b. 25 Jan. 1774, bp 13
                Mar. 1774, md. 13 Nov. 1800
                MARY PETTINGILL.
           720. HANNAH, b. 17 May 1776, d.
                1831, md. 14 Mar. 1799
                SIMEON TYLER. 6 children.
           722. LYDIA, b. 7 Feb. 1779, bp 9
                July 1779, d. young.
           723. NATHANIEL, b. 4 July 1781, d.
                17 Mar. 1827, md. 23 June
                1809 SARAH HOPKINS.
           724. JOHN, b. 16 Oct. 1783, d. 1810
                age 27 at Ipswich, School
                Master?
           725. LYDIA, b. 13 Mar. 1786, d. 16
                Feb. 1852, md. 3 Jan. 1810
                ENOCH GOULD.
           726. ELIJAH, b. 22 July 1788, md. 16
                June 1814 SALLY EASTMAN.
           727. JOSEPH, b. 2 Nov. 1792.

310. THOMAS ROWELL [ELIJAH 102] He was born 20
Feb. 1748. Enlisted Rev. War Feb. 1776 at
Poplin, N.H. Pvt. Capt. Sanborn Co., Col. Task
Reg't. Received pension #11,319. In 1832 age 85
resident of New Chester, N.H.

311. JOHN ROWELL [ELIJAH 102] He was born 3
Dec. 1750 at South Hampton, N.H. and died 14
June 1822 at Andover, N.H. He married first 10
Aug. 1770 ANNA CURRIER at Kingston, N.H. He
married second 31 August 1776 DOLLY/DOROTHY

LEAVITT. She born 11 Mar. 1756 and died 4 Mar. 1831 at Andover.

Children: 1st Wife:
    730. JUDITH, b. 24/27 Feb. 1771, at
      So. Hampton, N.H.
2nd Wife: 731. ANNA/NANCY, b. 20 Dec. 1777, d.
      June 1855, md. 13 Nov. 1800
      MOSES BROWN.
    732. JUDITH, b. 15 May 1780, d. 14
      May 1818, md. BENJAMIN
      JUDKINS.
    733. DOLLY, b. 16 May 1782, d. 1
      Dec. 1873, md. Capt. LAWRENCE
      ELLIS.
    734. ELIZABETH, b. 4 July 1784, d.
      1825, md. 17 Feb. 1813 Dea.
      JOSEPH FELLOWS at Andover.
    735. JOHN, b. 24 Feb. 1787, d. 7
      Feb. 1792.
    736. MOSES, b. 4 Oct. 1788, d. June
      1870, md. 6 July 1814 LYDIA
      GREELEY.
    737. JOHN, b. 30 May 1793, md. 22
      May 1817 SALLY FIFIELD.
    738. ENOCH, b. 1 Mar. 1796, d. 6
      Apr. 1801.
    739. POLLY, b. 1 Feb. 1800, d. 24
      Aug. 1802.

315. JOHN ROWELL [JOHN 103] He was born 15 Nov. 1737 at Salisbury, Mass. and died 2 May 1786, aged 49 years at Epping, N.H. He Married 1760 HANNAH WINSLOW, d/o ELISHA & MARY (SLEEPER) WINSLEY. She born 5 Apr. 1741 at Kingston and died 11 Dec. 1819 at Brentwood, N.H.

Children: 740. SARAH, b. 31 Aug. 1762, md. 14
      May 1786 LEVI TILTON.
    741. JOHN, b. 11 July 1764, d. 27
      Jan. 1844, md. 5 Jan. 1792
      MEHITABLE THYNG, m.2, 26 Feb.
      1812 ANNA S. SHUTE.

742. JEMIMA, b. 29 Aug. 1766, md. 17
     Feb. 1785 NATHANIEL BROWN.
743. JONATHAN, b. 4 May 1769, md. 19
     Sep. 1793 MARY PHILBRICK.
744. MARY, d. 20 Dec. 1870, md. 19
     Apr. 1809 THOMAS MARSTON.
745. ABRAHAM, d.y.
746. ABRAHAM, b. 1776, d. 13 Oct.
     1863, md. 23 June 1818 LOVEY
     SIMPSON.
747. ENOCH PAGE, b. 3 Oct. 1780, d.
     Nov. 1848, md. 13 Nov. 1801
     Mrs. SARAH (SALLY) MASON.
748. BENJAMIN, d. 29 Nov. 1848, md.
     12 Feb. 1805 MIRIAM CLIFFORD.
749. HANNAH, b. 9 Aug. 1776, d. 29
     Aug. 1835, md. 20 Nov. 1800
     NATHANIEL MORRILL.

320. DAVID ROWELL [JOB Jr 104] He was born 25
Nov. 1742 at Epping, N.H. and died 30 Mar. 1820
at Derryfield. He married 6 April 1766 Mrs.
SARAH/SALLY CHENEY REMICK, widow of ISAAC, d/o
DANIEL & HANNAH (DUSTIN) CHENEY. She born 1738.
In 1778 moved to Manchester. He had a log house
on Old Falls Road. Occ. farmer. Rev. War
service, Pvt. from Goffstown. Sons David,
Zebedee and Isaac went to Maine.

Children: 750. DAVID, b. 1 Oct. 1766, m.1, 8
               Mar. 1792 JANETTE DICKEY,
               m.2, 8 Mar. 1794 SARAH
               SPAULDING.
          751. MARY, b. 18 Jan. 1768.
          752. SARAH, b. 5 May 1769.
          753. JOB, b. 24 Feb. 1771, d. 1843,
               m.1, 26 Dec. 1799 ABIGAIL
               POLLARD, m.2, Mrs. BETSY B.
               DINSMORE.
          754. ISAAC, b. 17 May 1770, d. 10
               Dec. 1827, md. HANNAH
               RICHARDSON.

755. ZEBEDEE, b. 1775, md. 25 May
     1801 JUDITH HAMBLETT.
756. MERIBEE, b. 11 Apr. 1782, md.
     27 Nov. 1809 or 6 Feb. 1810
     JOHN CROSBY at Bedford, Me.
757. JONATHAN,
758. JOHANNA

322. JONATHON ROWELL [JOB Jr 104] He was born
11 Oct. 1753 at Salisbury and died 11 or 26 Dec.
1831, or 18 Dec. 1833 at Strafford, Vt. He
married first, 27 Feb. 1776 MEHITABEL WELLS at
Litchfield, N.H. She born 1756 and died Nov.
1785 Strafford, Vt. He married second 5 June
1787 HANNAH NEWMAN. She born 29 Mar. 1764 and
died 4 Aug. 1863. Occ. Grist Mill owner. Rev.
War service N.H. Res. Goffstown, Strafford and
Tunbridge, Vt.

Children: 760. JOHN, b . 15 Feb. 1778, md.
                 1806 HANNAH ROBERTS.
            761. LOIS, b. 20 Feb. 1780, md. 5
                 Mar. 1801 DARIUS TYLER.
            762. MEHITABLE, b. 18 Jan. 1791, md.
                 14 Feb. 1820 STEPHEN BURBANK.
            763. DAVID, b. 1 Feb. 1795, md.
                 ANNIS CAMP.

323. ABRAHAM ROWELL [THOMAS 105] He was born 3
Dec. 1743 at South Hampton, N.H. and died 29
Jan. 1815 at Hopkinton, N.H. He married at
Sutton 5 April 1764 ELIZABETH EASTMAN, d/o
JONATHAN & MARTHA (ALLEN) EASTMAN of Salisbury.
She born 6 June 1743 and died 9 Aug. 1832.
Signed Assoc. Test in 1776. Public Service in
Rev. War. His will dated 7 Dec. 1813, proved 24
Feb. 1815. Wife and all children named. MOSES
and SAMUEL named executors. Inventory taken 2
Apr. 1816 amounted to $362.20 [v.22, p.583] Res.
Hopkinton, N.H.

Children: 765. THOMAS B., b. 25 Nov. 1764, d.
                 20 Dec. 1833, md. 13 July
                 1788 LYDIA HAWES/HOUSE.

ROWELL FAMILY - NEW ENGLAND
6th Generation

766. JONATHAN, b. 25 Oct. 1766, d.
     1827, md. 1789 ACHSAH FLOOD.
767. JACOB, b. 22 Sep. 1768, d. 6
     Dec. 1833, m.1, SUSANNA
     _____, m.2, 17 Feb. 1820 SARA
     DANFORTH.
768. SALLY, b. c1768.
769. POLLY, b. c1771.
770. ABRAHAM, b. 17 Oct. 1770, d. 8
     Oct. 1829, md. 21 Sep. 1797
     SARAH WALDRON.
771. BETSEY/BETTE, b. 22 Nov. 1772,
     d. 7 Sep. 1810, md. 29 June
     1793 SAMUEL KENDRICK.
772. ISAAC, b.1 Nov. 1774, d. 7 July
     1845, m.1, _____ STRONG, m.2
     JOSHUA TILLATSON?
773. MOSES, b. 29 Nov. 1776, d. 25
     Mar. 1858, m.1 TAMESIN
     EASTMAN, m.2, JAMIESIN
     EASTMAN.
774. SARAH, b. 6 Sep. 1778, m.1,
     _____ WELLS, m.2, THOMAS
     MESSER.
775. SAMUEL, b. 15 Nov. 1780, d.
     1858, md. 16 Oct. 1806 POLLY
     (PATTY?) COLBY.
776. MOLLY, b. 10 Sep. 1782, d. 10
     May 1827, md. 30 Jan. 1800
     WHITCHER SARGENT or WILLIAM
     WHITTIER SARGENT.
777. HANNAH, b. 3 Jan. 1785, md. 13
     Sep. 1804 BENJAMIN COLBY.
778. NANCY ANN, b. 13 Nov. 1786, md.
     Nov. 1811 EBEN GOVE.

331. STEPHEN ROWELL [ASA 111] He was born 8 Mar.
1779 and died 13 Feb. 1855 at Thetford, Vt.
Buried in Post Mill Cemetary. He married HANNAH
HOUSE. She born c1777 in Vt. 1850 census at W.
Fairlee, Vt. Probable children:

Children: 780. ASA, b. 1803.

ROWELL FAMILY - NEW ENGLAND
6th Generation

781. RENSCLAIR, b. c1812, md.
THANKFUL AYERS.
782. SIMEON, b. 7 Dec. 1822, d. 8
Jan. 1896.
783. TIMOTHY H., b. c1827, d. 21
Jan. 1863, md. 19 Aug. 1847
AMANDA F. LATHROP.
784. BENJAMIN HOUSE, b. 4 July 1814.

333. DARIUS ROWELL [ASA 111]   He was born 10
June 1783 and died 13 Feb. 1855. Buried at
Thetford, Vt. He married 29 Dec. 1812 POLLY
MORAY at W. Fairlee, Vt.

337. HEZEKIAH ROWELL [PHILIP 112]   He was born
27 Apr. 1781 at Salem, N.H. and died 22 July
1852 at Hamden, Maine. He married 21 Dec. 1809
SARAH HASKELL, d/o IGNAUS & MARY (STICKLAND)
HASKELL at Deer Island, Me.   Justice of Peace
many years. Rep. General Court Boston 1810. 1850
census at Deer Is. Res. Deer Is. and Castine,
Me. Many deeds, most with Haskell family.

Children: 785. MARY STICKLAND, b. 25 July
1810, d. 21 Sep. 1818.
786. IGNATIUS HASKELL, b. 26 Feb.
1812, d. 1 June 1821.
787. PHILIP REDINGTON, b. 15 Oct.
1814, md 9 Oct. 1836
CLEMENTINE OSGOOD.
788. SARAH ELIZABETH, b. 21 July
1817, md. 22 Apr. 1842 JOHN
B. WILSON of Bangor, Me.
789. MARY DORCUS, b. 8 Dec. 1819,
md. 1 July 1841 SAMUEL HILL.
790. HARRIET BECK, md. 24 Dec. 1843,
WILLIAM B. WALKER.
791. HEZEKIAH SMITH, b. 20 Sep.
1824, d. 13 Jan. 1826.
792. MARTHA HASKELL, b. 23 July
1826, md. 1856 ALEXANDER
NELSON NOYES as 3rd Wife.

793. CAROLINE HASKELL, b. 27 Mar.
1829, md. WILLIAM B. WALKER.
after her sisters death.
794. HELEN MARIA, b. 5 Oct. 1831,
md. 10 Oct. 1863 ABRAM TAPLEY
LORD.
795. SARAH E., b. 1833.
796. MARY D., b. 1835.
797. HARRIET Z.C., b. 1837, md. 24
Dec. 1843 WILLIAM B. WALKER
of Boston.

340. JOSEPH ROWELL [PHILIP 112] He was born 7
May 1787 at Salem, N.H. and died 7 Jan. 1870 at
Montpelier, Vt. He married first 17 Mar. 1812
at Plaistow, N.H. ANN BARTLETT. She born 20 May
1791 and died 2 July 1833 at Waterville, Vt. He
married second 28 May 1834 Mrs. SUSAN PIERSON
McFARLAND at Haverhill. She born 1798. Occ.
blacksmith, hotel keeper, farmer & merchant.
1850 census at Troy, Vt.

Children by 1st wife:
798. FANNY, b. 25 Dec. 1814, md. 26
Aug. 1834 JAMES W. WHEELER.
799. MARY ANN, b. 18 Apr. 1817.
800. ADONIRAM JUDSON, b. 7 Nov.
1822, d. 24 Dec. 1864 md. 15
June 1841 LUCY ANN
RICHARDSON.
801. HARRIET, b. 25 Sep. 1824.
802. EMILY FISK, b. 22 Sep. 1822,
md. 28 Dec. 1842 WARREN
FULLER.
803. JOSEPH BARTLETT, b. 25 July
1827.
804. ELIZA, b. 4 Oct. 1829.
805. ADALINE, b. 6 June 1832, md.
HENRY PEARSON.
by 2nd wife:
806. ISAAC HENRY., b. 8 Nov. 1835.
807. SARAH ELIZABETH, b. 16 Oct.
1837.

ROWELL FAMILY - NEW ENGLAND
6th Generation

341. JOHN REDINGTON ROWELL [PHILIP 112] He was
born 24 July 1790 at Salem, N.H, and died 18
Mar. 1870 at Salem. He married first DORCUS
WHEELER, m.2, 20 Dec. 1817 RHODA G. HARRISON.
She born 1796 in N.J. Res. Salem, N.H. Occ.
farmer. 1850 census.

Children: 810. HARRIET ANN, b. 20 June 1823,
md. 2 Mar. 1841 PHILIP
ABBOTT.
811. CAROLINE JANE, b. 10 June
1826.
812. GRIDLEY BRYANT, b. 5 Aug.
1829, md. MARY _____. 1848 in
militia. Occ. shoemaker.
813. WHITTEMORE, b. 20 Sep. 1833.
814. WALTER BELFOUR, b. 20 June
1838. Civil War. Co. H, 1st
N.H. Regt. Served 31 months.

350. LEMUEL ROWELL [LEMUEL 116] He was born
1781 and died 18 Feb. 1850 at Greenwich, N.Y. He
married SALLY _____. She died 27 Mar. 1854, age
76 yrs. Res. Greenwich, N.Y.

Children: 815. LEMUEL, b. 1806, d. 1887, md.
MELINDA AMANDA FULLER.

351. EDMUND RANDOLPH ROWELL [LEMUEL 116] He was
born 1783 at Salem, N.H. and died 1827 at
Fisherville, N.H. He married 9 July 1823 JOANNA
N. COCHRAN. She died 3 Dec. 1831 [28-9-5] Occ.
physician. Admin. of estate granted to JOANNA of
Pembroke 20 Dec. 1827. [v.3, p.175] Inv. 16 Jan.
1828 $106.52. Res. Allentown, N.H.

Children: 820. EDMUND, b. 1826, d. 3 Jan.
1859 at Deerfield, md. 16
Nov. 1848 OLIVE M. REYNOLDS.
Occ. shoe maker.

352. CHARLES ROWELL [LEMUEL 116] He was born
1785 at Salem, N.H. and died 11 Jan. 1867 at

ROWELL FAMILY - NEW ENGLAND
6th Generation

Allentown, N.H.   He married 9 Feb. 1809 MARY
(POLLY) DAVIS at Croydon. She died 23 Jan. 1859.
[76-7-0] Occ. Farmer. 1850 Census at Allentown,
N.H.

Children: 824. CYNTHIA K., b. 1813, d. 20 July
                1881, md. 16 Sep. 1839 JACOB
                W. WOODS. Had: MARY 1841.
           825. EDWARD P., b. c1815, md.
                LUCINDA _____.
           826. MARY J., md. GEORGE MARSTON.
           827. LUCINDA, md. JOHN R. PERKINS.
           828. LOIS, b. 30 July 1826, md. 30
                July 1846 DAVID HAYES/HAINES.
           829. CHARLES T.,
           830. SHERBORNE B., d. 1 Apr. 1896
                [74y] at Sunapee, N.H.
           831. WARREN, b. c1819, md. 9 June
                1844 RUTH MATILDA COGSWELL.
           832. FRANKLIN B., b. 1821, md. 8
                Nov. 1846 MARY ANN JENKINS.

353. SHERBORNE B. ROWELL [LEMUEL 116] He was
born 1788 at Salem, N.H. and died 15 Mar. 1859
at Croydon, N. H. [70-10-10]. He married ANNA
WITHERSPOON. She born 1789 at Franciston, N.H.
and died 11 Apr. 1874, age 85. Res. Croydon,
N.H. 1850 census at Croydon.

Children: 835. EDMUND R., b. 18 Feb. 1814,
                will proved Sep. 1885.
           836. ELIZABETH, b. c1816, d. 1 July
                1894, unmd.
           837. SHERBURNE B. Jr, b. 21 Mar.
                1824, md. CLARA P. GEORGE.
           838. LYDIA, b. c1830, md. _____
                BATCHELDER.
           839. CLEMENTINE, b. c1832, md. 21
                Dec. 1859 PRESTON REED.
           840. ROSE E., md. prob. CHARLES
                FRENCH.
           841. CHARLES, b. 27 Mar. 1835, md.
                MARY ABBIE SANBORN.

366. **DAVID ROWELL [JOSIAH 123]** He was born 25
Aug. 1769 at Salem, Mass. and died 13 April 1813
or 21 Oct. 1834. He married first 7 May 1794
MARY BROWN by Amos Wood J.P. of Weare, N.H. She
born 25 May 1774 d/o **JOSIAH & DEBORAH (CORLISS)
BROWN.** Settled in Weare in 1764. Removed to
Croydon by 1803, where she was killed by
lightning. He married second 12 Oct. 1804 **DOLLY
LOVERING** of Deering at Weare. by Rev. Wm Sleigh.
She born 1785 and died Sep. 1824. He died of
spotted fever at Croydon. Res. Weare, Croydon
and Salem, N.H. His will dated 13 Sep. 1830,
proved 2 Dec. 1834. Wife not named. All
children except SALLY named. Son DAVID of
Deering named executor. [v.37, p.230]

Children: 845. **ANNA**, b. 23 Sep. 1794, md. 23
                   Sep. 1812 **EBENEZER LOVERIN
                   Jr.**
              846. **JUDITH**, b. 4 Sep. 1796, md. 6
                   Apr. 1815 **STEPHEN GOODALE.**
              847. **HILLIARD**, b. 6 May 1798, d. 26
                   Dec. 1864, md. 3 Apr. 1825
                   PHILENA KENSITON.
              848. **MERCY**, b. 1800, d. 21 Oct.
                   1831.
              849. **STEPHEN**, b. 27 June 1802, d. 8
                   Sep. 1874, md. 31 Mar. 1829
                   KERON H. BARTLETT.
by 2nd Wife:
              850. **SARAH**, b. 12 Jan. 1805.
              851. **DAVID**, b. 20 Aug. 1807, md. 25
                   Nov. 1830 **BELINDA HADLOCK.**
              852. **BETSY L.**, b. 1808, md. **WILLIAM
                   SMITH.**
              853. **SALLY**, b. 1810.

367. **AMOS ROWELL [JOSIAH 123]** He was born 30
Sep. 1773 at Salem, N.H. and died 1836. He
married 12 July 1795 **DOLLY GRIFFIN**, d/o **RICHARD
& SARAH (BATCHELDER) GRIFFIN** of Croydon. She
born 12 July 1774 and died 18 Jan. 1847. Res.
Croydon and Salem.

ROWELL FAMILY - NEW ENGLAND
6th Generation

Children: 855. LEVI, b. 18 Oct. 1795, d. 11
Jan. 1881, md. 10 Oct. 1825
MARY LEAR.
856. ABIGAIL, b. 11 Nov. 1797, d. 29
Mar. 1816.
857. GILMAN, b. 6 July 1800.
858. SARAH, b. 12 Sep. 1801.
859. ELIZA, b. 10 Nov. 1804, d. 5
Apr. 1854, md. JOHN LEAR,
m.2, 25 Aug. 1839 LEVI PIERCE
860. ELMIRA, b. 24 July 1807, d. 1
July 1827.
861. ANNA, b. 31 Mar. 1809, d. 5
Apr. 1816.
862. ROXANA, b. 20 Apr. 1814, d. 31
Jan. 1859, md. ? 16 Jan. 1834
SAMUEL C. BURNHAM at Goshen.
863. LOVINA, b. 3 Aug. 1816, d. 2
Oct. 1851, md. EVANS MESSER.

368. RICHARD ROWELL [JOSIAH 123] He was born 13
Jan. 1776 at Salem, N.H. and died there 12 Nov.
1846. He married MARY CORLISS. Res. Salem, N.H.

Children: 865. DANIEL HOLMAN, b. 1 Aug. 1809,
md. 10 Sep. 1842 HARRIET
BURRELL.
866. RICHARD H, b. 1821, d. 23 June
1854, md. 10 Apr. 1843 DORCUS
C. RICHARDSON.
867. MARY C., md. JOHN PARTRIDGE.

369. JONATHAN ROWELL [JOSIAH 123] He was born
14 Apr. 1781 and died 18 Dec. 1833. He married 6
Mar. 1806 LIVINIA ROWELL. (#378)

370. PETER CLEMENT ROWELL [JOSIAH 123] He was
born 12 Jan. 1794 at Salem, N.H. and died 24
Feb. 1876 at Hooksett, N.H. He married 18 Aug.
1814 SUSAN EASTMAN. She born 1794 in Mass. and
died 25 Dec. 1850, age 58 yrs. Res. Hooksett and
Suncock, N.H. Occ. farmer. 1850 census at
Hooksett.

Children: 870. **BARTLETT C.**, b. 1818, d. 6 Oct.
1864, md. 8 Sep. 1840 **BOLINDA
APPLETON**.
871. **ALBERT S.**, b. 1820, d. 12 July
1880. Shoemaker in 1850.
872. **PETER C.**, b. 1822, md. 10 Sep.
1851 **MARY H. ORDWAY**.
873. **CHARLOTTE**, b. 17 Aug. 1824, d.
12 Mar. 1847.
874. **LAURA A.**, md. 27 May 1835 **JACOB
FOWLER**.
875. **HORACE HILL**, b. 9 Jan. 1830
876. **EMILY**, b. 1832, alive 1850.
877. **FRANCES M.**, b. 2 Dec. 1836, md.
JOHN S. DRAKE.
878. **GILMAN**,

376. **MOSES DUTY ROWELL [WILLIAM 125]** He was
born 5 Oct. 1778 at Salem, N.H. and died 16 Nov.
1857 [78-9-16] at Tunbridge, Vt. He married 17
Jan. 1808 at Boston **LUCY ANN ADAMS**. She born 29
Dec. 1787 and died 13 Sep. 1865. He served in
War of 1812. 1850 census at Tunbridge, Vt.

Children: 880. **ADAM**, b. 9 Mar. 1810, d. 9 Mar.
1881, md. 26 Jan. 1842 **MARY
M. MARTIN**.
881. **ELIZA R.P.**, b. 25 Mar. 1811, d.
31 May 1901, md. 20 Feb. 1834
PAYNE DURKEE, 3 ch.
882. **GEORGE WASHINGTON**, b. 21 Nov.
1813, d. 14 Oct. 1853, md. 30
Mar. 1837 **SUSAN CUSHMAN**.
883. **MARY**, b. 22 Feb. 1816, d. 9
Mar. 1890, md. 27 Dec. 1840
or 3 Mar. 1841 **WILLIAM
WATERMAN**. Had a son.
884. **LUCY ANN**, b. 5 Feb. 1818, d. 26
Jan. 1842, md. 3 Mar. 1841
JOHN DUTTON, no ch.
885. **NATHANIEL LEWIS**, b. 20 Feb.
1820, d. May 1903. md. 2 Dec.
1841 **SUSANNA DUTTON**.

886. SUSAN M., b. 8 Feb. 1822, md.
     AMASA DUTTON, 2 ch.
887. JANE B. , 6 Apr. 1824, md. 11
     Dec. 1843 HORACE CHATFIELD.
     4 ch.
888. MOSES DUTY Jr., b. 5 Apr. 1824,
     d. 26 Sep. 1888, md. SUSAN E.
     WIGHT.
889. WILLIAM, b. 1826.
890. SARAH E., b. 9 Sep. 1830, d. 11
     July 1870, md. 19 Dec. 1853
     JOEL CRANDALL, 4 ch.

379. JAMES ROWELL [WILLIAM 125] He married 12
Apr. 1821 REBECCA CHASE.

children: 895. JOHN C., md. SARAH DUSTON

381. CALEB ROWELL [WILLIAM 125] He was born
about 1787. He married MARY G. HUBBARD or
HOBART. She born about 1791. Res. Quincy, Mass.
1816.

Children: 900. THADDEUS M.H., b. c1816 in
              N.H., d. 1900 Mass, md. 1843
              MARY A. LOUGEE.

384. GEORGE WASHINGTON ROWELL [WILLIAM 125] He
was born 16 Oct. 1794 at Salem, N.H. and died 21
Jan. 1873 at Tunbridge, Vt. He married 13 May
1818 RUTH CARTER, d/o CYRUS & ADELIA (LADD)
CARTER. She born 9 Feb. 1802 and died 3 Oct.
1898 at Quechee, Vt. 1850 census at Tunbridge,
Vt.

Children: 910. ABIAH, b. 1819, d. 1899, md.
              25 Sep. 1843 ORIN CHATFIELD.
              3 children.
          911. CHASE HALL, b. 15 Dec. 1822,
              d. 13 May 1898, md. 16 Mar.
              1847 SARAH ANN HILL.
          912. HANNAH L., b. 5 Sep. 1825, d.
              15 Feb. 1877, md. 22 June
              1844 ROBERT M. BLAKE. 5 ch.

913. **RUTH**, d. abt. 1845, md. 1842
     GEORGE WALES. No children.
914. **CYRUS CARTER**, b. 1831, d. 9
     Mar. 1909, md. 19 Feb. 1859
     AMELIA A. GIFFORD.
915. **GEORGE WASHINGTON Jr.**, b. 9
     Jan. 1833, d. c1918, md. 18
     Sep. 1864 **JANE HARTSHORN**.
916. **MARCIA C.**, b. c1835.
917. **MARCELLUS C.**, b. 27 Jan. 1837,
     d. 27 June 1906, md. 16 Mar.
     1858 **HELEN MARCIA HOWE**.
918. **ELIZA JANE**, b. 28 Dec. 1839,
     md. 28 Feb. 1871 **SAMUEL H.
     PEMBER**. 3 children.
919. **EMMA M.**, b. 29 Aug. 1842, d.
     Mar. 1922, md. 20 July 1862
     JOHN TYLER SISCO. 4 ch.
920. **MARY ELLEN/MARIA F.**, b. 1843?,
     d. 5 Apr. 1864, md. 7 Oct.
     1857 **HIRAM SANBORN**.
921. **ADELIA**, d.y.

412. **DANIEL MERRILL ROWELL** [JONATHAN 130] He was
born 28 June 1811 at Montville, Me. and died
there 14 Sep. 1888. He possibly married 1st 10
May 1829 **ELIZA WHITTEN**. He married 2nd 12 Aug.
1835 **HANNAH C. VOSE**. He married 3rd 2 Feb. 1878
Mrs. HANNAH VOSE. Occ. farmer. 1850 census at
Montville, Me.

Children: 929. **ELBRIDGE**, b. 1830, d. 3 Mar.
                1863, md. **MARTHA BROWN**.
           930. **GEORGE W.**, b. 15 June 1836, d.
                25 Jan. 1879, md. **Mrs. ABBIE
                McFARLAND**.
           931. **EBENEZER**, b. 29 Nov. 1837/8, d.
                5 Aug. 1863.
           932. **JONATHAN**, b. 6 Sep. 1839, d. 28
                Aug. 1862.
           933. **EZEKIEL P.**, b. 12 Apr. 1842, d.
                16 Sep. 1920, md. 19 Oct.
                1864 **MARY FRANCES WHITTEN**.

ROWELL FAMILY - NEW ENGLAND
6th Generation

934. HELEN/ELLEN M., b. 26 Aug.
1844, d. Feb. 1890.
935. SARAH F., b. 11 Jan. 1846, d.
8 Sep. 1920, md. 18 Feb. 1865
ALBION H. CLEMENTS.
936. EDWARD L., b. 27 Dec. 1848, d.
16 Jan. 1849, md. MARIA MORSE
937. ADOLPHUS M., b. 7 Mar. 1855, d.
18 Dec. 1863.
938. ALFRED H., b. 29 May 1850, d.
27 Apr. 1852.
939. LUELLA C., b. 13 May 1858, d.
9 July 1923, md. GEORGE
BROWN.

413. JESSE SHAW ROWELL [JONATHAN 130] He was
born 15 Oct. 1813. He married 25 Dec. 1836
HANNAH B. WRIGHT. She born 1818. Occ. farmer.
Res. Montville, Me.

Children: 940. ALMOND M.J., b. 1839, md. 7
Jan. 1860 JULIE E. COMBS.
941. DENNIS A., b. 1849.

427. DAVID ROWELL [JESSE 131] He was born 17
April 1823 at Jefferson, Me. and died 20 March
1890. He served in the Civil War, 21st Me.
Reg't. He married 11 Sep. or 7 Dec. 1845 MARY
JANE KENNEDY. She born c1828 and died 23 July
1893. Res. Jefferson, Me. Occ. farmer. 1850
Census.

Children: 945. DORINDA, b. c1845.
946. ETTA MAY, md. 22 Sep. 1890,
ROSCOE A. SHERMAN.

428. Rev. PARIS ROWELL [JESSE 131] He was born
31 Oct. 1825 at Jefferson, Me. and died 14 May
1894. He married 21 Sep. 1855 at New Castle
ALMIRA P. HODGKINS. She born c1827 and died 21
June 1887. Occ. blacksmith. Res. at Searport in
1860.

Children: 950. GEORGE PRATT, b. 1858, d. 13
                July 1889, md. 19 Aug. 1882
                MARY C. BEARCE.

430. LORENZO DOW ROWELL [JAMES 132] He was born
4 Oct. 1811 and died 27 Mar. 1899. He married 7
Jan. 1837 SUSAN HICKS FREEMAN. She born 28 Feb.
1818 and died 13 June 1891. Occ. joiner. 1850
census at Frankfort, Me.

Children: 952. JAMES FREDERICK, b. 5 Mar.
                1842, d. 1 Feb. 1902, md. 9
                Oct. 1867 EMMA FOSTER
                FREEMAN.
           953. CHARLES POTTER, b. 6 Feb. 1844,
                m.1, 16 Nov. 1871 MARY H.
                WOOD, m.2, 12 Dec. 1877
                LILLIS J. RYDER. Bangor, Me.
           954. WALTER HENRY, b. 23 July 1859,
                md. 8 Aug. 1885 SARAH A.
                NEWTON at Bangor, Me.

433. JAMES HARVEY ROWELL [JAMES 132] He was born
11 Feb. 1817 and died 1884. He married 1st SARAH
J. CANNERY or KENNEY. He married 2nd 11 April
1847 MARY E. CLARK, d/o WILLIAM CLARK. She born
1823 and died 1895. Occ. Clergyman. Res.
Atkinson, Me. 1850 Census at Sebec, Me.

Children: 955. JAMES EDWIN, b. 1842, md. 24
                July 1869 HARRIET ALFARATA
                MARTIN.
           956. WESLEY D., b. 1844, md. MARTHA
                E. CURRIER.
by 2nd wife:
           957. FRANK E., b. 15 Mar. 1849, md.
                13 May 1873 ABBIE M. SARGENT,
                d/o HECTOR & MARY D. SARGENT.
                Had twins who d.y.
           958. WILBER F., md. MARY _____.

435. BENJAMIN FRANKLIN ROWELL [JAMES 132] He was
born about 1820. He married 9 Mar. 1840 SARAH
BEAN, d/o ISAAC & SALLY (EVERETT) BEAN. Res. at
Montville, Me. in 1860.

Children: 960. SARAH A., b. 1841.
            961. ELIZA, b. 1844.
            962. JAMES, b. 1846.
            963. HENRY FRANK, b. 1849, md. MARIA
                 ELIZA BOWKER.
            964. GEORGE FREEMAN, b. 1853, d.
                 1907, md. EUNICE H. HOLBROOK.

437. AARON HOLBROOK ROWELL [JAMES 132] He was
born 1828 and died 18 Nov. 1901 at Lawrence,
Mass. He married MARY TAPLEY. Occ. joiner.

Children: 965. FRANK, d.y.
            966. FRANK ABBOTT, md. ADDIE WINN.
                 Had: HATTIE, d.y.

443. OLIVER PERRY ROWELL [RUFUS 133] He was born
7 Sep. 1826. He married GEORGIANN PENDLETON
BURCH.

Children: 970. HANNAH ELIZABETH,
            971. CHARLES ABBOTT,
            972. GEORGE RUFUS, md. MARY A.
                 _____.
            973. CLARA LOUISE,
            974. WALTER PERRY, md. 1 Nov. 1894
                 CORA EATON.
            975. JULIA EDITH,
            976. FRANK, d.y.
            977. MARINA, d.y.

446. ALBERT H/S. ROWELL [RUFUS 133] He was born
13 Jan. 1834. Had wife CLARA _____. Res.
Rockport, Me.

Children: 980. ROSELIND E., b. 28 Mar. 1859.
            981. ELLEN M., b. 27 Nov. 1862.

455. **BENJAMIN/BENNING W. ROWELL Sr.** [JOHN 94?]
He was born about 1756. He married **LUCY HORN**.
Occ. miller. He lived at Oxford, N.H., Vermont,
Livingstone Co., N.Y. 1828, moved to Wis. by
1843. Manufactured plows there.

Children: 985. **JOHN**, bp. 10 Oct. 1782, md. 23
Nov. 1799 **SALLY MOORE**.
986. **BETHEWEL C.**, b. c1797. Service
War of 1812. 4 & 5th US Inf.
Pension SC-5129.
987. **JARED M.**,
988. **BENNING/BENJAMIN Jr.**, b. 30
Apr. 1787, md. **TAMSON
BARRON**.
989. **GEORGE**,
990. **SAMUEL**, bp. 14 Sep. 1786 at
Oxford, N.H.
991. **DANIEL**,
992. **POLLY**,
993. **LUCY**,
994. **DEBORAH**,
995. **ELIZABETH**,

SEVENTH GENERATION

503. **MOSES ROWELL** [CHRISTOPHER 159] He was born 11 June 1764 at Newton, N.H. and died 14 Nov. 1846 at Loudon, N.H. He married first 6 April 1788 **ELLICE (ALICE) CURRIER** at Amesbury, Mass. She born 9 Feb. 1768 and died 9 May 1795. He married second 7 Mar. 1799 **NANCY LEAVITT**, d/o **JONATHAN & NANCY (TILTON) LEAVITT**. of Chichester, N.H. She born 9 Sep. 1777 and died 15 Dec. 1868. Moses served in the N.H. Militia in the Rev. War. Named in 1790 census at Loudon [3-3-7] Res. Loudon, N.H. His will dated 9 May 1845, proved 4 Dec. 1846. Named wife NANCY, sons: JOHN, MOSES Jr., and ASA, daughters: RUTH and SALLY. Sons RUFUS and CYRUS named executors. 1850 census at Loudon.

Children by 1st Wife:
     1000. **CAPT. JOHN**, b. 20 Jan. 1790, d. 19 July 1872, md. 6 May 1819 **ESTHER LAKE**.
     1001. **MOSES Jr.**, b. 21 Mar. 1793, d. 19 Jan. 1865, md. 21 Mar. 1821 **SOPHIA FRENCH**.
by 2nd wife:
     1002. **NANCY**, b. 17 July 1800 or 1802, d. 14 May 1838.
     1003. **MICAJAH**, b. 30 Mar. 1802/3, d. 11 Aug. 1829.
     1004. **RUTH**, b. 18 Apr. 1804, d. 7 Nov. 1864, md. 22 Jan. 1832 **JOHN LAKE**. Had: LOUISE, b. 1842.
     1005. **ASA TILTON**, b. 13 Feb. 1806, d. 23 Apr. 1875, md. 2 Dec. 1835 **ABIGAIL S. MOULTON**.
     1006. **HARRIS**, b. 10 July 1808, d. 15 July 1835.
     1007. **CYRUS**, b. 14 Apr. 1811, d. 24 July 1884, md. **JUDITH SANBORN**.
     1008. **RUFUS**, b. 6 Apr. 1814, d. 29 Nov. 1891. Single in 1850.

ROWELL FAMILY - NEW ENGLAND
7th Generation

1009. **SARAH/SALLY LANGMEAD**, b. 26
Mar. 1817, d. 18 Dec. 1895,
md. **THEOPHILUS BLAKE MARTIN**

504. **THOMAS ROWELL** [CHRISTOPHER 159] He was
born 13 Sep. 1767 and died in 1846. He married
27 Nov. 1794 or 26 Jan. 1799/1800 **LYDIA WILLIAMS**
at Lebanon, N.H. Went down Mississippi River.
Worked as shoe maker in New Orleans. Returned to
New England. Res. Lebanon, N.H. & Hartford, Vt.

Children: 1010. **JOHN**, b. 9 June 1796, d. 6
Nov. 1800.
1011. **ZIBA MORSE**, b. 26 Mar. 1798,
d. 1860, md. **FRANCES SEARS**.
1012. **ASNETH/ASANATH**, b. 26 June
1800 at Orange, N.H.
1013. **HANNAH**, b. 5 May 1802.
1014. **CHRISTOPHER CLARK**, b. 8 Aug.
1806, md. **MARY A. HUNTER**.
1015. **LYDIA ABBOTT**, b. 2 Nov. 1807.
1016. **JOHN ADAMS**, b. 14 Nov. 1809,
twin.
1017. **JAMES MADISON**, b. 14 Nov.
1809, twin.
1018. **daughter**, b. 1812.

505. **CHRISTOPHER ROWELL Jr.** [CHRISTOPHER 159]
He was born 22 Aug. 1769 at Newton, N.H. and
died at West Concord, N.H. 9 Sep. 1847 age 78
yrs. He married 27 Oct. 1798 **LYDIA ABBOT**, d/o
JABEZ & HEPZIBAH (STEVENS) ABBOT of Concord. She
born 1773 and died 23 Mar. 1841. Occ. farmer and
shoemaker. Res. W. Concord, N.H.

Children: 1020. **IRA**, b. 29 May 1797, d. 14
June 1876, m.1, 30 Jan. 1824
ELIZABETH THOMPSON, m.2, 9
Apr. 1828 **REBECCA KIMBALL**.
1021. **THOMAS**, b. 12 Aug. 1799, d. 20
Apr. 1832, md. **BRIDGET W.
FARNUM**.
1022. **Child**, d. 1802 at Concord.

506. JOHN ROWELL [CHRISTOPHER 159] He was born
27 Apr. 1772 and died 1796 at West Concord, N.H.
Unmd. Res. Lebanon, N.H.

507. MICAJAH ROWELL [CHRISTOPHER 159] He was
born 6 May 1774. He married 12 Nov. 1804
ELIZABETH SAVAGE, d/o STEPHEN SAVAGE. She born
31 Oct. 1784 in Conn, died 21 July 1847 at
Edenboro, Ohio. Res. Littleton, N.H. 1799 -
1816. Occ. farmer.

Children: 1030. ELIZA, b. 5 May 1806.

513. STEPHEN ROWELL [JACOB 160] He was born
about 1764. He married PHEOBE LITTLEFIELD. Res.
Frankfort, Me. in 1796.

Children: 1035. JACOB, b. 1796, d. 1883, md.
1816 WATEY PARSON.

519. JACOB ROWELL [JACOB 160] He was born 5
June 1773 at Newton, N.H. He married RUTH
CURRIER. Occ. farmer. In 1850 census had wife
HANNAH FAVOR. She born 1778. Res. Newton, N.H.

Children: 1039. JACOB, b. 25 July 1796.
1040. BETTE, b. 31 July 1800.
1041. LYDIA, b. 28 Jan. 1805, s.p.
in 1850.
1042. MYRON P., b. c1809, d. 10 Aug.
1886, md. ELIZA A BOSWELL.
1043. JOHN RAN, b. 9 Oct. 1813.

523. JOSEPH ROWELL [WILLIAM 161] He was born 15
Mar. 1767 and died 14 Nov. 1842. He married 15
Feb. 1803 HANNAH CHASE in Cornith. Called Rev.
in Vital Records. Res. Cornith, N.H.

Children: 1044. ELIZA, b. 27 Feb. 1804
1045. JONATHAN EDWARDS, b. 3 June
1806, md. 17 Aug. 1835
CAROLINE E. WHITE.
1046. MARIA CHASE, b. 3 Apr. 1808.

1047. DANIEL CHASE, b. 25 Aug. 1810.
1048. MARTHA LAURENCE, b. 9 Nov.
1812, md.30 Nov. 1836 EDWIN
LOCKE.
1049. GEORGE BERKELEY, b. 22 Jan.
1815, md. 7 Apr. 1842
MELVINA J. CHAPIN.
1050. TIMOTHY DWIGHT, b. 19 Dec.
1817, md. 23 Oct. 1845
MERIEL W. WILLARD.
1051. JOSEPH, b. 22 Apr. 1820.
1052. SAMUEL NEWELL, b. 21 Nov.
1821.
1053. CAROLINE ELIZABETH, b. 21 Nov.
1823.
1054. HARRIET LOUISE, b. 22 Jan.
1826.

525. WILLIAM ROWELL [WILLIAM 161] He was born 10
Oct. 1770 and died 10 Feb. 1823 at Salisbury,
Mass. He married 31 Dec. 1795 ELIZABETH
TEWKSBURY/TUXBURY at Salisbury, Mass. Some
sources say he married 2nd, 8 Feb. 1806 REBECCA
CLOUTMAN d/o JOSEPH & HANNAH (BECKER) CLOUTMAN
at Salem, Mass. She born 1781 and died 23 Dec.
1847. Res. Newton, N.H. See #536.

Children: 1055. MARIANNA/MARY ANN, b. 25 Jan.
1811, d. 1 Mar. 1881, md. 3
Sep. 1833 MOSES CARR Jr, md.
30 Apr. 1835 MORSE TEXBURY.
1056. ABIGAIL M.T., b. 9 Sep. 1795,
md. DANIEL CHASE Jr. 2 Ch.

527. JOSHUA ROWELL [WILLIAM 161] He was born 6
July 1774 at Newton, N.H. and died 17 July 1838,
age 63 years at Newton. He married SARAH
PEASLEE. Res. Newton, N.H.

Children: 1057. EDMUND, b. 9 Oct. 1803, md
1835 ELEANOR MARSHALL
1058. POLLEY, b. 17 Aug. 1809.
1059. LUCY, b. 6 Nov. 1811.

1060. **ANN**, b. 27 Aug. 1817.

529. **BENJAMIN ROWELL** [WILLIAM 161] He was born
8 Apr. 1778 at Newton, N.H. and died 18 Jan.
1856. He married first **PHEBE HOYT**. He married
second **RUTH** _____. Res. Newton, N.H.

Children by 1st Wife:
      1061. **HANNAH MORSE**, b. 19 Oct. 1803.
      1062. **RUTH HOYT**, b. 2 Aug. 1805.
by 2nd Wife:
      1063. **WILLIAM**, b. 1 July 1807, md.
         MERCY W. HARRIS.
      1064. **OTIS ROBERTSON**, b. 14 June
         1809, md. 1836 **ELVIRA WEED**.
      1065. **SALLY STUART**, b. 21 June 1811.
      1066. **ANNA**, b. 24 Aug. 1813.

536. **WILLIAM ROWELL** [THOMAS 171] He was born
1780 and died Feb. 1823, ae 43 yrs. He perhaps
married 8 Feb. 1806 **REBECCA CLOUTMAN**, d/o **JOSEPH
& HANNAH (BECKER) CLOUTMAN** at Salem. She born
1781 and died 23 Dec. 1847 at Salem. See #525.

Children: 1070. **FREDERICK**, b. c1800, md. 2
         Dec. 1838 **MARY ANN BURKE**.

545. **DANIEL ROWELL** [WILLIAM 180] He was born
1763 or 1765 and died 1847. He married 1788
NANCY NEAL d/o **Capt. JAMES NEAL** at Salisbury.
She born 1770. Rev. War service, Pvt. N.H.
served 3 years. Enlisted Feb. 1781 at Epping,
N.H., 2nd Reg't N.H., Col Reid Co. Commanded by
his father. Pension mentions wife and 12
children. No battles.

Children: 1074. **daughter**, B. 1797
         1075. **WILLIAM**, b. 1797, md. 27 Jan.
         1818 **LUCIA PORTER**.

551. **MOSES ROWELL Jr.** [MOSES 189] He was born
4 July 1800 and died 2 Feb. 1849 at Bath, N.H.
He married first 14 April 1831 **HANNAH MERRILL
MARTIN**. He married second 15 Feb. 1827 **ABIGAIL**

BANFIELD of Newbury, Vt. She born c1797 and died 2 Feb. 1870 at Bath. Res. Bath, N.H. 1850 census at Bath.

Children by 1st Wife:
        1077. WILLIAM,
        1078. ADALINE,
        1079. FINATHA,
by 2nd Wife:
        1080. GEORGE B., b. 24 Mar. 1830, d.
              21 Dec. 1870, m.1, LESTINE
              MERRILL, m.2, LOUISE CHIPMAN
        1081. MARTHA PAYTON, b. 26 Dec.
              1827, md. 19 Feb. 1848 MOSES
              CLARK at Newbury, Vt.
        1082. MARY P., b. 29 Mar. 1832, md.
              30 Mar. 1854 WILLIARD R.
              PARKER. 1 ch.
        1083. ABIGAIL, b. 3 May 1835, d.
              Mar. 1843.
        1084. HARRIET ALDUSTA, b. 25 Feb.
              1838, md. DAMON HALL. No ch.

555. IRA B. ROWELL [RICHARD 190] He was born 1803 in N.Y. and died 1893. He married in 1827 MARIA LUCY FORD of Ontario Co., N.Y. Occ. farmer. Res. Naples, Ontario Co., N.Y. and in 1842 came to Wisconsin. Settled at Lisbon. Had a farm. Later moved to Hartford where wife died. Then moved to Menomanee Falls. Manufactured plows. Last three children born in Wisconsin. 1850 census in Washington County.

Children: 1090. JOHN KENDRICK, b. 1828,
                 Salesman I.B.Rowell Co.
           1091. LEWIS FORD, b. 1829.
           1092. ELIJAH GIBSON, b. 1831, horse
                 breeder, Hartford.
           1093. IRA BENJAMIN, b. 19 Jan. 1833,
                 md. ELIZA OSBURN.
           1094. GUILFORD DUDLEY, b. 1834.
           1095. MARY MILTON, b. 1836.
           1096. ALPHONSO DWIGHT, b. 1839.

1097. LUCY MATILDA, b. 1841, md.
MIKE BUSH, Liv. at Milw.
1098. GEORGE WAYLAND, b. 1843, d.
1934, md. MARY WALSH.
1099. CHARLES SHOLL, b. 1845, d.
infancy, age 5 yrs.
1100. HORACE VINCENT, B. 1847, farm
Impl. dealer, Hartford, Wis.

556. PHINEAS ASHLEY ROWELL [RICHARD 190] He was
born 1807 and died 1875. He married c1849
ELIZABETH SHEPARD. Res. Lockport, N.Y.

Children: 1101. CHARLES WALTER, b. 1850, d.
1896, md. 1879 SARAH MARIA
COOPER.

other children: son 1799, dau. 1800,
dau. 1804, dau. 1805, dau. 1806,
dau. 1808, son 1810, son 1812, dau.
1815 and dau. 1817. names unknown.

561. PHILIP ROWELL [JACOB 202] He was born 1762
and died 8 June 1838. He married 22 Nov. 1792
ANNA JOHNSON. Res. Amesbury, Mass.

Children: 1110. JACOB, b. c1794, md. 17 Sep.
1817 POLLY STEVENS.
1111. PHILIP, b. 27 Nov. 1806, md.
13 Nov. 1830 MARY J. WELLS.
1112. EDWARD, b. 24 June 1808.
1113. ANN, b. 20 Oct. 1810, md. 5
Oct. 1831 HIRAM STEVENS.

566. JACOB ROWELL [JACOB 202] He was born 30
Oct. 1771 and died 6 Feb. 1853. He married 22
Nov. 1804 ABIGAIL JONES, d/o JOHN JONES of
Andover, Mass.. Res. Amesbury, Mass. 1850
census.

Children: 1120. JOHN, b. 28 Jan. 1806.
possibly md. 1832 SARAH M.
STEWART.
1121. ELIZABETH, b. 8 Feb. 1807.

1122. JACOB, b. 10 Dec. 1809,
     Possibly md. 1839 IRENE ANN
     JONES.
1123. REBEKAH, b. 1 Nov. 1812, md. ?
     28 Dec. 1844 STEPHEN C. GREY
1124. SAMUEL, b. 22 Aug. 1815,
     Possibly md, 1841 LYDIA J.
     NEAL.
1125. CHARLES, b. 24 Oct. 1817, md.
     9 Nov. 1842 RUTH ANN HEALEY.
1126. GEORGE S., b. 16 Sep. 1819,
     md. 27 Jan. 1840 MARY
     ELIZABETH COLBY, m.2,
     REBECCA JONES.
1127. ABIGAIL J., b. 15 Sep. 1821.
1128. SARAH, b. 27 Jan. 1824.
1129. MARY, b. 23 Nov. 1825.

568. JAMES ROWELL [JACOB 202] He was born 28 Sep. 1775 or 1776. He married 4 July 1800 PHEBE JARVIS. Res. Salisbury, Mass. She living 1850 with son Tim at Vasselboro, Me.

Children: 1140. JAMES, b. 21 Sep. 1808, md. 23
     Sep. 1831 SARENA FLANDERS.
1141. ANNA, b. 14 June 1810.
1142. TIMOTHY, b. 6 Jan. 1812, md.
     SARAH BRYANT.

571. JOSEPH ROWELL [MOSES 207] He was born 2 Feb. 1766. He married 30 July 1796 MARY COLBY. Occ. shoe maker. 1850 Census at Monmouth, Me.

Children: 1145. MOSES, b. 1794, md. SARAH ____.
1146. BELINDA, b. 1810.
1147. JOSEPH P., b. 1815.

572. MARK ROWELL [MOSES 207] He was born 22 Feb. 1776. He married 18 Feb. 1805 LYDIA WORTHAM. Res. Salisbury, Mass. Admin. estate 14 Sep. 1818 granted to EZEKIEL WORTHER. [v.44, p.509]

Children: 1150. MOSES, b. 11 Nov. 1805,
possibly md. 10 Sep. 1834
MARY STEVENS, d/o Capt. Wm
STEVENS in Amesbury, MA.

580. AARON ROWELL [THOMAS 217] He was born 1770
in Me. and died 1846. He married 5 Sep. 1795
POLLY PUTNEY/PUDNEY at Bradford, Vt. She born
1773 and died 26 Nov. 1849 [76-2] at Maidstone.
He married second 10 July 1830 ESTHER ORDWAY at
Jackson, N.H. She born c1805 in Me. Occ.
joiner. 1850 census at Lancaster, N.H. Res. of
Bradford, Vt.
Children: 1152. JANE, b. 19 Feb. 1796.
1153. RUTH, b. 6 Dec. 1797.
1154. BETSY, b. 8 Nov. 1799, md. 8
Jan. 1824 WARREN GAGE.
1155. HANNAH, b. 3 Sep. 1800, d.
1894, md. Jan. 1830 JOHN
COLBY at Bradford, Vt.
1156. MARY, b. 19 Feb. 1802.
1157. RUHANAN, b. 15 June 1804, md.
4 Jan. 1822 WILSON CARR.
1158. WILLIAM, b. 1805, d. 1857, md.
20 Nov. 1828 BELINDA ROGERS.
1159. SABINA, b. 9 Dec. 1808, d. 15
July 1850 [41-7].
1160. SALLY, b. 12 July 1811, md.
4 Nov. 1832 CLEFTON HATCHER.
1161. MENGARY, b. 3 Dec. 1813.

588. ELIJAH ROWELL [AARON 218] He was born 8 May
1765. He married 10 Nov. 1792 OLIVE POND.

590. MOSES ROWELL [AARON 218]. He was bapt. 22
May 1774. He married first 24 June 1798 SALLY
FREELAND at Hopkinton, N.H.   Res. Southboro,
Mass. Moved to Corinth, Vt. He married second 5
July 1818 RUTH BROWN at Corinth, Vt.

Children 1st Wife:
1170. AARON, b. 23 Apr. 1799.
1171. LYDIA, b. 25 Feb. 1802.
1172. HIRAM, b. 2 May 1803.

ROWELL FAMILY - NEW ENGLAND
7th Generation

     1173. **LEONARD F.**, b. 19 Apr. 1807,
          d. 13 Aug. 1866, md. 13 Dec.
          1829 **SARAH LOUISE KIMBALL.**
     1174. **LOUISE**, b. 8 Sep. 1809.
     1175. **MIRIAM**, b. 25 Apr. 1812.
by 2nd Wife:
     1176. **EMILY B.**, b. 4 Nov. 1818, md.
          27 Dec. 1842 **WARREN FULLER**
          at Waterville, Vt.
     1177. **ALONZO**, b. 18 Sep. 1822.
     1178. **HIRAM**, b. 11 July 1824, d. 20
          Apr. 1834 [9-6-13].
     1179. **CROMWELL G.**, b. 29 Aug. 1826,
          md.? 29 Nov. 1849 **HARRIET F.**
          MAYNARD at Framington, Mass.

596. **JACOB ROWELL** [PHILIP 224] He was born 28 Sep. 1793. Had wife **PATTY** in 1850 census at Salisbury. She born c1796 in Mass. Occ. farmer.

Children: 1185. **MARY**, b. c1835.

609. **EDWARD ROWELL** [DANIEL 232] He was born 24 May 1769 at E. Kingston and died about 1825 at Percy, N.H. He married 24 April 1794 **ABIGAIL SMITH**, d/o Capt. **CALEB & HANNAH (WADLEIGH) SMITH**. She born c1776 at Raymond. He was a farmer and Innkeeper at Percy. Selectman 1801 - 1825. Town clerk 1803 and J.P. Res. Percy/Starke, N.H.

Children: 1190. **DANIEL**, b. 30 Jan. 1796, d. 2
              May 1813.
          1191. **ABIGAIL**, b. 12 Oct. 1797, d.
              unmd, 29 Feb. 1876 at Stark,
              N.H.
          1192. **JUDITH**, b. 8 May 1800, md.
              JAMES STONE.
          1193. **HANNAH**, b. 19 Feb. 1803, d. 29
              Jan. 1886, md. **SAMUEL**
              ROBBINS. 4 children.
          1194. **JINNE** (m), b. 11 Feb. 1805.
          1195. **EDWARD Jr.**, b. 14 Jan. 1807,
              d. unmd. 19 Feb. 1876.

1196. GEORGE W., b. 7 May 1809, md.
    18 Aug. 1850 ELIZABETH F.
    CHAPMAN.
1197. SUSANNAH, b. 5 July 1813, m.1,
    JABISH P. CURRANT, m.2, 12
    May 1867 JUSTUS POTTER.
1198. HARRIET, b. 13 Apr. 1815, md.
    27 Apr. 1836 JOSEPH
    LEIGHTEN.
1199. JAMES M., b. 24 Sep. 1817, d.
    13 Oct. 1843 LAURA WAID.

610. JONATHAN ROWELL [DANIEL 232] He was born 14
May 1771 at Weare, N.H. and died 31 Oct. 1863/7
at Littleton. He married 4 Mar. or 31 Aug. 1799
SALLY HOSKINS, d/o ELKANAH HOSKINS. She born 21
Mar. 1780 and died 6 Sep. 1866. Occ. farmer,
Innkeeper, J.P., Selectman 1811-1815 & 1832,
Whig, Cong. Church. Signed petition 1797 at
Warrenville. Res. Starke, Littleton, N.H. & by
1804 at Waterford, Vt. 1850 census at Littleton.

Children: 1200. JONATHAN BARNEY, b. 3 Feb.
    1800, d. 28 Sep. 1850 md.
    22 Jan. 1828 CYNTHIA ABBOTT.
1201. ANNA, b. 21 Jan. 1802, d. 3
    Feb. 1889 at Barnet, Vt.,
    md. 29 Sep. 1832 ROSWELL
    SARTWELL. Had: LOIS ANNE.
1202. LOIS, b. 13 Jan. 1804, d. 20
    Jan. 1883, md. Dec. 1834
    CHARLES F. GREGORY. 2 ch.
1203. MINDWELL, b. 29 Jan. 1806, d.
    22 Sep. 1850, md. 30 May
    1839 ASA E. RANKIN. 2 dau.
1204. GUY CARLTON, b. 15 Feb. 1808,
    d. 17 Mar. 1891, md. 12 Feb.
    1835 CLARISSA DAVIS RANKIN.
1205. BENJAMIN FRANKLIN, b. 5 Feb.
    1810, d. 25 Sep. 1860, md. 6
    July 1837 CHARITY ABBOT.
1206. RICHARD, b. 21 Feb. 1812, d.
    24 Aug. 1813.

1207. RICHARD, b. 22 Jan. 1814, d.
        16 Oct. 1884, md. 1853 MARY
        (NANCY) BARNARD.
1208. SALMON HOSKINS, b. 2 July
        1816, d. 16 Jan. 1900, md. 4
        Jan. 1846 CORDELIA M. BALLOU
1209. JOSHUA, b.29 Nov. 1818, d. 6
        June 1853, md. 31 Mar. 1853
        MARY R. CHASE, d/o MILLER
        CHASE of Swansee.
1210. IRA, b. 12 Jan. 1821, d. 15
        Feb. 1823.
1211. ADELINE, b. 24 Feb. 1823, d. 6
        Oct. 1897, md. 5 Apr. 1853
        Dr. EPHRAIM PURDY. 4 ch.
        Res. Cinn., Ohio.

612. DANIEL ROWELL Jr. [DANIEL 232] He was born
5 Sep. 1776 at Barrington, N.H. and died 25 June
1843 at Starke. He married 31 Aug. 1799
MEHITABLE SMITH, d/o CALEB & HANNAH (WADLEIGH)
SMITH. She born 14 Sep. 1780 at Raymond, N.H.
and died 27 Oct. 1853. Had lot #14 at Percy in
1803. Selectman many times. Res. Starke, N.H.
and Percy, Vt.

Children: 1212. SARAH, b. 7 Feb. 1801, d. 15
                    Aug. 1882, md. 31 July 1826
                    ENOCH C. RICH. 14 children.
            1213. LEVI, b. c1802, d.y.
            1214. CALIB, b. 17 Apr. 1804, md. 13
                    Nov. 1826 MARY BANFIELD.
            1215. MIRIAM, b. 8 Mar. 1806, md. 17
                    Aug. 1826 RUFUS SPAULDING.
            1216. JOSHUA, b. 30 May 1808, d.
                    1881, md. 7 Mar. 1829 SYBIL
                    EUNICE SPAULDING.
            1217. LOIS, b. 19 Mar. 1810, d. 30
                    Oct. 1886, md. 10 May 1830
                    DANIEL MILES, 4 children.
            1218. LYDIA M., b. 26 July 1812, d.
                    6 Nov. 1861, md. 11 Jan.
                    1838 JOSEPH HINDS. 7 ch.

1219. DANIEL, b. 3 Dec. 1814, d. 22
      May 1881, md. 18 Feb. 1838
      CHARLOTTE POTTER.
1220. NANCY S., b. 3 Mar. 1817, d.
      25 Jan. 1894, md. Oct. 1852
      ALEX WENTWORTH Jr.
1221. Dr. ISAAC, b. 1818, md. NELLIE
      HALE.
1222. MARY, b. 1820.
1223. LEVI, b. 15 Sep. 1822, d. 29
      June 1869, md. CAROLINE
      McFARLAND.
1224. CHARLES W., b. 5 July 1824,
      md. 20 June 1846 SARAH B.
      HAMMOND.

616. Dr. RICHARD F. ROWELL [DANIEL 232] He was
born 1788. He married 22 Aug. 1822 MELINDA A.
MILLER. She died 1 Aug. 1855 [51yr]. Vermont
State Legislature 1840 - 1841. Res. Waterford,
Vt. 1850 census at Waterford.

Children: 1225. CAROLINE H., b. 21 Aug. 1827,
                 md 1866 JEREMIAH B. TAYLOR
                 as 2nd wife.
           1226. RICHARD C., b. 28 Oct. 1829.
                 1850 machinist.
           1227. ABNER, twin, b. 13 Dec. 1831,
                 d. 6 Nov. 1870.
           1228. AUGUSTA ADELIA, twin, b. 13
                 Dec. 1831, md. 28 May 1857
                 JOHN FITCH SPAULDING.
           1229. Col. HENRY WARD, b. 16 Jan.
                 1834, d. 1899, md. 11 Oct.
                 1855 ACHSAH B. TAYLOR. 1850
                 Census, Occ. machinist.
           1230. GEORGE B., b. 14 Apr. 1836.
           1231. DENISON P., b. 17 Sep. 1838.
           1232. WILLIAM H., b. 20 Dec. 1840,
                 d. 7 Mar. 1841.
           1233. DANIEL M., b. 30 Mar. 1842,
                 md. 28 May 1862 ADELINE D.
                 WHITTING.

ROWELL FAMILY - NEW ENGLAND
7th Generation

1234. ADELAIDE E., b. 29 May 1845,
    md. 3 Mar. 1864 RONALD A.
    KENNEDY.
1235. JAMES H.,
1236. CARDINE, md. 1866 JUDEDIAH
    CASWELL.

620. ABRAHAM ROWELL [RICE 261] He was born 1761
at Nottingham, N.H. He married BETSEY _____.
Res. at Nottingham.

Children: 1237. NEHEMIAH, b. 1789, d. 29 Mar.
           1872, md. 23 Nov. 1815
           ELIZABETH BROWN.
       1238. ABRAHAM, b. 1791, Vet. War of
           1812.

627. RICE RICHARDSON ROWELL [RICE 261] He was
born 1782 at Nottingham, N.H. and died 1840. He
married SARAH SPINNEY, before 1810 at Harrison,
Me. Occ. storekeeper and surveyor of roads.

Children: 1240. WILLIAM C., b. 1812, d. 1874,
           m.1, 1832 MARY NASH, m.2,
           1841 SARAH PLUMMER.

637. RICE ROWELL [WILLIAM 269] He was born 27
Apr. 1789 at Thomaston, Me. and died 1863. He
married first 8 Feb. 1816 SALLY DUNNING, d/o
ROBERT & ELIZABETH (BUCKLIN) DUNNING. She born
14 Oct. 1796 and died 14 July 1839. He married
second 30 Dec. 1839 Mrs. EUNICE (DAVIS) ALLEN.
She born c1785. He married third 1856 SALLY
(HOLMES) ALLY. Occ. ship caulker. In 1850
census. All children by 1st wife.

Children: 1255. ELIZA D. (ELIZABETH?), b. 23
           Mar. 1816, d. July 1899, md.
           18 Jan. 1842 DAVID A.
           CROCKET.
       1256. WILLIAM, b. 22 Mar. 1819, d.
           28 Jan. 1902, md. 20 Mar.
           1842 MARY ELLEN BARTLETT.

1257. ROBERT D., b. 21 Mar. 1821,
      d. 6 Apr. 1831.
1258. RUTH ANN, b. 29 Dec. 1824, d.
      2 Jan. 1872, md. 25 Dec.
      1845 ROBERT H. HEARD. 6 ch.
1259. MARGARET, b. 26 Oct. 1827, d.
      2 Apr. 1841. Killed by
      lightning.
1260. WARREN RAYBURN, b. 24 Oct.
      1829, d. 24 Oct. 1894, md.
      8 Apr. 1852 HANNAH ANN
      FALES.
1261. LUTHER HAYDON, b. 19 Nov.
      1834, d. 18 May 1917, md.
      27 Mar. 1856 SARAH WHITTIER
      MATTHEWS.
1262. HANNAH HAYDON, b. 19 Nov.
      1836, d. 19 Nov. 1916, md. 27
      July 1864 ISREAL J. MILLAY.
1263. MARY D,, b. 14 July 1839, d.
      17 Dec. 1925, md. 26 Jan.
      1870 GEORGE L. PUTNAM.

642. ENOCH ROWELL [ENOCH 273] He was born 14
March 1779 and died 9 Sep. 1839 at Albany, Vt.
He married 1 Mar. 1809 BETSY HODGES, d/o NATHAN
& BETTY (BOSWORTH) HODGES. She died 4 Sep. 1865.
Came 1813 to Albany, Vt. Occ. farmer. Selectman
1816-1820. Did he have a 1st wife?

Children: 1264. ZUAR, b. 2 Dec. 1804.
          1265. SILOAM, b. 10 Apr. 1806.
          1266. ZELDA, b. 27 June 1808.
          1267. MARY, b. 27 Apr. 1810.
          1268. JUDITH, b. 2 Apr. 1813, md. 7
                Nov. 1861 SILAS HOVEY.
          1269. BETSEY, b. 1 Apr. 1816.
          1270. MIRIAM MIRANDA, b. 12 May 1820
          1271. ENOCH, b. 18 Oct. 1835, d. 28
                June 1900, md. VIOLA ROWELL
                [#1267]

646. DANIEL ROWELL [ENOCH 273] He was born c1786
and died 26 Oct. 1848 [62-3] He married 17 July
1811 MERCY JOHNSON, d/o JOSHUA JOHNSON at
Iresbury, Vt. She born c1791 and died 16 Sep.
1863 at Albany, Vt. Selectman at Albany 1824 &
1836. Res. Iresbury, Vt.

Children: 1272. ZELIMA, b. 17 Apr. 1813.
     1273. MILLISEN M., b. 22 Apr. 1815.
     1274. GUY ELBRIDGE, b. 21 May 1818,
       md. 28 Jan. 1846 BETSY C.
       PAGE.
     1275. ENOCH, b. 18 July 1821, d. 7
       July 1886, m.1, CAROLINE
       LEAVITT, m.2, 20 Oct. 1869
       ROXANNE F. NORCROSS.
     1276. DANIEL C., b. c1829, d. 8 Oct.
       1834 [4-9].
     1277. FANNA/FANNY, md. 29 June 1837
       LEVI MESSER at Bradford, Vt.

647. WILLIAM ROWELL [ENOCH 273] He was born 23
Jan. 1791 at Plainfield, N.H. and died 1 Aug.
1871 [82-6] at Albany, Vt. He married 22
March 1818 SALLY LEAVITT. She born c1796 and
died 4 Sep. 1873 [73-11] at Hatley, Canada.
Selectman at Albany 1822, 1826-8, 1837 and 1846-
7. Had 5 children.

Children: 1278. MARY, b. 6 Oct. 1820, d. 17
       Feb. 1825.
     1279. JANE, b. c1831.
     1280. VIOLA, b. 23 Sep. 1837, d. 16
       June 1914, md. ENOCH C.
       ROWELL [#1264].

649. SAMUEL ROWELL [ENOCH 273] He was born 10
July 1793 and died 7 July 1850. He married 2
Mar. 1825 MARY MOORE. She born c1806. Occ.
farmer. 1850 census at Plainfield, N.H.

Children: 1281. HENRY J., b. 1826.
     1282. HIRAM J., b. 1831.

1283. **EMELINE P.**, b. 1832.
1284. **SARAH**, b. 1834.
1285. **ENOCH**, b. 1835.
1286. **JULIA E.**, b. 1838, d. 9 Sep.
1844 [5 yrs]
1287. **MINERVA J.**, b. 1840.

651. **ELIPHELET ROWELL** [ENOCH 273] He was born 28 Feb. 1796 and died 11 May 1875 [75 yr]. He married **SALLY TRUE**. She born 1791 and died 17 Feb. 1852 [60 yr]. 1850 census at Albany, Vt. Both buried at Albany, Vt.

Children: 1288. **SEN.** (m), b. 1819.
1289. **LUCINDA**, b. 1820, m.1, 21 Jan. 1851 **ERASTUS FAIRMAN?**
1290. **LEVI**, md. 29 Feb. 1868 **MARY S. SPAULDING.**
1291. **K. WILLIAM**, b. 1830, d. 14 Mar. 1870, md. 29 Nov. 1855 **LOIS P. ROWELL.**
1292. **TYLER M.**, b. 17 July 1832, d. 19 Feb. 1902, md. 1 June 1855 **ISABELLA ANDERSON.**

652. **CONVERSE ROWELL** [ENOCH 273] He was born 20 May 1798 and died 11 Nov. 1889. He married 25 Mar. 1825 **ORPHAR CHAMBERLIN**, d/o **AARON CHAMBERLIN**. She born c1803 in Vermont. Selectman 1835-6. Signed petition 1823 and 1826 at Albany, Vt. 1850 census at Albany, Vt.

Children: 1293. **CONVERSE WILLARD/ WILLARD CONVERSE**, b. 10 Jan. 1830, md. 6 Jan. 1883 **LAUELLA PRIEST.**
1294. **SARAH M..** b. c1837.

658. **ABIJAH ROWELL** [ELIPHELET 276] He was born 10 Oct. 1795 at Livermore Falls, Maine and died 6 April 1885. He married 30 Oct. 1816 **SOPHIA (WARREN) LEATHE**, d/o **MOSES WARREN**. She born 24 Mar. 1792 at Watertown, Mass. and died 29 May

ROWELL FAMILY - NEW EGLAND
7th Generation

1888, age 97 years at Livermore. Occ. farmer.
1850 census at East Livermore, Me. 1st settler
there.

Children: 1295. ABIGAIL B.. b. c1819.
           1296. Major ELIPHELET, b. 28 May
                 1822, md. 1844 ELLEN FRANCES
                 SMITH.
           1297. JOHN A., b. c1829. Bricklayer
                 in 1850 census.
           1298. EDWIN W., b. c1835, md. ? 26
                 July 1864 ARAXZENE I.
                 BRACKET.

663. SAMUEL ROWELL [SAMUEL 288] He was born 8
Oct. 1778 at Weare, N.H. and died 28 Dec. 1871
at Lancaster, N.H. He married 29 Oct. 1805 at
Dorchester MARY ATWOOD, of Milton, Mass. She
died 6 May 1879. Settled in Chester, N.H. Occ.
farmer and tax collector. Moved to Concord, Vt.
in 1817. 1850 census with son William at
Amesbury, Vt.

Children: 1299. RODNEY, d. 22 May 1826 [21 yr]
           1300. SAMUEL, b. 1808, d. 13 Oct.
                 1883, md. 1834 CAROLINE
                 PAGE.
           1301. WILLIAM, b. 1811, d. 25 Aug.
                 1891, md. 1841 ABIGAIL
                 CHAFFEE.
           1302. JAMES COLWELL, b. 1813, md.
                 1842 ANN POOR.
           1303. JOHN PAGE, b. 1816, d. 1850
                 RUTH M. BARNES.
           1304. GEORGE WASHINGTON, b. 1819,
                 d. 1898, md. 1844 MARCIA A.
                 CHADBURN.
           1305. BETSY, md. _____THOMPSON.
           1306. FREDERICK, b. 11 June 1820, d.
                 9 Dec. 1899, md. 29 Jan.
                 1846 ROSALINE A. BANFILL.
           1307. MARY A., md. _____ MOORE.
           1308. EDWIN, d. infancy.
           1309. SARAH, d. infancy.

1310. HARRIET, d.y.

664. **BETSEY ROWELL [SAMUEL 288]** She was born 4 Aug. 1780 and died 2 Jan. 1869 at Passumpsic. She married Jan. 1797 **SOMERS GOODELL** of Pomfort, Vt. He born 25 May 1773. Occ. farmer. He died at Lynne 18 Oct. 1845. She married second 1850 Rev. **LEWIS FISHER**. Baptist clergy.

Children: i. **SARAH D.**,
          ii. **ALANSON**, b. 20 Sep. 1802.
        iii. **RUFUS**,
       iv. **SAMUEL R.**,
        v. **ELVIRA**,
      vi. **CAROLINE**,
     vii. **SOMERS**,
    viii. **ADONIRAM J.**,
      ix. **SUSAN C.**,

665. **DUSTIN ROWELL [SAMUEL 288]** He was born 1782 at Weare, N.H. and died 1 July 1866. He married 1808 **JANE GORDON**, d/o **ROBERT & ANN (BUNTING) GORDON**. She born 20 Feb. 1779 at Chester, N.H. and died 12 Dec. 1835 at Lyndon, Vt. Occ. farmer. In 1850 census he was single living at Wolfborough, N.H.

Children: 1311. **POLLY**, b. 25 Aug. 1809, d. 5 Oct. 1809.
             1312. **MARY**,
             1313. **NANCY**, md. _____ **ADAMS**.
             1314. **ELSIE L.**, md. _____ **PARKER**.
             1315. **CLARISSA W.**, md. _____ **BLAISDELL**.
             1316. **ELIZABETH**,
             1317. **CHARLES HARVEY**, b. 1820, d. 1872, md. 1847 **ANN HEMINGWAY**.
             1318. **ELVIRA W.**, md. _____ **FELLOWS**.

666. **LYDIA ROWELL [SAMUEL 288]** She was born 7 Mar. 1785 at Weare, N.H. She married **JONATHAN JENKINS**, s/o **LEMUEL JENKINS**. She died 29 oct. 1874 at Kirby, Vt.

Children: i. FREDRICK,
          ii. LOREN,
         iii. SAMUEL,
          iv. DUSTIN L.,
           v. ELIZABETH,
          vi. LOUISE M.,
         vii. JONATHAN, b. 21 Apr. 1820, twin.
        viii. LYDIA C., b. 21 Apr. 1820, twin.
          ix. AUSTIN,
           x. JOEL,
          xi. MARY L.,
         xii. JOHN L.,
        xiii. DANIEL R.,

667. SARAH ROWELL [SAMUEL 288] She was born 1787 at Weare, N.H. She died at Boston 10 June 1855. She married 1820 at Newburyport, Mass. AARON SARGENT. He born 1786 and died 22 Jan. 1822 ?

Children: i. ELIZABETH W.,
          ii. SARAH R.,
         iii. STEPHEN P.,
          iv. SAMUEL R.,
           v. AARON C.,

668. MARY ROWELL [SAMUEL 288] She was born 5 Dec. 1791. She married 27 Dec. 1814 Rev. JOHN LORD, Methodist Clergyman. He was son of JAMES & HANNAH (NICHOLS) LORD. He born 19 June 1791 at Fryeburg, Me. and died 2 Aug. 1858 at Portland, Me. She died 24 Sep. 1850.

Children: i. DIANTHA AMELINE, b. 8 Nov. 1821,
               d. 15 Nov. 1821.
          ii. JOHN R.,
         iii. MARY M.

669. JAMES COLWELL ROWELL [SAMUEL 288] He was born 27 Nov. 1793 at Weare, N.H. and died 7 June 1857. He married 24 Apr. 1817 at Chester, N.H. OLIVE A. WIGGIN, d/o JOSEPH & BETSY (FRENCH) WIGGIN. She born 26 Dec. 1793 and died 28 Mar. 1856. He married second at Manchester, N.H. Mrs. MARY SMITH. Served in War of 1812. Received a

land grant for his service. Pension No. W.C.
102151. Methodist. Res. 1826 Amoskeag Valley,
1833 moved to Auburn and 1847 to Londonderry.

Children: 1319. GEORGE W., b. c1817.
           1320. SARAH E., b. c1818, md. _____
                 EVANS.
           1321. CHARLES WESLEY, b. 1820, d. 16
                 Apr. 1894, md. 20 June 1847
                 SARAH B. HAMMOND.
           1322. WILLIAM HENRY, b. 25 Feb.
                 1822, d. 18 July 1824.
           1323. JOHN PAGE, b. 25 Feb. 1822, d.
                 28 Dec. 1832.
           1324. OLIVE, b. 6 Apr. 1824, d. 3
                 Feb. 1832.
           1325. MARY L.,
           1326. OLIVE ANN, b. 12 Dec. 1833.

670. JOHN PAGE ROWELL [SAMUEL 288] He was born
15 Oct. 1796 at Chester, N.H. and died 20 Mar.
1875. He served in 17th N.H. Reg't in War of
1812. Enlisted age 18 for defense of Portsmouth
Capt. of militia later at Chester. He married 10
May 1820 BETSY EMERSON, d/o JAMES & NANCY
EMERSON of Chester. She born 3 Oct. 1796. Moved
1828 to Amoskeag. Employed at mill there. Served
in legislature in 1843. Methodist class leader.
Democrat. Occ. farmer. 1850 census at
Manchester.

Children: 1327. JOHN LORD, b. 20 Apr. 1821, d.
                 18 July 1853, md. 7 Oct.
                 1847 BETSY C. SARGENT.
                 Business man, Manchester.
           1328. EPHRAIM KELLEY, b. 21 Nov.
                 1822, d. 5 Oct. 1896, md.
                 25 Apr. 1847 MARY AMANDA
                 DAVIS. (AMANDA SMITH?)
           1329. ELIZABETH E., b. 20 Mar. 1825,
                 d. 15 yrs.
           1330. STEPHEN SARGENT, b. 14 Nov.
                 1827, d 18 Nov. 1827

1331. **WILLIAM HENRY**, b. 31 Dec.
1828, d. 11 Mar. 1829.
1332. **FRANK D.**, b. 1832, d. 12 Apr.
1862 [20 yr] at Manchester.
1333. **JAMES R.**, b. 25 Aug. 1833, d.
2 Sep. 1837.

680. **JOHN ROWELL** [ELIPHELET 294] He was born 15
July 1778 at Bow, N.H. He married **SARAH** _____.
Res. Bow, N.H.

Children: 1334. **EDITH**, b. 30 July 1795, md. 25
Dec. 1816/7 **AARON COLBY**.
1335. **JOHN PARKER**, b. 19 July 1797.

682. **ELIPHELET ROWELL** [ELIPHELET 294]   He was
born 3 Feb. 1782. Possibly the Eliphelet Rowell
in the 1850 census at Lubec, Washington County,
Maine. Had wife **MERCY** _____. She born c1783 in
Maine.

Children: 1336. **ALMOND**, b. c1824.

683. **JOSEPH ROWELL** [ELIPHELET 294]   He was born
13 Oct. 1784. He married **OLIVE** _____. She born
1784. Named in 1810 Census at Bow, N.H.   Occ.
farmer. 1850 census at Weld, Me.

Children: 1337. **SILOAM/SYLVANUS?**, b. 4 Nov.
1804, m.1, 20 Oct. 1833
RHODA A. POWERS, m.2, 28
Oct. 1855 **ARVILLE STORER**
at Weld. Occ. Cabinet Maker
1338. **CHARLES**, b. 21 June 1807.
1339. **BETSY BEARD**, b. 21 Apr. 1809,
md. 12 Apr. 1839 **HIRAM
WHEELER**.
1340. **JOSEPH Jr**, b. 30 Oct. 1811.
1341. **FANNY MORGAN**, b. 25 Dec. 1813
at Croydon.
1342. **JAMES**, b. 9 July 1817.

ROWELL FAMILY - NEW ENGLAND
7th Generation

1343. **ISAAC CLOUGH**, b. 24 Nov. 1820
at Bow.
1344. **AUGUSTA**, (f) b. 1822.
1345. **NATHAN PALMER**, b. 24 Sep.
1824, d. 1882, md. **MARY S.
KITTRIDGE.**

686. **JAMES ROWELL** [ELIPHELET 294] He was born 28
April 1795. He married 12 April 1821 **REBECCA P.
CLARK** at Hampstead. She born c1802. Occ. farmer.
1850 census at Derry, N.H.

Children: 1346. **JOHN C.**, b. 1828.
1347. **ADALINE J.**, b. 1837.
1348. **ELISA N.**, b. 1844.

687. **AMOS ROWELL** [ELIPHELET 294] He was born 9
Jan. 1797/8, or 6 Feb. 1804. He died 5 Mar. 1867
at Littleton, N.H. He possibly married 1st 17
Sep. 1818 **BETSY JOHNSON** at Bow, N.H. He married
7 Apr. 1822 at Bath **BETSY (ELIZABETH) CHASE**, d/o
ROBERT CHASE. She born 10 Oct. 1791 at Bath and
died 25 Mar. 1865 at Littleton. Methodist. Occ.
cabinet maker. Res. Littleton by 1826. 1850
census.

Children: 1350. **JANE C.**, b. 17 July 1823, md.
1 Apr. 1845 **JOHN COLBY
QUIMBY.**
1351. **FANNY ROSS**, b. 4 May 1827,
m.1, **CHARLES C. BARRETT.**
1352. **MARY ANN**, b. 4 Oct. 1830, m.1
ENOCH STRATTON.

690. **STRATTON ROWELL** [PETER 295] He was born
1791 and died 1878. He married **OLIVE BURTCH**, d/o
EDEE & CATHERINE (BECKER) BURTCH. She born 1791
and died 1874.

Children: 1353. **WILLIAM**, b. 1820, d. 1906, md.
ELEANOR JANE BROWN.

- 117 -

1354. RACHEL, b. 1822, d. 1888, md. 30 Nov. 1842 JOHN STRONG, 6 children.

1355. CATHERINE, md. GEORGE BLAKE, 13 children.

1356. LAVISA, md. WILLIAM V or C. BROWN, 2 children.

1357. ELIZABETH, md. JOSEPH MEADOWS Jr., 3 children.

1358. PERMALIA, b. 1830, d. 1875, m.1, CHAMLIN HALLOCK 3 ch., m.2, Mr. ALLEN, 3 ch.

1359. DANIEL, m.1, MARY THOMPSON, m.2, LAVINA LAZENBY.

1360. STRATTON, md. 11 Mar. 1860 ELIZA HUNT at Ossining, NY.

1361. ADAM, b. 1840, md. SARAH ANN MEADOWS.

1362. DURINDA, b. 1843, d. 1931, md. EMANUEL BROWN, 13 children.

691. PERLEY MARSH ROWELL [PETER 295] He was born 15 Sep. 1793. He married 24 Sep. 1818 PAMELIA JOHNSON in Chenango, N.Y. Moved to Mich. summer 1837.

Children: 1365. AMASSY, b. 1820, d. 1849, md. MARTHA McCOY.

1366. PERLEY MARSH, b. 1822, md. EMILY L. FARGO.

1367. CHARLES C., b. 1824.

1368. GEORGE, b. 1826, md. 10 Oct. 1854 JULIETTE GALE.

1369. SARAH J., b. 1828, md. 20 Jan. 1847 JOHN REED.

1370. AMANDA,

702. JONATHAN ROWELL [JOB 307] He was born 1 Aug. 1763 at Hampstead, N.H. He married 13 Sep. 1784 OLIVE TUXBURY. She died 27 Apr. 1838. Pvt. Capt. Gilman's Reg't, Col. Reid, N.H. Militia. No battles. Received pension. Res. Windsor Co., Vt. after war.

Children   1371. **MIRIAM**, b. 1789, d. 22 Jan.
1869, md. **FULLER SMITH**.

703. **MOSES ROWELL** [JOB 307] He was born 11 June
1765. He married first c1792 **ABIGAIL WARNER**. She
born 27 Sep. 1770. He married second 10 Dec.
1799 **BETSY MANN** at Windsor, Vt. He died 31 Aug.
1830. She was born 12 Sep. 1773 and died June
1852. Buried at Cambridge, Me. Family named in
1800 U.S. Census at Andover, Vt. [2002/3001].

Children: 1372. **ASABEL/ASHEL** (m), b. 10 Apr.
1793.
1373. **MOSES**, b. 3 Dec. 1794.
1374. **MIRIAM**, b. 25 Nov. 1796.
1375. **HANNAH**, b. 4 June 1799, twin.
1376. **RACHEL**, b. 4 June 1799, twin.
1377. **ABIGAIL**, b. 25 May 1801.

705. **ELIJAH ROWELL** [JOB 307] He was born 9 April
1769 at Hampstead, N.H. and died 26 July 1847 at
Bradford, Vt. [77 yr] He married **SARAH WHITTIER**
of Weare, N.H. She died 10 March 1847 [70 yr].
Removed to Bradford, Vt.

Children: 1378. **ELIJAH**, b. 1795, d. 14 Aug.
1828 [33 yr]
1379. **RALPH**,
1380. **RANSON**, b. c1833, md. 28 Dec.
1850 **HARRIET FRENCH**.
1381. **PHEBE**, md. 19 Oct. 1834 **SAMUEL
ROOMER**.
1382. **ESTHER**,
1383. **FANNY**, md. 19 Dec. 1819 **JAMES
MANN**.
1384. **RUFUS**, b. c1803, d. 14 Dec.
1881, md. 13 Feb. 1834 **BETSY
PRESCOTT**.

706. **AARON ROWELL** [JOB 307] He was born 19 Nov.
1771 at Hampstead, N.H. and died 1 Mar. 1846 at
Maidstone, Vt. He married 18 Nov. 1802 **EUNICE
BLOOD**. Occ. farmer. Res. Weare, N.H.

Children: 1385. **AARON** Jr., b. 18 Feb./July
1803.
1386. **SARAH**, b. 3 Oct. 1805

709. **ROBERT EMERSON ROWELL** [JOB 307] He was
born 3 Aug. 1779 and died 17 June 1857, ae 78.
He married 25 Mar, 1800 **HANNAH C. WHITTIER**, d/o
ASA WHITTIER. She died 27 Feb. 1858 [86-6]. 1850
census at Vershire, Vt.

Children: 1396. **JOHN**, md. 31 Dec. 1837 **ELIZA
BUCK**.
1397. **JESSE**, b. 20 May 1805.

715. **ABEL ROWELL** [NATHANIEL 309] He was born 22
Dec. 1765 at South Hampton, N.H. He married 19
July 1789 **SUSANNA KIMBALL**. [MERRILL?] Res. at
Warner and Hopkinton, N.H. Petition of REBECCA
ROWELL that her brother BENJAMIN supported by
Town is in a state of mental disarrangement and
pray appt. of guardian, 6 Nov. 1828 [v.6, p.188]
Inv. of BENJAMIN $275.00 taken 23 Dec. 1828.

Children: 1398. **REBECCA**, b. 21 Dec. 1789 or
1790.
1399. **BENJAMIN**, b. 8 Apr. 1792, d.
26 Aug. 1864, d.s.p, insane.
1400. **STEPHEN**, b. 8 Mar. 1794. Occ.
carpenter 1850 single.
1401. **JUDITH**, b. 5 Aug. 1796.

719. **MOSES ROWELL** [NATHANIEL 309] He was born
25 Jan. 1774, bp 13 Mar. 1774 at South Hampton,
N.H. and died before 1850. He married 13 Nov.
1800 **MARY PETTINGILL**. She born c1773 in Mass.
1850 census at Hopkinston, N.H.

Children: 1402. **MANLEY A.**,
1403. **LYDIA C.**, b. c1810.

723. **NATHANIEL ROWELL** [NATHANIEL 309] He was born 4 July 1781 at Hopkinton, N.H. and died 17 Mar. 1827. He married 23 June 1809 **SARAH HOPKINS.**

726. **ELIJAH ROWELL** [NATHANIEL 309] He was born 22 July 1782 at Hopkinton, N.H. He married 16 June 1814 **SALLY EASTMAN.**

736. **MOSES ROWELL** [JOHN 311] He was born 4 Oct. 1788 and died June 1870. He married 6 July 1814 **LYDIA GREELEY**, d/o **BENJAMIN GREELEY.** She die 22 June 1877 [85-2-6]. Occ. farmer. 1850 Census. Res. Andover, N.H.

Children: 1405. **BENJAMIN GREELEY**, b. 2 May 1815, md. **ABIGAIL A. MASON.**
1406. **JOHN**, b. 22 Sep. 1817.
1407. **MOSES WARREN**, b. 15 May 1821, md. 17 June 1847 **ELIZA H. DURKEE.**
1408. **ELIZA JANE**, b. 2 May 1824, md. 1 Dec. 1842 **W.J. FELLOWS.**

737. **JOHN ROWELL** [JOHN 311] He was born 30 May 1793. He married 22 May 1817 **SALLY FIFIELD.** She born 1798. Occ. cabinet maker. U.S. Census 1850-1860. Res. Franklin, N.H.

Children: 1410. **JOHN HIRAM**, b. 1818, md. June 1843 **MARTHA A. BATCHELDER.**
1411. **HORACE N.**, b. c1824.
1412. **WILLIAM LYMAN**, b. 1828, md. 1854/5 **CAROLINE ARAVESTA BROWN.**
1413. **THOMAS M.**, b. c1830.

741. JOHN ROWELL [JOHN 315] He was born 11 July
1764, bp 1774 and died 27 Jan. 1844. He married
first 5 Jan. 1792 MEHITABLE THYNG of Brentwood,
N.H. She born 1769 and died 1811. He married
second 26 Feb. 1812 ANNA S. SHUTE. She born 1782
and died 25 Mar. 1855. His will dated 26 June
1841, proved 20 Mar. 1844. Names wife and all
children. Son ADDISON named executor. Daughters
ANNA HICKEY and MEHITABEL CONCORD named as
deceased. [v.69, p.147] Res. Brentwood, N.H.
Widow in 1850 census.

Children: 1415. REBECCA G., b. 1792, md. 31
                  Dec. 1818 HENRY SWASEY.
            1416. JOHN Jr., b. 1794, d. 1852,
                  md. 13 Sep. 1820 or 4 Mar.
                  1822 DEBORAH SMITH.
            1417. JAMES, b. 1796, d. before
                  1841, md. 11 May 1823
                  LOIS VARNEY.
            1418. ANN L., b. 1798, md. 5 Sep.
                  1822 P.H. HICKEY.
            1419. PETER T., b. 1801.
            1420. MEHITABLE F., b. 1803, md. 18
                  Dec. 1836 JAMES COLCARD.
            1421. ISAAC, b. 1805.
            1422. JACOB H., b. 4 Dec. 1807, md.
                  23 Mar. 1832 EVERLINE H.
                  ROBINSON, m.2, 26 Nov. 1842
                  EMERETT PRESCOTT.
            1423. CHARLES LEWIS, b. 1810, md
                  1835 MARY A. SANDERS/SANBORN
            1424. ADDISON, b. 1813, d. 27 Dec.
                  1871, md. 11 Jan. 1835
                  ELIZA B. SHUTE.

746. ABRAHAM ROWELL [JOHN 315] He was born 1776
and died 13 Oct. 1863. He married 23 June 1818
LOVEY SIMPSON. She born c1797. In 1850 Census at
Newport, Me.

Children: 1425. ANN M., b. c1837.

ROWELL FAMILY - NEW ENGLAND
7th Generation

747. ENOCH PAGE ROWELL [JOHN 315] He was born 3
Oct. 1780 at Epping, N.H. and died Nov. 1848. He
married 13 Nov. 1801 SARAH (SALLY) MASON at
Chichester, N.H.   She born c1784. Res. at
Loudon, N.H.

Children: 1426. JOHN WINSLOW, b. 3 Mar. 1813,
              d. 1864, md. MARTHA LORD
              STEVENS or 17 May 1835 SARAH
              STEVENS at N. Hampton, N.H.
          1427. JOSEPH MASON, b. 2 Aug. 1817,
              md. 30 Jan. 1840 MARY ANN
              JOHNSON.

748. BENJAMIN ROWELL [JOHN 315] He was born
c1782 and died 29 Nov. 1848. He married 12 Feb.
1805 MIRIAM CLIFFORD. In 1850 Census with son
Isaac at Newport, Me.

Children: 1428. ISAAC, b. 1814, Occ. laborer.

750. DAVID ROWELL [DAVID 320] He was born 1 Oct.
1766 Goffstown, N.H. and died 25 April 1836 at
Madison, Me. He married first 8 Mar. 1792
JANETTE DICKEY at Francestown, N.H. who died
after only one year of marriage. He married
second 8 Mar. 1794 SARAH SPAULDING, d/o WILLIAM
& MARY (GREEN) SPAULDING at Francestown, N.H.
She born 13 Nov. 1768 at Pepperall, Mass. and
died 2 June 1828. Both buried at Skowhegan, Me.
All children by 2nd wife.

Children: 1429. DAVID SPAULDING, b. 9 Apr.
              1795, d. 8 July 1872, md. 16
              Apr. 1826 RACHEL JEWETT.
          1430. JONATHAN, b. 29 Aug. 1796,
              unmd.
          1431. WILLIAM, b. 25 June 1798, d.
              14 Dec. 1867, md. 18 Oct.
              1832 LUCINDA FLETCHER.

1432. ISAAC, b. 23 Mar. 1800, d. 4
Feb. 1874, md. RACHEL
MONTGOMERY.
1433. JANE, b. 15 Mar. 1802, md. 30
Mar. 1826 JOHN WHITTEN. Had:
JOHN 1817-1894.
1434. MYRA, b. 19 Apr. 1804, d. 9
Jan. 1886, md. 18 Apr. 1830
WILLIAM WHITTEN. 4 ch.
1435. SALLY, b. 11 Nov. 1805, d. 24
June 1893, md. SIMON
MERRILL.
1436. WASHINGTON, b. 16 Mar. 1808,
d. 8 Feb. 1864, md. MARY
SMITH.
1437. BETSY, b. 1 Sep. 1811, d. 20
Sep. 1828.
1438. HIRAM, b. 8 Nov. 1813, d. 26
Mar. 1850.

753. **JOB ROWELL [DAVID 320]** He was born 24 Feb.
1771 at Goffstown, N.H. and died 12 April 1843
at Dunbarton, N.H. He married first 26 Dec. 1799
at Derryfield **ABIGAIL POLLARD.** He married second
11 Nov. 1830 at Goffstown **BETSEY B.**, widow of
ROBERT DINSMORE. Occ. farmer, pilot, boatman,
N.H. Militia. Res. 1797 in Manchester. In 1837
he bought farm at Dunbarton, N.H. His will
dated 25 May 1839, proved 4 Apr. 1843. Names
wife and children. [v.16, p.138] Res.
Derryfield, N.H.

Children: 1439. ELIZABETH, b. 20 Mar. 1803.
1440. DANIEL, bp 1 May 1804, d.
1840, 1829 HANNAH STEVENS.
1441. JOSEPH MELCHOIR, b. 11 Apr.
1807, d. 17 Dec. 1894.
1442. SARAH, b. 20 Mar. 1805, md.
ISAAC A. DINSMORE.
1443. ABIGAIL, b. 8 May 1811, d. 2
Feb. 1896 at Manchester.
1444. HANNAH, b. 2 May 1813.
1445. MARY, b. 16 Aug. 1817.

ROWELL FAMILY - NEW ENGLAND
7th Generation

1446. JOHN P., b. 4 Apr. 1809, d. 24
        July 1873, unmd.
1447. WALTER P., b. 16 Aug. 1815.
1448. LEONARD, b. 7 June 1820, d. 17
        Nov. 1883, md. 12 May 1844
        ANN STUART RAY.
by 2nd wife:
1449. LEWIS, b. 25 Feb. 1833.

754. ISAAC ROWELL [DAVID 320] He was born 17 May
1770 in N.H. and died 14 Dec. 1827 at Hartland,
Me. He married HANNAH RICHARDSON at Goffstown,
N.H. She born 1777 and died 1858.

Children: 1450. JOHN, b. 23 Nov. 1799, d. 10
                  Dec. 1870, m.1, MARY HUFF,
                  m.2, Mrs. BACON w/o JOSIAH
                  BACON.
           1451. ISAAC, b. 25 Dec. 1803, d. 19
                  Mar. 1836, unmd.
           1452. SARAH, b. 4 Mar. 1805, d.
                  c1810.
           1453. MERIBAH, b. 9 Sep. 1807, d. 18
                  Oct. 1837, md. Capt. WILLIAM
                  T. WILLEY.
           1454. ELMIRA, b. 2 Aug. 1808, d. 18
                  Oct. 1847, md. 5 July 1833
                  ISREAL S. BIGELOW. 4 ch.
           1455. CHARLES, b. 27 Sep. 1811, d.
                  21 June 1886, md. JANE MOON.
           1456. ABRAM M., b. 16 Aug. 1813, d.
                  28 Oct. 1837, unmd.
           1457. HANNAH, b. 10 Dec. 1815, d. 11
                  Oct. 1837, unmd.
           1458. DAVID, b. 27 Mar. 1819, d. 1
                  Feb. 1894, m.1, 27 Dec. 1843
                  MARTHA JANE LITTLEFORD, m.2,
                  16 Sep. 1865 MARY F. AYER.

755. ZEBEDEE ROWELL [DAVID 320] He was born 1775
and died 8 Feb. 1833. He married 25 May 1801
JUDITH HAMBLET In 1802 moved to Dracut, Mass.

ROWELL FAMILY - NEW ENGLAND
7th Generation

Later to Solon, Maine. Served in Rev. War with
Gen. Stark.

Children: 1459. FREDERICK, b. 5 Oct. 1801, d.
                 12 Feb. 1853, md. 26 Mar.
                 1819 SOPHIA WOODS.
           1460. GEORGE B., b. 19 Feb. 1800, d.
                 20 May 1873, md. 1 Apr. 1833
                 SARAH PARKMAN, m.2, 20 Dec.
                 186_ CHARLOTTE WENTWORTH.
           1461. DAVID, b. 1806, d. 19 Dec.
                 1866, md. 1830 MARY
                 BUTTERFIELD.
           1462. ZEBEDEE Jr., b. 4 July 1808,
                 d. 19 Mar. 1879, md. 1 Feb.
                 1840 BETHEL SARAH AYER.
           1463. BENJAMIN FRANKLIN, b. 1 May
                 1815, d. 4 Jan. 1888, md.
                 CLIMERA WHITTIER. No ch.
           1464. DANIEL C., b. 15 Feb. 1818, d.
                 29 Mar. 1894, unmd.
           1465. CHARLES, b. 3 Dec. 1811, d. 20
                 Sep. 1866, md. 16 Mar. 1839
                 PHEBE HAWTHORNE.
           1466. ELBRIDGE, b. 16 May 1813, d.
                 20 Feb. 1845, md. SOPHIA
                 WESTON.
           1467. ELIZABETH PERHAM, b. 30 Sep.
                 1820, d. 27 July 1887, md.
                 BARNET EATON. 3 ch.

760. JOHN ROWELL [JONATHAN 322] He was born 15
Feb. 1778 at Litchfield, N.H. and died 14 Aug.
1847 at Strafford, Vt. He married 20 Nov. 1806
HANNAH ROBERTS at Strafford, Vt. She born 11 May
1784 and died 27 Apr. 1835 at Strafford.

Children: 1468. AMANDA, b. 21 Sep. 1807, m.1,
                 SAMUEL MORDEN, m.2, BERT
                 ELEAZER.
           1469. JOHN MIRANDA, b. 27 Jan. 1809,
                 md. 2 Mar. 1835 MEHITABLE
                 STEVENS FELLOWS.

1470. BETSY, b. 4 Dec. 1813, md.
_____ GAGE.
1471. ELBRIDGE JERRY, b. May 1815.
1472. HANNAH, b. 6 Aug. 1818, md. 9
July 1844 WEST ROBERTS.
1473. DARIUS TYLER, b. 29 May 1822,
d. 4 Feb. 1870, md. 1846
EMELINE R. ROBERTS.

763. DAVID ROWELL [JONATHAN 322] He was born 1
Feb. 1795 and died 2 Nov. 1869 at Bethel. He
married 5 Dec. 1815 ANNIS CAMP at Tunbridge,
Vt. Possibly the same DAVID ROWELL found at
Waterville, New York who had a wife Polly. She
died 8 May 1848, age 47 years. Occ. farmer.

Children: 1474. HIRAM, b. 1824, d. 10 June
1904, m.1, ELLEN FLYNN, m.2,
EUNICE T. ARNOLD, m.3,
ADELINE LEE HAPGOOD.
1475. NATHANIEL P., b. 4 Jan. 1825,
d. 11 Apr. 1897, md. 7 Sep.
1851, md. LUCINDA DUSTIN.
1476. HORACE, b. 1841, md. MALINDA
DUSTIN.
1477. HAMILTON,
1478. HENRY GEORGE WASHINGTON,

765. THOMAS B. ROWELL [ABRAHAM 323] He was born
25 Nov. 1764 [or 13 Dec. 1765] at South Hampton,
N.H. and died 20 Dec. 1833. He married LYDIA
HOWE. Some sources say her names was HAWES or
HOUSE. She born 10 Apr. 1769 at Sutton, N.H. or
12 Nov. 1769 and died 15 Oct. 1856 at Hatley,
Canada. Res. at Sutton, N.H. Moved to Hatley,
Quebec about 1802.

Children: 1479. ELIZABETH (BETSY), b. 10 Apr.
1789.
1480. LUDDIA/LYDIA, b. 30 July 1790
at Sutton.
1481. POLLY/MOLLY R., b. 24 Jan.
1794.

ROWELL FAMILY - NEW ENGLAND
7th Generation

1482. THOMAS, b. 20 May 1796, d.
      c1875, md. 1817 LYDIA
      LEAVITT.
1483. MARY, b. 20 Oct. 1798.
1484. NATHAN, b. 4 Mar. 1801, md.
      ANNE LEAVITT.
1485. LUCY, b. 15 Aug. 1803, md. 13
      Mar. 1823 JOHN LEAVITT, 11
      children.
1486. KENDRICK, b. 2 Nov. 1806, m.1,
      SARAH JONES, m.2, PLUMA
      ROWELL
1487. PHEBE, b. 4 Mar. 1809, md.
      c1829 LUKE WADLEIGH.

766. JONATHAN ROWELL [ABRAHAM 323] He was born
25 Oct. 1766 at South Hampton, N.H. and died
1827. He married 1789 ACHSAL FLOOD of Warner,
N.H. Res. at Sutton. His will dated 23 Apr.
1827, proved 31 July 1827. Son SILAS executor.
Wife and all children named. Inv. 12 Sep. 1827,
$1857.91. [v.1, p.428] The will of ACHSAL dated
16 June 1840, proved July 1847. Son DANIEL named
executor. [v.17, p.450] Occ. farmer.

Children: 1488. COMFORT, b. Sep. 1789, md.
                 c1817 JAMES PEASLEE.
           1489. DANIEL F., b. 5 Mar. 1791.
           1490. SILAS, b. 19 Apr. 1793, d.
                 1832, m.1, HANNAH POTTER,
                 m.2, BETSY P. OBER.
           1491. RACHEL ANNIS, b. 13 Aug. 1799,
                 d. 18 Sep. 1804.
           1492. CUTLER, b. 4 Nov. 1802, d. 9
                 Oct. 1804.
           1493. IRA, b. 6 Oct. 1807, md. 17
                 May 1832 HANNAH KENDRICK.

773. MOSES ROWELL [ABRAHAM 323] He was born 29
Nov. 1776 and died 25 Mar. 1852. He married
first 26 Nov. 1801 TAMESON EASTMAN at Hopkinton,
N.H., d/o BENJAMIN & ANNA EASTMAN. She born 17
Dec. 1777. He married second JAMEISON EASTMAN.
Res. Hopkinton, N.H. 1850 census living with son
ISAAC.

Children: 1494. TRUEWORTHY, b. 8 Apr. 1802.
1495. ABRAHAM, b. 4 Feb. 1803, d. 23
June 1811, age 7.
1496. JOHN PETTINGILL, b. 19 Apr.
1805, md.? 10 Sep. 1831
SUSAN P. COLMAN in Boston.
1497. BENJAMIN, b. 19 Jan. 1806.
1498. MANLEY A., b. 28 Mar. 1807, d.
20 July 1875.
1499. ELIZABETH, b. 10 June 1808.
1500. ABRAHAM, b. 4 Dec. 1810, d. 1
May 1865 at Memphis, Tenn.
Single in 1850 census.
1501. ISAAC, b. 19 Apr. 1813, d. 15
Apr. 1887, md. 20 Feb. 1840
HARRIET R. ADAMS.
1502. ALBERT GALLATIN, b. 14 Sep.
1815, d.y. age 5 yrs.
1503. ACHSA, b. 30 Jan. 1819, d.
infancy.
1504. ROXANA, b. 28 June 1823,
single 1850 census.

775. SAMUEL ROWELL [ABRAHAM 323] He was born 15
Nov. 1780 at So. Hampton, N.H. and died 3 Jan.
1858, ae 77. He married 16 Oct. 1806. POLLY
(PATTY?) COLBY. She born 10 Aug. 1777 and died
27 Dec. 1866, [68-4-17]. Moved in 1820 to Sutton
from Hopkinton, N.H. All buried at Sutton, N.H.

Children: 1505. NICHOLAS, b. 13 Oct. 1807, d.
26 Aug. 1883, md. 1835
HANNAH M. CHENEY.
1506. SALLY, b. 21 June 1811 or 3
Dec. 1811, md. 17 Nov. 1835
THOMAS CHENEY
1507. HANNAH, b. 12 Aug. 1813, d. 7
Mar. 1889, never married.
1508. ANNA/ANNIE, b. 9 Mar. 1817,
md. 1841 ICHABOD HAZEN.
1509. SAMUEL, b. 20 Feb. 1820, d.
1860 or 1906, md. 1846 NANCY
WHITTIER.

780. **ASA ROWELL [STEPHEN 331]** He was born 5 Sep. 1803 and died 15 Oct. 1869 [66-1-14] at Waterbury, Vt. He married 19 Feb. 1820 **THANKFUL AYERS**. Res. West Fairlee, Vt.

Children: 1510. **GILMAN**, b. 1837, md. 27 June 1858 **ELLEN A. BRINK**.

781. **RENSCLAIR ROWELL [STEPHEN 331]** He was born c1812. He married **RELIEF TITUS?**, d/o **SALLY TITUS**. She born c1810. 1850 census. Res. West Fairlee, Vt.

Children: 1511. **SALLY/SARAH**, b. 1836, md. 25 Nov. 1860 **TITUS C. _____**.
1512. **LORAINE M.**, b. c1837, md. 8 Aug. 1856 **JOSEPH W. BROOKS**.
1513. **GEORGE H.**, b. c1838, md. 11 Dec. 1858 **JANE M. ALDRICH**.
1514. **PATRICIA A.**, b. c1840.

782. **SIMEON ROWELL [STEPHEN 331]** He was born 7 Dec. 1823 and died 8 Jan. 1896. He married first **PATIENCE/PATRICIA _____**. She died 17 April 1883 [75-8]. He married second **JULIA _____**. She died 13 July 1902 [68 yr]. 1850 census at West Fairlee, Vt.

783. **TIMOTHY H. ROWELL [STEPHEN 331]** He was born c1827 and died 21 Jan. 1863 in Civil War. He married 19 Aug. 1847 **AMANDA LATHROP**. She born c1827. 1850 census Thetford, Vt.

Children: 1515. **ELIZA**, b. 20 Sep. 1849, d. 24 Mar. 1850.
1516. **ALICE**, b. 26 Apr. 1860.
1517. **ADDA F.**, b. 1 July 1863.
1518. **URBANE F.**, b. 1865, md. **MINNIE B. WEBB**.

787. **PHILIP REDINGTON ROWELL [HEZEKIAH 337]** He was born 15 Oct. 1814 at Castine, Me. He married

24 Sep. 1836 **CLEMENTINE OSGOOD** in Newburyport.
Res. Deer Is. and Castine, Me.

Children: 1520. **HENRY PLANT**, b. 4 June 1838.
           1521. **MARY STRICKNEY**, b. 13 June
                1840.
           1522. **WILLIAM REDINGTON**, b. 4 Mar.
                1842.
           1523. **LEWIS PHILIP**, b. 3 Feb. 1844.
           1524. **JOHN KIRBY**, b. 19 Mar. 1846,
                md. **CLARA HATCH**.
           1525. **JOSEPH**, b. 7 Sep. 1848.

800. **ADONIRAM JUDSON ROWELL** [JOSEPH 340] He was
born 4 Dec. 1818 at Waterville, Vt. and died 24
Dec. 1864 at Montpelier, Vt. He married 15 June
1841 at Methuen, Mass. **LUCY ANN RICHARDSON**. She
born 1818 at Methuen and died 1895 at North
Troy. Capt. Civil War. Received fatal illness.
Famous orator and politician. Underground
railroad agent.

Children: 1530. **WILLIAM R.**, b. 18 Mar. 1844,
                d. Oct. 1897, md. **IMOGENE**
                CLEASON.
           1531. **GEORGE BARKER**, b. 30 Mar.
                1846, d. 1918, m.1, 1 Jan.
                1873 **ISODORE DARLING**, m.2,
                1891 **ESTHER R. GRANT**.
           1532. **EDWARD**, d. 27 Feb. 1860 [4-5]

812. **GRIDLEY BRYANT ROWELL** [JOHN R. 341] He was
born 5 Aug. 1829. He married **MARY A.B.** _____.
Res. Salem, N.H.

Children: 1535. **CHARLES NELSON**, b. 27 July
                1852.

831. **WARREN ROWELL** [CHARLES 352] He was born
about 1819. He married 9 June 1844 **RUTH MATILDA
COGSWELL**. Occ. farmer. 1850 census at Tamsworth,
N.H. later at Winona, Minn.

Children: 1536. **MARY A.**, b. c1848.
1537. **FRANK SHERBURNE**, b. 23 Oct.
1837.

832. **FRANKLIN B. ROWELL** [CHARLES 352] He was
born about 1821. He married 9 Nov. 1846 **MARY ANN
JENKINS**. She born 1822. 1850 census at Pembroke.

Children: 1538. **CHARLES F,,** b. 1850.

847. **HILLIARD ROWELL** [DAVID 366] He was born 6
May 1798 at Weare, N.H. and died 26 Dec. 1864,
age 66 yrs. Settled at Croydon. Occ. farmer. He
buried at Eastman cemetery at Sunapee. He
married 3 April 1825 **PHILENA KENISTON**. She born
2 Nov. 1802 at Weare and died 15 Feb. 1841 at
Croydon. He married 2nd 27 June 1841 **LUCY DAVIS**
at Croydon. Occ. farmer. Res. Croydon, N.H. In
1850 census had wife **LUCY** age 50 yrs.

Children: 1540. **DANFORTH**, b. 1826.
1541. **HILLIARD**, b. 1827.
1542. **ALBERT**, b. 1828, md. **SARAH
HAMMOND.**
1543. **EBEN,** b. 1829.
1544. **DAVID**, b. 1830, d. 17 July
1838.
1545. **SYLVESTER**, b. 16 Jan. 1831, d.
15 Oct. 1896, md. 25 Mar.
1860 **SARAH C. DOW.**
1546. **DAVID CALIF,** b. 1833. [some
sources call him DERRIL
CALEF]

849. **STEPHEN ROWELL** [DAVID 366] He was born 27
June 1802 at Croydon and died Sep. 1877 at
Newport, N.H. He married first 31 Mar. 1829 at
Weare **KERON H. BARTLETT;** married second **IRENE B.
BARTLETT;** and married third **MARY R. WOODBURY.**
Occ. farmer, wool growing, teacher. Res.
Croydon, Weare and Newport. 1850 census at
Weare.

ROWELL FAMILY - NEW ENGLAND
7th Generation

Children: 1550. RICHARD S., b. 19 Dec. 1833,
           md. SARAH M. STEVENS.
           1551. ALMOND BARTLETT, b. 19 Sep.
           1838/1844?, d. 1907, md.
           MABEL J. SANBORN.
           1552. GEORGE F., b. 1846.
           1553. FRANKLIN PIERCE, b. 26 Aug.
           1850, d. 1927, md. 9 June
           1874 ELIZA I. YOUNG.
           1554. IRVING GREELEY, b. 1851/1854?,
           d. 1927, md. MARY EUNICE
           FULTON.

851. DAVID ROWELL [DAVID 366] He was born 20
Aug. 1807 at Weare, N.H. He married 25 Nov. 1830
BELINDA HADLOCK of Deering by David Harriman,
Clergyman of Weare. She died 8 June 1880 [68 yr]
Occ. carpenter. 1850 census at Lebanon, N.H.

Children: 1560. D.L. (m), b. c1832.
           1561. C.C. (m), b. c1835.
           1562. A.D. (m), b. c1838.
           1563. J.A. (f), b. c1841.
           1564. ANNE, d. 10 Mar. 1883 [40 yr]
           1565. L.J. (f), b. c1846.

855. LEVI ROWELL [AMOS 367] He was born 18 Oct.
1795 and died 11 Jan. 1881. He married 10 Oct.
1825 MARY LEAR, d/o JOSEPH LEAR. She born 1802
in Me. and died 22 Nov. 1881 [78-3-4] at
Croydon. Occ. shoe maker. In 1850 Census had
wife BETSY born c1812. Res. Goshen and Sunapee.
N.H.

Children: 1567. AMOS, b. 20 Sep. 1827, d. 11
           July 1868, md. 15 Nov. 1854
           EMILY F. WHEELER.
           1568. EUGENE A., b. c1848, d. 5 Mar.
           1885 [36-11-24] at Claremont

865. DANIEL HOLMAN ROWELL [RICHARD 368] He was
born 1 Aug. 1809. He married 10 Sep. 1842
HARRIET BURRELL at Haverhill, Mass. She born
1821 in N.H. Occ. shoe maker. 1850 Census at
Haverhill..

Children: 1569. LOUISE, b. c1843.
1570. HARRIET, b. c1844.
1571. LAURA, b. c1846.
1572. JEFFERSON WASHINGTON, b. 27
        Jan. 1848, d. 27 Sep. 1848.
1573. JOHN, b. 1849.

866. RICHARD H. ROWELL [RICHARD 368]   He was
born 1821 and died 23 June 1854. He married 10
Apr. 1843 DORCUS C. RICHARDSON of Chester, N.H.
Occ. shoe maker. 1850 census at Salem, N.H.

Children: 1574. FRANCES LAVINA, b. 1 Apr.
        1847.

870. BARTLETT C/H ROWELL [PETER 370] He was born
1818 at Allentown and died 6 Oct. 1864. He
married 8 Sep. 1840 BOLINDA S. APPLETON, d/o
ROBERT APPLETON. She died 21 May 1891 [70-1-21].
Res. Hookset, N.H. Occ. mason.

Children: 1575. _____, b. c1841.
1576. JOHN, b. c1843.
1577. dau., b. c1845.
1578. GEORGE A., b. c1847, d. 8 Oct.
        1893 [45-9-4]
1579. SUSANNA, b. 23 May 1850.
1580. dau., b. 2 Mar. 1852.
1581. dau., b. 4 May 1854.
1582. son., b. 22 July 1857.
1583. WARREN C., d. 26 Dec. 1876
        [11-3-18]

871. ALBERT S. ROWELL [PETER 370] He was born
1821 and died 12 July 1880 at Lebanon. He
married HARRIET _____. Occ. shoe maker. Res.
Lebanon, N.H. 1850 census at Hooksett, N.H.

Children: 1584. CHARLES A., b. 28 Nov. 1859,
        md. 2 Aug. 1882, div. 1 May
        1908 HELEN J. _____.

ROWELL FAMILY - NEW ENGLAND
7th Generation

872. PETER C. ROWELL [PETER C. 370] He was born
1822 at Hooksett, N.H. He married 10 Sep. 1851
MARY H. ORDWAY. Res. Newton, N.H.

880. ADAMS ROWELL [MOSES D. 376] He was born 9
Mar. 1810 at Salem, N.H. and died 9 Mar. 1881 at
Tunbrdige, Vt. He married 26 Jan. 1842 MARY M.
MARTIN, d/o JAMES & MARY (COFFREN) MARTIN. She
born 6 Aug. 1820 and died 3 July 1883 at Bethel.
Vt. 1850 census at Tunbridge, Vt.

Children: 1585. LUCY A./LUCINDA, b. 27 June
                  1845, md. 16 Jan. 1869
                  THOMAS K. MOXLEY. 1 child.
           1586. MARY SOPHIA, b. 21 July
                  1847/8, d. 9 Feb. 1894, md.
                  29 Apr. 1879 HOLMAN K.
                  HASTINGS. 2 children.
           1587. ADDIE C., b. 10 Feb. 1854, d.
                  30 July 1905, md. Mar. 1880
                  J. LOREN MADGETT, 1 child.

882. GEORGE WASHINGTON ROWELL [MOSES D. 376] He
was born 21 Nov. 1813 at Tunbrdige, Vt. and died
there 14 Oct. 1853. He married 30 Mar. 1837
SARAH CUSHMAN, d/o FRANK CUSHMAN, or SARAH
CURTIS, d/o CYRUS & POLLY (BRIGHTON) CURTIS. She
born 28 Dec. 1814 and died 21 Mar. 1899 at
Boston. 1850 census at Tunbridge, Vt. He was
called "2d". Buried Central Cemetary.

Children: 1590. GEORGE WYLIE, b. 24 Mar. 1838,
                  md. 6 Apr. 1859 EMELINE JANE
                  OSMAN.
           1591. SARAH JANE, b.15 Nov. 1839, d.
                  23 Apr. 1874, md. 24 Mar.
                  1859 ROMAYN D. CRANDELL or
                  DOUGLAS R. CRANDELL, 5 ch.
           1592. EMILY FRANCES, b. 22 Aug.
                  1841, d. 17 Apr. 1897, md. 4
                  Apr. 1866 EDWIN CRANDELL.
           1593. CHARLES ADAM, b. 18 June 1843,
                  d. Civil War 29 Apr. 1865,
                  disease, Pvt. Co. H or M,

11th Reg't, Vt. Buried
Central Cem. Tunbridge, Vt.
1594. **MARY ELLEN**, b. 9 Mar. 1847, d.
21 Oct. 1892, md. 12 Oct.
1870 **ORLANDO M. KING**. 1 son.
1595. **MOSES DUTY**, b. 4 Apr. 1849, d.
18 Feb. 1926, m.1, 1870 **Mrs.
EMMA FOSTER DIAMOND**, m.2, 6
Feb. 1878 **IDA BELLE TURNER**.
1596. **ABBIE MELISSA**, b. 6 Feb. 1853,
d. 8 Aug. 1922, md. 26 May
1870 **CARY C. FOSTER** at
Tunbridge, Vt.

885. **NATHANIEL LEWIS ROWELL** [MOSES D. 376] He
was born 20 Feb. 1820 and died May 1903. He
married 2 Dec. 1841 at Royalton, Vt. **SUSANNA
DUTTON**, d/o **JOHN G. & ABIGAIL (MOXLEY) DUTTON**.
She born 27 Sep. 1822 and died 3 Jan. 1896.
Quaker. Res. Tunbridge, Vt. in 1850 census.
Commisioned 1st Lt. Co. B, 2nd Vt. Inf. 26 May
1849.

Children: 1600. **WILBER FISKE**, b. 10 Oct. 1842,
d. 2 Dec. 1902, md. 16 Mar.
1870 **LUELLA T. WILMOT**, 3 ch.
1601. **ALFRED**, b. 16 July 1855, d.
1928, md. 21 May 1879
FRANCES C. LYMAN.
1602. **NATHANIEL Jr.**, b. 8 Nov. 1865,
d. 18 Jan. 1918, m.1, 1884
SARAH F. COX, m.2, 11 Dec.
1895 **ANNA AUGUSTA BROWN**.

888. **MOSES DUTY ROWELL Jr.** [MOSES D. 376] He
was born 5 Sep. 1824 at Tunbridge, Vt. and died
26 Sep. 1888. He married **SUSAN E. WIGHT**, d/o
LYMAN & SALLY (MORRILL) WIGHT. She born 1828 at
Warren, Vt. and died 30 Apr. 1889 at Tunbrdige,
Vt. He served in Mexican War. Received pension
therefrom 8 Apr. 1887, #A11196. 1850 census at
Tunbridge, Vt. single. Enlisted 2 Sep. 1861
Civil War, Co. H, 1st N.H. Regt. Pvt/Corp.

Children: 1605. SYLVIA ENADA, b. 20 Apr. 1854,
d. 7 July 1939, unmd.
1606. JAMES MADISON, b. 9 Apr. 1855,
d. 2 Sep. 1925, md. 18 Apr.
1878 LIZZIE NOYES.
1607. FRANCES ELIZABETH, b. 7 Sep.
1856/7, md. 1 Jan. 1883
HARRY W. CHAPMAN, 1 ch.
1608. JULIA ANNETTE, b. 22 Sep.
1858, md. NATHAN D. CHACE.
1609. GEORGE W., b. 26 Jan. 1860, d.
29 Mar. 1941, unmd.
1610. HEBER MOSES, b. 11 Feb. 1869,
md. ELIZABETH FRENCH.

889. WILLIAM ROWELL [MOSES D. 376] He was born
about 1826 and was probably the son of Moses D.
Rowell. He had a wife named SARAH born C1827 in
N.H. Occ. farmer. In 1850 census he lived next
to father Moses D. and his 3 brothers at
Tunbridge, Vt.

Children: 1612. WILLIAM Jr., b. 1848.

895. JOHN C. ROWELL [JAMES 379] He married SARAH
DUSTON, d/o MOSES & ADBIN (SHEPARD) DUSTIN. She
died 26 July 1900 [64 yr]. Res. Derry, N.H.

Children: 1615. ETTA M., b. 1860, d. 17 July
1880.
1616. WILMOT G., b. 2 Apr. 1862, d.
2 Apr. 1882 [28-8-7], md.
LIDA McKINNY.
1617. MYRTA VIOLA, b. 22 July 1868,
d. 30 Jan. 1869.
1618. JOHN F., b. 14 Dec. 1869, d.
6 July 1876.

900. THADDEUS M. H. ROWELL [CALIB 381] He was
born about 1816 at Quincy, Mass. and died 27
Jan. 1900 at Tewksbury, Mass. He married 24 Dec.
1843 MARY A. LOUGEE d/o ROBERT LOUGEE at Quincy.
She born 1823 at Pittsfield, N.H. and died 11
Jan. 1883 at Boston. Res. Boston.

Children: 1620. EDWARD, b. 1844.
1621. WILLIAM HENRY, b. 16 Mar.
        1845, d. 1885, md. 17 Aug.
        1865 MARTHA M. HELLEUR.
1622. BENJAMIN FORH, b. 16 May 1846,
        md. CATHERINE McGRAIL.
1623. ANNIE M., b. 1858.

911. CHASE HALL ROWELL [GEORGE W. 384] He was
born 15 Dec. 1822 at Tunbridge, Vt. and died 13
May 1898 there. He married 16 Nov. 1847 SARAH
ANN HILL, d/o IRA & SARAH (FLINT) HILL. She born
10 June 1821 and died 17 Aug. 1890 at Kansas
City, Mo.

Children: 1625. IRA HILL, b. 27 Jan. 1848, d.
        24 Jan. 1906, md. 12 Sep.
        1869 EVELYN ELDORA
        HARWOOD/HOWARD.
1626. MARTIN CHASE, b. 14 Mar. 1851,
        d. 6 Feb. 1934, md. 19 May
        1874 CHARLOTTE H. WARNER, or
        LUCY E. SHONION.
1627. SARAH HILL, b. 5 June 1854, d.
        26 Feb. 1911, unmd.
1628. JAMES PERRIN, b. 1 Dec. 1856,
        d. 22 Feb. 1857.
1629. EDGAR WITTERS, b. 10 Aug.
        1858, md. EVE LOUISE KING.
1630. MARY ISABELLE CARTER, b. 10
        Aug. 1860, d. 1 Sep. 1924,
        md. 25 Sep. 1883 EDWIN J.
        McWAIN. 5 ch.

914. CYRUS CARTER ROWELL [GEORGE W. 384] He was
born 1831 and died 9 Mar. 1909, age 78-9-19. He
married 19 Feb. 1859 at Tunbridge, Vt. AMELIA
GIFFORD, d/o ZIBA & LYDIA (MORRILL) GIFFORD.
She born 1837 and died 19 May 1914 [76-0-19].
Occ. farmer. Res, Tunbridge, Vt.

Children: 1632. ORVIS ABBOTT, b. 7 Mar. 1859,
        md. 15 May 1886 MINNIE E.
        ABBOTT.

1633. **CYRUS ELMER**, b. 24 Feb. 1861,
d. 10 Feb. 1922, md. 17 Oct.
1906 **JENNIE LANGMEAD**.

915. **GEORGE WASHINGTON ROWELL Jr.**[GEORGE W. 384]
He was born 9 Jan. 1833 at Tunbridge, Vt. and
died about 1918 at Columbia, N.H. He married 18
Sep. 1864 **JANE HARTSHORN**, d/o **CYRUS & BETSY
(RICE) HARTSHORN** of Royalton, Vt. She born 8
Nov. 1844 and died 6 Apr. 1911. He served as a
Sgt.in Civil War. Enlisted 22 Apr. 1861 and was
discharged 10 Sep. 1862 wounded.

Children: 1635. **WARD ADAMS**, b. Apr. 1868, d.
18 Oct. 1918, md. **LIZZIE
ADLER.**
1636. **GEORGE CYRUS**, b. 1872, md
abt. 1905 **EVA LAIRD.**
1637. **WALTER EVERETT**, b. 5 Feb.
1876, md. 3 July 1899
MYRTLE BLODGETT.
1638. **MINNIE BELL**, b. 17 Aug. 1880,
md. 28 Feb. 1899 **ALBERT B.
BLODGETT.** 5 ch.

917. **MARCELLUS CHANDLER ROWELL** [GEORGE W. 384]
He was born 27 Jan. 1837 at Tunbridge, Vt. and
died 27 June 1906 at Panama, N.Y. He married 16
Mar. 1858 **HELEN MARIA HOWE**, d/o **RHINO M. &
LOVINA (SEVERENCE) HOWE**. She born 12 May 1843.
Served in Civil War, Pvt. Co. H. 7th Inf. Res.
Tunbridge, Vt. and Clymar, N.Y.

Children: 1640. **WILL MARCELLUS**, b. 23 Aug.
1859, d. 15 Jan. 1896, md.
13 Oct. 1886 **ROSE E. COVEY.**
no ch.
1641. **MARY**, b. 29 July 1869, md. 6
Apr. 1898 **JAMES D. GLIDDEN**,
Had: **RUTH IRENE.**

929. **ELBRIDGE ROWELL** [DANIEL M. 412] Possible
son of Daniel if he had a first wife Eliza
Whitten. He was born 1830 and died 3 March 1867

ROWELL FAMILY - NEW ENGLAND
7th Generation

at Falmouth, Va. He married **MARTHA BROWN**, d/o
SEWELL BROWN. She born 1835 and died 11 Aug.
1859. Res. Montville, Me.

Children: 1645. **ORVILLE E.**, b. Apr. 1856, d.
16 Oct. 1859.
1646. **HERBERT EDGAR**, b. 11 Mar.
1858, d. 8 May 1904, md. 10
Jan. 1880 **OLIVE F. JACKSON.**

950. **GEORGE PRATT ROWELL** [PARIS 428] He was
born 8 Feb. 1858 and died 13 July 1889. He
married 19 Aug. 1882 **MARY C. BEARCE** at Bristol.
She born 1858 and died 1942.

Children: 1650. **GEORGE**, b. 11 Sep. 1889, d.
1889.

956. **WESLEY D. ROWELL** [JAMES H. 433] He born
1844. He married **MARTHA E. CURRIER** at Kittery,
Maine.

Children: 1655. **FRANK E.**, b. 25 Feb. 1867, md.
RUTH W. DURFEE.

963. **HENRY FRANK ROWELL** [BENJAMIN F. 435] he was
born 1849. He married **MARIA ELIZA BOWKER.**

Children: 1660. **MAUD ELIZABETH**, b. 1882.
1661. **HENRY F.**, b. 1868.
1662. **WALTER**, b. 1869.
1663. **ETHEL MAY**, b. 1872.
1664. **ALBUNTUR**, b. 1874.
1665. **LILLIAN/LILLIS**, b. 4 Aug.
1876.
1666. **BESSIE,**
1667. **BEN,**

964. **GEORGE FREEMAN ROWELL** [BENJAMIN F. 435] He
was born 1853 at Montville, Me. and died 1907.
He married **EUNICE H. HOLBROOK.**

Children: 1670. **WILLIAM E.**, b. c1886, d. 1918,
md. EDITH _____.

ROWELL FAMILY - NEW ENGLAND
7th Generation

972. GEORGE RUFUS ROWELL [OLIVER P. 443] He
married MARY A. _____.

Children: 1675. OLIVE, md. ARTHUR BOLTZ.
1676. OLIVE F., md. GEORGE D. WELSH.
1677. DAISY (ELSIE), md. GEORGE
BERRIE.

974. WALTER PERRY ROWELL [OLIVER P. 443] He
married 1 Nov. 1894 CORA RAYMOND EATON. Res.
Neponset, Mass.

Children: 1680. WALTER RAYMOND, b. 29 Aug.
1896, md. 30 Sep. 1922
HATTIE/NETTIE LEE WILSON.
5 children.

985. JOHN ROWELL [BENJ. 455] He was baptized 16
Oct. 1782 at Oxford, N.H. He married 23 Nov.
1799 SALLY MOORE.

Children: 1710. IRA,
1711. MARK, b. 10 Aug. 1809, md. 25
July 1833 ABIGAIL H. GOODWIN
1712. SAMUEL,
1713. BETHEWAL,
1714. DIADAMA, b. 26 Feb. 1805, md.
SILAS GROVER.
1715. JOHN S., b. 1 Apr. 1827, md.
MARY MARTHA BELLE/BALL.

988. BENNING W. ROWELL [BENJ. 455] He was born
30 Apr. 1787 at Wentworth, N.H. and died at Eau
Claire, Wisconsin. He married TAMSON BARRON in
Vermont. She born c1789 and died 13 Oct. 1862.
Res. Bath, N.H. and Livingstone Co., N.Y. Served
War of 1812.

Children: 1720. CAROLINE, b. 11 Dec. 1813, md.
OLIVER P. PENNOCK, went to
Eau Claire, Wis. in 1862.
1721. JOHN C., b. 1819, md. MARY
RATHBONE.

1722. JANE, b. 1823, md. ALEXANDER
      CHEESEBROUGH.
1723. BENNING, b. 1825, md. ANGELINE
      SNYDER.
1724. TAMESON, b. 1828, md. JOHN
      BARREN.
1725. ANDREW J., b. 6 Sep. 1833, md.
      ANNA VAN PRESSER.
1726. FLETCHER B., b. 12 Oct. 1835,
      d. 27 July 1907, md. June
      1856 CLARINDA CRANDELL in
      N.Y.
1727. FRANCIS, b. 1840, md. SADE
      SMITH.
1728. GEORGE, b. 1842, md. NANCY
      REDSTONE.
1729. BETSEY, b. 1844, md. DAVID
      THORN.
1730. EMILY, b. 1846, md. ELINUYER
      SOUTHMAID.
1731. ALMIRA, b. 1848, unmd.

998. SAMUEL ROWELL [MOSES 236?]   He was born
Dec. 1777 at Amesbury, Mass. and died 3 Mar.
1861. He married 25 Nov. 1802 JUDITH CORLISS.
She born 1782 and died 24 July 1833. He married
second 15 May 1834 HANNAH WOODWARD. She born
c1797. Children born at Salem, N.H.

Children: 1785. POLLY CLEMENT, b. 24 June
                 1803.
           1786. JACOB, b. 1 Nov. 1805, d. 27
                 Feb. 1887.
           1787. DANIEL CORLESS, b. 25 Aug.
                 1808, prob. md. 13 July 1862
                 ELIZA RICH of Manchester,
                 N.H.
           1788. THOMAS ASHBURY, b. 3 Oct.
                 1811, d. 25 Feb. 1891, md. 4
                 May 1862 MARY A. GILLINGHAM
           1789. ELIZABETHA C., b. 14 Nov.
                 1823, md. 18 June 1846 HENRY
                 T. KIMBALL at Methuen,
                 Mass.

999. JACOB ROWELL [UNKNOWN] He married POLLY
_____. Did she or her daughter married 2nd 22
Nov. 1812 DAVID BURTON? Res. Andover and
Windsor, Vt.

Children: 1790. JACOB Jr., b. 18 Feb. 1793,
                md. MARY GRAIGEN.
           1791. MARY/POLLY, b. 23 Dec. 1794,
                md. 24 Jan. 1815 DAVID
                BARTON Jr.
           1792. ARTEMUS, b. 14 Dec. 1796, md.
                18 Nov. 1817 BETSY SWALLOW.
           1793. ROSWELL, b. c1800, d. 10 Dec.
                1855, md. REBECCA _____.

EIGHTH GENERATION

1000. **JOHN ROWELL [MOSES 503]** He was born 20 Jan. 1790 and died 19 July 1878. He married 6 May 1819 **ESTHER LAKE**. She born c1792. Occ. farmer. 1850 census at Loudon, N.H.

Children: 2000. **REBECCA E.**, b. 9 Aug. 1835, d. 12 Sep. 1858.

1001. **MOSES ROWELL Jr. [MOSES 503]** He was born 21 Mar. 1793 and died 19 Jan. 1865. He married 21 March 1821 **SOPHIA FRENCH**. Res. Loudon, N.H. Occ. farmer. 1850 census at Loudon, N.H.

Children: 2001. **PERLEY W.**, b. 1823, md. 1869 **CAROLINE CLARK**.
2002. **JOHN F.**, b. 1826.
2003. **SARAH ANN**, b. c1833.

1005. **ASA TILTON ROWELL [MOSES 503]** He was born 13 Feb. 1806 at Loudon and died 23 April 1875 at Chichester, N.H. He married 2 Dec. 1835 at Salem, Mass. **ABIGAIL SMITH MOULTON**, d/o JACOB S. & NANCY (TILTON) MOULTON. She born 16 Aug. 1809 at Chichester and died 28 Oct. 1864 there. Both buried in Edgerly-Knowlton cemetary. Occ. farmer. 1850 census at Chichester, N.H.

Children: 2005. **WILLIAM H.**, b. 16 Mar. 1837, d. 27 Mar. 1842.
2006. **EDWARD P.**, b. 28 Sep. 1839, d. 29 Feb. 1840.
2007. **ANN BRAY**, b. 14 Mar. 1841, d. 29 Jan. 1934, md. 8 May 1872 **DANIEL T. YEATON** of Epsom. Authors Great Grandparents.
2008. **WILLIAM TILTON**, b. 6 Apr. 1843, d. 12 Jan. 1897, md. 17 June 1866 **LIZZIE M. STONE**.
2009. **MARY J.**, b. 14 Sep. 1848, d. 1 Mar. 1870, d.s.p.

ROWELL FAMILY - NEW ENGLAND
8th Generation

2010. JOHN ANDREW, b. 16 Oct. 1850,
d. 9 Aug. 1922, m.1, 5 July
1875 ALMA NARCISSA HOLMES,
m.2, 28 Sep. 1870 CLARA
HALE.

1006. HARRIS ROWELL [MOSES 503] He was born 10
July 1808 and died 15 July 1835 at Salisbury.
Occ. shoemaker and tanner. His will 28 July
1835. Inventory dated 27 Oct. 1835, $1175.28.
Brother CYRUS named executor. [v.3, p.433]

1007. CYRUS ROWELL [MOSES 503] He was born 1
April 1811 and died 24 July 1884. He married
JUDITH B. SANBORN. She born 31 May 1814 and died
21 Aug. 1888. Served as executor of brother
HARRIS' estate. Res. Loudon, N.H.

Children: 2011. BENJAMIN H., b. c1834.
           2012. ELECTRA, b. c1841.
           2013. MOSES P., b. 19 July 1848, d.
                 23 Jan. 1893, md. CORA
                 ETOIL.
           2014. son, b. 18 May 1851.
           2015. son, b. 15 Nov. 1853.
           2016. GEORGANNA, b. 1855.
           2017. dau., b. 17 Aug. 1857.
           2018. dau., b. 28 May 1859.

1011. ZIBA/ZEBA MORSE ROWELL [THOMAS 504] He was
born 26 Mar. 1798 at Lebanon, N.H. and died 1860
in Oregon. He married 1828 at Plymouth, Mass.
FRANCES SEARS. She born 1802 and died 1884. They
moved frequently. In 1853 the family migrated by
covered wagon to Oregon. Settled at Hillsboro
County, Ore. Occ. shoemaker and farmer. Had a
farm called "Scholls". 1850 Census at Rock
Island, Illinois.

Children: 2020. SUSAN FRANCES, twin b. 5 Sep.
                 1829 at Lowell, Mass., d.
                 1852 in Illinois.
           2021. THOMAS CLARK, twin b. 5 Sep.
                 1829, d. 1857 in Oregan.

2022. **LOUISA MARIA,** b. 12 Nov. 1832
         Hartford, Vt. d. 1855
         Scholls, Ore., md. 1852
         JAMES KAMPH at Port Bryon,
         Ill. Had: ROSALTHIA F., d.y.
2023. **LYDIA WILLIAMS,** b. 26 May 1834
         at Hartford, Vt., d. 1919
         Portland, Ore., md. 1853 at
         Port Bryon, Ill. **JACOB SMITH
         LaRUE.**
2024. **JAMES BARTLETT,** twin b. 1836
         at St. Joseph, Mich., d.
         1916 Newberg, Ore., md.187_?
2025. **JOHN DANIEL,** twin b. 1836, d.
         1896, md. 1874 **REBECCA JACK**
         in Washington Co., Ore.
2026. **ZIBA ARETUS,** b. 1840, in Ill.
         d. 1866, md. 1861 **ELIZABETH
         ELLEN HARRIS.**

1014. **CHRISTOPHER CLARK ROWELL [THOMAS 504]** He
was born 8 Aug. 1806 and died 8 Feb. 1892 [85-
6]. He married **MARY A. HUNTER.** She born 23 Feb.
1809 and died 21 Nov. 1886. Res. Sharon, Vt.
Only names of three of twelve children are
known. May have had a 1st wife **EMILY** who died 8
Mar. 1834 age 27 buried at Hartford, Vt.
cemetary. Probably other children.

Children: 2039. **BARTON,** b. c1832.
               2040. **CHARLES CHRISTOPHER,** b. 1837,
                        d. 1932, m.1, _____, m.2,
                        1866 **LOTTIE L. VANCE,** m.3,
                        EMMA D. PENDLETON, m.4,
                        CHARLOTTE ANN EASTMAN.
               2041. **HENRY VALENTINE,** b. 1838, d.
                        1925, md. **EMMA J. JAQUITH.**
               2042. **NEVA HUNTER,**

1017. **JAMES MADISON ROWELL [THOMAS 504]** He was
born 14 Nov. 1809, twin. lived at Eula, Ore.
Moved first to Vermont, then to Oregan. Occ.
farmer and teacher. He engaged in the Cayuse
War.

1020. **IRA ROWELL** [CHRISTOPHER 505] He was born
29 May 1797 at West Concord, N.H. and died 14
June 1876 there. He married first 30 Jan. 1824
ELIZABETH THOMPSON. She died 28 April 1826 age
29 yrs. at Concord. He married second 9 April
1828 **REBECCA KIMBALL**, d/o **EDWARD & ELIZABETH
(McALLISTER) KIMBALL** at Pembroke. She born 4
Jan. 1808 and died 13 Dec. 1871. Occ. farmer,
school teacher 17 years, Deacon North
Congregational church for 47 yrs, Selectman
1842-3, Representative General Court 1861-2.
Res. West Concord, N.H. near end of Penacock
Lake. 1850 census at Concord, N.H.

Children: 1st Wife:
   2070. **THOMPSON**, b. 21 Apr. 1825, d.
      18 Oct. 1881, md. 1849 **MARY
      ANN LEMFEST**.
2nd Wife: 2071. **WILLIAM KIMBALL**, b. 9 Nov.
      1828, d. 22 Nov. 1888, m.1,
      27 Nov. 1855 **MARY A. FLINT**,
      m.2, **HELEN MARIA TENNEY**.
      Occ. farmer.
   2072. **ELIZABETH THOMPSON**, b. 21 Sep.
      1832, d. 8 Jan. 1844.
   2073. **EDWARD THOMAS**, b. 14 Aug.
      1835, d. 4 Aug. 1892, md.
      1870 **CLARA S. WEBSTER**.
   2074. **JAMES HARRIS**, b. 16 May 1838,
      d. 8 Apr. 1903, md. 21 June
      1866 **MARY ANN FISKE**.
   2075. **MARY CLARK**, b. 16 Mar. 1841,
      d. 2 Mar. 1909, unmd.
   2076. **REBECCA KIMBALL**, b. 3 Sep.
      1843, m.1, **ANDREW S. FARNUM**,
      m.2, 1877 **ANDREW SHERBURNE**,
      3 children.
   2077. **CHRISTOPHER IRA**, b. 4 Dec.
      1846, d. 3 June 1849.

1021. **THOMAS ROWELL** [CHRISTOPHER 505] He was
born 12 Aug. 1799 at Concord, N.H. and died 20
Apr. 1833. He married 27 Mar. 1829 at Concord,

N.H. **BRIDGET W. FARNUM**, d/o **PETER C. FARNUM**. She married second **TIMOTHY E. HOIT**. Res. Pembroke, N.H.

Children: 2080. **PETER CHANDLER FARNUM**, b. 18 July 1828, d. 20 July 1839.
2081. **LYDIA**, b. 18 June 1830, d. 25 Aug. 1846.

1035. **JACOB ROWELL** [STEPHEN 513] He was born 1796 at Frankfort, Me. and died 1883. He married 9 March 1817 **WAITY/WATEY PIERSON/PARSONS** of Bristol, Me. He served in War of 1812. Received pension #SC-24853. Res. Montville and Dixmont, Me. 1850 Census at Dixmont, Me.

Children: 2100. **REUBEN P.**, b. 1817, d. 1866 at Saco. Me.
2101. **JOANNA**, b. 1819, d. 1904, md. 18 Apr. 1839 **NEHAMIAH WEYMOUTH**.
2102. **STEPHEN**, b. 1822, d. 1839 at Dixmont, Me.
2103. **WATEY**, b. 1824, d. 1899.
2104. **JOHN**, b. 1827, d. 4 Nov. 1859, at Hopewell [32-6-4] md. 1853 ____. Had: **EDWIN D.** & **JOHN**.
2105. **JACOB**, b. 1829, d. 1881.
2106. **DANIEL**, b. 1831, d. 1911, md. 1854 **MARY MILLER JACKSON**.
2107. **WILLIAM**, b. 1833, d. 1913, md.
2108. **MARCUS**, b. 16 July 1835, d. 1879, md. 9 July 1859 **VERTA PRESCOTT**.
2109. **ORINDA P.**, b. 1837, d. 1925, md. 1865 **WILLIAM JOHNSON**.
2110. **PHOEBE**, b. 1839, d. 1841.
2111. **ALPHEUS/ALTHEUS**, b. 20 July 1842, d. 1898, md. 23 Feb. 1867 **CASSANDRA BICKFORD**.
2112. **ELIAS D.**, b. 5 May 1844, d. 1885.

2113. **ESTHER**, b. 1846, d. 1926, m.1,
10 May 1866 **ASHLEY YOUNG**,
m.2, 1900 **ED TARR**.

1042. **MYRON P. ROWELL** [JACOB 519] He was born
c1809 and died 10 Aug. 1886 [77-8-6] He married
ELIZA A. BOSWELL. Res. Newton.

Children: 2120. **CHARLES M.**, b. 8 Jan. 1853.
2121. **JOHN N.**, b. 4 Apr. 1858.

1045. **JONATHAN EDWARD ROWELL** [JOSEPH 523] He was
born 3 June 1806. He married 17 Aug. 1835
CAROLINE E. WHITE, d/o JAMES WHITE at Cornish,
N.H. She died 22 Feb. 1864 [57 yr]. 1850 census
at Claremont, N.H.

Children: 2125. **GEORGE EDWARD**, b. 16 May 1841,
md. 1 Sep. 1862, div. Oct.
1890 **SARAH E. _____**.
2126. **HENRY LOUIS**, b. 26 Aug. 1843.
2127. **ELLEN M.**, b. 1844.

1057. **EDMUND ROWELL** [JOSHUA 527] He was born 9
Oct. 1803 at Newton. N.H. and died probably at
Lynn, 8 Feb. 1891 or 19 April 1872. He married
30 April 1835 at East Kingston, N.H. **ELEANOR
MARSHALL**, d/o RUTH MARSHALL of Hampstead. She
born c1807 and died 5 Oct. 1860 age 99-6-0. Res.
Kensington, N.H. Possibly m.2, **JANE S. _____**.
1850 census at Kensington, N.H. Occ. farmer.

Children: 2140. **AMOS**, b. 28 Aug. 1837, d. 9
Aug. 1865, md.**ISABEL AUSTIN**.
2141. **EDMUND M.**, b. 16 July 1842, d.
5 Oct. 1863 at London, Ky.
Civil War, md. 1 Jan. 1861
MARY L. BROWN. She m.2,
JOSEPH M. AUSTIN. No ch.
2142. **RUTH ANN**, b. 5 Oct. 1844, md.
2 June 1863 **JOHN P. GREEN**.

1063. **WILLIAM ROWELL** [BENJAMIN 529?] He was born
1 July 1807. He married **MERCY W. HARRIS**. She

born c1811. Occ. carpenter. 1850 Census at Amesbury, Mass.

Children: 2148. **WILLIAM**, b. 26 June 1838.
2149. **IDA LUCY**, b. 15 Aug. 1846.

1064. **OTIS ROBERSTON ROWELL** [BENJAMIN 529] He was born 14 July 1809. He married first 22 Dec. 1836 **ELVIRA WEED**. She died 16 May 1839, age 26-7-0. He married second **SARAH** _____. Res. Newton, N.H.

Children: 1st Wife:
2150. **ELBRIDGE BROOKS**, b. 17 June 1838, d. 18 June 1845, age 7 yrs.
by 2nd Wife:
2151. **ELBRIDGE BROOKS**, b. 1 Apr. 1857.
2152. **BENJAMIN**, b. 15 Dec. 1858.

1070. **FREDERICK ROWELL** [WILLIAM 536] He was born c1800. He married 2 Dec. 1838 **MARY ANN BURKE** or **MARGARET BROCK** at Salem. Res. Salem, Mass.

Children: 2155. **FREDERICK**, b. 5 May 1839, md. **CLARA ELLEN SANGER**.

1080. **GEORGE B. ROWELL** [MOSES 551] He was born 1828 at Bath and died there 21 Dec. 1870. He married **LESTINE B. MERRILL**, d/o **JOSEPH & ROSANA (JOHNSON) MERRILL**. She died 31 Oct. 1892. Res. Bath, N.H.

Children: 2160. **KILBURN M.**, b. 3 Apr. 1870, d. 19 Feb. 1871.

1091. **LEWIS FORD ROWELL** [IRA 555] He was born 1829. He married _____. Occ. farmer. Res. Wisconsin, Lewis Co., Minnesota.

Children: 2165. **CHARLES**,
2166. **JOHN**,
2167. **LEWIS**,

2168. IRA,
2169. BELLE,
2170. SUSAN,

1093. **IRA BENJAMIN ROWELL** [IRA 555] He was born 1833. He married 1861 **ELIZA OSBURN**. She died after 11 months. In 1863 went to Calif. Returned in 1865 to Wis. He married second 31 Jan. 1866 **LOUISA CHIPMAN**, dau. of **JOHN B. CHIPMAN**. Occ. farmer and manufacturer. Mason, Methodist. Republican. Res. Menomonee Falls, Wis.

Children: 2175. **MABEL M.**, d. 3 Dec. 1893, md.
            MYRON WEDISH.
         2176. **HARRY H.**,
         2177. **EDITH L.**,

1094. **GUILDFORD DUDLEY ROWELL** [IRA 555] He was born 1834. He married _____. Occ. farmer. Partner in Valley Iron Works, Appleton, Wisc. Res. Beaver Dam, Wis.

Children: 2178. **DUDLEY**,
         2179. **HATTIE**,

1096. **ALPHONSO DWIGHT ROWELL** [IRA 555] He was born 1839. He married _____. Occ. farmer. Partner Hartford Plow Works. Res. Hartford, Wis.

Children: 2180. **GUY**,
         2181. **JULIETTE**, b. 2 Sep. 1857.

1098. **GEORGE WAYLAND ROWELL** [IRA 555] He was born 1843 and died 1934. He married **MARY WALSH** of Wisconsin. Occ. farmer and manufacturer with firm of I.B. Rowell. Res. Menomonee Falls, Wis.

Children: 2182. **DONNA**,
         2183. **JOHNNY**,
         2184. **BELLE**, d. young
         2185, **IRA WAYLAND**, b. 1878, d. 1946,
               md. 1900 **LIDA RIEDENBACH**.
         2186. **MARIA BLANCH**, b. 1880. Occ.
               Secretary

2187. STELLA MAE, b. 1882, md. FRED
ELLINGTON.
2188. FRANK FORD, b. 1884, d. 1945,
md. 1911 MINNIE MacEVANS.
2189. GEORGE WALSH, b. 1886, md.
1918 MARY E. BERIGAN.
2190. WALLACE ARTHUR, b. 1888, d.
1954, md. 1919 MARIE
MEDENNES.

1101. CHARLES WALTER ROWELL [PHINEAS 556] He
was born 1850 at Lakeport, N.Y. and died 1898.
He married 1879 SARAH MARIA COOPER, d/o Gen.
COOPER, U.S. Army. He grad. from West Point,
Class of 1874. Was Capt. 2nd Reg't U.S.
Infantry. Veteran of Indian Wars. Killed in
action at Santiago, Cuba. Res. Lockport, N.Y.

Children: 2200. FRANK WHEATON, b. 1880, d.
1947, md. 1904 GERTRUDE
MERCER.
2201. CHARLES WALTER, b. 1884, West
Point Class 1910.
2202. ASHLEY QUINSTEAD, b. 1886.

1110. JACOB ROWELL [PHILIP 561] He was born
c1794. He married 17 Sep. 1817 POLLY STEVENS.

Children: 2205. ANNA JACKSON, b. 25 Aug. 1823,
md. 7 May 1845 JOSEPH H.
PETTINGILL.
2206. LYDIA DEAN, b. 28 Dec. 1825.
2207. MARY STEVENS, b. 7 May 1831.
2208. MARY ESTHER, b. 24 Feb. 1835.

1120. JOHN ROWELL [JACOB 566] He was born 28
Jan. 1806. He married 18 Sep. 1832 SARAH M.
STEWART. She born 1814. Occ. shoe maker. Res.
Amesbury, Mass. 1850 census.

Children: 2210. JOHN STEWART, b. 15 Nov. 1833.
2211. SARAH ANN, b. 24 Jan. 1840.

1122. JACOB ROWELL [JACOB 566] He was born 10
Dec. 1809. He married 9 Feb. 1834 IRENE ANN
JONES. She born 1814. Occ. laborer. Res.
Amesbury, Mass. 1850 census.

Children: 2212. MARY REBECCA, b. 9 July 1839.
2213. GEORGE JONES, b. 3 Apr. 1841.
2214. ABBIE ELIZABETH, b. 13 Apr.
1843.

1124. SAMUEL ROWELL [JACOB 566] He was born 22
Aug. 1815 in Mass. He married 13 Aug. 1841 LYDIA
J. NEAL. She born c1815 in Maine. Occ. painter.
1850 census in Portsmouth, N.H.

Children: 2215. JACOB HAM, b. 13 Apr. 1843.
2216. ABBY ELIZABETH, b. 13 Apr.
1843.
2217. LYDIA L.D., b. 27 July 1845.
2218. OLIVER D., bp. 18 Oct. 1847.
2219. JOHN, b. 20 Aug. 1859.

1125. CHARLES ROWELL [JACOB 566] He was born 24
Oct. 1817. He married 9 Nov. 1842 RUTH ANN
HEALEY. She born c1819. 1850 census at Lawrence,
Mass.

Children: 2220. JACOB A., b. 5 Aug. 1840.
2221. ANN MARIA/ANNABEL H., b. 21
Sep. 1844.
2222. CHARLES, b. 12 July 1848.

1126. GEORGE S. ROWELL [JACOB 566] He was born
16 Sep. 1819 and died about 1871. He married
first 27 Jan. 1840 MARY ELIZABETH COLBY in
Salisbury. He married 2nd REBECCA JONES. Occ.
hardware merchant. Res. Amesbury, Mass.

Children: 2225. JULIUS V., b. 7 Nov. 1840.
2226. GEORGE H.P., b. 3 Feb. 1842.
2227. MARY An, b. 5 June 1843, md.
25 Nov. 1867 JAMES JOHNSON.

2228. **MOSES T.**, b. 20 Jan. 1845,
d.15 Dec. 1920, md. **MARY W.
ELLIOT.**
2229. **WILLIAM**, b. 6 Jan. 1847.
2230. **EMILY JANE**, b. 25 Aug. 1848.
2231. **JOHN F.**, b. 18 Jan. 1860, md.
2 Apr. 1891 **MINNIE T. BEAN.**

1140. **JAMES ROWELL [JAMES 568]** He was born 21
Sep. 1808. He married 23 Sep. 1831 **SARENA
FLANDERS.** She born c1813. In 1850 census. Res.
at Amesbury, Mass.

Children: 2233. **MARY AUGUSTA**, b. 23 Feb. 1833.
2234. **ABIGAIL F.**, b. 29 Nov. 1835.
2235. **JAMES CYRUS**, b. 14 Sep. 1840.
2236. **JAMES ALFRED**, b. 28 May 1843.
2237. **CYRUS W.**, b. 25 June 1848.

1142. **TIMOTHY ROWELL [JAMES 568]** He was born 6
Jan. 1812 at Salisbury, Mass. He married **SARAH
BRYANT.** She born c1810 in Maine. In 1850 census.
Occ. carpenter. Res. at Vasselboro, Me.

Children: 2238. **JAMES HENRY.**, b. 27 Sep. 1839.
2239. **SARAH ELLEN**, b. 29 Mar. 1842.
2240. **TIMOTHY BRYANT**, b. 9 May 1845,
md. 21 Nov. 1872 **ELLA M.
HOLLAND**, m.2, 1 Sep. 1880
ELIZABETH C. LATHORP.
2241. **ANNA**, b. 20 Jan. 1849, md. 2
Sep. 1872 **GEORGE FRANK
ABBOTT.**

1145. **MOSES ROWELL [JOSEPH 571]** He was born
c1794. Had wife **SARAH _____**. She born c1798 in
Me. Occ. farmer. 1850 Census at Monmouth, Me.

Children: 2242. **GREEN L.**, b. c1834.
2243. **GEORGE F.**, b. c1834.

1150. MOSES ROWELL [MARK 572] He was born 11
Nov. 1805. He probably married 22 Mar. or 10
Sep. 1834 MARY ANN STOVER, d/o Capt. WILLIAM
STOVER in Amesbury, Mass.

Children: 2245. CHARLES WILLIAM, b. 1 Nov.
           1837.
           2246. CHARLES, b. 14 Oct. 1838.

1158. WILLIAM ROWELL [AARON 580] He was born
1805 at Lancaster, N.H. or New Miford, Me. and
died there in 1857. He married 20 Nov. 1828
BELINDA ROGERS, dau. of THOMAS & LYDIA (HALL)
ROGERS at Lancaster. She born 1803 at Derry and
died 1878. Occ. carpenter and builder, Free
Baptist, Democrat. Res. Caledonia, Vt. 1850
census at Lancaster, N.H.

Children: 2250. LYDIA D.A., b. 1833.
           2251. WILLIAM LYMAN, b. 31 Oct.
           1834, md. 4 Apr. 1856
           MARTHA LeGRO.
           2252. JAMES M., b. 1836.
           2253. LEVI W., b. 1838, md. FANNIE
           T. ESTABROOK.
           2254. VICTORIA A., b. 1840, md.
           MILES C. GRAY.
           2255. CATHERINE E., b. 1842.
           2256. ELLEN M., b. 1844.

1173. LEONARD F. ROWELL [MOSES 590] He was born
19 Apr. 1807 at Corinth, Vt. and died 13 Aug,
1866 at Berlin, Vt. He married 13 Dec. 1829 at
Haverhill SARAH LOUISE KIMBALL. She died 8 Sep.
1866, age 57-8. They moved from Haverhill to
Berlin, Vt. about 1844. Occ. farmer.

Children: 2270. HIRAM LEONARD, b. 21 Jan.
           1837, d. 26 Mar. 1916, md.
           CLARA F. BATCHELDER.
           2271. GARDNER P., b.____, d. 19 Sep.
           1905, md. 3 Feb. 1871 ELLA
           H. ANDREWS.

ROWELL FAMILY - NEW ENGLAND
8th Generation

2272. **GEORGE F.**, d. 4 Apr. 1892 at
      E. Kingston [60-11-28]
2273. **AARON**, b. 26 Jan. 1846, d. 20
      Mar. 1926, md. 10 Feb. 1871
      ANNA WILSON.
2274. **LYDIA A.**, md. 4 Aug. 1867
      CHARLES L. ANDREWS.
2275. **WARREN H.**, b. 10 Mar. 1844, d.
      21 Oct. 1862. Civil War.
2276. **CHARLES F.**, b. 2 May 1850, d.
      9 June 1910, md. 17 Jan.
      1874 **ANNA WINTERS.**
2277. **HATTIE M.**, md. 8 Feb. 1873
      HENRY C. REED.
2278. **JOHN W.**, b. 9 June 1835, md. 1
      Aug. 1858 **MARY L. WHEELER** or
      BELLE LENOX?
2279. **CAROLINE L.**, md. 19 May 1872
      A.E. GOODNOUGH.

1199. **JAMES M. ROWELL** [EDWARD 609] He was born
24 Sep. 1817 and died 13 Oct. 1834. He married
LAURA WAID, d/o **JOHN & LAURANA (POTTER) WAID.**
She born 23 May 1825 and died 3 Aug. 1890. She
married 2nd 22 April 1846 **ALBION WHEELER** of
Milan and married 3rd 10 Aug. 1853 **AMOS K,
CROSS.** By him she had:

Children: i. **FRANK POTTER CROSS**, b/d. 1854.
          ii. **LAURANA POTTER CROSS**, b. 1857, d.
              1871.

1200. **JONATHAN BARNEY ROWELL** [JONATHAN 610] He
was born 3 Feb. 1800 at Waterford, Vt. and died
28 Sep. 1850 at Danvers, Illinois. He married 22
Jan. 1828 **CYNTHIA ABBOTT**, d/o **MOSES & LUCY
(WILLIS) ABBOTT.** She married second 21 Feb. 1860
JOHN HAY. Res. Haverhill and Danvers, Ill. 1850
Census at McLean Co., Illinois. Moved to
Illinois c1835.

Children: 2300. **MARY JANE**, b. 27 June 1829, d.
               8 Sep. 1848.

ROWELL FAMILY - NEW ENGLAND
8th Generation

2301. IRA, b. 20 May 1831, d. 4 May
1898, Ill., md. 16 Nov. 1869
LAVINA CARLOCK.
2302. JONATHAN HARVEY, b. 10 Feb.
1833, d. 15 May 1908 md.
1866 MARIA SANFORD WOODS.
5 children.
2303. LUCY MARIA, b. 27 Jan. 1835,
d. 16 Apr. 1849.
2304. CHARLES CARROLL, b. 11 Dec.
1836, d. 4 July 1899, md.
c1851 MARGARET RAYBURN.
Had grocery at Danvers, Ill.
2305. WILLIAM FRANKLIN, b. 15 Sep.
1838, d. 13 May 1912, md. 24
Oct. 1867 MARY ISABELL
DICKINSON.
2306. MILO A., b. 13 Dec. 1840, d.
12 Jan. 1922, md. 13 Dec.
1859 (SARAH) LOUISE COYNER.
2307. GEORGE BARNEY, b. 13 Dec.
1842, d. 27 Dec. 1907, md.
22 Dec. 1881 ADELPHIA
WARLOW.
2308. CHESTER, b. 7 Oct. 1844, d. 23
May 1912, md. 25 Aug. 1872
Mrs. NELLIE HALE ROWELL
[#1221]
2309. ALBERT ABBOTT, b. 30 May 1848,
md. 22 Dec. 1878 NANCY ANN
BOOTH, d/o STEPHEN BOOTH.

1204. GUY CARLTON ROWELL [JONATHAN 610] He was
born 15 Feb. 1808 at Waterford, Vt. and died 17
Mar. 1891 at Bloomington, Ill. He married 12
Feb. 1835 CLARISSA DAVIS RANKIN, d/o Gen. DAVID
& PERSIS (DANIEL) RANKIN. She born 21 Jan. 1809
at Littleton, N.H. and died 3 Nov. 1873 at
Bloomginton, Ill. Occ. farmer. Signed petition
1837 at Concord, Vt. Moved to Illinois in 1863.
Appointed Lt. 1st Co. Light Inf., 33nd Req't
N.H. Militia 4 June 1844. 1850 census at
Littleton, N.H.

- 157 -

Children: 2320. FRANCES HARRIET or HARRIET
           NEWELL, b. 15 Nov. 1835 at
           Concord, Vt., d. 12 Jan.
           1924, md. 23 Apr. 1863
           GEORGE P. ELY. 2 children.
       2321. CLINTON, b. 12 Nov. 1838, d. 1
           Nov. 1907, md. 12 Nov. 1868
           CAROLYN M. FARRIS.
       2322. FRANK F., b. 11 June 1850, d.
           31 June 1890 at Bloomington.
       2323. HELEN EDNA, b. 26 May 1852, d.
           11 Nov. 1932 at Los Angeles,
           md. 30 May 1878 WILLIAM J.
           WASHBURN, b. 1852, No ch.

1205. BENJAMIN FRANKLIN ROWELL [JONATHAN 610]
He was born 5 Feb. 1810 at Littleton, N.H. and
died 25 Sep. 1860 at Danvers, Illinois. He
married 6 July 1837 CHARITY ABBOTTS, d/o MOSES &
LUCY (WILLIS) ABBOTTS of Bath, N.H. She born 7
July 1811 and died 5 July 1876. Res. Moved to
Illinois 1838. All children born there. White
Oak Grove, Illinois. 1850 Census in McLean Co.

Children: 2325. JONATHAN, b. 10 Feb. 1838, d.
           10 Aug. 1863 in Civil War at
           Vicksburg of typhoid fever.
       2326. LUCY AMANDA, b. 10 Aug. 1839,
           d. 13 May 1867, md. 8 June
           1864 CYRUS M. BENSON.
       2327. SARAH ADELINE, b. 26 Apr.
           1841, d. 28 May 1913, md.
           I. LOUIS STANBUS.
       2328. HATTIE/HARRIET, b. 10 Apr.
           1844, d. 30 Apr. 1863, of
           smallpox.
       2329. MOSES FRANKLIN, b. 26 Oct.
           1848, d. 16 July 1913, md.
           20 May 1875 ALMA SUSAN
           BOWEN.

1207. RICHARD ROWELL [JONATHAN 610] He was born
22 May 1814 at Stark, N.H. and died 16 Oct. 1884
at Bloomington, Illinois. He married 15 Dec.

1853 **NANCY BARNARD.** She born 28 Oct. 1824 in Ohio and died 27 July 1891 at Bloomington. Occ. farmer.

Children: 2330. **LOIS,** b. 16 Nov. 1855, d. 17 Jan. 1920, md. 7 Feb. 1878 **JAMES W. JOHNSON,** 3 ch.
2331. **EMMA,** b. 25 Feb. 1857, d. 11 Nov. 1885.
2332. **CLARK,** b. 10 Mar. 1862, d. 5 Apr. 1869.

1208. **SALMON HOSKINS ROWELL [JONATHAN 610]** He was born 2 July 1816 at Littleton, N.H. and died 16 Jan. 1900 at Peacham, Vt. He married 4 Jan. 1846 **CORDELIA M. BALLOU,** d/o **OTIS BALLOU** of Waterford, Vt. She born 23 Apr. 1820 and died 20 Feb. 1897. Occ. carpenter and farmer. Selectman 1841-2. State legislature 1846-7. Lt. Col. 32nd Reg't N.H. Militia 19 June 1840. 1850 census at Littleton. 1850 Census at Peacham, Vt.

Children: 2334. **OTIS FILLMORE,** b. 20 Aug. 1848, d. 19 June 1874, md. 29 Sep. 1870 **ELLA HOOKER.** Postmaster, Stewart, Iowa.
2335. **ADALINE CORDELIA,** b. 22 Apr. 1857, d. 29 Oct. 1910, md. 8 Mar. 1876 **WILLIAM V. McLAUGHLIN.** Res. Peacham.
2336. **SALMON HARVEY,** b. 26 Mar. 1860, d. 2 June 1877.
2337. **HATTIE EDITH,** b. 26 Mar. or 4 Aug. 1862, d. 15 Apr. 1901, md. 8 Oct. 1880 **ELIJAH W. LYFORD,** 1 ch. Res. Barnet, Vt.
2338. **RICHARD CLARK,** b. 25 Oct. 1865, d. 22 June 1928, md. 25 Oct. 1886 **MARGARET BUNDY,**

1209. **JOSHUA ROWELL [JONATHAN 610]** He was born 29 Nov. 1818 and died 6 June 1853 at Falls River, Mass. He married 31 Mar. 1853 **MARY R.**

ROWELL FAMILY - NEW ENGLAND
8th Generation

CHASE. Occ. wood worker. Res. Falls River, Mass.
No children.

1214. CALIB ROWELL [DANIEL 612] He was born 17
Apr. 1804 at Percy, N.H. He married 13 Nov. 1826
MARY BANFIELD of Bath, N.H. Res. Malden, Vt.

Children: 2340. HARRIET, b. 11 May 1827, d. 2
                 Dec. 1890, md. 22 Apr. 1846
                 CAPT. CHARLES COLE. 6 ch.
           2341. GEORGE B., b. 27 Feb. 1829, d.
                 9 Feb. 1905, md. 13 Nov.
                 1851 LOUISE COLE. His 2nd
                 cousin.
           2342. HARVEY, b. 1834, d. 21 Feb.
                 1891, md. 3 Sep. 1853 CORA
                 ALMIRA COLE.

1216. JOSHUA ROWELL [DANIEL 612] He was born 30
May 1808 at Percy, N.H. (now Starke) and died 9
Mar. 1881 at Abbotsford, Quebec. He married 7
Mar. 1829 at Starke SYBIL EUNICE SPAULDING, d/o
PHINEAS & POLLY (BAKER) SPAULDING. She born 18
Apr. 1804 and died c1891/2. Both buried in
Methodist cemetary at Abbotsford. Occ. owned a
sawmill and tavern. Removed to Canada about
1839.

Children: 2345. LOVINA, b. 22 May 1830, md.
                 JOHN BAIRD, 7 ch.
           2346. SPAULDING, b. 21 Nov. 1831, d.
                 24 May 1877, md. MARTHA BALL
           2347. JEANNETTE KOFFRAN, b. 30 Mar.
                 1833, d. 20 May 1915, md.
                 ELMAN JACKMAN.
           2348. EMMELINE, b. 27 Feb. 1835, d.
                 infancy.
           2349. EMMELINE, b. 6 Jan. 1837, d.
                 infancy.
           2350. ISAAC SMITH, b. 13 Aug. 1838,
                 d. 13 Apr. 1907, md. 28 July
                 1868 MYRA WILBER.
           2351. CLARK, b. 14 Nov. 1840, d.
                 infancy.

2352. SENECA PAIGE, b. 8 Jan. 1843,
d, 17 Jan. 1917, md. HELEN
WATSON.
2353. JOSHUA, b. 6 Nov. 1844, md.
1902 JULIE ROWELL. [#2358]
2354. SYBIL EUNICE, b. 25 July 1848,
d. 10 Dec. 1915, S. HENRY
KENT. 2 dau.

1219. DANIEL ROWELL [DANIEL 612] He was born 3
Dec. 1814 at Percy, N.H. and died 22 May 1881
there. He married 18 Feb. 1838 CHARLOTTE POTTER,
d/o AARON & HANNAH (MILES) POTTER. She born 7
Oct. 1818 at Percy and died 9 Feb. 1862. 1850
census at Stark, N.H.

Children: 2355. MARTHA E., b. 11 June 1843, d.
30 Mar. 1862.
2356. MARY ANN, b. 1850, d. 1928,
md. GILMAN H, FARRAR.
2357. CORA, b. 1855, md. HENRY
STEVENS of Lundenburg, Vt.
adopted daughter;
2358. JULIA, b. 1 June 1857, d. 16
Apr. 1914, md. JOSHUA ROWELL
Jr. [#2353]

1221. Dr. ISAAC ROWELL [DANIEL 612] He was born
about 1818 at Percy, N.H. and died 4 Jan. 1871
at San Francisco, Calif. He married 31 Mar. 1860
NELLIE HALE. She born 17 Jan. 1837 died 25 June
1884 at Fresno, Calif. She married second in 25
Aug. 1873 Dr. CHESTER ROWELL [# 2308] Prominent
Prof. of Medicine at the U. of Pacific. Masonic
lodge.

Children: 2360. FRANK A., b. 25 Oct. 1863, d.
9 Apr. 1898, md.14 Sep. 1887
ELIZABETH JOHNSON.
2361. IMOGENE, b. 4 Dec. 1866, d. 25
Nov. 1933, md. 25 Nov. 1895
Dr. JOHN R. ELDRIDGE. Had;
CARLTON & HELEN R.

1223. LEVI ROWELL [DANIEL 612] He was born 15
Sep. 1822 at Percy, N.H. and died 22 June 1869
at Stark [48-5-7]. He married 2 May 1846
CAROLINE McFARLAND, d/o DANIEL M. & PATTY
CRAWFORD (BELL) McFARLAND. She born 21 Apr. 1824
and died 11 Feb. 1902. She married second 23
Jan. 1874 JOHN ROBERTS at Starke, N.H. Occ.
farmer, Selectman 1846 and 1855. Res. 1850
census at Starke.

Children: 2362. DANIEL M., b. 1848, d. 17 June
                  1862.
            2363. LOVINA MEHITABLE, b. 8 Nov.
                  1850, d. 3 Sep. 1923, md. 19
                  June 1867 FREEMAN THOMAS
                  POTTER, Had: NELLIE E., b.
                  1860, d. 1894.

1224. CHARLES W. ROWELL [DANIEL 612] He was
born 5 July 1824 at Percy, N.H. He married 20
June 1847 SARAH B. HAMMOND at Manchester, N.H.

1229. HENRY WARD ROWELL [RICHARD F. 616] He was
born 16 Jan. 1834 at Waterford, Vt. and died
1899 at Washington, D.C. He married 11 Oct. 1855
ASHSAH B. TAYLOR, d/o SAMUEL TAYLOR. She born 18
Apr. 1837 at Springfield, Vt. Methodist. Est.
"Peoples Journal" 6 June 1855. Treasurer Grafton
Co. 1858-9. Chief of Agricultural Div. of the
Census Bureau till 1867. Republican. Member of
AF & AM. Res. Littleton, N.H. Moved to Rockford,
Illinois.

Children: 2364. ELIZABETH/LIZZIE M., b. 24
                  July 1858, md. 1 May 1879
                  M.F. SAWYER. Res. Iowa City.
            2365. CHARLES H., b. 20 Aug. 1864,
                  md. 6 Sep. 1886 ANNIE E.
                  MARCEY. Res. Iowa City, Ia.
                  Occ. merchant.
            2366. ALICE C., b. 28 Mar. 1868, d.
                  1 Jan. 1872.

1233. DANIEL ROWELL [RICHARD F. 616] he was born
30 March 1842. He married 28 May 1862 ADELINE D.
WHITTING. Occ. shoemaker. Res. Concord, Vt.

Children: 2367. CATE, b. 30 Nov. 1867.

1237. NEHEMIAH ROWELL [ABRAHAM 620] He was born
1789 at Nottingham, N.H. and died 29 Mar. 1872
at Sutton, age 82 years. He married 23 Nov. 1815
at Peerfield, N.H. ELIZABETH BROWN, d/o
ELIPHELET & ABIGAIL (NORTHFIELD) BROWN. She born
1792 and died 16 Nov. 1858 at Nottingham, N.H.

Children: 2368. JOHN COLBY, b. 1835, d. 1919,
md. 1864 MARY ELIZABETH
CLARK.

1238. ABRAHAM ROWELL [ABRAHAM 620] He was born
1791 at Nottingham, N.H. He served 60 days in
the War of 1812 from Deerfield, N.H.

1240. WILLIAM C. ROWELL [RICE 627] He was born
1812 at Harrison, Me. and died 1874. He married
first 8 Mar. 1834 MARY NASH of Portland, Me. He
married second 6 June 1840 SARAH H. PLUMMER of
Portland. Occ. boot maker and violinist. Res.
Portland, Me.

Children: by 1st Wife:
2369. SARAH, b. 1833, d. 13 June
1841.
2370. MARY ANN, b. 13 Nov. 1835, d.
young.
2371. daughter, d. young.
2nd Wife: 2372. ALEXANDER, b. 6 Aug. 1842, d.
1905, md. 1867 SUSAN ELLEN
JENKINS, Civil War Service.
2373. SARAH, b. 1844, md. _____
JOHNSON. Moved to Manhatten,
Kansas.
2374. WILLIAM, b. 1842, d. 1887,
Civil War Service. 31st Me.
Vol. Inf.

1256. **WILLIAM ROWELL** [RICE 637] He was born 22
Mar. 1819 in Maine and died 28 Jan. 1902. He
married 20 Mar. 1842 **MARY ELLEN BARTLETT**. She
born 1822. Occ. ship caulker. 1850 census at So.
Thomaston, Me. Moved to Ohio.

Children: 2400. **ADELPHUS**, b. 12 Feb. 1843, d.
14 Jan. 1912, unmd at Ord,
Nebr.
2401. **ALMENEZER C.**, b. 5 Apr. 1845,
d. 10 Nov. 1919, md. 28 Dec.
1871 in Ohio **MARTHA SPOONER**.
No children.
2402. **FRANK B.**, b. 12 May 1847, d.
1916 or 1940, md. 1 Dec.
1910 **MAUD PHILBRICK**. No ch.
2403. **RICE**, b. 12 Jan. 1852, d. 29
Oct. 1852.
2404. **HENRY S.**, b. 17 Nov. 1853, d.
2 Dec. 1853.
2405. **NELLIE**, b. 21 Sep. 1856, d. 30
Mar. 1915, md. 21 Oct. 1882
MINGERSON COOMBS, 2 ch.
2406. **MARGARET D.**, b. 1 Nov. 1858,
d. 23 Dec. 1901, md. 5 Aug.
1883 **EDWARD BOYER**, 2 ch.
2407. **MARY E.**, b. 1856.

1260. **WARREN RAYBURN ROWELL** [RICE 637] He was
born 24 Oct. 1829 and died 24 Oct. 1894. He
married 8 Apr. 1852 **HANNAH ANN FALES**. Res.
Thomaston, Me.

Children: 2420. **AVA**, b. 30 Mar. 1853, d. 26
May 1855.
2421. **WARREN RAYBURN Jr.**, b. 18 Feb.
1856, d. 28 Mar. 1932, unmd.
2422. **NATHAN CLIFFORD**, b. 27 Apr.
1857, d. 29 Mar. 1873 unmd.
2423. **MABEL ATWOOD**, b. 3 Oct. 1865,
d. 1951/2, unmd.
2424. **ETHAN ALLEN**, b. 17 Feb. 1876,
d. 1952, unmd.

ROWELL FAMILY - NEW ENGLAND
8th Generation

1261. LUTHER HAYDEN ROWELL [RICE 637] He was
born 19 Nov. 1834 at Thomaston, Me. and died 18
May 1917. He married 27 May 1856 SARAH WHITTIER
MATTHEWS of Lincoln. She died 10 Sep. 1887 [43-
8-13]. Res. Thomaston, Maine.

Children: 2430. FRED RICE, b. 29 Dec. 1856, d.
               27 Apr. 1904, md. 16 Jan.
               1884 MARY FLORANCE STETSON.
               No children.
           2431. IDA MAY, b. 10 May 1859, d. 2
               Oct. 1907, md. 17 Mar. 1885
               WILLIAM CROSBY. No children.
           2432. MARK EDWIN, b. 15 Sep. 1863,
               d. 15 Sep. 1939, md. 19 Feb.
               1883 ALICE MAY SNOW.
           2433. SARAH ELIZA, b. 10 Jan. 1871,
               d. 6 Jan. 1875.
           2434. RALPH ROBERT, b.24 Apr. 1880,
               m.1, 8 June 1905 ELLA G.
               NEWELL, divorced, m.2, 1929
               MABEL McKAY.

1271. ENOCH C. ROWELL [ENOCH 642] He was born
18 Oct. 1835 at Plainfield, N.H. and died 28
June 1900. He married VIOLA ROWELL [#1266]
Daughter of WILLIAM & SALLY (LEAVITT) ROWELL.
She born 23 Sep. 1837 and died 16 June 1914.
Came to Albany, Vt. in 1851. Capt. 1st Vt. Reg't
Militia Aug. 1866. Res. Albany, Vt.

Children: 2438. WILLIAM OWEN, b. 1865, State
               Legislatur 1900.
           2439. CAROLINE VIOLA, b. 20 Aug.
               1860.
           2440. MARY V., b. 15 May 1869.

1274. GUY ELBRIDGE ROWELL [DANIEL 646?] He was
born 21 May 1818 at Albany, Vt. He married 28
Jan. 1846 BETSY C. PAGE. She born c1826.
Selectman 1849-1850, 1857 & 1865. Occ. farmer.
1850 Census at Albany, Vt.

ROWELL FAMILY - NEW ENGLAND
8th Generation

Children: 2442. ORVILLE, b. c1847.
           2443. WALLACE, b. Feb. 1850.
           2444. CARRIE FLORANCE, b. 5 Aug.
                 1859, md. 1 Nov. 1884 JAMES
                 BUNKER at Nashua, N.H.
           2445. NELLIE M., b. 4 June 1865, md.
                 15 June 1895 EDWARD C. GOULD
           2446. child, b. 17 Apr. 1862.
           2447. IRENE B., b. 15 Apr. 1868.
           2448. WILLIAM W., b. 14 May 1852,
                 md. MARY HESTER 8 ch.

1275. ENOCH ROWELL [DANIEL 646] He was born 18
July 1821 in N.H. and died 7 July 1886 intestate
at Albany, Vt. [Prob. Ct. 5:2344]. He married
first CAROLINE LEAVITT, d/o NATHANIEL & DEBORAH
LEAVITT. She died 13 April 1869 [49-9] at
Albany, Vt. He married 2nd 20 Oct. 1869 ROXANNA
F. NORCROSS. Buried in Rowell Cem. at Albany.
1850 Census at Albany, Vt.

Children: 2449. EUGENE, b. 1848.

1291. K. WILLIAM ROWELL [ELIPHELET 651] He was
born 1830 and died 14 March 1870 [39-9] He
married 29 Nov. 1855 LOIS P. ROWELL [# ??] She
born 22 June 1838 and died 16 Sep. 1927. Will
Orleans District Court 4:987. Res. Albany, Vt.

Children: 2450. WELMA E., b. 21 Mar. 1857.
           2451. EDWARD EVERETT, b. 20 May
                 1865, d. 28 May 1894, md. 25
                 Nov. 1891 INEZ E. THOMPSON.
           2452. MARY L., b. Nov. 1867.

1292. TYLER ROWELL [ELIPHELET 651] He was born
17 July 1832 and died 19 Feb. 1902 intestate at
Albany, Vt. [Prob. Ct. 8:4433]. He married 1
June 1855 ISABELLA ANDERSON. She born 26 June
1833 and died 16 Jan. 1921.

ROWELL FAMILY - NEW ENGLAND
8th Generation

Children: 2454. **EDNA JANE**, b. 20 Sep. 1865, d.
18 Sep. 1866.

1293. **WILLARD CONVERSE ROWELL** [CONVERSE 652] He
was born 10 Jan. 1830. He married 6 Jan. 1883 at
Albany, Vt. **LAUELLA PRIEST**.

Children: 2455. **ENOCH JOHN**, b. 6 Jan. 1886, d.
1938, md. 5 Oct. 1922
MILDRED A. BROWN. 4 ch.
2456. **FRANK PLUMBY**, b. 14 Feb. 1888,
md. **GEORGIANNE** _____.
2457. **JOHN**,

1296. Major **ELIPHELET ROWELL** [ABIJAH 658] He was
born 28 May 1822 at Livermore, Maine and died 31
Oct. 1903 in Minn. He married 2 Dec. 1844 **ELLEN
FRANCES SMITH**, d/o Capt. **SAMUEL SMITH** at
Kennebec. She born 22 June 1826 and died 27 Oct.
1876. Occ. printer. Published "Hallowell
Gazette". Served as Paymaster of Army during the
Civil War. Appointed by Lincoln. Post Master 12
years. Mayor of Hollawell 1890. Baptist. Res.
Hallowell and Kennebec, Me.

Children: 2458. **GEORGE SMITH**, b. 12 Mar. 1846,
md. 27 Mar. 1871 **LYDIA E.
GALLAGHER**.
2459. **EDMUND P.**, b. 13 Apr. 1848.
2460. **LIZZIE F/W.**, b. 30 Aug. 1850.
2461. **EMELINE P.**, b. 3 Aug. 1854.
2462. **ELLEN F.**, b. 30 Aug. 1857, d.
25 Mar. 1886.
2463. **WILLIAM W.**, b. 20 Feb. 1861,
md. 11 Sep. 1885 **FLORANCE M.
JOHNSON**. Went to Minn.
2464. **LILLIE P.**, b. 3 Aug. 1868.

1298. **EDWIN W. ROWELL** [ABIJAH 658] He was born
c1835 at East Livermore, Me. He married 26 July
1864 **ARAXZENE I. BRACKET**, d/o **SAMUEL & LOUISE
(INGRAHAM) BRACKET**. Baptists. Res. Lewiston, Me.

Children: 2465. IVY LOUISE, b. 11 Feb. 1875,
            md. FRED W. HILTON.

1300. SAMUEL ROWELL [SAMUEL 663] He was born 30
May 1808 at Chester, N.H. and died 28 Oct. 1883
at Lancaster, N.H. He married 15 Jan. 1834
CAROLINE EVELINE PAGE, d/o ENOS & ASENETH PAGE.
She born 23 Dec. 1814 at W. Concord, Vt. Occ.
farmer, cotton mill employee. Res. Concord, Vt.,
Manchester 1845, So. Natick 1862, later Milford,
Mass.

Children: 2470. HARRIET MOORE, b. 22 Dec.
                  1834, d. 1917, md. HORACE A.
                  WHITE. No children.
            2471. BERNICE ADALINE, b. 27 Sep.
                  1836, d. 1917, md. 11 Jan.
                  1859 HENRY O. KENT. 2 ch.
            2472. GEORGE PRESBURY, b. 4 July
                  1838, d. 1918, m.1, 1862
                  SARAH B. EASTMAN, m.2, 1891
                  JEANETTE RIGNEY HALLACK.
                  Res. New York City.
            2473. PERSIS ANN, b. 22 Mar. 1840,
                  d. 1918-1919, md. 28 May
                  1874 Dr. FREDERICK P.
                  MARVIN. No children.

1301. WILLIAM ROWELL [SAMUEL 663] He was born
1811 at Chester, N.H. and died 1891. He married
23 Feb. 1841 ABIGAIL CHAFFEE at Chelmsford. She
born 1822. Occ. farmer. Res. Concord, Vt. and
Lancaster, N.H. 1850 census at Amesbury, Vt.

Children: 2485. EMILY, b. c1841.
            2486. CELIA BELINDA, b. 27 June
                  1843, md. 17 Dec. 1866
                  PHILATUS H. EASTMAN

1302. JAMES CALDWELL ROWELL [SAMUEL 663] He was
born 17 Dec. 1813 at Chester, N.H. He married
14 Nov. 1842 ANN POOR, d/o WILLIAM & ANN
(TRAVERS) POOR. She born 6 June 1818 at
Branfield, Me. She died 8 Sep. 1886. Occ.
farmer. Res. Lowell, Mass., Concord, Manchester
and Littleton, N.H. Gave church bell 1900 at
Littleton. Republican. Unitarian Church.

Children: 2488. MELISSA ANN, b. 30 Jan. 1844,
                     d. 23 Jan. 1846.
            2489. ELIZABETH A., b. 5 May 1848,
                     md. 19 June 1869 LUTHER DOW
                     SANBORN.
            2490. JAMES HERBERT, b. 29 Sep.
                     1850, d. 12 Nov. 1866.
            2491. CAROLINE LUVIA, b. 6 May 1855,
                     md. JOHN A. FOGG.

1303. JOHN PAGE ROWELL [SAMUEL 663] He was born
1816 at Waterford, Vt. He married 1850 RUTH M.
BARNES of Graveton and Portage, N.Y. In 1837 he
walked to Ohio with 2 brothers. He returned.

Children: 2495. HIRAM VANDALIA, b. 1851, md.
                     1875 MARY A. GREENWOOD.
            2496. MARY E., md. _____ GARDNER.

1304. GEORGE WASHINGTON ROWELL [SAMUEL 663] He
was born 1819 at Lyndon, Vt. and died 1898. He
married 1844 MARCIA A. CHADBURN. She born c1823.
Served in Civil War 1861-1865 as Pvt. in N.Y.,
moved to Wisconsin and in 1873 to Kinsley,
Kansas, then to Great Bend, KS. As a youth he
spent 6 years on a whaling cruise. Occ. farmer.
1850 Census at Lyman, Hancock Co., Maine.

Children: 2497. RODNEY, d. infancy.
            2498. CHARLES HENRY, b. 1846, d.
                     1864 Civil War.

ROWELL FAMILY - NEW ENGLAND
8th Generation

2499. EDWARD ALONZO, b. 1848, d.
1896, md. 1870 JANETTE H.
CROSS.
2500. MARY E., md. _____ SOWARDS.

1306. FREDERICK ROWELL [SAMUEL 663] He was born
11 June 1820 at Kirby, Vt. and died 9 Dec. 1899
at Whitefield. He married 29 Jan. 1846 at
Manchester ROSELINE A. BANFILL. Occ. farmer and
store keeper. Went to Boston in 1857 then to
Nadick, Mass. in 1865. In 1871 moved to
Whitefield, N.H. 1850 Census at Concord, Vt.

Children: 2501. ELIZABETH MELISSA, d. infancy.
2502. CHARLES EMERY, b. 2 May 1849,
d. 1904, md. ARLETTA E.
BOLLES.
2503. CLARA LILLIAN, b. 12 Jan.
1851, md. 10 Aug. 1870
CHARLES B. EASTMAN.
2504. EDWARD EVERETT, b. 28 Oct.
1853, m.1, 1870 ELLA
WILBARD or WILLARD, m.2,
1892 ADELINE SKELDING.
2505. MARIETTA A., md. _____
EASTMAN.
2506. ALICE M.,
2507. BERTHA E., md. _____ THAYER.

1317. CHARLES HARVEY ROWELL [DUSTIN 665] He was
born 1820 at Lyndon, Vt. and died 1872. He
married 1847 ANN HEMINGWAY. He graduated from
Dartmouth in 1845. Occ. Doctor. Res. of Maine.
1850 Census at Hancock, Me.

Children: 2540. CHARLES S., b. 1849, md. 21
May 1890 FRANCES S. ALLEN.
2541. EDWARD, d. infancy.
2542. ALONZO, b. 1854, single 1898
in California.
2543. JULIA, md. _____ LORD.

1321. CHARLES WESLEY ROWELL [JAMES C. 669] He was born 1820 at Chester, N.H. and died 16 April 1894 at Manchester. He married 20 June 1847 SARAH B. HAMMOND. Occ. farmer. In 1849 went to Calif but returned in 1851 to Manchester, N.H.

Children: 2560. CHARLES WILLIAM, b. 1852, m.1, 25 Sep. 1876 MARY E. STARKE, div. 1 June 1894, m.2, 1895 ADELINE PINGREE.
2561. HERBERT SIDNEY, b. 1854, md. 1896 BESSIE GREEN.
2562. CLARA L., b. 1858, md. 30 Oct. 1879 FRANK B. KNOWLTON.
2563. LOIS ALMA, d. infancy.
2564. GRACE L., md. _____ GARLAND.
2565. JAMES FRANCIS, b. 1868, unmd 1891.
2566. HENRY IRVING, b. 24 Aug. 1870, md. 1891 MARGARET B. MADDON.

1327. JOHN LORD ROWELL [JOHN P. 670] He was born 20 Apr. 1821 at Chester, N.H. and died 1853. He married 7 Oct. 1847 BETSY C. SARGENT. Occ. grocery business and cotton mill employee. Res. 1847 Hooksett, 1850 to Manchester, N.H. His estate 2 Aug. 1853 [v.54, p. 382] CHARLES STARK app. Admin. widow and bro. EPHRAIM declined. JOHN SARGENT named guardian of ELLA FRANCES minor. Inv. $1864.56 personel property and $1400 house, land and stable. 1850 census at Manchester, N.H.

Children: 2580. ELLEN FRANCES (ELLA F.?), b. 25 Oct. 1848, md. _____ PULSIFER.
2581. HENRY GAULT, d. infancy.

1328. EPHRAIM KELLEY ROWELL [JOHN P. 670] He was born 21 Nov. 1822 at Hooksett, N.H. and died 5 Oct. 1896. He married 27 Apr. 1847 MARY AMANDA DAVIS, d/o ROBERT & LUCINDA (GOULD) DAVIS. She born 30 May 1827 at Hooksett and died 30 Sep. 1892 at Manchester, N.H. In 1842 he moved to

Manchester. Active in business next 24 years.
Real estate. He occupied the family homestead
after 1876. Democrat. Some sources say he
married **AMANDA SMITH**. Occ. "restorator." 1850
census at Manchester, N.H.

Children: 2585. **ROLAND**, b. 22 Feb. 1849, d.
                  16 Nov. 1906, md. 5 Sep.
                  1883 **SARAH ALIDA CROSBY**.
            2586. **CHARLES EDGAR**, b. 1851.

1337. **SILOAM/SILVANUS ROWELL** [JOSEPH 683] He was
born 4 Nov. 1804. He married. Res. Grand Isle,
Me. Occ. cabinet maker. 1850 census at Weld, Me.

Children: 2589. **SAVELLE**, (f), b. 1842.
            2590. **JAMES P.**, b. 1848.

1345. **NATHAN PALMER ROWELL** [JOSEPH 683] He was
born 24 Sep. 1824 at Bow, N.H. and died 1882. He
married **MARY S. KITTREDGE**, d/o **Rev. JAMES
KITTREDGE** of Weld, Me. Occ. Baptist minister.

Children: 2591. **JAMES FRANK**, b. 21 Dec. 1852,
                  DDS, md. 4 Mar. 1877 **ABBIE
                  J. KENNEDY**.
            2592. **CHARLES F.**,

1365. **AMASSY ROWELL** [PERLEY M. 691] He was born
3 Aug. 1822 at Hamliton Co., N.Y. and died at
sea on way to California during the gold rush on
S.S. McKinnon 8 Dec. 1851. He married 1848
MARTHA McCOY of Vt.

Children: 2593. **WILLIAM EDWIN**, b. 9 Jan.
                  1850, md. 31 Oct. 1872
                  SUSAN WORDEN.
            2594. **CHARLES PITT**,
            2595. **MARY**,

1366. **PERLEY MASON ROWELL** [PERLEY M. 691] He was
born 1822. He married **EMILY LOUISE FARGO**. Res.
Owosso, Mich.

Children: 2596. HARRIET PHEBE, md. FRANCIS
                  LABODIE.

1380. RANSON ROWELL [ELIJAH 705] He was born
c1833 at Clarksville, N.H. He married 28 Dec.
1850 HARRIET FRENCH.   She born c1831. Occ.
shoemaker. Res. Rummy, N.H. and Albany, Vt.

Children: 2597. ALVAH R/B., b. 15 Dec. 1850/1.
            2598. MARY C., b. 24 Sep. 1852.
            2599. SARAH J., b. c1856.
            2600. LAURA B., b. c1858.
            2601. FRANK W., b. c1859.

1384. RUFUS ROWELL [ELIJAH 705]   He was born
c1803 and died 14 Dec. 1881. He married 13 Feb.
1834 BETSY E. PRESCOTT. She born c1805 and died
1 Jan. 1864 at Corinth, Vt. [57-9]. Possibly
married 2nd 1865 MARIE C. UNDERWOOD. She born 10
Sep. 1824 and died 5 Sep. 1905. Occ. farmer.
1850 Census at Bradley, Vt.

Children: 2602. WILLIAM H,, b. 2 Nov. 1836.
            2603. ADELPHUS P., b. 13 Nov. 1834,
                  d. 1910, md. 26 Nov. 1854
                  ANNE E. THUMBER.
            2604. ORANGE, b. 19 Mar. 1840, d.
                  1903, md. ALMA/ALVINE _____.
            2605. BYRON, b. 23 Sep. 1842.
            2606. ERASTUS N., b. 27 Jan. 1846.
            2607. LYDIA ANN, b. 30 Aug. 1848, d.
                  13 Jan. 1864 [15-4].

1385. AARON ROWELL [AARON 706] He was born 18
Feb. or July 1803 at Weare, N.H. Perhaps same
at Springfield, N.H. in 1850 Census. Had wife
BETSEY born c1803. Occ. shoemaker.

Children: 2608. JACOB, b. c1827.
            2609. JESSE, b. c1829.
            2610. AUGUSTUS, b. c1835.
            2611. RICHARD, b. c1839.
            2612. BETSY J., b. c1841.

1396. JOHN ROWELL [ROBERT 709] He was born at
Corinth, Vt. He married 31 Dec. 1837 ELIZA BUCK.
Res. Tunbridge, Vt.

Children: 2613. ERASTUS B., b. 8 Jan. 1832, d.
            1 Apr. 1895, md. FRANCELIA
            ATKINS.

1405. BENJAMIN GREELEY ROWELL [MOSES 736] He was
born 2 May 1815. Probably married ABIGAIL A.
MASON. Res. Mineral, Bureau Co., Illinois.

Children: 2614. JOHN M., b. 6 Apr. 1846.
            2615. HENRIETTA A., b. 22 Aug. 1849.
            2616. JAMES ROBY, b. 17 June 1852.
            2617. BENJAMIN GREELEY, b. 27 Aug.
            1857.
            2618. ADDIE H., b. 10 Mar. 1869.

1407. MOSES W. ROWELL [MOSES 736] He was born 15
May 1821. He married 17 June 1847 ELIZA H.
DURKEE. Res. Andover, N.H.

Children: 2619. ALDORA J., b. 1851.
            2620. GEORGE A., b. 1858.
            2621. ARTHUR J., b. 21 Sep. 1863.

1410. JOHN HIRAM ROWELL [JOHN 737] He was born
1818. He married 1 June 1843 MARTHA A.
BATCHELDER at Hooksett, N.H. She born about
1821. Occ. iron founder. 1850 census at
Franklin, N.H.

Children: 2622. CLARA ELIZABETH, b. 7 Apr.
            1846.
            2623. MARY ANN, b. 28 Oct. 1854.
            2624. CHARLIE HIRAM, b. 14 Mar.
            1857.

1412. WILLIAM LYMAN ROWELL [JOHN 737] He was
born 1828. He married 1854/5 CAROLINE ARAVESTA
BROWN, d/o JOSEPH & BETSY BROWN. She born 22
June 1836 at Chester, Vt. and died 6 Jan. 1916
[79-7-14] at Franklin. Res. Franklin.

ROWELL FAMILY - NEW ENGLAND
8th Generation

Children: 2625. WILLIAM C., b. 6 Aug. 1857,
                  md. MINA SWALLOW.
            2626. CHARLES GUY, b. 18 Nov. 1863,
                  m.1, DOLLE E. BEAN, m.2,
                  LETTIE MAY BROWN.

1416. JOHN ROWELL [JOHN 741] He was born 1798.
He married 17 Sep. 1820 or 4 March 1822 DEBORAH
SMITH. 1850 census at Brentwood, N.H. with wife
HANNAH (b. c1798).

Children: 2627. SMITH A., b. 1828.
            2628. ELLEN M., b. 1836.
            2629. DEBORAH, b. 1838.
            2630. JOHN, b. 1845.

1417. JAMES ROWELL [JOHN 741] He was born 1796
and died before 1850. He married 11 May 1823
LOIS VARNEY, d/o HUMPHRY & ELIZABETH (PIERCE)
VARNEY. She born 6 Mar. 1801.   Owned land in
Exeter. Estate Admin. by JOHN ROWELL [v.80, p.
28] Res. Brentwood and Exeter, N.H. Widow in
1850 census at Brentwood, N.H.

Children: 2640. ANNE E., b. c1824.
            2641. REBECCA, b. c1828.
            2642. CATHERINE P., b. c1833.
            2643. JAMES R., b. c1839.
            2644. EMMA J., b. c1846.
            2645. CHARLES C., b. 1849.

1421. ISAAC ROWELL [JOHN 741] He was born 1805
and died 21 Dec. 1868 at Brentwood, N.H.   Name
of wife was ELLEN. She born c1805 in N.H.   1850
census at Brentwood, N.H.

Children: 2650. ADALINE, b. c1832.
            2651. MARY E., b. c1835.
            2652. ISAAC H., b. c1840.
            2653. ADDISON, b. c1845.
            2654. FRANK, b. 30 Nov. 1846, d. 8
                  Apr. 1933, md. MARY
                  GARLAND.

1422. **JACOB H. ROWELL** [JOHN 741] He was born 4
Dec. 1807 at Brentwood, N.H. and died 23 Nov.
1883. He married 28 Mar. 1832 **EVELINE H.
ROBINSON**. She born 8 Sep. 1807 at Wolfborough,
N.H. and died 1 July 1842. He married second 26
Nov. 1842 **EMERETT PRESCOTT**. She born 18 Dec.
1823 at Newport, Me. and died 26 Jan. 1890 or 24
Jan. 1896.

Children: 2670. **ELMIRA ADALINE**, b. 14 June
1834, d. 31 Jan. 1923, md.
May 1865 **HARRY WILLIAMS**.
2671. **JOHN EDWIN**, b. 25 Jan. 1838,
d. 31 May 1920, md. 24 Apr.
1861 **MARIETTA FRENCH**. She d.
1929.
2672. **ANGELIA MARCELLA**, b. 21 Jan.
1842, d. 10 May 1904, md. 20
Feb. 1859 **WILSON HOOK**.
2673. **ABBIE S.**, b. 6 Nov. 1849, d.
19 May 1870, md. 13 Aug.
1868 **SUMNER GRAVES**.

1423. **CHARLES LEWIS ROWELL** [JOHN 741] He was
born 1810. He married 14 Oct. 1834 or 22 Sep.
1835 **MARY ANN SANBORN**, d/o **JOHN & HANNAH (HOYT)
SANBORN**. She died 3 Jan. 1885 [67 yr]   Res.
Amesbury, Mass.

Children: 2691. **CHARLES E.**, b. 8 Mar. 1836.
2692. **LAURA F.**, b. 6 Oct. 1837.
2693. **JOHN SANDBOURN**, b. 5 Oct.
1842.
2694. **ALDEN AUGUSTUS**, b. 20 Mar.
1846.
2695. **MARY AUGUSTUS**, b. 13 Oct.
1848.

1424. **ADDISON S. ROWELL** [JOHN 741] He was born
1813 and died 27 Dec. 1871. He married 11 Jan.
1835 at Brentwood **ELIZA B. SHUTE**. She born
c1814. Owned land in Exeter and Poplin, N.H. in
1847. Occ. farmer. 1850 census at Brentwood,
N.H.

Children: 2698. AMBROSE, b. 1835, d. 22 Nov.
1885, md. MARY A. GORDON.
2699. MIRIAM, b. c1838.
2700. JOHN SHUTE, b. 7 Mar. 1842,
md. 15 Feb. 1864 ROSELVINA
BELKNAP.
2701. ADDISON, b. c1850.

1426. JOHN WINSLOW ROWELL [ENOCH 747] He was
born 3 Mar. 1803 and died 1864 at Loudon, N.H.
He married MARTHA LORD STEVENS, d/o NATHANIEL &
BETSY (SMITH) STEVENS. She born 18 Sep. 1822 at
Stratham, N.H. and died 5 June 1891 at Lynn,
Mass. Occ. cordwainer. 1850 census at Lynn,
Mass. [one source says he married 17 May 1835 at
N. Hampton, N.H. SARAH STEVENS]

Children: 2702. JOHN B., b. 1828.
2703. SARAH E., b. 1836.
2704. EMILY J., b. 1840.
2705. NATHANIEL J., b. 1841.
2706. ENOCH P., b. 1843.
2707. BENJAMIN, b. 1844.
2708. BENJAMIN WINSLOW, b. 18 Aug.
1845, d. 22 Aug. 1927, md. 5
Dec. 1871 SUSAN A. NEWHALL.
2709. JOSEPH W., b. 1847.
2710. ALBERT P., b. 1848.

1427. JOSEPH MASON ROWELL [ENOCH P. 747] He was
born 2 Aug. 1817. He married 30 Dec. 1840 MARY
ANN JOHNSON at Lynn, Mass. He married 2nd 15
Jan. 1854 SARAH JANE CLEVELAND. Occ. cordwainer.
1850 census. Res. Lynn, Mass.

Children: 2712. HARRIET NEWHALL, b. 9 Apr.
1842.
2713. MARY ANN, b. 26 Feb. 1845.
2714. SARAH IRENE, b. 9 July 1847.
2715. FRANCES ADELAIDE, b. 3 Oct.
1848.
2716. WINSLOW H/J., b. 3 Feb. 1853,
md. 17 Nov. 1875 CARRIE
MATILDA FELT in Lowell, MA.

by 2nd wife:
  2717. **ELTON CLEVELAND**, b. 3 Mar.
   1861.
  2718. **WALTER ADAMS**, b. 8 Dec. 1868.

1429. **DAVID SPAULDING ROWELL** [DAVID 750] He was
born 9 Apr. 1795 and died 29 Mar. 1879. He
married 16 Apr. 1826 **RACHEL JEWETT**, d/o **JAMES &
MIRIAM (WALKER) JEWETT**. She born 15 Mar. 1804 at
Solon, Me. and died 29 Mar. 1879 at Madison, Me.
Occ. farmer. 1850 census at Madison, Me.

Children: 2719. **DAVID JEWETT**, b. 1 Mar. 1827,
      d. 28 Aug. 1905, md. 21 Sep.
      1857 **MARY PLUMMER**.
    2720. **SALLY**, b. 17 Jan. 1829, d. 27
      Feb. 1859, md. **MILTON
      LANGLEY**. 1 child.
    2721. **JAMES GREEN**, b. 5 Mar. 1831,
      d. 1 Nov. 1899, md. 25 Apr.
      1856 **JANE S. HAMBLETT**.
    2722. **FLAVIS L.**, b. 25 May 1833,
      d.y.
    2723. **EDWARD**, b. 18 Oct. 1835, d. 3
      Jan. 1857.
    2724. **WILLIAM HARRISON**, b. 1838, d.
      12 Jan. 1842.
    2725. **ALBERT**, b. 7 Mar. 1841, d. 21
      Oct. 1919, md. 12 Mar. 1873
      CARRIE KINCAID. (1857-1939)
    2726. **WILLIAM HENRY**, b. 11 Jan.
      1843, d. 25 Apr. 1916, m.1,
      16 May 1891 **ABBIE F. BROWN**,
      (1849-1903), m.2, **LYMA
      PRESCOTT** (1864-1940).
    2727. **NELSON**, b. 4 Aug. 1846, d.
      1939, md. 18 Jan. 1886 **LAURA
      F. POTTER** (1853-1935). Had:
      VIVIAN, d.y.

1432. **ISAAC ROWELL** [DAVID 750] He was born 23
Mar. 1800 and died 4 Feb. 1874. He married
RACHEL MONTGOMERY, d/o **ROBERT & JANE MONTGOMERY**.

She born 1807 and died 1868. Occ. farmer. 1850
census at Madison, Maine.

Children: 2730. **JOHN W.**, b. 1834, d. 1868.
           2731. infant,
           2732. infant,
           2733. **SARAH M.**, b. 11 June 1842, d.
                  28 Sep. 1911.
           2734. **ELLEN**, b. 26 Aug. 1844, d. 1
                  Sep. 1884, md. **THOMAS
                  GRAVES.** 3 children.
           2735. **MYRA**, b. 17 Aug. 1846, d. 16
                  June 1929, md. 15 Sep. 1885
                  MELVILLE ARNOLD.
           2736. **GEORGE W.**, b. 15 Dec. 1848, d.
                  2 Mar. 1921, md. **ETTA SMITH**
                  (1861-1924)
           2737. **WILLIAM**, b. 7 Feb. 1853, d. 18
                  Jan. 1918, md. 30 Dec. 1884
                  ZETTA E. SOULE.

1436. **WASHINGTON ROWELL** [DAVID 750] He was born
16 Mar. 1808 Madison, Me. and died 8 Feb. 1864.
He married **MARY SMITH.** She born c1816 in Me. and
died 1866. 1850 census at Skowhagen, Maine.

Children: 2740. **MARY**, b. 12 May 1841, d. 15
                  May 1923, m.1, **EUGENE
                  TAYLOR**, m.2, **GEORGE W.
                  BEAN.**
           2741. **JANE/JENNIE E.**, b. 28 Aug.
                  1842, md. 1 July 1865 **DENNIS
                  LOWELL.** Res. Florida.
           2742. **ELLEN MARIA**, b. 29 Jan. 1844,
                  d. 22 July 1933, md. 10 Oct.
                  1863 **ABRAM L. LORD.** 4 ch.
           2743. **SARAH**, b. 20 Mar. 1845, d. 22
                  Dec. 1860.
           2744. **OLIVE**, b. 5 May 1846, md. 23
                  Nov. 1875 **FRANK M. COTTON.** 1
                  child.

2745. **SIMON M.**, b. 28 Apr. 1847, d.
10 Feb. 1936, md. 12 Oct.
1873 **JENNIE E. POTTLE.**
(1852-1930)
2746. **DAVID**, b. 23 Aug. 1848, d. 7
Jan. 1861.
2747. **HIRAM CHENEY**, b. 25 May 1850,
d. 18 Nov. 1941, md. 8 Mar.
1876 **ADA E. BLODGETT.**
2748. **FRANK**, b. 15 May 1852, d. 15
Oct. 1925.
2749. **LESTER ALBERT**, b. 23 Sep.
1854, d. 26 Apr. 1897, md. 9
Jan. 1889 **MINA BELLE LESLIE.**
2750. **EUGENE**, b. 17 June 1858, d. 24
Oct. 1884.
2751. **FRED**, b. 8 Feb. 1860, unmd.
Res. California.

1440. **DANIEL ROWELL [JOB 753]** He was born 1804
at Manchester, N.H. and died 1840. He married
1829 **HANNAH STEVENS** of Manchester. Occ. farmer.
Res. Manchester on Black Brook Rd.

Children: 2753. **ABBIE MARIA**, b. 1830, md.
_____ **CALDWELL.**
2754. **JAMES S.**, b. 1831, d. 1858,
md. **EMILY MARTIN.**
2755. **CHARLES DINSMORE**, b. 1833, d.
1910, md. 1862 **ELIZABETH
MARTIN.**
2756. **GEORGE**, b. 1835, d. young.
2757. **SARAH JANE**, b. 1837, d. young.
2758. **HENRY S.**, b. 1839.

1441. **JOSEPH MELCHOIR ROWELL [JOB 753]** He was
born 11 Apr. 1807 at Manchester and died 1894.
Attended 1828 Pinkerton Acadamy at Derry, N.H.
Had wife named **JANETT.** She born 1810. Occ.
teacher at Amoskeag Falls, Deputy Sheriff in
1850 at Manchester, N.H. Res. Falmouth, Me. and
Ottumwa, Illinois in 1854.

Children: 2760. **MARY J.**, b. 1834.

2761. ABBY, b. 1837.
2762. ELLEN, b. 1840.
2763. JOSEPH F., b. 1841, d. 1892,
      md. 1872 MARY F. ROCKWELL,
      2 children.

1448. LEONARD ROWELL [JOB 753] He was born 7
June 1820 at Manchester, N.H. and died 1883. He
married 1844 ANN STUART RAY of Dunbarton, N.H.
She born 12 May 1821 at Hopkinton. Went west a
few years but returned to Manchester. Occ.
contractor, builder till 1871. Became station
agent at Goffstown, N.H. till his death. Res. at
Dunbarton and Goffstown. 1850 census at
Dunbarton, N.H.

Children: 2765. NANCY POLLARD, 2 Jan. 1847, d.
                 1866, unmd.
           2766. HIRAM DAVIS, b. 28 Dec. 1849,
                 d. 1878, unmd.
           2767. WALTER AARON, b. 1856, d. 10
                 June 1879, unmd.
           2768. ANNE MARIA, b. 26 Apr. 1857,
                 d. 23 Oct. 1883, unmd.
           2769. HENRY LEONARD, b. 1861, md.
                 1888 NELLIE L. HADLEY.
           2770. WILLIAM STINSON, b. Sep. 1863,
                 d. 1917, md. CORA RICHARDS.

1450. JOHN ROWELL [ISAAC 754] He was born 22
Nov. 1799 in N.H. and died 10 Dec. 1870. He
married first MARY HUFF. She born 1806 and died
25 Nov. 1869. He married second Mrs. HANNAH
BACON, widow of JOSIAH BACON. She died 3 Dec.
1877 [77-11] All children by 1st wife.

Children: 2780. LORENZO D., b. Mar. 1830, d.
                 14 Apr. 1866, md. Mrs. SARAH
                 GILMAN. Had: MIRTIE F., d.y.
           2781. JOHN ORLANDO, b. 1831, d. 9
                 Jan. 1899, md. JANE (JENNIE)
                 MITCHELL.
           2782. ALMYRA, b. 1834, d. 19 June
                 1855.

2783. **CHARLES W.**, b. 4 Dec. 1835,
d. 20 Nov. 1907, md. **ROSE
ANN STARBIRD.**

2784. **ALFRED**, b. Mar. 1837, d. 27
Oct. 1858.

2785. **KESIAH**, b. 22 May 1839, d. 4
Dec. 1912, md. **JOHN FURBUSH.**
3 children.

2786. **LYMAN**, b. 1841, moved to
Calif. Had: **MILLARD.**

2787. **THOMAS BARTON**, b. 6 Aug. 1843,
d. 10 June 1913, md. **HARRIET
N. WHEELER.**

2788. **LIZZIE H.**, b. 1 Feb. 1846, d.
9 Aug. 1870.

2789. **ABBY**, b. 17 June 1848, d. 26
Nov. 1870.

1458. **DAVID ROWELL** [ISAAC 754] He was born 27
May 1819 and died 1 Feb. 1894. He married first
27 Dec. 1843 **MARTHA JANE LITTLEFORD.** She died 5
Oct. 1864. He married second 16 Sep. 1865 **MARY
F. AYERS.**

Children: 2800. **CAROLINE PRESCOTT**, b. 9 Nov.
1845, md. 13 Jan. 1863
WILLIAM A. TOWLE. 2 ch.

2801. **CLARA FLORANCE**, b. 27 Oct.
1848, d. 20 Mar. 1931, m.1,
HENRY HURLBUT, m.2, **BURLEIGH
SALISBURY.** 1 child.

2802. **MARIBAH ELLA**, b. 28 Mar. 1852,
md. 30 Oct. 1877 **JOSEPH F.
IRELAND.** 1 ch. Res. Minn.

1459. **FREDERICK ROWELL** [ZEBEDEE 755] He was born
5 Oct. 1801 at Dracot, Maine and died 12 Feb.
1853 at Solon, Me. He married first 26 March
1829 **SOPHIA WOOD.** She born 8 July 1809 and died
28 March 1878. She married 2nd, 1 Nov. 1854
JAMES M. WILDER. She married 3rd, 19 Nov. 1867
WILLIAM BURGESS of Fairfield. She died 30 Nov.
1875. Probably town clerk 1849 at Hartland, Me.
Res. Solon, Me.

ROWELL FAMILY - NEW ENGLAND
8th Generation

Children: 2805. SYBIL S., d. 1869, md. 1855
SEXTUS HEBERT (1832-1868).
1 child.
2806. ABEL W., b. 12 Mar. 1832, d. 5
Oct. 1909, m.1 26 Mar. 1854
ALMEDA W. BURNS, m.2, 1 June
1887 Mrs. LYDIA B. McFARLAND
2807. FREDERICK Jr., b. 6 Oct. 1834,
d. 24 Mar. 1860, md. 1857
EMILY WILSON. Went to Calif.
2808. ZEBEDEE, b. 3 Apr. 1840, d. at
sea 29 Mar. 1864, went to
Calif.
2809. CAROLINE WOOD, b. 28 Dec.
1842, d. 19 Mar. 1926, md.
AMOS GERALD. 1 child.
2810. HELEN S., b. 6 Dec. 1844, d.
30 Nov. 1865, md. 3 Dec.
1862 ALBERT HARBILL.

1460. GEORGE B. ROWELL [ZEBEDEE 755] He was
born 19 Feb. 1804 and died 20 May 1873. He
married first April 1833 SARAH PARKMAN. She born
24 Sep. 1807 and died 16 Mar. 1880. He married
second 30 Dec. 1850 CHARLOTTE WENTWORTH. She
born 12 May 1822 and died 22 Oct. 1895. Res.
East Solon, Maine.

Children: 2815. JOHN HAMBLETT, b. 10 Mar.
1834, d. 14 July 1911, md.
20 Nov. 1856 SOPHIA ATWOOD.
2816. SARAH, b. 7 Jan. 1835, d. 23
Feb. 1909, md. 12 Apr. 1855
EDWARD SAVAGE. 5 ch.
2817. GEORGE, b. Apr. 1837, d Sep.
1839.
2818. ELBRIDGE, b. 25 Feb. 1839, d.
20 May 1898, md. 12 Dec.
1877 ARVILLA AMES.
2819. ELIZABETH, b. 1 Apr. 1841, d.
29 Jan. 1923, md. 4 Nov.
1861 WILLIAM HARVILLE. 8 ch.

2820. **WILLIAM PARKMAN**, b. 3 Feb.
1843, d. 2 June 1920, md. 17
Mar. 1867 **SARAH WILLIAMS**.
2821. **DANIEL CHENEY**, b. 6 Dec. 1844,
d. 2 Dec. 1893, md. 1 May
1875 **ALICE COBURN**.
2822. **SUMNER**, b. 7 Feb. 1847, d. 15
June 1914, md. 15 June 1872
CAROLYN ROUNDY.

1461. **DAVID ROWELL** [ZEBEDEE 755] He was born
1806 and died 19 Dec. 1886. He married 1830 **MARY
BUTTERFIELD**. She born 1805 and died 29 May 1891.
Occ. farmer. 1850 census at Cornville. Res. East
Solon, Maine.

Children: 2825. **LEVI DAKIN**, b. 13 Feb. 1832,
d. 18 Sep. 1901, m.1, 1860
NAOMI DURRELL or **SOMES**,
(1836-1860), m.2, 4 Feb.
1862 **MARY DURRELL** her
sister. She m.2, **S.R. KING**.
2826. **LUTHER**, b. 5 Nov. 1833, d. 10
Mar. 1908, md. 1860 **LOVINA
DAWIN**. (1834-1889)
2827. **JOSEPH**, b. 1835, d. 19 Mar.
1837.
2829. **ALMEDA**, b. 1837, d. 15 Apr.
1917, md. **LLEWELLYN EATON**. 7
children.
2830. **DAVID Jr.**, b. 4 Aug. 1839, d.
31 Oct. 1920, md. 20 Nov.
1871 **DORA CHANEY**. Civil War
Service. 1 child.
2831. **BENJAMIN**, b. 1841, d. 1 Mar.
1856.
2832. **EBEN**, b. 22 July 1843, d. 27
Jan. 1909, md. 4 Dec. 1864
MARY KNIGHT.

1462. **ZEBEDEE ROWELL Jr.** [ZEBEDEE 755] He was
born 4 July 1808 and died 19 Mar. 1879. He
married 1 Feb. 1840 **BETHEL SARAH AYER**. She born

9 June 1812 and died 22 Oct. 1882. Res. So.
Solon, Maine.

Children: 2835. RUEL E., b. 6 Nov. 1840, d. 21
Apr. 1922, md. 29 Nov. 1876
VIOLA FARRAR. (1852-1936)
2836. ANTOINETTE, b. 23 June 1844,
d. 4 Sep. 1924, md. 1 Jan.
1872 GALEN KINCAID. 1 ch.
2837. HARLOW KILGORE, md. 29 Oct.
1873 EMMA PEIRCE.

1465. CHARLES ROWELL [ZEBEDEE 755] He was born
3 Dec. 1811 and died 20 Sep. 1866. He married 16
March 1839 PHEBE HAWTHORN. She born 23 July 1818
and died 19 June 1897. Res. Brighton, Me. Occ.
farmer. 1850 census at Brighton, Maine.

Children: 2839. ENOCH H., b. 22 Dec. 1839.
2840. SARAH, b. 22 Dec. 1839, d. 24
Feb. 1842.
2841. WILLIAM HENRY, b. 7 Feb. 1842,
md. 4 Mar. 1910, md. ELLEN
_____.
2842. SUMNER, b. 29 Mar. 1844, d. 17
Aug. 1899, md. MARY WHITTER.
2843. ALLEN, b. 29 Nov. 1845, d. 14
Feb. 1918, md. 10 June 1882
MARY SNOW.
2844. ELLEN, b. 28 Mar. 1848, d.
1923, md. LEONARD CORSON. 3
children.
2845. SARAH A., b. 20 Feb. 1850, d.
16 Apr. 1918, md. 29 Jan.
1886 as 3rd wife, WARREN
LOOMIS.
2846. CHARLES FRANKLIN, b. 1 May
1855, d. 1907. Calif.

1466. ELBRIDGE ROWELL [ZEBEDEE 755] He was born
16 May 1813 and died 20 Feb. 1888. He married 15
Feb. 1845 SOPHIA WESTON. She born 23 Jan. 1814
and died 16 Feb. 1901. Res. Madison, Maine.

ROWELL FAMILY - NEW ENGLAND
8th   Generation

Children: 2847. **EBEN VAUGHN**, b. 6 Nov. 1847,
               d. 21 July 1864.
           2848. **REBECCA JUDITH**, b. 25 Aug.
               1849, d. 27 Nov. 1884, md.
               27 June 1872 Dr. **DAVID S.
               HUNNEWELL**. 5 ch.
           2849. **ELIZABETH**, b. 23 Jan, 1852, d.
               27 Mar. 1886, md. **FRANK
               DINSMORE**.

1469. **JOHN MIRANDA ROWELL** [JOHN 760] He was
born 27 Jan. 1809 at Strafford, Vt. He married 2
May 1835 **MEHITABLE STEVENS FELLOWS**, d/o
EBENEZER FELLOWS at Tunbridge, Vt. She born 25
Nov. 1815 at Deerfield, N.H. and died 5 Feb.
1869. Buried East Hill Cemetary. 1850 census at
Tunbridge, Vt.

Children: 2850. **HENRY STEVENS**, b. 22 June
               1837, d. 1 Mar. 1842.
           2851. **SARAH JANE**, b. 1841.
           2852. **EDGAR ALLEN**, b. 25 Feb. 1843,
               d. 12 Dec. 1892, m.1, 29
               Jan. 1869 **MARY HELEN HORNER**,
               m.2, **HATTIE HORNER**. Civil
               War, Corp. Co. D, 12th Vt.
               Inf.
           2853. **EMILY AMANDA**, b. 5 Oct. 1845,
               md. 7 Mar. 1877 **CHARLES R.
               HOUSTON**. 6 children.
           2854. **SARAH ANN**, b. 20 July 1847,
               m.1, **ANDREW J.P. DOW**, m.2,
               WILLIAM BOND.
           2855. **IDA FRANCES**, b. 27 Jan. 1849,
               md. 25 Apr. 1868 **GEORGE
               WASHINGTON DOW**.
           2856. **JOHN S.**, b. 1849, d. Sep. 1849
           2857. **HERBERT LESLIE**, b. 18 Dec.
               1852, md. 28 Feb. 1880 **KATE
               ISABEL DOW**.

1473. **DARIUS TYLER ROWELL** [JOHN 760] He was born
29 May 1822 and died 4 Feb. 1870 at Strafford,
Vt. He married 23 Nov. 1846 **EMELINE R. ROBERTS**.

ROWELL FAMILY - NEW ENGLAND
8th Generation

She born 1831. Occ. farmer. Res. Windsor Co.,
Vt. 1850 census at Strafford, Vt.

Children: 2858. FLORA ESTELLE, b. 21 June
1860.

1474. HIRAM ROWELL [DAVID 763] He was born about
1826 at Westville, N.Y. and died 10 June 1904 at
Malone, N.Y. He was buried in Maplewood
Cemetary. He married 2 June 1878 at Nashua, N.H.
ELLEN FLYNN. He married second 27 Feb. 1876
EUNICE J. ARNOLD, d/o JOSHUA & EUNICE (LOBDELL)
ARNOLD. She born 1853 at Malone. He married
third 27 Feb. 1896 ADELINE LEE HAPGOOD at Fay,
N.Y.

Children by 1st Wife:
        2860. SARAH A., b. 1850, md. 10 Sep.
              1870 GEORGE P. GILBERT.
        2861. ADNIRON (m), b. 1852.
        2862. ELIZA (LIDA), b. 1857, d. 19
              Mar. 1875.
        2863. BENTON, b. 1859.
by 2nd Wife:
        2864. IDA M., b. 1872, d. 1953, md.
              DANA HAPGOOD. Had: HOWARD M.
              1904, LAWRENCE 1909.

1475. NATHANIEL P. ROWELL [DAVID 763] He was
born 4 Jan. 1825 at Westville, N.Y. and died
there 11 April 1893. He married 7 Sep. 1851
LUCINDA DUSTIN, d/o JONATHAN & MARY (AVERY)
DUSTIN. She born about 1831 and died 4 June
1901. He served in Civil War, Co. D, 98th N.Y.
Inf.

Children: 2865. WALLACE M., b. 1853, d. 1917,
              md. ALMA STEENBERRY.
          2866. EDA, b. 1859, md. ___ WILDER.
          2867. MARY, b. 1861, md. ORVILLE
              RHOADES. Had twins.

- 187 -

1476. HORACE ROWELL [DAVID 763] He was born 1841
at Westville, N.Y. He married MALINDA MAY
DUSTIN, d/o JONATHAN & MARY (AVERY) DUSTIN. She
born 27 March 1839 and died 21 Dec. 1914 at
Norwich, Conn. Res. Franklin, N.Y.

Children: 2870. ADA, b. 1863, md. WILLIAM
                 BOBO.
           2871. ALICE, b. 1868 in Ill., md.
                 A.J. GODDARD?
           2872. GEORGE HENRY, b. 1870, md. 4
                 June 1890 EMMA F.
                 DEGGENDORF, m.2, 20 Oct.
                 1904 JENNIE ELIZABETH
                 HENDERSON.
           2873. JENNIE, md. WILLIAM L. HAYES?

1482. THOMAS ROWELL [THOMAS 765] He was born 20
May 1796 at Fisherville, N.H. and died about
1875 in St. Lawrence Co., N.Y. He married 1817
LYDIA LEAVITT of Hadley, Quebec. She born 1794
at Exeter, N.H. Res. Hadley, Que. and
Fisherville, N.Y.

Children: 2875. ALBERT KENDRICK, b. 1830, d.
                 c1921, m.1, AVIS COLLINS
                 BRISTOL, m.2, MARTHA _____.
           2876. NATHAN, b. c1832, d. c1923,
                 md. MAUD _____.
           2877. JEFFERSON,
           2878. MARIA, md. _____ SAMPSON.
           2879. ELMORE,
           2880. ERASTUS,

1483. NATHAN ROWELL [THOMAS 765] He was born 4
Mar. 1801 at Fisherfield, N.H. and died 1877. He
married about 1833 ANNE LEAVITT. Res. Hadley,
Quebec.

Children: 2885. ABIGAIL, b. 1836, md. _____
                 PERKINS.
           2886. WIEAR LEAVITT, b. 30 Aug.
                 1838, d. 1911, md. 1856
                 THURSEY AYER, 4 ch.

ROWELL FAMILY - NEW ENGLAND
8th Generation

2887. PHEBE, b. 21 Apr. 1840, d.
      1919, md. c1861 CHARLES B.
      PECK.
2888. LAURA, b. 21 Apr. 1844, md.
      _____ ABBOTT.
2889. THOMAS, b. 1848, d. 1918, md.
      JANE WITCOMB JACKSON.
2890. WILLIAM NATHAN/WALLACE?, b.
      Jan. 1850, d. y.
2891. EVA, b. 28 May 1855, md. JOHN
      PARKER ATKINSON.

1486. KENDRICK ROWELL [THOMAS 765] He was born
2 Nov. 1806 at Hatley, Que. and died 1871. He
married first SARAH JONES. He married second
PLUMA ROWELL.

1490. SILAS ROWELL [JONATHAN 766] He was born
19 Apr. 1793 at South Sutton, N.H. and died
1832. He married first HANNAH POTTER and married
second BETSY PILLSBURY OBER of Sutton. His will
dated 5 Jan. 1832 and proved Feb. 1832. Wife
BETSY and three children named. [v.8, p.195]
JOHN PILLSBURY named executor.

Children: 1st Wife:
      2895. LORINDE, b. 20 Sep. 1820, md.
            21 Oct. 1841 GEORGE C. EATON
by 2nd Wife:
      2900. GEORGE SILAS, b. 9 Apr. 1827,
            md. 6 Nov. 1850 HEPSIBAH
            BEAN.
      2901. CHARLES PARKER, b. 23 Apr.
            1828, d. 1922, m.1, 1862
            CLARA ANN COUCH, m.2, 1870
            LUCRETIA ABIGAIL EASTMAN.
            1850 single at Sutton.

1493. IRA ROWELL [JONATHAN 766] He was born 6
Oct. 1807 and died in 1837. He married 17 May
1832 HANNAH KENDRICK. His will dated 20 May 1837
and proved 4 June 1837. Names wife HANNAH. She
named executrix. Res. Sutton and Concord. IRA

ROWELL [#1020] appointed guardian of minor son
23 Nov. 1841.

Children: 2902. THOMPSON,

1496. JOHN PETTINGILL ROWELL [MOSES 773] He was
born 19 April 1805 at Hopkinston, N.H. Possibly
married 10 Sep. 1831 SUSAN P. COLEMAN in Boston.
Had wife LYDIA in 1850 census. Occ. farmer.

Children: 2905. ALONZO, b. c1832, Farmer.
          2906. MARTIN, b. c1834, Shoemaker.
          2907. ABRAM, b. c1838,
          2908. LOVINIA, b. c1844.
          2909. LUCINDA, b. c1846.
          2910. MARY A., b. c1848.
          2911. GEORGE, b. 1848, md. ELLEN
                JANE CHAFFEE.

1501. ISAAC ROWELL [MOSES 773] He was born 19
Apr. 1813 and died 15 April 1887 at Hopkinton,
N.H. He married 20 Feb. 1840 HARRIET A. ADAMS,
d/o JAMES & LYDIA (JOHNSON) ADAMS of Henniker,
N.H. Occ. farmer. 1850 census at Hopkinton, N.H.

Children: 2912. JAMES A.,
          2913. HARRIET ELLA, b. 1846, d.
                infancy.
          2914. HARRIET ELLA, md. 24 Oct. 1866
                FRANK HOWLETT of Bradford.
          2915. MARY E., md. 9 June 1874
                GEORGE GOVE of Henniker.
          2916. CHARLES S., b. 26 June 1857,
                md. 22 Dec. 1882 FLORANCE S.
                GOODWIN.

1505. NICHOLAS ROWELL [SAMUEL 775] He was born
13 Oct. 1807 at Hopkinton, N.H. and died 1883.
He married 29 Sep. 1836 HANNAH M. CHENEY of
Bradford. She born 1810. 1850 census at Sutton,
N.H.

Children: 2917. **MARY ANN**, b. 1837, md. 1861
                 THOMAS ROBY.
           2918. **IRA F.**, b. 1839, md. 1868
                 RACHEL A. HOOK.

1509. **SAMUEL ROWELL** Jr. [SAMUEL 775] He was
born 20 Feb. 1820 at Sutton, N.H. and died there
14 Dec. 1906. He married Nov. 1846 **NANCY
WHITTIER** of Sutton, N.H. She born 1835 and died
23 Dec. 1871 at Sutton. Res. Sutton.

Children: 2920. **ASHSAH J.**, b. 4 June 1846.
           2921. **ACSAH**, b. Aug. 1848
           2922. **JOHN HENRY/HENRY A.**, b. 21
                 Aug. 1850, md. 30 Dec. 1878
                 LYDIA M. BUNTIN.
           2923. **CHARLES EDWIN**, b. 5 June 1852,
                 d. 23 Dec. 1905, md. 25 Dec.
                 1879 **ROSA L. WHEELER** or **ROSA
                 L. WOOLLEY.**
           2924. **LILLY**, b. c1854
           2925. **GRACE ANN**, b. 8 Sep. 1856.
           2926. **EMMA VIOLA**, b. 23 Mar. 1859.
           2927. **CORA DELL**, b. 20 Nov. 1861.
           2928. **SELENA MAY**, b. 2 Apr. 1864.
           2929. **CLINTON C.**, b. 20 Nov. 1867.

1522. **WILLIAM REDINGTON ROWELL** [PHILIP R. 787]
He was born 4 March 1842 at Castine, Me. He
married **ELIZABETH B. _____.** Res. Charleston,
Mass.

Children: 2930. **HENRY K.**, b. 1 June 1870.
           2931. **CLEMENTINE OSGOOD**, b. 11 Oct.
                 1872.

1524. **JOHN KIRBY ROWELL** [PHILIP R. 787] He was
born 19 Mar. 1846. He married **CLARA HATCH.** Res.
Castine, Me.

Children: 2932. **MABEL**, b. 9 Dec. 1879.
           2933. **CLEMENTINE**, b. 11 Oct. 1881.

ROWELL FAMILY - NEW ENGLAND
8th Generation

1530. **WILLIAM R. ROWELL** [ADONIRAM 800] He was
born 18 Mar. 1844 at Troy, Vt. and died Oct.
1897 at Methuen, Mass. He married **IMOGENE
CLEASON**, d/o **DANIEL & DELIA M.** (KENDALL)
CLEASON. He served in the Civil War, 3rd Batt.
Vt. Light Artillary. Was State Legislator 2
years. Moved 1886 to Methuen, Mass. Occ. lawyer.
Republican. Masonic Lodge.

1531. **GEORGE BARKER ROWELL** [ADONIRON 800] He
was born 30 March 1846 at North Troy. Vt. and
died 1918 at Orleans, Vt. He married first 1
Jan. 1873 **ISODORE DARLING**, d/o **DANIEL & SUSAN**
(PERKINS) **DARLING**/ She died 30 August 1876. He
married second 1 Sep. 1891 **ESTHER ROWAN GRANT** of
Pembroke, Ontario, d/o **HUGH & JANE** (ROWAN)
GRANT. She born 1867 and died 1952. Occ. Doctor,
Banker and business man. Served in Civil War.
1873 moved to Iresburg, Vt. Res. Orleans, Vt.
1892.

Children: 2935. **HUGH GRANT**, b. 1892, md. 1921
           SARA M. DENNIS.
           2936. **GEORGE BARKER** Jr., b. 1896,
           md. 1925 **MARION C. SMITH.**
           2937. **ADONIRAN JUDSON,**

1541. **HILLIARD ROWELL** [HILLIARD 847] He was
born 1827. Res. at Croydon, N.H.

Children: 2938. **ELLEN**, b. 1853, d. Sep. 1870.

1542 **ALBERT ROWELL** [HILLIARD 847] He was born
1828. He married **SARAH HAMMOND**. Res. Pittsburg,
N.H.

Children: 2939. **daughter**, b. 9 Feb. 1859.

1545. **SYLVESTER ROWELL** [HILLIARD 847] He was
born 16 Jan. 1831 at Croydon and died 15 Oct.
1896. He married 25 Mar. 1860 **SARAH C. DOW**, d/o

LORENZO DOW of Croydon. She born 28 Apr. 1836.
Occ. farmer and stone mason, cattle dealer. Had
600 acre farm. Res. Croydon, N.H.

Children: 2940. SARAH JENNIE, b. 25 Nov. 1861,
                 md. REUBEN G. SMITH.
           2941. JOHN WESLEY, b. 8 Sep. 1864,
                 md. Sep. 1885 E. BELLE
                 COLBY. Lumber business at
                 Sunapee, N.H.
           2942. HILLIARD ELMER, b. 29 Apr.
                 1867.
           2943. DAVID SELWIN, b. 30 May 1870,
                 md. ANNIE M. SAWYER.

1550. RICHARD S. ROWELL [STEPHEN 849] He was
born 1833. He married SARAH M. STEVENS.

Children: 2950. CLARA MARIA, b. 1858.
           2951. ALMON BARTLETT, b. 1859, d.
                 1907, md. MABEL J. SANBORN?
           2952. GEORGE A.,

1551. ALMON BARTLETT ROWELL [STEPHEN 849] He
was born 1839 and died 1907. He married MABEL
JOSEPHINE SANBORN.

1553. FRANKLIN PIERCE ROWELL [STEPHEN 849] He
was born 26 Aug. 1850 at Weare, N.H. and died
1927. He married 9 June 1874 ELIZA I. YOUNG of
Manchester, d/o SAYWARD J. & MARTHA (IRELAND)
YOUNG. She born April 1848. Educated at
Francestown Academy. Occ. machinist in
Manchester. Had Grist mill at Newport, N.H.
Republican. In General Court of N.H. in 1893-4.
Congregational church member. Prominent citizen,
Director 1st National Bank, V.P. Newport Savings
Bank. Res. Weare, N.H.

Children: 2960. ARTHUR S., b. 26 Oct. 1876, d.
                 1951, md. 26 Oct. 1898
                 BESSIE JOSLYN.

2961. STEPHEN FRANKLIN, b. 4 Oct.
1878, d. 1948, md. 1929
VIOLA J. BROCK.
2962. LENA GERTRUDE, b. 1880, md.
1910 WESTON P. LORD.
2963. IRVING WILLIS, b. Apr. 1885,
d. 1943, md. 1907 EDITH AMY
GLIDDEN.
2964. JESSE RICHARD, b. Apr. 1890,
md. 1914 LAURA M. WILMARTH.

1554. IRVING GREELEY ROWELL [STEPHEN 849] He
was born 1851 or 1854 and died 1927. He married
MARY EUNICE FULTON, d/o JOSEPH W. & LUCY A.
FULTON. Res. Weare, N.H.

Children: 2970. ALICE MABEL, b. 1880, md.
_____ FRENCH.
2971. CHARLES WARREN, b. 1883.
2972. FRANK FULTON, b. 1885, d.
1957, md. HELEN CLARKE.
2973. EUNICE MARY, b. 1887, md.
_____ GAMSBY.
2974. JOHN IRVING, b. 1890, md. 1919
ELIZABETH PITKIN.

1590. GEORGE WYLIE/WILLIS ROWELL [GEORGE W. 882]
He was born 24 Mar. 1838 and died out west. He
married 6 April 1859 at Tunbridge, Vt. EMELINE
JANE OSMAN, d/o AMANDER & MARY (CILLEY) OSMAN
(OSMOND). She born 1841. Occ. farmer. Res.
Tunbridge, Vt. Moved out west.

Children: 2980. NELLIE S. (NORA), b. 20
Mar. 1859.
2981. LUELLA VANLORA, b. 15 Nov.
1860.
2982. GEORGE WYLIE, b. 17 July 1862.
2983. MINNIE ESTELLE, b. Aug. 1864.
2984. WILL,
2985. FRANK,

1595. MOSES DUTY ROWELL [GEORGE W. 882] He was
born 4 Apr. 1849 at Tunbridge, Vt. and died 18
Feb. 1926 at Royalton, Vt. He married first 28
Sep. 1870 Mrs. EMMA FOSTER DIAMOND, d/o ORSON &
TRIPHENA (SMITH) FOSTER. She born 2 Aug. 1841
and died 11 Aug. 1873. He married second 6 Feb.
1878 IDA BELLE TURNER, d/o LEANDER & LAURA
TURNER. She born 16 Nov. 1857. Res. Tunbridge.

Children by 1st Wife:
            2986. CHARLES FOSTER, b. 5 Aug.
                  1873, d. 25 May 1961, md.
                  4 Oct. 1899 MARGARET B.
                  MOORE.
by 2nd Wife:
            2987. EMMA BELLE, b. 9 May 1880, md.
                  19 July 1909 ARTHUR AINSLEY
                  ABBOTT, 2 ch.
            2988. GLENN ELLIS (MOSES), b. 23
                  Apr. 1886, d. 5 Sep. 1955,
                  md. 28 Oct. 1914 RETA
                  ABBOTT.

1600. WILBER FISKE ROWELL [NATHANIEL L. 885] He
was born 10 Oct. 1842 at Tunbridge, Vt. and died
2 Dec. 1902 at Strafford. He married 16 Mar.
1870 at South Royalton, Vt. LUELLA THERESA
WILMOT, d/o ALONZO W. & JANE J. (CADY) WILMOT.
She born 9 Mar. 1847 at Troy, N.Y. and died 22
Mar. 1916 at Burlington, Vt. Occ. grocer. Res.
West Fairfield, Vt.

Children: 2990. MARGUERITE, b. 29 Sep. 1874,
                 d. 2 Oct. 1961, md. 22 Mar.
                 1908 AUGUSTUS I. SARGENT,
                 2 children.
           2991. KATHERINE MAUDE, b. 22 Mar.
                 1870, d. 7 Feb. 1902, md. 2
                 Jan. 1899 GEORGE CHASE. No
                 children.
           2992. JENNIE LENA, b. 9 Oct. 1883,
                 d. 25 Apr. 1949, md. 9 Oct.
                 1918 THOMAS BRADLEE, No ch.

1601. **ALFRED ROWELL** [NATHANIEL L. 885] He was born 16 July 1855 at Tunbrdige, Vy. and died 1928. Buried at Nashua, N.H. He married 21 May 1879 at Tunbridge, Vt. **FRANCES C. LYMAN**, d/o **JASPER & NANCY (EMERY) LYMAN**. She born 13 Oct. 1853 at Duxbury, Vt. and died 1921.

Children: 2993. **BERNICE F.**, b. 9 Aug. 1884, md. 22 Jan. 1917 **JOHN M. STONE** Jr. No children.
2994. **EARL STANLEY**, b. 16 Dec. 1889, d. 1938, md. 14 Apr. 1917 **ANNE F. FLOOD**. No ch.

1602. **NATHANIEL LEWIS ROWELL** Jr. [NATHANIEL L. 885] He was born 8 Nov. 1864 at Tunbridge, Vt. and died 18 Jan. 1918 at Derby, Vt. He married first 1884 at Massawippi, Quebec **SARAH FRANCES COX**, d/o **CARLOS & CHARLOTTE (GRANT) COX**. She born 1866 and died 3 June 1895. He married second 11 Dec. 1895 at Brownshill, Que. **ANNA AUGUSTA BROWN**, d/o **WILDER & SULA A. (SMITH) BROWN**. She born 27 Oct. 1872 and died 28 Dec. 1940. Res. Derby, Vt.

Children: 2995. **JESSIE DUTTON**, b. 14 Aug. 1888, d. 15 Jan. 1937, md. 9 Sep. 1908 **HUGH FAIRBROTHER** 3 children.
2996. **MABEL FRANCES**, b. 6 Sep. 1890, d. 18 Apr. 1946, md. 5 Nov. 1914 **CLYDE W. KITTREDGE**, 2 ch.
By 2nd Wife:
2997. **LEWIS WILDER**, b. 9 Sep. 1896, md. 1920 **DOROTHY JANE MANSFIELD**.
2998. **NATHANIEL LEROY**, b. 17 Feb. 1898, md. 1923 **MARION C. HAMILTON**.
2999. **DORIS SULA**, b. 16 May 1904, md. 26 May 1922 **CHARLES R. HASTINGS**. 7 children.
3000. **ROBERT CLARE**, b. 11 Nov. 1908, md 1931 **EMORY FRANCES KELLEY**

ROWELL FAMILY - NEW ENGLAND
8th Generation

3001. HAROLD LEON, b. 23 May 1910.

1606. JAMES MARTIN/MADISON ROWELL [MOSES D. 888]
He was born 9 Apr. 1855 and died 2 Sep. 1925. He
married 18 Apr. 1878 at Winooski, Vt. LIZZIE
NOYES, d/o JAMES SOLON & CYNTHIA (KNOX) NOYES.
She born 12 Oct. 1856 and died 23 Feb. 1926.
Res. Tunbridge, Vt.

Children: 3012. CALLA ETHEL, b. 8 Nov. 1879,
                  d. 29 Apr. 1953, md. 24 July
                  1901 JOHN H. McGETTRICK, 3
                  children.
            3013. ALICE WINIFIELD, b. 9 Sep.
                  1883, md. 28 Nov. 1934
                  DANIEL P. WALDO. No ch.
            3014. IDA MADGE, b. 17 Sep. 1885, d.
                  3 July 1948, md. 14 Sep.
                  1927 GEORGE STOCKTON. No ch.
            3015. DON NOYES, b. 3 Sep. 1890, d.
                  28 Sep. 1918 (WW1) illness.

1610. HEBER ROWELL [MOSES D. 888]   He was born
11 Feb. 1869. He married ELIZABETH FRENCH at
Kingston, N.H.

Children: 3016. DORIS SULA,

1616. WILMOT G. ROWELL [JOHN C. 895] He was born
2 Apr. 1862. He married LIDA McKINNY. Res.
Derry, N.H.

Children: 3017. JOHN W., b. 1877.

1621. WILLIAM HENRY ROWELL [THADDEUS 900] He was
born 16 Mar. 1845 at Weymouth, Mass. and died 14
Aug. 1885. He married 17 Aug. 1865 MARTHA M.
HELLEUR at Boston, d/o MATTHEW J. & RACHEL
(GILBERT) HELLEUR. She born 27 Mar. 1845 Nova
Scotia, Canada and died 16 Feb. 1925 at Boston.
Res. Boston, Mass.

Children: 3018. BENJAMIN F., b. 1866.

3019. **MATTHEW JOSEPH**, b. 1867, d.y.
3020. **MATTHEW JOSEPH**, b. 20 June
1871, md. **ADA CLARA GRANT**.
3021. **FREDERICK FRANK**, b. 2 Feb.
1873, d. 19 Dec. 1927, md.
1896 **ETTA S. MURCH**.
3022. **MARTHA MAY**, b. 5 Nov. 1875,
md. 28 Feb. 1895 **HENRY
WILLIAM GRANT**.
3023. **NICHOLAS M.**, b. June 1877, md.
17 Oct. 1892 **MARY A. McCABE**.
3024. **MABEL LOUISE**, b. 1880, md.
GEORGE F. MURCH.
3025. **ELIOT**, b. Sep. 1894, md. 17
Oct. 1916 **ALICE G. COREY**.

1625. **IRA HILL ROWELL** [CHASE H. 911] He was born
27 Jan. 1848 at Randolph, Vt. and died 24 Jan.
1906 at Williamstown, Vt.   He married 12 Sep.
1869 **EVELYN ELDORA HARWOOD**, d/o **NATHAN A. &
WEALTHY (MOODY) HARWOOD**. She born 8 Sep. 1851 at
Bristol, Vt. and died 20 June 1917 at Barre, Vt.
Res. Braintree, Orange Co., Vt.

Children: 3026. **ADA MAY**, b. 2 May 1871, d. 29
Apr. 1946, md. 5 Sep. 1897
AZRO A. REED. 2 ch.
3027. **ERSKINE PLINY**, b. 25 May 1877,
d. 2 June 1943, md. 22 June
1897 **LIZZIE B. PRESCOTT**.

1626. **MARTIN CHASE ROWELL** [CHASE H. 911] He was
born 14 Mar. 1851 at Randolph, Vt. and died 6
Feb. 1934. He married 19 May 1874 **CHARLOTTE H.
WARNER**, d/o **WILLIAM K. & DIANE (WOOD) WARNER**.
She born 28 Jan. 1851 and died 19 Dec. 1878. He
married 2nd, 19 Aug. 1881 **LUCY E. SHONION**, d/o
JEAN B. & CELESTE (TRADEAU) SHONION. at Milton,
Vt. She born 26 May 1856 at Milton, Vt. and died
13 Sep. 1943.

Children: 3030. **MYRTLE E.**, b. 1 Apr. 1882, d.
4 Dec. 1964, md. 21 June
1922 **EDWARD F. WAGNER**.

3031. BERTHA A., b. 5 Mar. 1887,
m.1, 14 Sep. 1910 FRANKLIN
A. SALISBURY, m.2, 27 Aug.
1950 EDWIN H. KIMBALL. Had:
ELEANOR 1912.
3032. RICHARD MARTIN, b. 12 Feb.
1892, d. Jan. 1981 in Fla.,
md. 6 Mar. 1916 FLORA ANN
McCUIN. Had: REGINA 1916.

1629. EDGAR WITTERS ROWELL [CHASE H. 911] He was
born 10 Aug. 1853 at Randolph, Vt. and died 31
Aug. 1930. He married 28 Aug. 1883 EVA LOUISE
KING, d/o WILLIAM P. & ELLEN (NOYES) KING. She
born 12 Feb. 1863 at Tunbridge, Vt. Res.
Carter, Vt.

Children: 3033. RALPH KING, b. 6 Dec. 1884, d.
21 Nov. 1966 md. 31 Oct.
1911 ELIZABETH SULLIVAN.
3034. GLENN EDGAR, b. 26 July 1888,
d. Jan. 1960, md. BERNICE S.
MacCORRISON. Had 3 children.

1632. ORVIS ABBOTT ROWELL [CYRUS C. 914] He was
born 7 Mar. 1859 at Tunbridge, Vt. He married
15 May 1886 MINNIE E. ABBOTT, d/o FRANK &
CHARLOTTE ABBOTT. She born 9 April 1869 at
Fayston, Vt. and died 6 April 1975 at
Northfield. Res. Tunbridge, Vt.

Children: 3035. NORA, b. 20 Feb. 1890, md.
HOMER H. CLOUGH. 6 ch.
3036. BLANCHE, b. 12 Mar. 1892, md.
8 Sep. 1908 FRANK SHEPARD.
2 children.
3037. CLIFTON, b. 10 Sep. 1895, unmd
3038. CHARLES, b. 5 Sep. 1896, md. 7
Oct. 1922 EDNA MORSE. No ch.
Served in WW1.
3039. PERLEY, b. 30 June 1899.
3040. GRACE C., b. 7 Mar. 1902, md.
20 Feb. 1925 ROBERT KNAPP.

1633. **CYRUS ELMER ROWELL** [CYRUS C. 914] He was born 24 Feb. 1860 and died 10 Feb. 1922. He married 17 Oct. 1906 **JENNIE LANGMAID**, d/o **FRANK & ELIZABETH (TURNBILL) LANGMAID**. She born 22 Sep. 1887 Brookton, Mass. Res. Tunbridge, Vt.

Children: 3041. **ELIZABETH MAY**, b. 24 Feb. 1908, md. **JOHN BOLES**. Had: **LOUISE MAY**.
3042. **LESLIE BENNETT**, b. 2 Oct. 1910.
3043. **MARY MILDRED**, b. 11 Jan. 1920.

1635. **WARD ADAMS ROWELL** [GEORGE W. 915] He was born April 1868 ar Lockport, N.Y. and died 18 Oct. 1918 at Fairview, Wash. He married **LIZZIE ADLER** of Honolulu, H.I.

Children: 3044. **JENNIE**, b. 1898, d. 1908.
3045. **GLADYS**, b. 1900.
3046. **EVA**, b. 1904.
3047. **WARD Jr.**, b. 1906.
3048. **JESSIE**, b. 1908.

1636. **GEORGE CYRUS ROWELL** [GEORGE W. 915] He was born 1878 at Strafford, N.H. He married c1905 **EVA LAIRD** at Bethel, Vt. At Godding, Idaho in 1926.

Children: 3049. **OLIVE LAIRD**, b. 7 May 1905.

1637. **WALTER EVERETT ROWELL** [GEORGE W. 915] He was born 5 Feb. 1876. He married 3 July 1899 **MYRTLE BLODGETT**, d/o **MILO R. & ISABEL (BROWER) BLODGETT**. Res. So. Columbia, N.H.

Children: 3050. **CLAUDE**, b. 8 May 1904.
3051. **CARROL**, b. Nov. 1906.

1646. **HERBERT EDGAR ROWELL** [ELBRIDGE 929] He was born 11 Mar. 1858 and died 8 May 1904. He married 10 Jan. 1880 **OLIVE FRANCES JAACKSON**.

Children: 3052. THEODORE EARL, b. 22 Oct.
1882, d. 31 Aug. 1962, md.
BESSIE MAE LOWE.

1655. FRANK E. ROWELL [WESLEY D. 956] He was
born 25 Feb. 1867. He married RUTH W. DURFEE,
d/o JOSEPH & CYNTHIA (COGGESHOE) DURFEE. She
born 23 May 1873.

Children: 3055. RAYMOND C., b. 23 Feb. 1897,
d. May 1973.
3056. MARIAN I., b. 27 Apr. 1898.

1680. WALTER RAYMOND ROWELL [WALTER P. 974] He
was born 29 Aug. 1896. He married 30 Sep. 1922
NETTIE LEE WILSON.

Children: 3060. EDITH EVELYN, b. 25 Oct. 1933,
md. Dr. DONALD M. TARDIFF.
3061. WALTER RAYMOND Jr., b. 30 Apr.
1925, md. EDITH SHOEMAKER.
3062. NORMA LOUIS, b. 22 July 1926,
md. GEORGE GREMILE.
3063. ROBERT LEE, b. 29 July 1932,
md. ELIZABETH ANN HELLSTROM.
3064. CHESTER OTIS, b. 30 Sep. 1935,
md. SHIRLEY ANN SULLIVAN.

1711. MARK ROWELL [JOHN 985] He was born 10 Aug.
1809 and died age 86 years. He married 25 July
1833 ABIGAIL HARRISON GOODWIN, d/o ETHAN & OLIVE
[BRANDIGE] GOODWIN. She was born 25 Sep. 1814
and died 7 Aug. 1846 at Hartland, Wis. He
married second _____ and married third
SOPHRONIA _____. She died 12 Mar. 1907,
Washington Co., Wis.

Children: 3065. IRA, b. 28 Oct. 1836, d. July
1886, md. 1868 MARY
THOMPSON.
3066. WALDEN, b. 22 July 1839, d. 20
Apr. 1904, md. 7 Nov. 1866
HATTIE M. ARNOLD.

ROWELL FAMILY - NEW ENGLAND
8th Generation

3067. CATHERINE/CALISTA OLIVE, b. 30
Mar. 1842, md. CHANNCEY M.
SKINNER.
3068. MARY, b. 15 Nov. 1844, d. 15
July 1846.
by 2nd wife:
3069. MARK Jr., d. 8 Oct. 1898.
3070. EMMA,
3071. PHILADELPHIA,

1715. JOHN S. ROWELL [JOHN 985] He was born 1
Apr. 1827 at Springwater, N.Y. He married 1
Jan. 1850 MARY MARTHA BELLE of Virginia. She
died April 1891. He married second MARY
SCHILLER. Came to Wisc. 1848. Located at
Hartland. Moved to Beaver Dam. Manufacturer
there. Mayor 1867. In spring of 1879 built 21'
boat named "Belle Rowell."

Children: 3072. THEODORE B., md. 17 Dec. 1872
CAROLYN NEWELL ROBINSON,
m.2, 31 Dec. 1892 _____.
3073. SAMUEL W. , b. 28 Jan. 1850,
md. 3 Sep. 1877 MARY
MILLAND.
3074. ELIZABETH M/B., md. 27 Mar.
1871.
3075. LILLIAN,
3076. FLORANCE BELLE, d. 25 Sep.
1882.
3077. FRANK,
3078. JAMES,
3079. JOSEPH NEWELL, md. MARY
BOREHARDT.

1727. FRANCIS M. ROWELL [BENNING 988] He was
born 1840. Had wife SADE SMITH. Res. Thetford,
Vt.

Children: 3080. MINNIE E., b. 15 June 1866.

1788. THOMAS ASHBURY ROWELL [SAMUEL 998] He was
born 3 Oct. 1811. He married 4 May 1862 MARY
GILLINGHAM. Res. Salem, N.H.

Children: 3081. **WILLIS S./SAMUEL WILLIS**, b.
c1864.
3082. **EMILY J.**, b. c1868, md. 5 Oct.
1884 **SAMUEL KELLY**.

1790. **JACOB ROWELL** [JACOB 999] He was born 18
Feb. 1793 at Andover, N.H. He married first 24
Feb. 1818 **MARY CRAIGEN**. She born 1795 and died 4
June 1866. He married second 6 Sept. 1869 **MARY
SEAVER**. She b. c1825. Res. Andover, Vt.

Children: 3090. **HENRY C.**, b. 24 May 1819.
3091. **ISAAC NEWTON**, b. 16 May 1821.
3092. **JACOB RODNEY**, b. 2 Apr. 1823.
3093. **MARTHA**, twin, b. 9 June 1825.
3094. **MARY**, twin, b. 9 June 1825,
md. **ASA ROSS** or 8 Sep. 1847
RUFUS ROSS.
3095. **WILLIAM**, b. 16 July 1827, md.
MARIA _____.
3096. **ELIZABETH J.**, b. 28 Aug. 1829.
3097. **ORLANDO**, b. 25 Mar. 1832.
3098. **ABRAM/AARON**, b. 15 Sep. 1835,
md.13 Mar. 1860 **ADELINE
MAY**, at Andover, Vt..
3099. **MARTHA A.**, b. 25 Oct. 1837,
md. _____ **BAILEY**.

1792. **ARTEMUS ROWELL** [JACOB 999] He was born
14 Dec. 1796 at Andover, N.H. He married 18
Nov. 1817 at Mason, N.H. **BETSY SWALLOW**. Res.
Mason, Hillsboro County.

Children: 3110. **MARY**, b. 7 Feb. 1813.
3111. **HENDERSON**, b. 3 Mar. 1820, md.
22 Oct. 1848 **HELLEN A.
BURGESS** at Acton, Mass.
3112. **ARTEMUS MILO**, b. 17 Oct. 1821.
3113. **JOHN HARRIS**, b. 18 Oct. 1823,
md. 18 May 1848 **HANNAH D.
LOWIS** at Royalton, Mass.
3114. **MARTHA**, b. 5 Oct. 1825.

3115. **LEANDER**, b. 5 Jan. 1828, md.
20 Dec. 1849 **SUSAN M.
FULLER**.

1793. **ROSWELL ROWELL** [JACOB 999]   He was born
c1800 and died 10 Dec. 1855. He married **REBECCA**
_____. She died 18 Oct. 1856 [49 yrs]. Both
buried at Pittsfield, Vt. Res. Landgrove, Vt.

Children: 3116. **WINCHESTER**, b. c1827, d. 11
                May 1861. [35-7]
            3117. **AUSTIN A.**, b. 1833, d. 4 May
                1879 [46-1-4], m.1, 28 Sep.
                1850 **MARTHA A. DAVIS**, (1839-
                1859), m.2, 3 Dec. 1865
                FANNY A. BAILEY. (1843-1879)
            3118. **SALOME**, b. 1835, md. 7 May
                1862 **MERRILL DAVIS**.

NINTH GENERATION

2001. **PERLEY WORCESTER ROWELL** [MOSES Jr. 1001]
He was born 1823 at Loudon, N.H. He married 1869
(SARAH) CAROLINE CLARK, d/o JOHN & ASEMETH
(WELLS) CLARK. She died 30 June 1889. Res.
Loudon, N.H.

Children: 5000. SARAH W.,
5001. GEORGE WILMER, b. 30 Dec.
1867, md. ETTA BELLE
PERKINS, 1 child.

2007. **ANN BRAY ROWELL** [ASA T. 1005] She was
born 14 Mar. 1841 at Chichester, N.H. and died
29 Jan. 1934 at Epsom. She married as second
wife **DANIEL T. YEATON**. [authors Great
Grandparents] Children named YEATON.

Children: 5010. **ALFRED DANIEL**, b. 5 Mar. 1874,
d. 22 Oct. 1956, md. 2 Oct.
1898 **EVELYN MAY WINKLEY**.
Had: GLADYS 1901-1991, DORIS
1905, **MARGARET** 1906-
1929.
5011. **MINOT ROWELL**, b. 26 July 1878,
d, 15 June 1957, md. 1902
HELEN GREEN. Had: KENNETH.
5012. **ALICE BERTHA**, b. 24 July 1883,
d. 19 June 1978, md. 25 Dec.
1906 **HARRY SILVER**. No ch.

2008. **WILLIAM TILTON ROWELL** [ASA T. 1005] He
was born 6 Apr. 1843 at Chichester and died 12
Jan. 1897. He married 17 July 1866 LIZZIE M.
STONE, d/o SIMON & SUSANNAH (DORMAN) STONE. She
born 19 June 1848 at Newfield, Me. He graduated
from Epsom H.S. Worked in 1864 at Amoskeag
Mills in Manchester, N.H.

Children: 5020. **ARTHUR WILLIAM**, b. 27 June
1870, d. 26 Dec. 1938, md.
1897 **ALICE O. SPAULDING**.
Had: BERTHA, MILDRED, LUCIAN

N., ADRIAN 1906, LEONARD
DEXTER 1909, EUNICE 1922, A
son died at birth.
5021. **MYRA LILLIAN,**

2010. **JOHN ANDREW ROWELL** [ASA T. 1005] He was
born 16 Oct. 1850 at Chichester and died 9 Aug.
1922 at Modesto, Calif. He married first 5 July
1875 **ALMA NARCISSA HOLMES.** She died 4 Mar. 1889.
He married second 28 Sep. 1890 **CLARA HALE.** Occ.
Cong. Minister.

Children: 5025. **Rev. WILFRED ASA,** b. 5 Mar.
1877, d. c1956, md. 5 June
1907 **TERESINE PECK.** She d.
1945. Had: **TERESINE** 1909-
1992.
5026. **MARION E,**
5027. **MAURICE H.,** Prof.
5028. **FLORANCE,** md. _____ **ANDRESEN.**
5029. **ALMA,** b. 1889.
by 2nd Wife:
5030. **HELEN,** md. **ARTHUR INGHAM.**
5031. **JOHN HALE.**

2013. **MOSES P. ROWELL** [CYRUS 1007] He was born
19 July 1848 and died 23 Jan. 1893. He married
CORA ETOIL. She born 20 Sep. 1859.

Children: 5032. **NELLIE LUELLA,** b. 29 June
1881, md. **JAMES MARTIN.**

2021. **THOMAS CLARK ROWELL** [ZIBA M. 1011] He was
born 5 Sep. 1829, a twin, at Lowell, Mass. and
died 1857 at Althouse, Jackson Co., Oregon.

2023. **LYDIA WILLIAMS ROWELL** [ZIBA M. 1011] She
was born 26 May 1834 at Hartford, Vt. and died
1919 at Portland, Ore. She married at Port
Bryon, Ill. **JACOB MITH LaRUE.** He born 1829
Chocton, Steuben Co., N.Y. and died 1866 at
Yamhill Co., Ore. In 1853 they went west with
her parents to Oregon. Children named LaRue.

Children: i. EMILY MARIA, b. 1854, md.
BERRICK G. GUILD.
ii. ZIBA MARCEL, b. 1857, m.2,
HATTIE FOLSOM.
iii. MARY ADELME, b. 1859, md. DAVID
I. KERD.
iv. LEONARD EUGENE, b. 1861, md.
MELVINA GRIMES.
v. BARTLETT ROBINSON, b. 1862, d.
1874.
vi. JOHN E.S., b. 1864, m.1, ABBIE
E. MEAL, m.2, LOUISE TAGGART.

2024. JAMES BARTLETT ROWELL [ZIBA M. 1011] He
was born 1836 a twin at St. Joseph, Mich. and
died 1916 at Newberg, Oregon. He married in 187_
??

2025. JOHN DANIEL ROWELL [ZIBA M. 1011] He was
born 1836 at St. Joseph, Mich. a twin and died
in 1896. He married REBECCA JACK in 1874 in
Washington Co., Ore. She born 1852 and died
1939. Res. Scholls, Oregon.

Children: 5040. FRANCIS ELMER, b. 1876, md.
1905 MINNIE B. SUTHERLAND.
Had: FRANCIS T. 1908.
5041. CARRIE MAY, b. 1877, d.
infancy.
5042. JAMES ALBERT, b. 1879, d.
1955, unmd.
5043. CASSIE HATTIE, b.1882, d. 1925
at Portland, Ore. md. 1902
THOMAS R. RADCLIFF.
5044. INA ILA ISA, b. 1889, d. 1956,
md. 1927 JOHN E. SUTHERLAND.

2026. ZIBA ARETUS ROWELL [ZIBA M. 1011] He was
born 1840 in Whiteside Co., Ill. and died there
in 1866. He married 1861 ELIZABETH ELLEN HARRIS.

Children: 5050. CORA F., b. 1865, d. young.

2040. **CHARLES CHRISTOPHER ROWELL** [CHRISTOPHER 1014] He was born 1837 and died 1932. He married first _____, and married second in 1866 **LOTTIE L. VANCE**, married third **EMMA O. PENDLETON**, and married fourth **CHARLOTTE ANN EASTMAN** of Berlin, Wis. Occ. RR Engineer.

Children: 2nd wife:
    5060. **NETTIE MAY**, b. 1868, md. _____BRENNEN.
    5061. **BESSIE LOTTIE**, b. 1872, md. _____ CULVER.
by 3rd Wife:
    5062. **JAMES ALBERT**, b. 1883, d. 1936, md. 1911 **JESSIE M. JOHNSON**. Had: **CHARLES HUGH** 1915, md. 1945 **MILDRED P. SPEER**.

2041. **HENRY VALENTINE ROWELL** [CHRISTOPHER 1014] He was born 1838 and died 1925. He married **EMMA JOSEPHINE JAQUATH**. Res. Malden and Medford, MA.

Children: 5065. **NEVA HUNTER**, b. 6 Feb. 1882, md. 19 Aug. 1905 **ERNEST M. HODGDON**.

2070. **THOMPSON ROWELL** [IRA 1020] He was born 21 Apr. 1826 at West Concord, N.H. and died 18 Oct. 1881 at Concord. He married 1849 **MARY ANN LEMFEST**, d/o **THOMAS & ABIGAIL (COBURN) LEMFEST** of Dracut, Mass. She born 1822 and died 17 March 1889 [67-7-10] at Concord. Occ. mason and builder. Res. 1850 census at Concord, N.H.

Children: 5070. **HENRY A.**, b. 30 Dec. 1850, m.1, **MARY BUNTIN**, d/o **WILLIAM BUNTIN**. She d. 1879. Had: 1 ch. d.y., m.2, 10 July 1883 **GRACE BOOTH**, d/o **GEORGE EDWIN & BETSY (UNSWORTH) BOOTH**.

5071. **WILLIAM**, b. 5 Mar. 1860, md. 3 Feb. 1883 **ANNIE PRESCOTT**. Had: **MARJORIE**, b. 1891, md. **JULIAN C. STEVENS**.

2071. **WILLIAM KIMBALL ROWELL** [IRA 1020] He was born 9 Nov. 1829 at West Concord, N.H. and died 22 Nov. 1886. He married first 27 Nov. 1855 **MARY AUGUSTA FLINT**, d/o **AMES & MARY (STICKNEY) FLINT** of Hampton, N.H. She born 18 Aug. 1834 at Compton, N.H. and died 23 June 1857. He married second April 25, 1861 **HELEN MARIA TENNEY** of Chester, N.H. He grad. from Dartmouth in 1855. Occ. school teacher at Paschum, Vt. Moved to San Francisco, Calif. Children by 2nd wife.

Children: 5075. **WILLIAM TENNEY**, b. Oct. 1862, d. Jan. 1883.
5076. **REBECCA AUGUSTA**, b. Jan. 1864, d. Oct. 1864.
5077. **HELEN FLINT**, B. 1866, md. **FRANCIS R. CURTIS** of Stratford, Conn. Moved to Loadsbury, Cal.
5078. **EDWARD MURREY**, b. 1868, d.y.
5079. **HENRY DURANT**, b. 1875, d.y.
5080. **MABEL CHESTER**, b. 1877, md. **NEWTON J. REED**.

2073. **EDWARD THOMAS ROWELL** [IRA 1020] He was born 14 Aug. 1835 at West Concord, N.H. and died 4 Aug. 1899. He married 8 Sep. 1870 **CLARA E. WEBSTER** of Lowell, Mass. He grad. from Dartmouth in 1861. Served in Civil War for 3-1/2 years in Burden's Sharpshooters. Twice wounded. Occ. Editor of Lowell Courier newspaper. Postmaster at Lowell in 1874, served 11-1/2 years.

Children: 5085. **SADIE WEBSTER**, b. 8 Oct. 1875, d. 19 May 1880.
5086. **EDWARD WEBSTER**, b. 29 Nov. 1878, d. 22 May 1880.
5087. **CLARA ALICE**, b. 8 Aug. 1881, grad. Smith College 1904.

2074. JAMES HARRIS ROWELL [IRA 1020] He was born 16 May 1838 at West Concord, N.H. and died 8 April 1908 at Concord. He married 21 June 1866 **MARY ANN FISK**, d/o **JOHN & ELIZABETH (KITTREDGE) FISK** of Concord. She survived him. Grad. Kimball Union Academy. Occ. in livery business 9 years, contractor for concrete, Treasurer Merrimac Co. 1876-7, Supt. Streets 1860-6, Comm. highways 1887-9. No children.

2104. JOHN ROWELL [JACOB 1035] He was born 1827 at Montville and died 1859 at Rock Island, Illinois. He married in 1853 _____.

Children: 5100. **EDWIN DEANE**, md. 15 June 1864 at Penobrest, Me. **FLORANCE BICKFORD**, 2 ch.

2105. JACOB ROWELL [JACOB 1035] He was born 1829 at Montville, Me. and died 1881 at Commonville, Wis. He married _____.

Children: 5105. **EVAN**,
          5106. **ALPHEUS**,
          5107. **LANCIL**,
          5108. **FRANK**,

2106. DANIEL ROWELL [JACOB 1035] He was born 1831 at Montville, Me. and died 1911 at Hampden. He married 1854 **MARY MILLER JACKSON**. Occ. wheelwright and cabinet maker.

Children: 5110. **MINNIE**, md. **ARTHUR HARDY**.
          5111. **LEROY**, b. 1857, d. 1923, md. 31 Dec. 1886 **ELSIE D. DUNTON**. Had: ADDIE M., HORACE D., WILLIAM F. & MARGARET L.
          5112. **ROSWELL**,

2107. WILLIAM ROWELL [JACOB 1035] He was born 1833 at Dixmont, Me. and died 1913 at Oak Hills, Illinois. He married _____.

ROWELL FAMILY - NEW ENGLAND
9th Generation

Children: 5115. ANNIE,
5116. JESSIE,
5117. WILLIAM,

2108. MARCUS ROWELL [JACOB 1035] He waas born
1835 at Dixmont, Me. and died 1879 at Lewiston,
Me. He married in 1859 VESTA PRESCOTT. Res.
Clinton, Maine.

Children: 5120. ARETUS, b. 30 Sep. 1863, md. 7
Nov. 1888 EMMEGENE REED.
5121. ELLA,
5122. MELVIN,

2109. ORINDA P. ROWELL [JACOB 1035] She was
born 1837 at Dixmont, Me. and died 1925 at
Clinton, Me. She married 1865 WILLIAM JOHNSON.

Children: i. ALICE JOHNSON, b. 1869, d. 1956.

2111. ALPHEUS ROWELL [JACOB 1035] He was born
20 July 1842 at Dixmont, Me. and died 1898. He
married 23 Feb. 1867 CASSANDRA BICKFORD. Sgt.
1st Maine Reg't Heavy Artillary 1862-5 in Civil
War. Occ. carpenter and builder. Member Maine
Legislature in 1894. Res. Clinton, Me.

Children: 5125. MINA, b. 1868, d. 1958.
5126. GERTRUDE, b. 1871, md.
BENJAMIN F. BEAN.

2113. ESTHER ROWELL [JACOB 1035] She was born
1846 at Dixmont, Me. and died there in 1926. She
married first 10 May 1866 ASHLEY YOUNG, married
second 1900 ED TARR. By first husband she had:

Children: i. BERT YOUNG, md. ANNIE _____.

2140. AMOS ROWELL [EDMUND 1057] He was born 28
Aug. 1837 and died 9 Aug. 1865. He married
ISABEL AUSTIN. Occ. photographer. Had Tin wagon.
Musician. Played at Ford's Theater night Lincoln
was shot.

Children: 5140. **MARY**, b. 27 Feb. 1861.

2155. **FREDERICK ROWELL** [FREDERICK 1070] He was born 5 May 1839. He married **CLARA E. SANGER**. She born 15 Dec. 1841. Res. Solon, Maine.

Children: 5150. **MARIETTA B.**, b. 21 Feb. 1862, md. 16 July 1890 **SAMUEL H. WILKENS**. 2 children.

2185. **IRA WAYLAND ROWELL** [GEORGE W. 1098] He was born 1878 and died 1946 at Battle Creek, Mich. He married 1900 **LYDIA RIEDENBACH** of Menomonee Falls, Wis. Occ. banker and manufacture.

Children: 5170. **KATHERINE**, b. 1913.
            5171. **MARTON O'CONNER**.

2188. **FRANK FORD ROWELL** [GEORGE W. 1098] He was born 1884 and died 1945. He married 1911 **MINNIE MacEVANS** of Wisconsin.

Children: 5180. **FORD OWEN**,
            5181. **ROBERT GEORGE**,

2189. **GEORGE WALSH ROWELL** [GEORGE W. 1098] He was born 1886. He married 1918 **MARY E. BERIGAN** of Omaha, Nebr. Occ. newspaper editor.

2190. **WALLACE ARTHUR ROWELL** [GEORGE W. 1098] He was born 1888 and died 1954. He married 1919 **MARIA MEDENNES** of Minneapolis. Occ. salesman.

2200. **FRANK WHEATON ROWELL** [CHARLES W. 1101] He was born 1880 in Idaho and died 1947. He married 1904 **GERTRUDE MERCER** of Woodside, N.J. Occ. military career. 2nd Lt. rose to Major Gen'l in 1938. Vet. WW1.

Children: 5200. **GERTRUDE MERCER**, b. 1905, md. 1928 _____ **DRESSLER**.
            5201. **FRANK WHEATON**, b. 1907, d. infancy.

5202. CATHERINE, b. 1909, md. 1927
_____ HEARN.
5203. VIRGINIA, b. 1915, md. 1935
_____ BROWN.
5204. FREDERICK MERCER, b. 1922.

2231. JOHN F. ROWELL [GEORGE S. 1126] He was
born 18 Jan. 1860. He married 2 Apr. 1891 MINNIE
T. BEAN. Res. Brentwood, N.H.

Children: 5225. GEORGE H., b. 20 Oct. 1891.

2240. TIMOTHY BRYANT ROWELL [TIMOTHY 1142]   He
was born 13 May 1845 at Vasselboro, Me.   He
married 1 Sep. 1880 ELIZABETH CHAMPION LATHROP.
She born 9 May 1855 and died 28 Sep. 1895 at
South Hadley Falls, Mass.

Children: 5230. ELIZABETH L., b. 10 Jan. 1882.
            5231. PHILIP L., b. 15 Feb. 1885.

2251. WILLIAM LAYMAN ROWELL [WILLIAM 1158] He
was born 31 Oct. 1834 at Gorham, N.H. He married
14 Apr. 1856 MARTHA A. LeGRO, d/o DAVID & SARAH
(HODGDON) LeGRO. She born 10 Apr. 1837. Occ.
carpenter. Enlisted Civil War 18 Oct. 1862 Pvt.,
Sargent 22 Nov. 1862. Served till 16 Apr. 1863.
Co. A, 7th N.H. Inf. Res. Manchester, N.H. Occ.
carpenter.

Children: 5240. AMOS FREMONT, b. 1 Feb. 1857,
                  d. 3 Aug. 1903. Editor of
                  Lancaster Gazette.
            5241. DAVID EUGENE, b. 1859.
            5242. CARRIE, b. 1862, md. GILBERT
                  E. LANE.
            5243. WILLIAM L. Jr., b. 1864, md.
                  ELIZA M. FRIDLEY?
            5244. ARTHUR W., b. 1870.

2253. LEVI W. ROWELL [WILLIAM 1158] He was born
1838 at Gorham, N.H. He married 7 July 1863
FRANCES T. ESTABROOK, d/o ALANSON & ELECTRA
ESTABROOK, of West Lebanon.   Occ. printer,

Granite State Press. Will probated 1886 at
Albany, Vt. [5:2392] Res. Johnsburg, Vt.

Children: 5245. **GEORGIE LENA,**
           5246. **WINIFRED.**

2270. HIRAM LEONARD ROWELL [LEONARD F. 1173] He
was born 21 Jan. 1837 at Haverhill, Mass. and
died 26 Mar. 1916 at E. Kingston, N.H. He
married 16 Sep. 1869 **CLARA FRANCES BATCHELDER,**
d/o **NATHANIEL & ABBIE (MARSH) BATCHELDER.** She
born 30 July 1848 and died 21 April 1935. He
served in Civil War, 2nd N.H. Inf. Reg't. Occ.
shoe maker. Res. Rochester.

Children: 5280. **ALBERT LEONARD,** b. 18 Feb.
                  1872, d. 9 Nov. 1939, md.
                  1912 **MELVINA McCARTHY.** Had:
                  NATHANIEL B. 1921. Hotel Mgr
           5281. **HARRIET FRANCES,** b. 26 Apr.
                  1873, md. 15 Sep. 1921
                  WILLIAM or **WALLACE L. TILTON**
           5282. **IRVING H.,** b. 7 Sep. 1875,
                  d. 24 Nov. 1893 E. Kingston.
           5283. **CHARLES WARREN,** b. 17 Sep.
                  1877.
           5284. **EDWARD STEVENS,** b. 30 Aug.
                  1879.
           5285. **WALTER GIFFORD,** b. 8 Apr.
                  1884, d. 16 Aug. 1884.
           5286. **ANNE TEWKSBURY,** b. 8 Aug.
                  1885, md. 1931 **ELDON PACKARD**
           5287. **MARION LUCRETIA,** b. 11 May
                  1889.
           5288. **ALLEN B.,** b. 29 June 1891, d.
                  17 Jan. 1894.
           5289. **FREDERICK BACHELDER,** b. 9 June
                  1895.

2278. JOHN W. ROWELL [LEONARD F. 1173] He was
born 9 June 1835 at Lebanon, N.H. He married 1
Aug. 1858 **MARY L. WHEELER,** d/o **Rev. LEONARD &
HANNAH (GILMAN) WHEELER.** Occ. lawyer, State
Senator, Judge 1882, Chief Judge 1902.

2301. IRA ROWELL [JONATHAN B. 1200] He was born
20 May 1831 at Haverhill, Mass. and died 4 May
1898 at Eureka, Illinois. He married 16 Nov.
1869 LAVINA CARLOCK. She born 17 Dec. 1839 at
Oak Grove, Ill. and died 9 Nov. 1917 at Des
Moines, Iowa.

Children: 5300. LILLY EDGERTON, b. 27 Sep.
1870, md. 29 Dec. 1892
Dr. OLYNTHUS BURROUGHS. Had:
LAWRENCE, RALPH T., ANNA
LAURA, MARGARET O., & ALFRED
5301. LAURA BELLE, b. 20 Dec. 1871,
d. 2 June 1889.
5302. LULA JOSEPHINE, b. 21 Nov.
1875, d. 12 Sep. 1896.
5303. EDITH IRENE, b. 30 June 1879,
md. 6 Aug. 1902 ROSCOE R.
HILL. Had: ROSCOE R.,
DOROTHY J., LUCILE E., &
EDITH F.
5304. IRA HOMER, b. 10 Oct. 1885,
md. 18 Mar. 1914 ELEANOR
WEBSTER. Had: CAROLYN,
ELIZABETH & HOMER W.

2302. JONATHAN HARVEY ROWELL [JONATHAN B. 1200]
He was born 10 Feb. 1833 at Haverhill, Mass. and
died 15 May 1905 at Bloomington, Illinois. He
married 1866 MARIA SANFORD WOODS. She born 14
Feb. 1843 at Alton, Ill. and died 8 Jan. 1916 at
Western Springs, Illinois. Occ. Lawyer. Eureka
College. Served in Civil War. Comander Co. C.,
17th Reg't Ill. Inf. Representative in Congress.

Children: 5305. CHESTER HARVEY, b. 1 Nov.
1867, d. 1948, md. 1 Aug.
1897 MYRTLE M. LINGLE.
Editor Fresno Republican
Newspaper. Had: CHESTER H.
Jr., CORA WINIFRED, MILDRED
MAY, BARBARA LOIS & JONATHAN
HARVEY.

5306. **CORA M.**, b. 20 Mar. 1869, md.
30 June 1902 **ALBERT C.
OLNEY.** Had: **MARGARET, CORA,
MARY JANE, & FREDRICK CHAS.**
5307. **LAWRENCE W.**, b. 2 Jan. 1871,
md. **ANNA HELEN WELCHER**, Had:
HELEN EVELYN.
5308. **ELMER O.**, b. 12 July 1873, md.
2 July 1902 **DELLA PAULI.**
Had: **DOROTHY JANE & AMY
ELIZABETH.**
2 children.
5309. **LAURA MAY**, b. 10 May 1879.

2304. **CHARLES CARROLL ROWELL [JONATHAN B. 1200]**
He was born 11 Dec. 1836 at Haverhill, Mass. and
died 4 July 1899 at Bloomington, Illinois. He
married about 1861 **MARGARET RAYBURN**. She born 22
May 1842 at Danvers, Ill. Res. Danvers.

Children: 5310. **KATE**, b. 31 Dec. 1861, md.
GEORGE MARTIN. Had: **RAYBURN,
VERNE M.**, GEORGE Jr.
5311. **WILLIAM SHERMAN**, b. 5 Dec.
1864, d. 31 Mar. 1945, md.
10 Sep. 1890 **MINNIE L.
DENTON.** Had: **MILO W.,
MARGARET E.**, & **GARNER R.**
5312. **CHARLES CARROLL**, b. 28 June
1869, d. 18 Oct. 1910, md.
31 Dec. 1890 **GERTRUDE W.
HALL.** Had: **MAURINE, FRANCIS
M., CHARLES HALL & JONATHAN.**

2305. **WILLIAM FRANKLIN ROWELL [JONATHAN B. 1200]**
He was born 15 Sep. 1838 at Woodville, N.H. and
died 13 May 1912 at San Jose, Calif. He married
24 Oct. 1867 at Danvers, Ill. **MARY ISABELLA
DICKINSON.** She born 26 Feb. 1847 and died 29
Aug. 1928 at San Jose, Calif. Civil War service,
Cpl. Co. D, 8th Miss. Regt.

Children: 5315. **FRANCES GERTRUDE**, b. 6 Dec.
1868.

5316. MILO LOREN, b. 12 Jan. 1871,
md. 28 June 1899 EVA LILLIAN
LAVERLY. Had: LOREN, MILO E.
WILLIAM F., MARGARET E., &
JUDITH F.
5317. MARY JANE, b. 6 Dec. 1873, d.
27 Sep. 1887.
5318. HARRY DICKINSON, b. 2 Oct.
1875, md. 1 June 1903
FANNY ROLAND. Had: FRANCES J
5319. EDNA ELLEN, b. 7 Dec. 1879,
md. 27 June 1914 WILLIAM
CLAYBOUGH. Had: MARY ELLEN,
EDNA E., CYNTHIA L. &
WILLIAM F.
5320. OLA LOIS, b. 12 Aug. 1882, md.
4 Nov. 1911 CLYDE H.
REYNOLDS. Had: GERTRUDE &
MATT C.
5321. JONATHAN, b. 25 July 1887, d.
19 Feb. 1889.
5322. ISABELL, b. 3 Oct. 1890, md.
12 Mar. 1915 STANLEY B.
SMITH. Had: FRANCES E.,
ALBERT, LOREN S. & LOIS I.

2306. MILO A. ROWELL [JONATHAN B. 1200] He was
born 13 Dec. 1840 at Woodville, N.H. and died 12
Jan. 1922 at Seattle. Wash. He married 13 Dec.
1869 SARAH LOUISE COYNER. She born 7 June 1846
Va. He served in Co. D, 8th Mo. Inf. in Civil
War. Occ. Merchant. Went to Seattle, Wash. Res.
Burlington, Kansas?

Children: 5325. ELIZABETH ABBOTT, b. Oct.
1870.
5326. daughter,
5327. JOHN HENRY, b. 1874, d. 1875.
5328. ELSIE, b. Apr. 1877, md. Dec.
1904 FRANCIS SMITH. Had:
LOUISE & ROWELL.
5329. STANLEY, b. 7 Aug. 1882, m.1,
DOROTHY HAWKINS, m.2, CLARA
McCULLOUGH.

2307. **GEORGE BARNEY ROWELL** [JONATHAN B. 1200]
He was born 13 Dec. 1842 at Woodville, N.H. and
died 27 Dec. 1907 at Fresno, Calif. He married
22 Dec. 1881 **ADELPHIA WARLOW**. She born 3 Dec.
1852 at Danvers, Illinois. She died 26 Feb. 1932
at Fresno, Cal. In 1866 crossed Great Plains.

Children: 5330. **BERNICE CYNTHIA**, b. 20 Dec.
                  1882, md. 28 Nov. 1906
                  ARTHUR L. DAHLGREN. Had:
                  DOROTHY B. & ARTHUR R.

2308. **CHESTER ROWELL** [JONATHAN B. 1200] He was
born 7 Oct. 1844 at Waterford, Vt. and died 23
May 1912 at Los Angelos, Calif. He married 25
Aug. 1872 Mrs. **NELLIE HALE ROWELL**, widow of Dr.
ISAAC ROWELL [#1220] his cousin. She born 17
Jan. 1837 and died 25 June 1883. Occ. Doctor.
Res. Fresno, Calif. Started Fresno newspaper 23
Sep. 1876. Civil War service. Battles of Shiloh
and Vicksburg. Served in Co. G, 17th Ill. Inf.
1909 mayor of Fresno, Cal.

2309. **ALBERT ABBOT ROWELL** [JONATHAN B. 1200] He
was born 30 May 1848 Essex Co., Vt. He married
22 Dec. 1878 **NANCY ANN BOOTH**, d/o **STEPHEN BOOTH**.
Served as Pvt. in Co. G, 17th Ill. Inf. Went to
York, Nebr. in 1871, then to Fresno, Cal. Member
Christian Chursh. Res. Selma, Cal.

2321. **CLINTON ROWELL** [GUY C. 1204] He was born
12 Nov. 1838 at Concord, Vt. and died 1 Nov.
1907 at St. Louis, Mo. He married 12 Nov. 1868
CAROLYN M. FERRIS, d/o **CHARLES FERRIS**. She born
April 1843 at Peru, N.Y. Dartmouth Coll. 1861-
2, Lawyer. Democrat. Res. St. Louis, Mo.

Children: 5335. **EUGENIA MAY**, b. 12 May 1870,
                  d. 1879.
            5336. **GRACE F.**, b. 24 Nov. 1873.
            5337. **CARLTON F.**, b. 9 June 1885.

2329. MOSES FRANKLIN ROWELL [BENJAMIN F. 1205]
He was born 26 Oct. 1846 at White Oak Park, Ill.
and died 16 July 1913 at Berwyn, Ill. He married
20 May 1875 ALMA SUSAN BOWEN, d/o ABRAHAM M. &
ELIZABETH (SCARFF) BOWEN.. She born 9 Oct. 1855
at Dayton, Oh. and died 5 Jan. 1931. Res.
Danvers, Illinois.

Children: 5338. HARRIET, b. 24 Feb. 1876, d. 4
                 Feb. 1938, md. 30 Dec. 1897
                 IRA J. HOFF. Had: FRANKLIN
                 R. & WILLIAM J.
           5339. IDA, b. 29 Oct. 1877, d. 17
                 Nov. 1947, md. 23 Aug. 1899
                 WILLIAM G. NEWELL. Had: IDA
                 B., ELEANOR, RICHARD,
                 FRANCES, BARIAN, ROBERT
                 WILLIAM & JOHN D.
           5340. BIRD, b. 16 Nov. 1879, d. 16
                 May 1964, md. Dec. 1918
                 CLYDE L. BURTON. Had:
                 JONATHAN.
           5341. LOIS, b. 11 Mar. 1882, d. 7
                 May 1966, md. 2 July 1930
                 WILLIAM F. SPENCER, 1 child.
           5342. CHARITY ELIZABETH, b. 24 Nov.
                 1887, d. 21 May 1963, md. 27
                 Nov. 1929 ALBERT E. KIRBY.

2338. RICHARD CLARK ROWELL [SALMON H. 1208] He
was born 25 Oct. 1865 and died 22 June 1938 at
Barnet, Vt. He married 25 Oct. 1886 MARGARET
BUNDY. She died 5 Dec. 1927 at Barnet, Vt.

Children: 5343. IMOGENE, b. 9 Dec. 1887, m.1,
                 4 July 1910 ALEXANDER E.
                 ROY, m.2, 22 Sep. 1923 GUY
                 COURGER. 1 dau.
           5344. JOSEPHINE, b. 22 Aug. 1890, d.
                 21 Jan. 1907.
           5345. HATTIE M., b. 17 Sep. 1892,
                 md. 17 Sep. 1912 CLARENCE
                 CALDWELL. 3 ch.

2341. **GEORGE B. ROWELL** [CALEB 1214] He was born
27 Feb. 1829 at Percy and died 9 Feb. 1905 at
Paxton. He married 13 Nov. 1851 at Starke, N.H.
his second cousin **LOUISE COLE**, d/o **JOSHUA &
AMANDA (HINDS) COLE**. She born 11 May 1832 at
Percy and died 11 Sep. 1879. Occ. Boat and shoe
manufacturer, Paxton, Me. 1899.

Children: 5346. **ELLA LOUISE**, b. 21 Jan. 1858,
            d, 1 May 1888, unmd. Born
            Spencer, Mass.

2342. **HARVEY ROWELL** [CALEB 1214]   He was born
c1834 at Walden, Vt. and died 21 Feb. 1891 in
Cuba. He married 3 Sep. 1853 his second cousin
CORA ALMIRA COLE, d/o **WEEDEN & MARGARET
(LEAVITT) COLE**. She born 29 June 1833 at Percy
and died 1873. Occ. locomotive Engineer.
Children born at Starke, N.H. Res. Walden,
Caledonia Co., Vt.

Children: 5347. **JULIUS J.**, b. 31 Mar. 1860, d.
            23 Sep. 1860.
            5348. **HENRY IRVING**, b. 31 Mar. 1860.
            5349. **AVERY EDSON**, b. 24 June 1863,
            liv. 1930, md. 21 Feb. 1891
            ANGIE SARAH GREEN, d/o
            **CHARLES & ROSE (ELLINGWORD)
            GREEN**. She b. 1868.
            5350. **FREDDIE GRANT**, b. 1 Feb. 1867.
            5351. **CHARLES H.**, b. 18 July 1865.
            5352. **LINDA ABBA**, b. 5 Feb. 1870.

2346. **SPAULDING ROWELL** [JOSHUA 1216]   He was
born 21 Nov. 1831 at Starke, N.H. and died 24
May 1877. He married **MARTHA BALL**, d/o **ALMON &
MARY ANN (AVERY) BALL**. She died 10 days before
her husband. Res. Abbottsford, Quebec.

Children: 5353. Dr. GEORGE BELL, b. 19 July
1858, d. 1921 at So.
Bernardine, Cal., m.1,
FLORENCE WOOD, divorced,
m.2, LOUISE _____. Had:
GEORGE BALL.
5354. CLARK, b. 1 Sep. 1861, d.
1890, md. MARGARET CRAIG.
Had: CLARENCE A. 1884,
THEROLD c1886.
5355. ALBERTA LUCINDA, b. 19 Oct.
1864, d. 30 Sep. 1952, md.
1 Oct. 1884 JAMES OTIS
RICHARDSON. Had: ETHEL M.,
EDITH I., SAMUEL S., HELEN
A. & JAMES K.
5356. SYBIL EUNICE, b. 22 May 1867,
d. 7 Oct. 1937, md. ORVIS
HARRISON JACKMAN as 2nd wife
5357. SYDNEY, b. 7 July 1872, d.
1954, m.1, ELIZABETH
BROUSSEAN, m.2, widow
MARGARET MUNRO. Had:
MILDRED, DOROTHY, & STUART.
5358. WILLIAM SPAULDING, b. 1 May
1877, m.1, CLARA RUFFING,
m.2, widow ANNE _____. Had:
GEORGE RUFFING. Res. Cal.

2350. ISAAC SMITH ROWELL [JOSHUA 1216] He was
born 13 Aug. 1838 at Stark, N.H. and died 13
Apr. 1907 at Cedaredge, Colo. He married 26 July
1868 MYRA WILBER, d/o JEFFERSON &
(ELIZABETH) ANNE (TRIM) WILBER at Ponca, Nebr.
She born 10 Oct. 1849 and died 4 Feb. 1914 at
Eureka, Calif.

Children: 5360. ALBERT CHESTER, b. 15 May
1869, d. 12 Aug. 1939, unmd.
5361. MINNIE IRENE, b. 23 Apr. 1871,
md. 23 Jan. 1889 FRANCIS M.
FICKES. Had: JAMES F.,
SUSAN B., ROSE M., HELEN G.
& DOROTHEA R.

5362. CHARLES PAIGE, b. 23 Sep.
1873, d. Jan. 1913, unmd.
5363. EUGENE CLARK, b. 25 Aug. 1875,
d. 22 Jan. 1956, m.1, June
1908 WINIFRED M. PEEBLES,
m.2, 9 June 1932 MINNIE
OLSON,
1 child.
5364. WILBER SPAULDING, b. 1880, d.
1959, 6 children.
5365. SYBIL ANN, b. 1882, d. 1948,
4 children.
5366. LOVINA PENELOPE, b. 1884, d.
1884.
5367. INA MARTHA, 1 child.
5368. PHOEBE LORETTA, b. 1891, d.
1891.
5369. ALFRED LEE, b. 1894, 1 child.

2352. SENECA PAIGE ROWELL [JOSHUA 1216] He was
born 8 Jan. 1843 and died 17 Dec. 1917 at
Abbottsford, Quebec. He married HELEN WATSON.
Occ. school principal in Montreal. Earned A.B.
from McGill University.

Children: 5370. Dr. WATSON JOSHUA, b. 10 Sep.
1875, d. Dec. 1956 md.
KATHERINE WARD. Had:
HARTLAND P. b. 1902.
5371. ARTHUR HOWARD, b. 8 July 1877,
md. NELLIE ROBERTS. Had:
HOWARD PAIGE, b. c1902, d.
1966, md. ANNE ARGNE. Had:
PAIGE, MARY E. & ANNE A.
5372. HELEN LOUISE, b. 15 Dec. 1878,
d. 8 June 1957, md. Dr.
WILLIAM WATSON, her 1st
cousin. Had: DAVID S., JOHN,
MARION, JEAN, PETER, WILLIAM
& PAULINE.
5373. JOHN SPAULDING, b. 25 Jan.
1883, d. 1935, unmd.

ROWELL FAMILY - NEW ENGLAND
9th Generation

2353. JOSHUA ROWELL Jr.[JOSHUA 1216] He was born
16 May or 6 Nov. 1844 and died Mar. 1882. He
married 5 Feb. 1902 JULIA ROWELL [#2338] adopted
daughter of DANIEL & CHARLOTTE (POTTER) ROWELL
[#1219] She born 1 June 1857 and died 26 Apr.
1919. Owned sawmill. Res. Fulford, Quebec.

Children: 5375. ELLEN, b. 8 Nov. 1872, d.y.
           5376. BYRON JOSHUA, b. 25 Mar.
                 1881, d. 10 Sep. 1950, md.
                 VIVIAN GIBB. Had: ETHEL,
                 BYRON ARTHUR 1912, DOROTHY
                 1914.

2360. FRANK A. ROWELL [Dr. ISAAC 1221] He was
born 25 Oct. 1863 and died 9 April 1898. He
married 14 Sep. 1887 ELIZABETH JOHNSON.

Children: 5377. NELLIE IMOGENE, b. 1886, md.
                 WALLACE MASON.

2368. JOHN COLBY ROWELL [NEHEMIAH 1237] He was
born 1835 at Nottingham, N.H. and died 1919. He
married 1864 MARY ELIZA CLARKE of Barrington,
N.H. Occ. farmer.

Children: 5378. ERASTUS CHASE, b. 1865, d.
                 1948, md. AGNES MAY SARGENT,
                 Had: BRIDGE RICE, 1898, MARY
                 SARGAENT 1905.
           5379. GEORGE HARVEY, b. 1867, md.
                 BELLE TUTTLE. No children.
           5380. WILBER JAMES, b. 1873, d.
                 1945, m.1, 1909 LAURA C.
                 CLEGG, m.2, 1945 ISABELLA
                 DEAN.

2372. ALEXANDER ROWELL [WILLIAM 1240] He was
born 6 Aug. 1842 at Portland, Me. and died 1905.
He married 1867 SUSAN ELLEN JENKINS of York, Me.
He served in 27th Maine Vol. Inf. in Civil War.
Res. So. Berwick, Me. Salmon Falls, N.H. and
Waltham, Mass.

Children: 5381. Col. MELVIN WESTON, b. 1868 at
            So. Berwick, Me., d. 5 Aug.
            1965 at Manchester, N.H.
            V.A. Hosp., buried at
            Northwood, N.H., Grad. West
            Point, Author of Register of
            Rowells books. Had: MELVIN
            WILSON, & JOSEPHINE by 1st
            Wife; Had: adopted dau.
            HUGUETTE & SUZANNE by JEANNE
            LONGCHAMPT.
            5382. LEWIS ALBRA, b. 1870, d. 1921,
            md. 1899 EMMA A. MENDIGO.
            Had: LEWIS WILLIAM, ALBERT
            EUGENE & ESTHER A.
            5383. WESLEY ALEXANDER, b. 1873, d.
            1934, twin.
            5384. LENA SUSAN, b. 1873, d. 1952,
            unmd, twin.

2375. JOHN A. ROWELL [JOHN 1242] He was born
1844 and died 1938. He married 1866 MARY CARTER.
Res. Brentwood, N.H.

Children: 5390. WALTER,
            5391. ALICE, md. _____ STEEVES.
            5392. GEORGE A., b. 1870.

2376. CHARLES EVERETT ROWELL [CHARLES L. 1243]
He was born 1836 and died 1919. He married
JUDITH M. GILE. Occ. grocer. Res. Merrimac Port.

Children: 5395. LAURA, b. 1866, md. EVERETT
            JEWELL.

2432. MARK EDWIN ROWELL [LUTHER H. 1261] He was
born 15 Sep. 1863 and died 15 Sep. 1939. He
married 19 Feb. 1888 ALICE MARY SNOW, d/o SAMUEL
B. & SOPHIE (KEEN) SNOW. She born 27 Sep. 1884?
and died 10 may 1954. Attended Colby Coll. Res.
Thomaston, Me.

Children: 5430. EVA MAY, b. 16 Sep. 1888, md.
            12 Feb. 1911 MAYNARD POST.

5431. FRED WILLIAM, b. 3 Sep. 1890,
 d. Feb. 1952, m.1, 1914
 HAZEL SHIPMAN, div. 1915,
 m.2, 24 Dec. 1918 IVA
 RUSSELL, WW1. Lt. aviation,
 Had: ROBERT WILLIAM.
5432. EDNA MABEL, b. 18 Sep. 1892,
 md. 1 Dec. 1913 ARCHIE
 RACKLIFF.
5433. son, d. 1894. died at birth.
5434. GRACE MATTHEWS, b. 27 June
 1895, d. 1954, md. 29 May
 1921 CHARLES H. CARR.
5435. LILLIAN BUCKLIN, b. 16 June
 1899, d. 1956.

2434. RALPH ROBERT ROWELL [LUTHER 1261] He was
born 24 Apr. 1880. He married first 8 June 1905
ELLA G. NEWELL. Divorced. He married second 1928
MABEL McKAY of Augusta. She born 15 Sep. 1901.
Grad. Washington Univ. Occ. lawyer. Elected to
Maine State legislature.

Children: 1st wife:
 5440. EVELYN ELIZABETH, b. 27 Mar.
 1906, md. 1928 PHILIP E.
 WHITAKER.
by 2nd wife:
 5441. IDA MABEL, b. 4 Feb. 1929, d.
 28 Mar. 1930.
 5442. PHYLLIS ALBERTA, b. 2 Mar.
 1931.

2455. ENOCH JOHN ROWELL [WILLARD C. 1293] He was
born 6 Jan. 1886 and died 6 Mar. 1938. He
married 5 Oct. 1922 MILDRED A. BROWN. Res.
Albany, Vt.

Children: 5465. PAULINE ESTHER, b. 11 Aug.
 1923.
 5466. ENOCH JOHN, b. 23 Apr. 1925.
 5467. WILLIAM BROWN, b. 10 July
 1926.

ROWELL FAMILY - NEW ENGLAND
9th Generation

5468. PHILIP WAYNE, b. 14 May 1928,
md. CAROLYN ANDERSON.

2456. FRANK PLUMBY ROWELL [WILLARD C. 1293] He
was born 14 Feb. 1888 at Albany, Vt. He married
GEORGIANNA BROCK. She born 1896 in Scotland.

Children: 5470. BEVERLEY E., md. 4 Feb. 1945
ARTHUR S. LITTLE Jr.
5471. NORMA BROCK, md. 4 May 1947
FREDERICK L. ANDREWS.
5472. JOYCE MAE, b. 13 May 1913, md.
29 May 1950 M. ALBERT SEWARD
Jr.
5473. FRANK CONVERSE, md. BARBARA
_____.

2458. GEORGE SMITH ROWELL [ELIPHELET 1296] He
was born 12 March 1846 at Hallowell, Maine. He
married 17 April 1871 LYDIA E. GALLAGHER, d/o
MICHAEL GALLAGHER of Presque Isle. He was editor
of the Portland Daily Advertizer.

2472. GEORGE PRESBURY ROWELL [SAMUEL 1300] He
was born 4 July 1838 at Concord, Vt. and died
1908. He married first 1862 SARAH B. EASTMAN. He
married second 1891 JEANETTE RIGNEY HALLACK. In
1863 he published the first complete directory
of U.S. newspapers. Res. Boston, Mass. and New
York City. Child by 1st wife.

Children: 5479. PERSIS E., Had: EVERETT B.M.

2495. HIRAM VANDELIA ROWELL [JOHN P. 1303] He
was born 1851 at Groveland, N.Y. He married 1875
MARY A. GREENWOOD. Occ. hotel keeper. Res.
Nunda, N.Y.

Children: 5480. GEORGIA A., b. 1876.

2498. CHARLES HENRY ROWELL [GEORGE W. 1304] He
was born 1846 at Boston and died 1864. Enlisted
in 4th N.Y. Heavy Artillery. Killed in action at
Petersburg, Va.

2499. EDWARD ALONZO ROWELL [GEORGE W. 1304] He
was born 1848 at Boston and died 1896. He
married 1870 JANETTE H. CROSS. Went to Kinsley,
Kansas and in 1873 to Great Bend, KS.

Children: 5485. ELIZABETH, b. c1871, md. _____
           PURCELL.

2502. CHARLES EMERY ROWELL [FREDERICK 1306] He
was born 2 May 1849 at Kirby, Vt. and died 29
March 1924 at Stamford. He married 1872 ARLETTA
EMELINE BOLLES, d/o JAMES & LOUISE (FIELDS)
BOLLES. She born 7 March 1854 at Dalton, N.H.
and died 21 Feb. 1932. Occ. Doctor. Res.
Stamford, Conn.

Children: 5490. JAMES FREDERICK, b. 1874, d.
                 1951, md. 1903 MAUD
                 NARBONEE. Had: DOROTHY,
                 ARLETTA, MAYE, CHARLES E.,
                 WILLIAM D. & EDITH.
           5491. GEORGE PRESBURY, b. 23 Nov.
                 1876, d. 18 Apr. 1935, md.
                 27 Aug. 1919 RUTH L. TUCKER.
                 No children. Went to Texas.
           5492. EDWARD EVERETT, b. 1878, d.
                 1947, md. 1921 MADELINE
                 GERONIMO. Occ doctor.

2504. EDWARD EVERETT ROWELL [FREDERICK 1306] He
was born 28 Oct. 1853 at Concord, Vt. He married
first 1876 ELLA WILLARD. He married second 1892
ADELINE SKELDING. Occ. Doctor. Res. new York
City, Chicago and Colorado. At Stamford, Conn.
in 1877.

Children: 5495. EDWARD EVERETT, b. 1876.
           5496. RODNEY WALLACE, b. 1893.
           5497. DOROTHY SKELDING, d. infancy.
           5498. DORIS, b. 1897.

2540. **CHARLES S. ROWELL** [CHARLES H. 1316] He was born 1849 at Lebanon, Me. He married 21 May 1890 **FRANCES (FANNIE) S. ALLEN.** Occ. lawyer. Res. Fairfield, Me. and Union, N.H.

Children: 5540. **CHARLES ALLEN,** d. infancy.
5541. **KATHERINE FRANCES,** b. 1895.

2560. **CHARLES WILLIAM ROWELL** [CHARLES W. 1321] He was born 1852 at Manchester, N.H. He married first 1876 **MARY E. STARKE.** He married second 1895 **ADDIE PINGREE.** Occ. farmer.

Children: 5560. **DUDLEY SAVORY,** b. 1877, d. 18 Nov. 1898, md. 1897 **FLORA A. CATE.**
5561. **WALTER STARK,** b. 1878, d. infancy.
5562. **ASHLEY HILL,** b. 1886, d. infancy.
5563. **JOHN PAGE STARK,** b. 1883.

2561. **HERBERT SIDNEY ROWELL** [CHARLES W. 1321] He was born 1854 at Manchester, N.H. He married 1896 **BESSIE GREEN.** Res. Manchester, N. H. 1898.

2565. **JAMES FRANCIS ROWELL** [CHARLES W. 1321] He was born 1868 at Manchester, N.H. Single in 1898. Res. Manchester.

2566. **HENRY IRVING ROWELL** [CHARLES W. 1321] He was born 1870. He married 1891 **MARGARET B. MADDEN.** Occ. house painter, Lt. in Militia. Res. Manchester, N.H.

Children: 5565 **MILDRED CATHERINE,** b. 14 Mar. 1902.

2585. **ROLAND ROWELL** [**EPHRAIN K.** 1328] He was born 22 Feb. 1849 at manchester and died there 16 Nov. 1906. He married in Chicago 5 Sep. 1883 **SARAH ALIDA CROSBY**, d/o **ALPHONSO & SARAH J. (FAIRFIELD) CROSBY**. She born 18 Nov. 1853. Author of book on "SAMUEL ROWELL & DESCENDANTS". Occ. lawyer, Court Clerk. No children.

2586. **CHARLES EDGAR ROWELL** [**EPHRAIM K.** 1328] He was born 1851 at Manchester, N.H. Single in 1898. Occ. Realtor. Res. Manchester, N.H.

2591. **JAMES FRANK ROWELL** [**NATHAN P.** 1345] He was born 21 Dec. 1852 at Weld, Maine. He married 4 March 1877 **ABBIE J. KENNEDY**, d/o **Hon. THOMAS KENNEDY**. Had 1 child who died young. Attended Portland Medical School. Occ. DDS.

2593. **WILLIAM EDWIN ROWELL** [**AMASSY** 1365] He was born 9 Jan. 1850 Oakland Co., Mich. He married 31 Oct. 1872 **SUSAN WORDEN** at Fenton, Mich.

Children: 5570. **BEN IRVING**,
           5571. **CHARLES EDWIN**, b. 7 Sep. 1885,
                  d. 18 June 1975, md. 23 Oct.
                  1907 **EMMA J. HAYES**. Had:
                  **VICTOR M, LAUREN EDWIN, AVON
                  MARION & THEO CHARLINE**.
           5572. **GEORGE AMASSY**,
           5573. **BLANCH**,
           5574. **ELSIE**,
           5575. **NELLIE**,
           5576. **GOLDA**,
           5577. **MARY**,
           5578. **VERNE**,

2603. **ADOLPHUS P. ROWELL** [**RUFUS** 1384] He was born 3 Nov. 1834 and died 1910. He married 26 Nov. 1854 **ANNE E. THUMBER**. She born 1836 and died 1914. Res. Corinth & Vershire, Vt.

Children: 5579. **FLORA A.**, b. 28 Nov. 1862, d.
5 Nov. 1899, md. **GEORGE H.**
BECKWITH.
5580. **BERTHA M.**, b. 29 Sep. 1865, d.
30 Mar. 1866.

2604. **ORANGE ROWELL** [RUFUS 1384] He was born
1840 and died 1903. He married **ALMA/ALVINA**
_____. Buried at Corinth, Vt.

Children: 5581. **FRED NELSON**, b. 15 Dec. 1869.

2613. **ERASTUS B. ROWELL** [JOHN 1398] He was born
8 Jan. 1837 and died 1 April 1895 at Manchester,
N.H. He married **FRANCELIA ATKINS.** Res.
Bennington, Vt.

Children: 5582. **ALANSON ERASTUS**, b. 14 Apr.
1866.

2654. **FRANK ROWELL** [ISAAC 1421] He was born 30
Nov. 1846 at Brentwood, N.H. and died 8 Apr.
1933. He married **MARY GARLAND** of Exeter, N.H.
Occ. farmer. Res. Brentwood, N.H.

Children: 5583. **CARRIE**, b. 1875, md. **C.S.**
SMITH.
5584. **HOWARD**, b. 17 Sep. 1877, d. 23
May 1953, md. **MABEL PIKE.**
Had: **MADELINE.**
5585. **GRACE**, b. 1881, md. 1903 **C.D.**
CARLISLE.
5586. **SIDNEY FOREST**, b. 11 May 1885,
md. **BERTHA STEVENS.** Had:
LEONA, ARTHUR, DORIS,
PRISCILLA & ROBERT.

2670. **ELMIRA ADALINE ROWELL** [JACOB H. 1422] She
was born 14 June 1834 at Newport, Me. and died
31 Jan. 1923. She married May 1865 **HARRY**
WILLIAMS. She married second 8 Oct. 1876 **ROBERT**
LESLIE.

Children: i. GEORGE KELLER WILLIAMS, b. 30
                 Mar. 1867.
            ii. JESSIE EVELYN WILLIAMS, b. 30
                 Sep. 1870.

2672. ANGELIC MARCELLA ROWELL [JACOB H. 1422]
She was born 21 Jan. 1842 and died 10 May 1904.
She married 20 Feb. 1859 WILSON HOOK.

Children: i. MYRA EVELINE HOOK, b. 3 Jan.
                 1860.
            ii. CLARA FRANCES HOOK, b. 4 Feb.
                 1862.
           iii. JACOB EDWARD HOOK, b. 28 Aug.
                 1864.
            iv. FREDERICK GEORGE HOOK, b. 13
                 Mar. 1867.
             v. ABBIE MARIE HOOK, b. 19 Oct.
                 1869.
            vi. WILLIAM SUMNER HOOK, b. 19 Sep.
                 1871.
           vii. WALTER ROWELL HOOK, b. 20 June
                 1874.

2698. AMBROSE ROWELL [ADDISON 1424] He was born
1835 and died 1885. He married MARY A. GORDON.
She died 1905. 7 children. Res. Brentwood.

Children: 5690. NORA,
             5691. FRED, b. 15 July 1869.
             5692. JACOB, b. c1870, d. 22 Apr.
                   1892 [21-6-16] Shoe maker at
                   Raymond, N.H.

2700. JOHN SHUTE ROWELL [ADDISON 1424] He was
born 7 Mar. 1842. He married 15 Feb. 1864
ROSELVINA BELKNAP. Res. Exeter Co., Mass.

Children: 5700. JOHN EDWARD E.M., b. 17 Mar.
                   1871.
             5701. CHARLES EVERETT, b. 7 Mar.
                   1871?
             5702. GRACE DARLING, b. 7 Feb. 1876.
             5703. ARTHUR B., b. 17 June 1887.

2708. **BENJAMIN WINSLOW ROWELL** [JOHN W. 1426] He
was born 18 Aug. 1845 at Chichester, N.H. and
died 23 Aug. 1927 at Lynn, Mass. He married 5
Dec. 1871 **SUSAN AUGUSTA NEWHALL**, d/o **HENRY
WILLARD & SUSAN H. (LEWIS) NEWHALL**. She died 2
Sep. 1919. No children. Occ. treasurer Boston
Mutual Life Ins. Co. Masonic Lodge. Methodist.

2719. **DAVID JEWETT ROWELL** [DAVID S. 1429] He
was born 1 Mar. 1827 at Madison, Me. and died 28
August 1905. He married 21 Sep. 1857 **MARY
PLUMMER**. She born 17 June 1835 and died 28 Sep.
1914. Res. Madison, Maine.

Children: 5705. **EDWARD F.**, b. 17 June 1866, d.
May 1915, md. 1893 **EFFIE
MERRILL**. (1870-1956)
5706. **ELMER B.**, b. 22 Dec. 1867, d.
5 May 1952, md. 18 Apr. 1900
EDA DAGGETT (1877-1963) Had:
GLADYS.

2721. **JAMES GREEN ROWELL** [DAVID S. 1429] He was
born 5 March 1831 and died 1 Nov. 1899. He
married 25 April 1856 **JANE SUSAN HAMBLETT**. She
born 26 Aug. 1836 and died 26 Dec. 1895. Both
buried at Solon, Maine.

Children: 5707. **HARLOW WOOD**, b. 12 Dec. 1858,
d. 8 May 1921, m.1, 19 Nov.
1890 **MINNIE E. HIGHT**. She d.
16 Feb. 1892, m.2, 25 Dec.
1894 **EMMA MARIA WESCOTT**
(1874-1950) Had: **HOWARD,
LEONA, HILDA & CURTIS**.
5708. **EMMA F.**, b. 16 Oct. 1860, d.
10 June 1886, md. 15 Aug.
1880 **WILLIAM H, WARD**. Had:
IVAN 1881.
5709. **ALBION K.**, b. 28 Jan. 1863, d.
18 Nov. 1938, md. 19 July
1890 **LULU JEANETTE STEVENS**
(1873-1958). Had: **FREEMAN E.**

b. 1882, d. 1885 and **ELINOR MAE**, b. 1891.

2725. **ALBERT ROWELL** [DAVID S. 1429] He was born 7 Mar. 1841 and died 21 Oct. 1919. He married 12 May 1873 **CORRIE KINCAID**. She born 24 Feb. 1857 and died 1939.

Children: 5710. **HERBERT**, b. 1875, d. 24 Apr. 1897, md. **LENA CORSON**. Had: DAVID, DONALD & DENA.
5711. **FLORANCE**, b. 1876, d. 1955, md. 25 Dec. 1895 **ARTHUR HEALEY**. 1 ch.
5712. **WALTER WOOD**, b. 6 Apr. 1878, d. 2 Sep. 1956, md. 29 Dec. 1909 **INEZ KEACH**. Had: HERBERT, ALICE, DOROTHY, WILLIAM, RUTH & NORMAN.
5713. **ANNE**, b. 1882, d. 14 Sep. 1898
5714. **HATTIE**, b. 24 Mar. 1888, d. 24 June 1964, md. 15 Mar. 1911 **HERBERT BOARDMAN**. 2 sons.

2737. **WILLIAM ROWELL** [ISAAC 1432] He was born 7 Feb. 1853 and died 18 Jan. 1918. He married 30 Dec. 1884 **ZETTA E. SOULE**. She born 10 Oct. 1863 and died 20 April 1927.

Children: 5720. **ALTA ERVEME**, b. 8 Oct. 1899.
5721. **MILDRED ALICE**, b. 8 June 1904, md. **ERNEST R. DUNLAP**. 5 ch.

2745. **SIMON M. ROWELL** [WASHINGTON 1436] He was born 28 Apr. 1847 and died 10 Feb. 1936. He married 12 Oct. 1873 **JENNIE E. POTTLE**, d/o JOHN D. & ELEANOR (NORTON) POTTLE. She born 3 Jan. 1853 and died 8 Aug. 1930.

Children: 5725. **FRANK L.**, b. 17 Dec. 1877, d. 16 Oct. 1923, md. 24 Jan. 1905 **MILDRED A. BEAR**. 1 ch.

2747. HIRAM CHENEY ROWELL [WASHINGTON 1436] He
was born 25 May 1850 at Skowhegen, Me. and died
18 Nov. 1941. He married 8 Mar. 1876 ADA E.
BLODGETT, d/o SAMUEL & LUCRETIA (MANN) BLODGETT.
She born 24 Oct. 1853 and died 5 May 1923 at
Berlin, N.H.

Children: 5726. CHENEY DEXTER, b. 12 Dec.
1876, d. 28 Sep. 1971 in
Ohio, md. ELSIE THOMAS.
2 children.
5727. NELLIE MARIE, b. 10 Dec. 1878,
md. 20 Sep. 1904 GEORGE
F. LOVETT.
5728. EUGENE DUNBAR, b. 2 Feb./9
July 1885, d. 1887.
5729. RENA L., b. 16 Jan. 1887, d.
22 Apr. 1934, md. 17 June
1918 CLARENCE G. ANDRUS.

2749. LESTER ALBERT ROWELL [WASHINGTON 1436] He
was born 23 Sep. 1854 at Skowhegen, Me. and died
26 April 1897 at Berlin, N.H. He married 9 Jan.
1889 MINA BELLE LESLIE d/o SAMUEL C. & MARY ANN
(DOLBIER) LESLIE. She born 8 Oct. 1862 and died
1917. Res. Lewiston, Maine. Spokane, Wash. in
1915.

Children: 5730. MINA, b. 27 Dec. 1889, d. 24
Dec. 1965, md. 17 July 1917
THOMAS H. McKAY. 4 ch.
5731. EDNA, b. 26 Oct. 1891, d. 11
May 1970, m.1, 1928 Capt.
J.O. FISHER (USN), m.2,
NATHANIEL MITCHELL.
5732. LESLIE EUGENE, b. 31 July
1896, d. 11 Oct. 1972, md.
27 June 1924 EVELYN MARTIN.
1 child.

2755. CHARLES DINSMORE ROWELL [DANIEL 1440] He
was born 1833 and died 1910. He married
ELIZABETH MARTIN of Goffstown. Occ. farmer. Res.
Goffstown & Concord, N.H.

Children: 5733. FRANCIS MARTIN, b. 1863, d.
1899, md. 1890 EMMA CHASE.
Had: ETTA MAY 1891.
5734. JAMES D., b. 1865, d. 1878.
5735. MARY L.. b. 1868, md. 1895
_____ EMERSON.
5736. ADDIE M., b. 1873, md. 1893
_____ EMERSON.

2763. JOSEPH F. ROWELL [JOSEPH M. 1441] He was
born 1841 at Manchester, N.H. and died 1892 or
1899 at Northampton, Mass. He married 1872 at
Southwick, Mass. MARY F. ROCKWELL. Occ. Railroad
Station Master at Northampton.

Children: 5737. ARTHUR B., b. 1874, d. 1945,
md. 1899 MAUD COOLEY. Had:
ELWYN J. & ELEANOR.
5738. JEANETTE,

2769. HENRY LEONARD ROWELL [LEONARD 1448] He
was born 1861 at Dunbarton, N.H. He married 1888
NELLIE L. HADLEY. Occ. Salesman. Res. San Diego,
Calif. No children.

2770. WILLIAM STINSON ROWELL [LEONARD 1448] He
was born Sep. 1863 and died 1917. He married
CORA RICHARDS of Goffstown. Occ. appointed
station master at Goffstown in 1883. Res.
Goffstown.

Children: 5739. MARJORIE, b. 1886.

2780. LORENZO ROWELL [JOHN 1450] He was born
March 1830 and died 14 April 1866. He married
Mrs. SARAH GILMAN.

Children: 5740. MIRTIE F., d.y.

2781. JOHN ORLANDO ROWELL [JOHN 1450] He was
born 1831 and died 9 Jan. 1899. He married JANE
(JENNIE) MITCHEL, d/o DAVID & ELIZA (JEWETT)
MITCHEL. She born 1845 and died 9 Aug. 1905.
Res. Hartland, Maine.

Children: 5742. **LULU BLANCHE**, b. 1877, d. 16
Feb. 1936, md. **CLARENCE W.
THOMAS.**
5743. **DAVID**, Had 2 children.

2783. **CHARLES W. ROWELL [JOHN 1450]** He was born
4 Dec. 1835 and died 20 Nov. 1907. He married
ROSE ANNE STARBIRD. She born 3 April 1838 and
died 20 Nov. 1905. Res. Hartland, Maine.

Children: 5745. **ALFRED ALPHANE**, b. 11 Apr.
1861, d. 1 Mar. 1935, md.
_____ .
5746. **MINNEOLA**, b. 6 May 1864, d. 22
May 1912.
5747. **MERTLE FRANCES**, b. 1874.
5748. **RALPH HAROLD**, b. 1879, unmd.

2787. **THOMAS BARTON ROWELL [JOHN 1450]** He was
born 6 Aug. 1843 and died 10 June 1913. He
married **HARRIET N. WHEELER**, d/o **WILLIAM &
ELIZABETH (FINSOM) WHEELER.** She born 15 July
1848 and died 10 Oct. 1951.

Children: 5750. **BARTHA M.**, b. 19 Sep. 1869, d.
5 June 1952.

2806. **ABEL WOOD ROWELL [FREDERICK 1459]** He was
born 12 March 1832 at Solon, Maine and died 5
Oct. 1909. He went to Calif. age 19 and again
later for 3 years. He married 1st 26 March 1854
ALMELA W. BURNS, d/o **SAMUEL & ANNIS (WESTON)
BURNS.** She born 1835 and died 21 March 1882. He
married 2nd, 1 Jan. 1887 **Mrs. LYDIA BASSETT
McFARLAND**, d/o **ALANSON BASSETT.** She born 1843 at
Solon and died 1932. Members Cong. Church.

Children: 5760. **NELLIE/ELLA F.**, b. 1 Sep.
1854, d. 30 July 1918, md.
14 Dec. 1878 **OBED A. CORSON.**
5761. **FREDERICK**, b. 17 Apr. 1857, d.
3 Mar. 1890.
5762. **ANNIE**, d. Mar. 1881, md.
DANIEL JEWETT.

5763. HERBERT B., b. 10 Oct. 1867,
d. 7 July 1936, md. Apr.
1898 ALMA MILLETT. Res.
Seattle.
5764. CAROLYN, b. 2 July 1869, d. 14
Dec. 1935, md. Capt. CHARLES
H. BRANTINGHAM.

2815. JOHN HAMBLETT ROWELL [GEORGE B. 1460] He
was born 10 March 1834 and died 14 July 1911. He
married 20 Nov. 1856 SOPHIA ATWOOD. She born 24
Jan. 1838 and died 13 Feb. 1919. Res. Solon, Me.

Children: 5765. ERNEST, b. 16 Mar. 1858, d. 14
Jan. 1860.
5766. HATTIE, b. 28 Nov. 1860, d. 21
Nov. 1917, m.1, 20 Sep. 1880
CHARLES WILSON, m.2, 9 Sep.
1916 SIDNEY BAKER. 4 ch.
5767. CORA, b. 28 Dec. 1863, d. 7
June 1922, md. 20 Dec. 1888
WRIGHT CRAM. 1 child.
5768. CLARENCE PARKMAN, b. 31 Mar.
1868, d. Mar. 1941, md. 20
June 1901 MABEL MARSHALL. 3
children.

2818. ELBRIDGE ROWELL [GEORGE B. 1460] He was
born 25 Feb. 1839 and died 20 May 1898. He
married 12 Dec. 1877 ARVILLA AMES.

Children: 5770. NELLIE, d. 1 July 1882 [0-2-
18]
5771. ETHELYN, b. 6 Jan. 1885, d. 23
Mar. 1982, md. CHARLES
JENKINS. 1 child.

2820. WILLIAM PARKMAN ROWELL [GEORGE B. 1460]
He was born 3 Feb. 1843 and died 2 June 1920. He
married 17 March 1867 SARAH WILLIAMS. She born
24 June 1846 and died 28 July 1919.

Children: 5775. GEORGE F., b. 14 Apr. 1868, d.
14 Oct. 1933.

ROWELL FAMILY - NEW ENGLAND
9th Generation

5776. **FLORANCE E.**, b. 11 Nov. 1871, d. 24 Aug. 1963.

2821. **DANIEL CHENEY ROWELL** [GEORGE B. 1460] He was born 6 Dec. 1844 and died 2 Dec. 1893. He married 1 May 1875 **ABBIE COBURN**. She born 23 Aug. 1850 and died 28 Feb. 1893.

Children: 5780. **MERMAN C.**, b. 5 Sep. 1876, d. Nov. 1902.
5781. **BLANCH ETHEL**, b. 2 Feb. 1878, d. 20 July 1878.
5782. **BERNICE L.**, b. 30 Sep. 1883, d. 1948, md. **LEON TITCOMB**. 1 child.

2822. **SUMNER ROWELL** [GEORGE B. 1460] He was born 7 Feb. 1847 and died 15 June 1914. He married 15 June 1872 **CAROLYN ROUNDY**. She born 2 Dec. 1845 and died 18 April 1927. Res. Solon, Maine.

Children: 5785. **CHARLES**, b. 17 Aug. 1873, d. 1947.
5786. **GUY PARIS**, b. 5 Mar. 1875, d. 31 Jan. 1894.
5787. **PERLEY ACTON**, b. 26 June 1877, d. 10 July 1948, md. **MYRTLE COOLEY**. 1 child.
5788. **CHISPA**, b. 2 Feb. 1882, d. 1960, md. 1927 **HUGH B. McFARLAND**.
5789. **LEROY ABRAM**, b. 12 Dec. 1888, d. 13 Jan. 1971, md. **MAUDE LOOMER**. 4 children.

2830. **DAVID ROWELL Jr.** [DAVID 1461] He was born 4 Aug. 1839 and died 31 Oct. 1920. He married 20 Nov. 1871 **DORA CHANEY**. She born 4 May 1852 and died 14 July 1919. Res. Solon, Maine.

Children: 5790. **ALSTON**, b. 9 Jan. 1873, d. 17 Dec. 1937, md. 17 Jan. 1907 **ETHEL HILTON**.

2832. EBEN ROWELL [DAVID 1461] He was born 22
July 1843 and died 27 Jan. 1909. He married 4
Dec. 1864 MARY KNIGHT. She born 28 July 1847 and
died 18 Oct. 1927. Res. East Solon, Maine.

Children: 5792. ETTA M., b. 22 Jan. 1867, d.
30 Oct. 1950, m.1, 3 Oct.
1888 HERBERT EATON, m.2, 18
Nov. 1909 GEORGE PIERCE.
2 children.
5793. HERMAN L., b. 17 Feb. 1870, d.
18 Mar. 1926, md. MARY
CORSON.
5794. NETTIE, b. 10 Oct. 1883, d. 5
Jan. 1974.

2837. HARLOW KILGORE ROWELL [ZEBEDEE 1462] He
was born 27 Sept. 1847 at Skowhegan, Me. He
married 29 Oct. 1873 EMMA PIERCE, d/o ELBRIDGE
F. & MARTHA (DORN) PIERCE. She born 20 Jan.
1851. Res. E. Madison, Maine.

Children: 5795. IVAN, b. 10 July 1877.

2842. SUMNER ROWELL [CHARLES 1465]   He was born
29 Mar. 1844 and died 17 Aug. 1899.   He married
MARY WHITTIER. She born 5 Feb. 1841 and died 10
Sep. 1928. Res. Brighton, Maine.

Children: 5796. ETHEL, b. 6 Mar. 1881, d. 3
July 1968, md. 20 July 1904
PERLEY E. WARD. 1 child.

2843. ALLEN ROWELL [CHARLES 1465]   He was born
29 Nov. 1845 and died 14 Feb. 1918. He married
10 June 1882 MARY SNOW. She born 1856 and died
1942. Res. Cornville.

Children: 5797. ERNEST, b. 22 May 1883, d. 21
Feb. 1963, m.1, 12 May 1910
MARTHA PHILBROOK, div., m.2,
IDA HOLWAY (1885-1953) 2 ch.

ROWELL FAMILY - NEW ENGLAND
9th Generation

5798. HAROLD, b. 2 Aug. 1888, d.
1954, md. 22 June 1912
NETTIE B. POLLARD. Had:
GORDON ALLEN 1906.

2852. EDGAR ALLEN ROWELL [JOHN M. 1469] He was
born 25 Feb. 1843 at Tunbridge, Vt. and died 12
Dec. 1892, 49 yrs. at Thetford, Vt. He married
29 Jan. 1869 MARY HELEN HORNER. He married 2nd
HATTIE HORNER. Res. Orange Co., Vt.

Children: 5813. JOHN, b. 20 Feb. 1871.
5814. MARY JOSEPHINE, b. 25 Oct.
1872.

2857. HERBERT LESLIE ROWELL [JOHN M. 1469] He
was born 18 Dec. 1852. He married 28 Feb. 1880
KATE ISABEL DOW.

Children: 5815. KATE MAE, b. 26 Sep. 1885, md.
14 Sep. 1910 HORACE GOODWIN.
5816. JENNIE MIRANDA, b. 22 Aug.
1888, md. 24 Aug. 1904
CLINTON GUY BOWEN.
5817. SARAH LILLIAN, b. 12 Feb.
1890.

2865. WALLACE M. ROWELL [NATHANIEL P. 1475] He
was born 1853 and died in 1918. He married ALMA
STEENBERG. She born about 1856 at Westville,
N.Y.

Children: 5820. JUDSON D., b. 1878.
5821. ARTHUR J., b. 1880, d. 1890
[10-4-6]
5822. EDSON H., b. 1882, d. 7 Mar.
1900.
5823. NATHANIEL H., b. 1883, d. 26
Aug. 1961, md. 1903 IDA
HUTCHINS, d/o EDWIN &
PAULINE (VIGOR) HUTCHINS.
She b. 14 Apr. 1885, d. 10
Oct. 1943. Had: GLADYS 1906,

MILDRED, BEARRICE 1913,
LUITE 1916 and DOROTHY 1924.

2872. GEORGE HENRY ROWELL [HORACE 1476] He was
born about 1870 at Westville, N.Y. and died in
New England about 1904. Declared dead 3 July
1913 Dubuque, Iowa. He married first 4 June 1890
at Dubuque EMMA FRANCES DEGGENDORF, d/o HUGO &
HELENE (WIENZIERL) DEGGENDORF. She born 28 July
1873 and died 18 July 1956. She married 2nd 26
Dec. 1927 AUGUST KLEIN at Mpls, Minn.

Children: 5830. HILDA MARIE, b. 21 May 1891,
            d. 12 June 1891.
          5831. BERTRAM GUSTAVE, b. 18 May
            1892, d. 31 Dec. 1972, md.
            SUSAN GRUBER. She b. 30 Oct.
            1894, d/o WOLFGANG W. & MARY
            (MARTS) GRUBER. Had: RAYMOND
            F. 1916, ROBERT A. 1927, and
            RICHARD JOHN 1933.
          5832. FREDERICK WILLIAM, b. 18 Feb.
            1894, d. 27 Aug. 1958, md.
            15 Oct. 1914 VERONICA B.
            FAY, d/o PETER J. & AMANDA
            (GLAWE) FAY. She b. 11 Apr.
            1897. Had: MIRIAM E. 1915,
            FAITH M. 1919, PHYLLIS J.
            1933 and JACQUELINE M. 1934.
          5833. MABLE, b. 31 Oct. 1897,
            stillborn.
          5834. MABLE, b. 31 Oct. 1899, d. 6
            Apr. 1977, md. 23 Aug. 1930
            JOHN PALMER.

2875. ALBERT KENDRICK ROWELL [THOMAS 1482] He
was born 1830 at Hatley, Quebec and died about
1921 at North Lawrence, N.Y. He married first
AVIS COLLINS BRISTOL. He married second MARTHA
_____. Res. North Lawrence, N.Y.

Children: 5840. ALICE, md. _____ JACKSON.

ROWELL FAMILY - NEW ENGLAND
9th Generation

5841. **CLAYTON FREMONT**, b. 1861, d.
1938, m.1, 1890 **LILY
KOSTOMLATSKY**, m.2, 1924
ZULEMA KOSTOMLATSKY. Had:
ALBERT RAY by 1st wife.
5842. **ERNEST CLINTON**, b. c1872, d.
c1947, md. **ALICE STETSON**.
Had: **HOPE**.

2876. **NATHAN ROWELL** [THOMAS 1482] He was born
about 1832 at Hatley, Quebec and died about 1923
at Santa Barbara, Calif. He married **MAUDE** _____.
Occ. Cong. Minister.

Children: 5844. **MURIEL**,
5845. **THOMAS**,
5846. **HUBERT N.**, Dr. Had: **RICHARD C.**

2886. **WIEAR LEAVITT ROWELL** [NATHAN 1484] He was
born 1833 at Ayers Cliff, Quebec and died 1911.
He married 1856 **THURSEY AYER**. Res. Hatley,
Quebec. Children born at Hatley.

Children: 5850. **HIRAM WALLACE**, b. 1857, md.
c1875 **ELLEN MAGOON**. Had:
FREDRICK & WIEAR LEWIS.
5851. **MARY JANE**, b. 1862, d.y.
5852. **WILBER NATHAN**, b. 1867, d.
1943, md. 1892 **MARY
SOUTHWICK**. Had: **GLAYDS M.**,
MILDRED M. & RALPH MERTON.
5853. **JENNIE**, b. 1874, md. **CHARLES
PERRY**.

2889. **THOMAS ROWELL** [NATHAN 1484] He was born
1848 at Hatley, Quebec and died 1918. He married
JANE WITCOMB JACKSON. Children born at Hatley.

Children: 5855. **ALBERT KENDRICK**, b. 1874, md.
1899 **JOSEPHINE MAUD TODD**.
Had: **FORREST, ALBERTA &
GERALD**.
5856. **CORA**, b. 1877.
5857. **GRACE**, b. 1882.

ROWELL FAMILY - NEW ENGLAND
9th Generation

5858. ARTHUR, b. 1884, unmd.

2900. GEORGE SILAS ROWELL [SILAS 1490] He was
born 9 Apr. 1827 in Mass. He married 6 Nov.
1850 HEPSIBAH CUTTING BEAN of Warner. Res.
Warner and Sutton, N.H.

Children: 5860. CHARLES AUGUSTUS, b. 23 May
           1851, md. 15 Apr. 1885
           EUGENIA A. WHITTMORE.
      5861. MARY ELLEN, b. 9 July 1854.
      5862. ABBY M., b. 9 Apr. 1859.

2901. CHARLES PARKER ROWELL [SILAS 1490] He was
born 1828 at So. Sutton, N.H. and died 1922. He
married first 1862 CLARA ANN COUCH. He married
second 1870 LUCRETIA ABIGAIL EASTMAN of
Whitefirld, N.H. Occ. hotel keeper, wood & coal
dealer. Res. Concord, N.H.

Children: 1st Wife:
      5865. WARREN SILAS, b. 1866.
by 2nd Wife:
      5866. CLARA ANN, b. 1874.
      5867. GEORGE EATON, b. 1876, d.
           1948, md. 1917 EVELYN A.
           PIPER. Dentist. Had: JOHN
           CHARLES 1918.

2916. CHARLES S. ROWELL [ISAAC 1501] He was born
26 June 1857. He married 22 Dec. 1882 FLORANCE
S. GOODWIN, d/o BENJAMIN & LUCY A. (VIXON)
GOODWIN. She died 19 Oct. 1898 [37-6-5]. Occ.
farmer. Post Master at Hopkinton, N.H. No
children.

2918. IRA F. ROWELL [NICHOLAS 1505] He was born
1839. He married 1868 RACHEL A. HOOK of
Claremont. Res. Sutton, N.H.

Children: 5870. HARRY F., b. 15 Sep. 1873.

2922. **HENRY A. ROWELL** [SAMUEL Jr. 1509] He was
born 21 Aug. 1850 at Sutton, N.H. He married 30
Dec. 1878 **LYDIA M. BUNTIN** of Concord, Mass.

Children: 5875. **FRANK HENRY**, b. Oct. 1878, d.
             18 Mar. 1879.

2923. **CHARLES EDWIN ROWELL** [SAMUEL Jr. 1509] He
was born 5 June 1852 and died 23 Dec. 1905 at
Colfax, Calif. He married 25 Dec. 1879 **ROSA**
LOUISE WOOLEY of San Francisco, Calif. She born
28 July 1862 and died 25 Nov. 1930 at
Sacramento. Occ. farmer and Rail Road Engineer.
Moved from Sutton, N.H. to Calif. Res.
Sacramento.

Children: 5880. **MAUD E.**, b. 1882.
             5881. **MABEL**, b. 1883, d.y.
             5882. **MABEL**, b. 1885.
             5883. **ETHEL**, b. 29 Sep. 1887, md.
                   JOSEPH CALDWELL.
             5884. **CHARLES LEWIS**, b. 15 Nov. 1889
                   [born RUBIN LEWIS] md. 1920
                   LEOLA FRANCES KERSHNER. Had:
                   EUGENE, LEONARD, ARNOLD,
                   CHARLES & NORMA L.
             5885. **ALYCE GERTRUDE**, b. June 1892,
                   md. **PAUL JONES**.

2935. **HUGH GRANT ROWELL** [GEORGE B. 1531] He was
born 1892 at Barton Landing, Vt. and died 1963.
He married 1921 at Battle Creek, Mich. **SARA**
MILLER DENNIS, d/o **Senator WILLIAM & Dr. AGNES**
DENNIS. Occ. Doctor. Grad. Phillips Exeter
Academy, Dartmouth, Harvard Medical School. Res.
Orleans, Vt.

2936. **GEORGE BARKER ROWELL Jr.** [GEORGE B. 1531]
He was born 1896 at Orleans, Vt. He married 1925
MARION C. SMITH, d/o **GEORGE WILBER & FRANCES**
SMITH of Bridgeport, Conn. Grad. Dartmouth
1918, Harvard Law School 1921. Lt. WW1. Res.
Cambridge, Mass.

ROWELL FAMILY - NEW ENGLAND
9th Generation

Children: 5890. DOROTHY FRANCES,

2960. ARTHUR S. ROWELL [FRANKLIN P. 1553] He was
born 26 Oct. 1876 at Newport and died 1951. He
married 26 Oct. 1899 BESSIE JOCELYN. Res.
Newport.

Children: 6030. RICHARD IRVING, b. 1 Sep. 1899
           6031. SAYWARD FRANKLIN, b. 7 Dec.
           1900.

2961. STEPHEN FRANKLIN ROWELL [FRANKLIN P. 1553]
He was born 4 Oct. 1878 at Newport and died
1948. He married 1929 VIOLA J. BROCK. Res.
Newport.

2963. IRVING WILLIS ROWELL [FRANKLIN P. 1553] He
was born Apr. 1885 at Newport and died 1943. He
married June 1907 EDITH AMY GLIDDEN.

Children: 6035. CHARLES IRVING, b. 1914.
           6036. JEAN ELIZABETH, b. 1916.
           6037. RUTH ELEANOR, b. 1919.

2964. JESSIE RICHARD ROWELL [FRANKLIN P. 1553]
He was born Apr. 1890 at Newport. He married
1914 LAURA M. WILMARTH. Occ. Manager & Treasurer
of Rowell Brothers, Inc., V.P. Brampton Woolen
Co., 6 terms in House and 2 terms in Senate.

Children: 6038. MALCOLM WILMARTH, b. 1914.
           6039. BERTHA MARGARITE, b. 1917.
           6040. DONALD ARTHUR, b. 1924, d.
           infancy.

2972. FRANK FULTON ROWELL [IRVING G. 1554] He
was born 1885 and died 1957. He married HELEN
CLARKE. Res. Buffalo, N.Y. and Sunapee, N.H.

Children: 6045. IRVING CLARKE, b. 1911, m.1,
           MARGARET ABNER, m.2, URSULA
           _____. Had: CAROLYN 1942 and
           DEBORAH 1957.

ROWELL FAMILY - NEW ENGLAND
9th Generation

6046. JOHN FULTON, b. 1913, d. 1954,
md. 1940 BONNIE HUMPHREY.
Had: JOHN H. & DANIEL.

2974. JOHN IRVING ROWELL [IRVING G. 1554] He was
born 1890. He married 1919 ELIZABETH PITKIN.
Service WW1. Occ. insurance agent. Res. Akron,
Ohio.

Children: 6050. MARY ELIZABETH, b. 1921, md.
1943 R.G. PAINE.
6051. ELEANOR PITKIN, b. 1922, md.
1947 D.E. McPHERSON.
6052. NANCY JANE, b. 1925, md. 1948
R.C. McPHERRIN.
6053. JOAN ALEXANDER, b. 1929, md.
1951 C.L. ABLE.

2986. CHARLES FOSTER ROWELL [MOSES D. 1595] He
was born 5 Aug. 1873 and died 25 May 1961 at
North Reading, Mass. He married 4 Oct. 1899 at
Waltham, Mass. MARGARET BRADFORD MOORE, d/o
BRADFORD & MARGARET (PARSONS) MOORE. She born 5
Oct. 1878.

Children: 6060. CHARLES FOSTER Jr., b. 11 Nov.
1900, md. 25 Sep. 1920 MABEL
OLIVE LIBBY. Had: FRANK,
DOROTHY, ALBERT & MARGARET.
6061. HOWARD HERBERT, b. 27 Jan.
1902, md. 12 Apr. 1924
ELOISE R. DAVIS. Had:
JACQUALINE EMMA 1924.
6062. PAUL, b. 26 Jan. 1903, d. 11
Feb. 1903.
6063. MARGARET BELLE, b. 20 Oct.
1905, d. 1 May 1907.
6064. MYRTA GIFFORD, b. 21 Sep.
1907, unmd 1926.

2988. GLENN ELLIS (MOSES) ROWELL [MOSES D. 1595]
He was born 23 Apr. 1886 at Tunbridge, Vt. and
died 5 Sep. 1955 at Royalton, Vt. He married 28
Oct. 1914 RETA ABBOTT, d/o DANIEL E. & ELBRA

(BLANCHARD) ABBOTT. She born 17 July 1888 and died 12 Feb. 1919. Res. Royalton, Vt.

Children: 6067. DRUCILLA, b. 16 Apr. 1915.
           6068. NORMA, b. 12 Feb. 1916, md. 9
           May 1948 RODNEY SWIFT,
           3 children.

2994. EARL STANLEY ROWELL [ALFRED 1601] He was born 16 Dec. 1889 at West Derby, Vt. and died 1938. Buried at Nashua, N.H. He married 14 Apr. 1917 at Nashua ANNA F. FLOOD, d/o JOHN C. & MARY (RIGNEY) FLOOD. She born 27 Oct. 1888 at Nashua. He enlisted in the submarine service in WW1. No children.

2997. LEWIS WILDER ROWELL [NATHANIEL L. 1602] He was born 9 Sep. 1896 at Brownshill, Quebec. He married 9 July 1920 at Cambridge, Vt. DOROTHY JANE MANSFIELD, d/o HENRY & ALICE (ATHERTON) MANSFIELD. She born 17 Nov. 1902 at Coventry, Vt. Served in WW1 in submarines. Discharged 13 Feb. 1919. Res. Derby and Wells River, Vt.

Children: 6070. REGINALD LEWIS, b. 21 Aug.
           1921, md. 25 Dec. 1944,
           VIRGINIA KEMMER. Had:
           REGINALD K. & JUDITH ANN.
           6071. NORMA JEAN, b. 11 Dec. 1929,
           md. 16 June 1951 JAMES K.
           NOBLE Jr., Had: ANNE R. &
           JAMES K.
           6072. SULA JANE, b. 28 Dec. 1941,
           md. 24 oct. 1959 DOUGLAS P.
           ROWE.

2998. NATHANIEL LEROY ROWELL [NATHANIEL L. 1602] He was born 17 Feb. 1892 at Masswsippi, Quebec. He married 12 Oct. 1923 at White River Junction, Vt. MARION C. HAMILTON, d/o PLINY J. & BESSIE (SAYWARD) HAMILTON. She born 28 July 1896 at Newport, Vt.

Children: 6075. JAMES HAMILTON, b. 19 Oct.
1924, md. 1 Feb. 1944
DOROTHY E. WHITE. Had: DAVID
ALAN 1954.
6076. MARGARET ANNE, b. 5 Dec. 1926,
md. 5 Apr. 1958 DONALD S.
ARNOLD Jr. Had: SUSAN E.,
DONALD S. & JAMES C.
6077. ROBERT LEE, b. 17 Feb. 1931,
md. 26 Sep. 1953 AUDREY
PERKINS. Had: ROBERT L. Jr.
& WILLIAM SIDNEY.

3000. ROBERT CLARE ROWELL [NATHANIEL L. 1602]
He was born 11 Nov. 1908 at Derby, Vt. He
married 24 June 1931 there EMORY FRANCES KELLEY,
d/o ORVILLE LEVI & LENA ANNIE (HITCHCOCK)
KELLEY. Res. Derby, Vt.

Children: 6080. RITA MAYE, b. 6 June 1933, md.
11 July 1954 PRESTON G.
HARRINGTON. No children.
6081. MARILYN CLARE, b. 19 Jan.
1935, md. 9 Nov. 1952
ROBERT N. TAPLIN. Had:
ROBERT D. & JANET LYNN.
6082. CAROLYN JUNE, b. 26 Nov. 1936,
md. 13 July 1957 ANDREW
THERRIEN, 1 child.

3001. HAROLD LEON ROWELL [NATHANIEL L. 1602] He
was born 23 May 1910 at Fairlee, Vt. He married
29 May 1930 at newport, Vt. GENEVA HAYES, d/o
GEORGE W. & ROSENA (WEBB) HAYES. She born 10 may
1908 at Newport, Vt.

Children: 6085. HAROLD LEON, b. 26 Aug. 1935,
md. 16 Nov. 1956 GAIL
SCHRIBNER. Had: KIM ELAINE
1953. Res. California.

3020. **MATTHEW JOSEPH ROWELL** [WILLIAM H. 1621]
He was born 20 June 1871 at Dorchester, Mass. He
married **ADA CLARA GRANT**. She born 25 March 1869
Nova Scotia. Res. Boston, Mass.

Children: 6090. **FLORANCE MAE**, b. 23 May 1894,
md. 23 May 1915 **RICHARD
BRIAR ROSS**.
6091. **WILLIAM GRANT**, b. 3 May 1904.

3023. **NICHOLAS M. ROWELL** [WILLIAM H. 1621] He
was born June 1877. He married 17 Oct. 1892 **MARY
A. McCABE** at Boston, Res. Boston. Mass.

Children: 6092. **WILLIAM N.**, b. 19 Feb. 1895.
6093. **JOSEPH A.**, b. Aug. 1897, d.
Feb. 1981.

3027. **ERSKINE PLINY ROWELL** [IRA HILL 1625] He
was born 25 May 1877 at Randolph, Vt. and died 2
June 1943 at Hartford, Conn. He married 22 June
1897 **LIZZIE B. PRESCOTT**, d/o **NEWELL & ALMIRA
(JACKSON) PRESCOTT**. She born 19 July 1878 at
Vershire, Vt. and died 19 Nov. 1941 at Hartford,
Conn.

Children: 6094. **GLADYS M.**, b. 23 Jan. 1899,
md. 11 Mar. 1922 **HAROLD A.
CHAPMAN**.

3033. **RALPH KING ROWELL** [EDGAR W. 1629] He was
born 6 Dec. 1884 at Randolph Center, Vt. and
died 21 Nov. 1966. He married 31 Oct. 1911
ELIZABETH SULLIVAN, d/o **THOMAS O. & CATHERINE
(DONNELLY) SULLIVAN**. She born 26 Dec. 1883. Res.
Bridgeport, Conn.

Children: 6095. **THOMAS EDGAR**, b. 3 May 1915,
d. 5 June 1915.
6096. **MARY**, b. 5 June 1919, md. 17
Dec. 1945 **HENRY H. CARSE**. 7
Children.

3034. **GLENN EDGAR ROWELL [EDGAR W.** 1629] He was born 26 July 1888 at Tunbridge, Vt. and died 11 Jan. 1962. He married 10 Dec. 1921 **BERNICE S. MacCORRISON,** d/o **FRANK DAVIS & LOU (DANIELS) MacCORRISON.** She born 31 Aug. 1901 at Concord, Mass.

Children: 6097. **JOHN CHASE,** b. 29 Apr. 1923, WW2, md. 30 June 1948 **INEZ E. FRASER.** Had; JOHN F. 7 **JANET C.**
6098. **WAYNE DANIELS,** b. 5 May 1925, WW2, md. 3 Sep. 1946 **GENEVIEVE H. RHOADES.** Had: **RICHARD W., HELEN G., MARY E., STEPHEN R. & ROBERT K.**
6099. **GAIL ELAINE,** b. 18 Dec. 1926, md. 19 June 1948 **COLIN M. ROBERTSON.** Had: SUSAN E., JAMES S., **MALCOLM C. & BRUCE.**

3052. **THEODORE EARL ROWELL [HERBERT B.** 1646] He was born 22 Oct. 1882 at Liberty, Me. and died 31 Aug. 1962. He married **BESSIE MAE LOWE,** d/o **SYLVANUS M. & MARGARET A. (WARD) LOWE.**

Children: 6104. **RUTH OLIVE,** md. **DONALD TAVERNER.**

3065. **IRA ROWELL [MARK** 1711] He was born 28 Oct. 1836 at Springwater, N.Y. and died July 1886 at Beaver Dam, Wis. He married 25 Nov. 1868 **MARY THOMPSON,** d/o **JOHN & MARY (INGRAM) THOMPSON** of Canada. Came to Wisc. 1842. Taught school near Hartford. Founded Beaver Dam Farm Machinery Co. 1867 with Uncle John S. [#1655] Had general store at Hartland. Moved 1864 to Beaver Dam.

Children: 6110. **JENNIE/MAYBELLE,** b. 15 Sep. 1870, d. Feb. 1950, md. **EDWARD BEICHL.** No ch.

6111. **WALLIE/WALDEN THOMPSON**, b. 5
Feb. 1873, d. July 1954,
md. **MAY BARNES**. No ch.
6112. **EDLA/ELLA INGRAM**, b. 23 Sep.
1878, d. Oct. 1958, md. 12
Dec. 1906 **RALPH E. INMAN**,
Had: **CATHERINE R.**, **THEODORE**
& **MARY**.
6113. **IRA CLARENCE**, b. 1 Feb. 1884,
d. Oct. 1958, md. _____.
Had 1 child, d.y.

3072. **THEODORE B. ROWELL** [JOHN S. 1715] He
married 17 Dec. 1872 **CAROLYN NEWELL ROBINSON** of
Beaver Dam, Wisc. She died 33 years. Res.
Watertown, Wisc.

Children: 6117. **FRANK**,
6118. **JAMES**,
6119. **JOSEPH NEWELL**,
6120. **ROBERT**,
6121. **LIBBIE**,

3079. **JOSEPH NEWELL ROWELL** [JOHN S. 1715] He
married **MARY BOREHARDT**.

Children: 6135. **THEODORE H.**,
6136. **EDNA MAY**,
6141. **FRED ABRAM**, b. 15 Nov. 1864,
d. 6 Jan. 1919, md. **ABBIE J.
ROUNDS**. Had: **JOHN ABRAM**
1887-1974, **LEE ORLANDO** 1886-
1907, md. **HELEN LAWRENCE**.
6142. **ANNIE MARIE**, b. 7 Dec. 1873,
d. 6 June 1948, md. **ELMER L.
SMITH**.
6143. **ALICE**,

3095. **WILLIAM ROWELL [JACOB 1790]** He was born
16 July 1827. He married **MARIA** _____.

Children: 6150. **EMMA MARIA**, b. 10 Dec. 1852.
            6151. **GEORGE HENRY**, b. 30 Feb. 1869.

3098. **ABRAM ROWELL [JACOB 1790]** He was born 15
Sep. 1835 at Windsor, Vt. He married 13 Mar.
1860 **ADELINE WAY**, d/o **FREDERICK & PERSIS
(COSSET) WAY.** Occ. farmer. Res. Andover, Vt.

Children: 6152. **ADA**, b. 22 Jan. 1861.

APPENDIX

Revolutionary War Service
New England Rowells

1. Asa Rowell Pvt. [111] N.H. Enl. 20 Sep. 1778 for 2 mo. 11 days. Capt. Samuel Atkinson Co. Stationed at Haverhill.

2. Benjamin Rowell [   ] From Fairlee, Vt. Capt Marston's Co. 1780-1. Paid £1..18..8.

3. Christopher Rowell [   ] Pvt. Enl. 5 Aug. 1778 for 28 days. Capt. Jesse Page Co., Col. Jacob Gales Regt., Cont. Army.

4. Daniel Rowell [235] N.H. Enlisted Feb. 1778 for 3 years from Epping, N.H. 2nd Reg't. Col. Reid under his father William Rowell. 1st Lt. 4th Co., Capt. David McDuffee Gen. Whipple's Brig. Enl. 17 Mar. 1781 Cont. Army. 21 yrs., 5', dark complexion. From Epping. Pvt. 3rd Co., 2nd Reg't. No battles. Pension S-40,364.

5. Daniel Rowell [545] Pvt. N.H., Sgt. Capt. Samuel Pierce. 5 Nov. 1775 at Pierce Is.

6. Daniel Rowell [275?] Capt., Me. d. at Jay, Me. 1834.

7. David Rowell [320] Pvt. Maine, Capt. Andrew Gilman's Co., Maine. Enlisted 19 Oct. 1776. Discharged 10 April 1777. Stationed on Penoscot River.

8. Eliphelet Rowell [97] Pvt. Mass.

9. Enoch Rowell Jr. [273] Pvt. & Sgt, from Candia, N.H. Capt. Thos. Cogginswall Co., Mass. Line Cont. service. Reg't of Col. Baldwin 1 yr. Jan. 1776 - Jan. 1777. Was at taking of Burgoyne in 1777. Sgt., Capt. Joseph Dearborn Co. exp. against Canada 1777 at Saratoga Capt. Moses Bakers Co. Pension W-16,393.

10. Isreal Rowell [115] Pvt. N.H., 3 yrs Col.
Geo. Reid. Enlisted Apr. 1777. Capt. Calib
Robinson Co., Corp. 3rd Co., 2nd N.H. Reg't
First commanded by Nathan Hale. Discharged
April 1780. Pension S-45,125. From North
Salem, N.H. Pvt. 5'6", 24 yrs old, 23 Apr.
1775 Capt. Elisha Woodbury Co., Col. John
Starks Regt. 3 mo., 16 days service. At
Bunker Hill.

11. Jacob Rowell [124?] Sgt. 1775 Capt. Winslow
Co., 3 Oct. to 2 Nov. 30 days. Sgt. Mass.
Capt. John Blunt's Co., Major Lithgo's
Militia detachment 10 Sep. 1779 to 10 Nov.
1779. Later res. Lincoln Co., Me.

12. James Rowell [117] b. c1763. From Salem,
N.H. Pvt. 5'8", 18 yrs, Mar. 1776 Capt.
Elisha Woodburg, Col. Starkes Reg't. N.H.
line served 1 yr. Enlisted 3 yrs Apr. 1777
under Capt. Calib Robinson. Discharged
April 1780 in Connecticut Battles of Fort
Montigomery 1776, wounded severely. At
Ticonderoga 6 July 1777. Taken prisoner for
3 months. Released by Anerican Troops. At
battles of White Plains and Monmouth.
Richard Dow Co., 3rd Co., 2nd. Batt. Col.
Geo. Ried Regt. Res. Vershire, Vt. 1820.
Pension S-41,101.

13. Job Rowell [307] From Hampstead, N.H., age
36, Occ. husbandman, 17 May 1775 to 4 Oct.
1775 Capt. Samuel Gilman's Co., Col. Poor's
Regt.

14. John Rowell [311?] Pvt., N.H. enl. 19 July
1777, discharged 18 Sep. 1777, 2 mo. Capt.
McConnell's Co. marched Pembroke to
Bennington & Stillwater. 1 Apr. 1778 Capt.
Timothy Barrow's Co. 10 July 1776 Pvt.
Capt. Samuel Nay's Co., Cont. Service.
From Bath, N.H. 1780 paid for scouting.
£2.11.0.

15. Jonathan Rowell [322] Pvt. N.H., served 1
    yr. 1 mo. 24 days. Enl. 26 Sep. 1776 Capt.
    Samuel McConnell's Co. 1780 Capt. John
    Powell's Vt. Co. 2 days Pd £0.2.8. Pension
    W-24,799. Blwt-13,183-160.

16. Jonathan Rowell [702] Pvt. N.H., Enlisted
    Hampstead, N.H. Capt. Gilman Reg't, Col.
    Reid. Served 10 mo. 24 days. June 1780.
    then 5 mo. 28 days June 1781 and 5 mo. No
    battles. Was at West Point. Pension S-
    22,476.

17. Jonathan Rowell [   ] Sgt. Capt. Nathanial
    Delamore Co., Col. John Abbott Reg't. Alarm
    Oct. 1781 (23 Oct. 6 Nov.) Paid £0..18..0.

18. Lemuel Rowell [116] From New Salem, N.H.
    Pvt. Mass. Served 2 yrs. Enlisted 2nd Cont.
    Reg't, Capt. Olmstead April 1775 at Salem,
    N.H. At Bunker Hill and 1776 expedition
    against Canada. May 1777 Capt. Jeremiah
    Dow's Co. Pvt. 1st Co., 3rd Regt Capt.
    Gray's Co., Col. Alex. Scammel's Regt. at
    Saratoga. In Gen. Sullivan's exp. against
    Indians. Pension W-17,563.

19. Moses Rowell [403] From Pembroke. Pvt.
    N.H. Col. George Reid. Cont. Service 4 Sep.
    1782. Capt. E. Frye. Pension W-1474.

20. Nehemiah Rowell [267] Pvt, N.H., 24 days
    service Aug. 1778 Rhode Is. Exp. Col. John
    Langdon Co. Light Horse Vol.

21. Peter Rowell [295] fifer, Mass., paid 12 s
    for 2 pair of shoes 10 Aug. 1775 by Col.
    Starke, if same man.

22. Philander Rowell [A34] Pvt. Conn. Capt.
    Pirear Co. Conn. Militia. Pension S-14,327.

23. Philip Rowell [112] Pvt., From Warner, N.H.
Enl. 15 Apr. 1777, 3 yrs. Disch. 10 Sep.
1778 for Inability. Col. Thos. Stickney's
Reg't. 4th. Co., 3rd Regt. Col. Alex.
Scammell's Regt.

24. Samuel Rowell [288] From Perry, N.H., 20
yrs, farmer N.H. 20 July 1777 Gen. Starke's
Brig. Marched to Charleston, 2 mo. 9 days.
returned sick. 8 July 1776 at Chimney
Point. 22 yrs, 5'8" Capt. Poor Co. 1 yr.
Enlisted 1 April 1778 for 1 year Capt.
Nathan Matthews Reg't. Joseph Cilley N.H.
line. Enl. 29 Nov. 1776, Discharged 26 Apr.
1779 in Conn. Battles Bunker Hill and White
Plains. Pd £60 for 9 mo.

25. Thomas Rowell [310] From Poplin, N.H., Pvt.
Capt. Sanborn, Col. Task. Served 9 mo.
Enlisted Feb. 1776 N.H. Militia Capt.
Nathan Brown Reg't. Col. David Gilman of
Pembroke marched to Portsmouth. Lt. Aug.
1778 Rhode Island Exp. Capt. Bayley's Co.,
Col. Kelly's Regt. 21 days. Marched 130
miles. Pension S-11,319.

26. William Rowell [125] Pvt. N.H. public
service. Cont. Army. Col. Stark, 9 mo.
service. No battles. Enlisted Apr. 1775 at
Salem, N.H. Capt. George Reid Reg't John
Stark. At Bunker Hill. Lived at Windham.

27. William Rowell [180] From Epping, N.H.
Promoted to Capt. 2 Apr. 1777. Capt. 6th
Co., 2nd Regt. N.H., Col. Nathan Hale.
Brevet Major, N.H. Land grant Blwt-
1774-300-Capt. 1780 Pd. £480.

28. William Rowell [269] Pvt. N.H. Capt.
Dearborn's Co. at Bunker Hill.

NOTE: Numbers in [ ] are Rowell ancestor
numbers.

APPENDIX

WAR OF 1812 ROWELL MEN

1. AARON ROWEL, [#2820] N.H. Militia, Pvt., Served 60 days, Capt. Thos. Currier Co.

2. ABRAHAM ROWELL, N.H. Militia, Pvt., Served 2 months, from Deerfield.

3. ASAHEL ROWELL, N.Y. Militia, Capt. L. Dume's Co., Pension WC-7007, Wife Phebe.

4. BETHAEL C./BATHEWEL ROWELL, [#910] N.H. Mil. Pvt., served 1 year, Capt. Joseph Flander's Co., Capt. Conkling, Capt. Foster's Co., 4th & 5th U.S. Inf., Pension SC-5129.

5. CHARLES ROWELL, N.H. Militia, Pvt., served 40 days, Capt. Edward Fuller's Co.

6. CHARLES ROWELL, N.H. Mil., Pvt., served 45 days, Capt. Asa Head's Co., from Pembroke.

7. DANIEL ROWELL, N.H. Mil., Pvt., served 1 yr., Capt. Joseph Flander's Co.

8. DAVID ROWELL, Vermont Militia, Battle at Plattsburg, from Tunbridge, Pension WO-31367, Wife Annie.

9. DAVID ROWELL, N.Y. Militia, Capt. Nathan Seward's Co., Pension WC-25984, Wife Polly.

10. ENOCH ROWELL, N.H. Mil., Pvt., served 60 days, from Guildford

11. ENOS ROWELL, N.H. Mil., from Bath, N.H.

12. HENRY W. ROWELL, N.H. Mil., Col., from Littleton, N.H.

13. HIRAM A. ROWELL, from Manchester, N.H.

14. JACOB ROWELL, [#1040] Pvt. Mass. Militia, Capt. Robert Thompson's Co., Entered at

APPENDIX

WAR OF 1812 ROWELL MEN

Montville. Served at Belfast. Pension
SC-24853 & SO-33175.

15. JAMES C. ROWELL, [#669] N.H. Militia, Capt.
Samuel Callen's Co., Pension WC-10451.

16. JAMES ROWELL, Lt. Mass. Capt. A Weston Co.,
Entered at Frakfort. Battle at Hampden Sep.
1-4, 1814.

17. JARED M. ROWELL, N.Y. Militia, Capt. R.
Tyler's Co., Pension WC-20220 & SC-601,
Wife Jemima.

18. JESSE ROWELL, [131?] Pvt. Mass. Capt. A.
Ridman Co., Entered at Jefferson. Served at
Wiscasset. Sep. 10-23, 1814.

19. JOHN ROWELL, Vermont Militia, Capt. Cyril
Chandler's Co., from Strafford, battle at
Plattsburg

20. JOHN ROWELL, [#670] N.H. Mil., served 10½
months, Capt. Bradley Bartlett's Co. &
Capt. John S. Davis' Co., Possibly the
John Rowell from New Chester who served
60 days in Capt. Reuben Noyes' Co.

21. JOHN ROWELL Jr, Pvt., Capt. Treat's Co.,
Capt. Pratt's Co., 21st & 5th U.S.,
Pension WC-16741 & SC-9577, Wife Martha.

22. JOHN ROWELL, Pvt. Mass. Capt. G. Paget Co.,
Entered at Jay. Served at Portland Sep. 14-
24, 1814.

23. JONATHAN ROWELL, Pvt. Mass. Capt. J.
Collins Co., Served at Wiscasset Sep. 24 to
Nov. 9, 1814.

24. MOSES ROWELL, Pvt. Mass. Capt. M. Boynton
Co., Entered at Monmouth. Sep. 13-17, 1814.

APPENDIX

WAR OF 1812 ROWELL MEN

25. MOSES D. ROWELL, from Manchester, N.H.

26. ROBERT ROWELL, Vt. Mil., Capt. Ira Corse's Co., from Vershire, battle of Plattsburg.

27. SAMUEL ROWELL, N.H. Mil., served 60 days, Capt. David Hayes' Co., from Windham.

28. STEPHEN ROWELL, Vermont Mil., Lt. Phineus Kimball Co., from West Fairlee, battle of Plattsburg.

29. THOMAS ROWELL, Pvt. Mass. Capt. D.R. Adams Co., at Boothbay June 21 to Sep. 28, 1814.

30. TRUMAN ROWELL, N.Y. Mil., Capt. John Smith, Pension WC-33441, Wife Lucy C.

Note: Numbers in [ ] are Rowell Ancestor Numbers.

APPENDIX

THE THOMAS ROWELL FAMILY OF CONNECTICUT

A **THOMAS ROWELL/ROWLE** first appeared about 1668 in Hartford County, Connecticut. He resided at Simsley and later at Windsor. No connection with the **THOMAS** and **VALENTINE ROWELL** early settlers of Salisbury, Mass. appears to exist. From various sources the following pedigree has been constructed.

A1. **THOMAS ROWELL**. He was born probably 1645-1650. He died 4 April 1708 at Windsor. He married 5 May 1669 **MARY DENSLOW**. She died 14 June 1739 at Windsor. Named in court case 7 May 1667. Complaint by Mercy Person. [NEHGR v.148] Res. at Simsburg and Windsor. May have 7 children:

Children: A2. **THOMAS**, b. Oct. 1671, md. 16 Mar. 1699 **VIOLET STEDMAN**.
A3. **ELIZABETH**, b. Mar. 1673.
A4. **DEBORAH**, b. 5 Jan. 1680, md. **CORNELIUS GILLETT**.
A5. **SAMUEL**, b. 16 June 1685, d.y.
A6. **ABIGAIL**, b. 10 Feb. 1686. Perhaps had **DANIEL** b. 3 Jan. 1709 at Middletown.
A7. **MARY?**, b. c1670, md. 25 Dec. 1696 **THOMAS MILLER**.

A2. **THOMAS ROWELL** [THOMAS A1] He was born Oct 1671 at Simsley, Ct. and died 28 Oct. 1741 at Windsor. He married 16 Mar. 1699 **VIOLET STEDMAN**. She died 1 Apr. 1751. Res. at Windsor, Ct.

Children: A8. **HANNAH**, b. 5 July 1700, d. 5 Jan. 1719/20.
A9. **ANN**, b. 24 Sep. 1703.
A10. **THOMAS**, b. 5 Dec. 1705, md. 7 Dec. 1743 **HANNAH ELMOR**.
A11. **SARAH**, b. 17 Sep. 1708.
A12. **SAMUEL**, b. 11 Mar. 1710, md. **ELIZABETH _____**.
A13. **JOHN**, b. 4 Apr. 1714, md. 4 Jan. 1743/4 **MARY FILLEY**.

APPENDIX

Thomas Rowell Family of Connecticut Cont.

A14. **DANIEL**, b. 11 Oct. 1717, md. 23
June 1736 **EUNICE BROWN**.
A15. **HANNAH**, b. 11 Feb. 1720.

A10. **THOMAS ROWELL [THOMAS A2]** He was born 5
Dec. 1705 at Simsley, Ct. He married 7 Dec. 1743
HANNAH ELMOR. She born 3 Mar. 1700. Possibly
father of **LOES**, born 17 Apr. 1749 at Hebron, Ct.

A12. **SAMUEL ROWELL [THOMAS A2]** He was born 11
Mar. 1710. He married **ELIZABETH** _____. Res.
Windsor, Ct.

Children: A21. **SAMUEL**, b. 29 May 1746, md. 9
June 1771 **CATHERINE FYLER**.
A22. **ELIZABETH**, b. 3 Apr. 1748.
A23. **JOB**, b. 15 Apr. 1752, md. **RUTH**
_____.
A24. **STEPHEN**, b. 21 Mar. 1755.
A25. **SILAS**, b. 2 Dec. 1759, md.
CHRISTIAN _____.
A26. **LUCINE/SUSINE**, b. 10 Mar. 1762.
A27. **CATE**, b. 9 Dec. 1766.
A28. **WILLIAM**, bp 29 Sep. 1771.

A13. **JOHN ROWELL [THOMAS A2]** He was born 4 Apr.
1714 and died 24 May 1776 [62y]. He married 4
Jan. 1743/4 **MARY FILLEY**. Res. Windsor, Ct.
Church member 1745 at Wintenbury, Conn.

Children: A30. **JOHN**, b. 20 Feb. 1744/5.
A31. **REUBEN**, b. 11 Oct. 1746, d. 11
July 1763.
A32. **MARTIN**, b. 18 Aug. 1748.
A33. **ROGER**, bp 26 Aug. 1750, md. 31
May 1778 **ANNE BUNCE**.
A34. **THOMAS**, b. 24 Dec. 1753.
A35. **PHILANDER**, b. 20 Dec. 1755, d.
5 Aug. 1818, md. 5 Jan. 1775
JOANNA HAZE/HAYES.
A36. **MARY**, bp 2 Nov. 1760.
A37. **REUBEN**, b. 11 July 1764.

Thomas Rowell Family of Connecticut Cont.

A14. DANIEL ROWELL [THOMAS A2] He was born 11
Oct. 1717 at Windsor, Ct. He married 23 June
1736 **EUNICE BROWN**. Res. Windsor, Ct.

Children: A36. **DANIEL**, b. 25 Apr. 1737, d. 20
Oct. 1741.
A37. **DAVID**, b. 6 Apr. 1739, d. 22
Oct. 1741.
A38. **ANNE**, b. 17 Mar. 1745, md. 30
Dec. 1761 **AMOS BURR?**
A39. **DANIEL**, md. 23 June 1775 **PHEBE
SPENCER**. Had: **CHLOE**, 1778.
A40. **HANNAH**, b. 9 Apr. 1758.

A21. SAMUEL ROWELL [SAMUEL A12] He was born 29
May 1746 at Windsor, Ct. He married 9 June 1771
CATHERINE FYLER at Bloomfield, Ct. Res.
Windsor, Ct.

Children: A41. **SAMUEL**, b. 22 May 1772.
A42. **JAMES**, b. 9 Apr. 1774.
A43. **LINDIA/LYNDA**, b. 11 Nov. 1775.
A44. **RACHEL**, bp 14 Dec. 1777.
A45. **STEPHEN**, bp 30 Apr. 1780.
A46. **AMELIA**, bp 29 Aug. 1784.
A47. **NATHAN**, bp 2 July 1786.

A22. JOB ROWELL [SAMUEL A12] He was born 15
Apr. 1752 at Windsor, Ct. He married **RUTH**
_____. Res. at Windsor, Ct.

Children: A48. **JOB**, b. 11 Aug. 1787.
A49. **RUTH**, b. 4 June 1789.
A50. **AMY**, b. 30 May 1791.
A51. **BILDAD**, b. 17 Aug. 1795.
A52. **LOOMIS**, b. 13 Apr. 1797.

A24. SILAS ROWELL [SAMUEL A12] He was born 2
Dec. 1759 at Windsor, Ct. He married **CHRISTIAN**
_____. Res. at Windsor, Ct.

Children: A53. **SILAS**, b. 19 Nov. 1785.

APPENDIX

Thomas Rowell Family of Connecticut Cont.

> A54. **CRISSE**, b. 4 Oct. 1787, d. 16
> Sep. 1788.
> A55. **CRISSE**, b. 11 Sep. 1789.
> A56. **BETTE**, b. 15 Aug. 1792.
> A57. **HIRAM**, b. 19 Oct. 1795, d. 25
> Apr. 1799.
> A58. **NABEY KING**, b. 2 May 1798.

A30. **JOHN ROWELL [JOHN A13]** He was born 20 Feb.
1744/5. Had probably the following children.

Children: A59. **MARTIN S.**, bp 2 Apr. 1772.
A60. **SIMON**, bp 16 July 1780.

A34. **PHILANDER ROWELL [JOHN A13]** He was born 20
Dec. 1755 at Windsor, Ct. he married 10 May
1773 or 5 Jan. 1775 **JOANNA HAZE/HAYES** at
Bloomfield, Ct. Served in Rev. War as a Pvt. in
Conn. Militia. He received a pension S-14327.

Children: A61. **PHILANDER**, b. 19 Oct. 1775, d.
5 Aug. 1818, md. **ZULIMA** __.
A62. **SOLOMAN**, b. 5 May 1776.
A63. **JESSE**, b. 4 Dec. 1777.
A64. **LEVY**, b. 24 Mar. 1780.
A65. **SUSANNA**, b. 20 Feb. 1782.
A66. **CHARLOTTE**, b. 20 Mar. 1785.
A67. **ODADORMAN**, b. 29 Aug. 1790.
A68. **GURDON/GORDON**, b. 13 Aug. 1792.
A69. **BIRAM**, b. 28 Sep. 1797.
A70. **FANNA**, b. 10 July 1801, md. 7
Aug. 1828 **LEMUEL PRUNWELL.**

A36. **DANIEL ROWELL [DANIEL A14]** He married 23
June 1775 **PHEBE SPENCER.**

Children: A71. **JUSTINE**, b. 30 June 1776.
A72. **DAVID J.**, d. 23 Aug. 1777, 16
months.
A73. **CLOE**, bp 18 Oct. 1778.
A74. **SUSANNA**, d. 17 Oct. 1784.

Unknown Conn. Rowell findings:

APPENDIX

Thomas Rowell Family of Connecticut Cont.

Eunice Rowell md. 10 May 1773 Isaiah Burr at
Windsor.
Elizabeth Rowell md. 18 Nov. 1790 Theophilus
Moore at Windsor.
Lucy Rowell md. 1 Jan. 1822 Jonathan Bow at
E. Hartford.
Martha Rowell md. 25 Apr. 1754 Samuel Fitch
at Windsor.
Olive Rowell md. 29 Apr. 1772 Isaac Bartlett
at Bloomfield.
Orma d/o Lusina Rowell b. 15 June 1784 at
Windsor.

Comments:

There are a number of other Rowell entries
scattered through early Connecticut records. But
they do not appear to be related to the above
Thomas Rowell family.

THE ENOS ROWELL FAMILY OF NEW HAMPSHIRE

Melvin W. Rowell in his books; The Register of Rowells (1957), p. 35-37 and Supplement to the Register of Rowells, (1959), p. 19 presents the Enos Rowell Family. Enos Rowell reportedly came to New England from Ireland via Spain shortly before the Revolutionary War. He settled at or near Piermont, N.H. The family resided in the extreme northern part of New Hampshire and in adjacent Vermont and Providence of Quebec, Canada. This Rowell Family appears to be unrelated to THOMAS and VALENTINE ROWELL of early Salisbury, Mass.

B1. ENOS ROWELL. Piermont and Pittsburg, N.H. He was born about 1750 in Ireland. Arrived in N.H. shortly before the Rev. War. Wife's name is unknown.

Children: B2. SAMPSON, b. 1772, d. 26 Apr. 1855.
           B3. son X,

B2. SAMPSON ROWELL [ENOS B1] He was born 1772 at Piermont, N.H. and died 26 April 1855 [82 yrs] at Pittsburg, N.H. He married PHEBE STOKES. She born c1777. Moved 1823 to Pittsburg, N.H. Occ. farmer. He served in the Indian Stream War 1832-6. Named in 1810 U.S. Census at Piermont. 1850 census at Pittsburg, N.H.

Children: B4. SON Y, possibly EDWARD, b. 14 June 1807 at Pittsburg, N.H.
           B5. DAVID T., b. 1808, md. ELIZABETH B. SMITH.
           B6. RHODA,
           B7. WELLMAN, b. 1813, d. 1872, md. HANNAH FLANDERS.

B3. SON X ROWELL [ENOS B1] He had at least the following sons.

Children: B8. MOSE, md. MARCISSIE PARKER.

APPENDIX

The Enos Rowell Family of N.H. Cont.

B9. JOHN, b. c1805, md. MALINDA
SMITH.

B4. SON Y ROWELL [SAMPSON B2] He married _____
COATES. Res. Johnsville, Quebec.

Children: B10. GEORGE,
           B11. MARY, twin b. 1827.
           B12. MARRIAM, twin b. 1827.
           B13. SIMEON,

B5. DAVID T. ROWELL [SAMPSON B2] He was born
1808 at Piermont, N.H. He married ELIZABETH B.
SMITH. She born 1814. 1850 census at Pittsburg,
N.H.

Children: B14. ELLEN FLANDERS, b. 16 Feb.
                1833, md. THOMAS MAYO.
           B15. LOIS M., b. 24 July 1834, md.
                18 May 1861 HARLAN CARR.
           B16. CHARLES, b. 14 Mar. 1836, d.
                1907, unmd.
           B17. GEORGE ALLEN (WILLIAM?), b.
                1838.
           B18. DAVID O., b. 1841, md. SARAH
                JACOBS.
           B19. SUMNER TOWNSEND, b. 1842, md
                JULIA BROWN.
           B20. LUCIOUS S., b. 2 July 1850, d.
                26 June 1907, md. 1894
                ELIZABETH VIOLA YERTAU.

B7. WELLMAN ROWELL [SAMPSON B2] He was born
1813 and died 1872. He married HANNAH FLANDERS.
She died 1880. Res. Pittsburg, N.H., Canaan, Vt.
and Hereford, Quebec.

Children: B21. EDWIN, b. 1834, d. 1864, unmd.
           B22. HENRY, b. 1836, d. 1915, md.
                MARIETTA PARKER.
           B23. ZEBULON F., b. 1838, d. 1906,
                md. MARGARET A. OWEN.

APPENDIX

The Enos Rowell Family of N.H. Cont.

> B24. **FRANKLIN B.**, b. 1840, d. 1905,
>   unmd.
> B25. **HIRAM**, b. 1842, d. 1867, unmd.
> B26. **MARIA**, b. 1844, d. 1870, unmd.
> B27. **MARY**, b. 1846, d. 1871, unmd.
> B28. **WELLMAN Jr.**, b. 1848, d. 1873,
>   unmd.
> B29. **FREEMAN**, b. 1850, d. 1855,
>   unmd.
> B30. **GEORGE**, b. 1855, d. 1877, unmd.

B8. **MOSE ROWELL** [SON W B3] He married **MARCISSIE PARKER**.

Children: B31. **PERSIS**,
           B32. **MARTHA ANN**,
           B33. **RUBY**,
           B34. **RANSOM**,
           B35. **IRA**,
           B36. **MARY ANN**,
           B37. **PARKER**, b. 1851, d. 1925.

B9. **JOHN ROWELL** [SON X B3] He born 1805 in N.H. He married **MALINDA SMITH**. She born 1805. 1850 census at Pittsburg, N.H. Res. Canada and Pittsburg, N.H.

Children: B38. **ALBERT**, b. 1831.
           B39. **EMILY**, b. 1834.
           B40. **BETSY**, b. 1836.
           B41. **SCHUYLER**, b. 1839, Civil War
                 Soldier.
           B42. **LITTLE JOHN**, b. 1843.
           B43. **DIANA**, b. 1846.
           B44. **FANNY**, b. 1848.

B17. **GEORGE ALLEN ROWELL** [DAVID T. B5] He was born 1838. Served in Civil War. Res. at Pittsburg, N.H.

Children: B45. **daughter**,
           B46. **daughter**,

APPENDIX

The Enos Rowell Family of N.H. Cont.

B18. **DAVID O. ROWELL [DAVID T. B5]** he was born 1842. He married **SARAH JACOBS**. Res. Stratford, N.H.

Children: B47. **EDGAR**,

B19. **SUMNER TOWNSEND ROWELL [DAVID T. B5]** He was born 1846. He married **JULIA BROWN**. Res. Stewartown, N.H. Served in Civil War.

Children: B48. **JESSIE**,

B20. **LUCIOUS S. ROWELL [DAVID T. B5]** He was born 1850 and died 1906. He married 1894 **ELIZABETH VIOLA YERTAU** of North Stratford, N.H. Occ. Insurance agent. Lt. WW1. Res. Stratford, N.H.

Children: B49. **WELLMAN H.**,b. 1896, md. 1919
        ETHEL BOYD.
        B50. **daughter**,
        B51. **KENNETH**, Lt. WW1.

B22. **HENRY ROWELL [WELLMAN B7]** He was born 1836 at Pittsburg, N.H. and died 1915 at East Hereford, Quebec. He married 1866 **MARIETTA PARKER**. Res. Hereford, Quebec.

Children: B52. **WALTER L.**, b. 1867.
        B53. **JENNIE E.**,

B23. **ZEBULON F. ROWELL [WELLMAN B7]** He was born 1838 at Pittsburg, N.H. and died 1906. He married 1862 **MARGARET A. OWEN**. Res. Hereford, Quebec.

Children: B54. **ELWIN E.**, b. 1861, d. 1921, md.
        1906 **SARAH E. BAXTER**.
        B55. **EDWIN C.**, b. 1864, d. 1927, md
        1891 **LULA B. CHASE**.
        B56. **ORVIN S.**, b. 1866, d. 1931, md.
        1902 **Mrs. EVA J. EVANS**.
        B57. **IDA MAY**, b. 1868, d.y.

APPENDIX

The Enos Rowell Family of N.H. Cont.

B58. **FRANK I.**, b. 1870, d. 1947, md.
1903 **VIOLA J. BENNETT**.
B59. **IDA M.**, b. 1873.
B60. **BURTON Z.**, b. 1875.
B61. **VERA L.**, b. 1882.

B49. **WELLMAN H. ROWELL** [LUCIOUS B20] He was born
1896 at North Stratford, N.H. He married 1919
ETHEL BOYD of Lachute, Quebec. Occ. dealer saw
and lawn mowers. Res. Derby, Vt. 2nd Lt. WW1.

Children: B62. **KENNETH F.**, b. 1920, md. 1943
BARBARA BOND, WW2, Had 4 dau.
B63. **BARBARA**, b. 1930.

B51. **WALTER L. ROWELL** [HENRY B22] He was born
1867 and died 1948. He married 1897 **ESTHER M.
WESTON**. She died 1939.

Children: B64. **DORIS M.**, b. 1897.
B65-6. twin sons still born.

B53. **ELWIN E. ROWELL** [ZEBULON B23] He was born
1863 at Pittsburg, N.H. and died 1921. He
married 1906 **SARAH E. BAXTER**. Res. Boston, Mass.

Children: B67. **RAYMOND LESLIE**, b. 1908.

B54. **EDWIN C. ROWELL** [ZEBULON B23] He was born
1864 at Pittsburg, N.H. and died 1927. He
married 1891 **LULA B. CHASE**. Occ. farmer. Res.
Hereford, Quebec.

Children: B68. **HAROLD G.**, b. 1892, md. 1930
FLORA KEMPTON, WW1.
B69. **CELYON**, b. 1896, d. 1947, md.
M. KATHRYN KINNEY, WW1.
B70. **IRVIN E.**, b. 1898, d. 1921,
WW1.
B71. **EDNA**, b. 1900.

The Enos Rowell Family of N.H. Cont.

B55. **ORVIN S. ROWELL [ZEBULON B23]** He was born 1866 at Pittsburg, N.H. and died 1931. He married 1902 **Mrs. EVA J. EVANS.** Res. Boston and Hereford, Que. No children.

B57. **FRANK I. ROWELL [ZEBULON B23]** He was born 1870 at Hereford, Quebec and died 1947. He married 1903 **VIOLA J. BENNETT.**

Children: B72. **SYLVIA E.**, b. 1904.
          B73. **WILSON O.**, b. 1907.
          B74. **JOHN B.**, b. 1909, md. 1939 **MARABELLE G. BROWN.**
          B75. **WELLMAN A.**, b. 1914, Canadian Army WW2.

B62, **KENNETH ROWELL [WELLMAN B49]** he was born 1920. He married 1943 **BARBARA BOND**, d/o **WILLIAM G. & DORIS (BLANCHARD) BOND** of Newport, Vt. Occ. vet. WW2. 1959 Commander U.S. Navy Air Arm. Res. Derby, Vt.

Children: B76. **SANDRA,**
          B77. **JUDY,**
          B78. **BARBARA,**
          B79. **PATTY,**

B65. **HAROLD G. ROWELL [EDWIN B54]** He born 1892 at Hereford Hill, Quebec. He married 1930 **FLORA KEMPTON.** Soldier WW1. Served in Germany. Res. Hanover, N.H.

Children: B80. **DONALD B.**, b. 1931.

B66. **CELYON ROWELL [EDWIN B54]** He was born 1896 and died 1947. He married **KATHRYN KINNEY.** Soldier WW1. Res. Lancaster, Pa.

Children: B81. **ANNABELLE K.**, b. 1924.
          B82. **JAMES E.**, b. 1927, md. 1949 **JACQUELINE BRUST.**
          B83. **DOROTHY E.**, b. 1930.

APPENDIX

Enos Rowell Family of N.H., Cont.

B84. **CHARLES EDWARD**, b. 1934, md.
1956 **JOSEPHINE DeTRILIO**.
Marine Corp. 1953-8, Sgt.
B85. **FRANCIS G.**, b. 1938.

B71. **JOHN B. ROWELL** [FRANK B57] He was born 1909 at Hereford, Quebec. He married 1939 **MARABELLE G. BROWN**. Res. Canaan, Vt. Sherbrooke, Que.

Children: B86. **JOANNE E.**, b. 1940.
B87. **AVERY I.**, b. 1942.

B77. **DONALD B. ROWELL** [HAROLD G. B65] he was born 1931 at Hanover, N.H. He married 1953 **BEVERLY CAMP**. Res. Carmichael, Calif.

Children: B88. **TERRY ANN**, b. 1954.

B79. **JAMES E. ROWELL** [CELYON B66] He was born 1927 at Lancaster, Pa. He married 1949 **JACQUELINE BRUST**. Res. Lancaster, Penn.

Children: B89. **LINDA MARIE**, b. 1955.

APPENDIX

ROWELL FAMILY OF SOUTH CAROLINA

Col. Melvin Rowell in his book The Register of Rowells (1957) on page 37 says that nine Rowell's came to the Carolina's on the ship SPUR, during Colonial times. Regretfully he didn't give us more information nor name his source. He states that: "the recurance of certain given names [Jacob, David, Valentine and William] in both this line and in the line of Thomas' of Mass. seems to indicate a possible connection back in Old England" [or New England].

The author searched for possible connection back in County Warwickshire, England. Regretfully no connection was found in Warwickshire records for the Atherstone/Mancetter area. The Rowell family at Atherstone had died off by the year 1700 which predates the probable arrival in South Carolina.

In the NEHGR vol. 134 pg 91 (1980) is given a list of nine ROWELL'S who came to South Caroline about 1770. They reportedly came from a place called "Newingland." They are suppose to be brothers and sisters. The parents names are not given.

Oliver Rowell, b. c1741
Mary Rowell, b. c1743
Valentine Rowell, b. 1747
Jane Rowell, b. 1749
William Rowell, b. 1751
Jacob Rowell, b. c1754
Elizabeth Rowell, b. 1756
David Rowell, b. 1758
Calib Rowell, b. 1761

In the 1790 census for South Carolina there were some 30 Rowell names listed with additional names in North Carolina. That seems to indicate they had been there for several generations. Yet

APPENDIX

ROWELL FAMILY OF SOUTH CAROLINA

the earliest Rowell record I found was the marriage of William Rowl to Ann Sprunton on 20 July 1761 at Charlestown.

Combining Col. Melvin Rowell's information with that from other sources, the following tentative pedigree is presented:

C1. **VALENTINE ROWELL**, He was born about 1747. Emigrated perhaps in 1770. Named in 1790 and 1800 census at Georgetown District.

Children: C10. **VALENTINE Jr.**, b. c1761, md.
                NANCY ANN BAKER

C2. **JACOB ROWELL**. Georgetown. Born perhaps about 1743. Name of his first wife is unknown. He married 2nd Mrs. Palmer or Polson. Named in 1790 census. Res. Marion Co., S.C. in 1809.

Children: C11. **WILLIAM**,   (went west)
                C12. **DAVID**, b. c1778, d. c1853, md.
                REBECCA PHILIPS.

C3. **DAVID ROWELL**, Georgetown. He was born about 1758. Emigrated perhaps in 1770. He married about 1780 **ELIZABETH LONG**. She born 1761 at Barnwell. Named in 1790 census at Georgetown District.

Children: C13. **JAMES**, b. c1785.
                C14. **LEVI**, b. c1787.
                C15. **VALENTINE**, b. c1789, md. **EVA _**.
                C16. **JONAS**, b. c1793, md. 1825
                ISADORA JACKSON.
                C17. **DAVID**, b. 1795, d.y.
                C18. **ALFRED**, b. 1796.
                C19. **DAVID**, b. 5 Apr. 1806, md.
                CLARA WYNN.

C10. **VALENTINE ROWELL Jr.** [VALENTINE C1] He was born about 1761. He married **NANCY ANN BAKER**. Served in Rev. War with Gen'l Francis Marion.

APPENDIX

ROWELL FAMILY OF SOUTH CAROLINA

Served in State Legislature 1812 - 1822. Named
in 1790 census at Georgetown. 1810 census in
Marion District.

Children: C20. **WILLIAM BASCOMB**, b. 28 Mar.
1800, d. 22 May 1880, m.1,
ELIZABETH AVANT, m.2, **MARTHA
BRANTLEY**.
C21. **CORNELIUS DePRE**, d. 13 Mar.
1831, md. **SUSAN SWEET**.

C12. **DAVID ROWELL** [JACOB C2] He was born about
1778 and died about 1853. He married **REBECCA
PHILIPS**. Res. Marion Co. S.C. in 1809. Named on
tax rolls.

Children: C22. **JACOB**,
C23. **WILLIAM L.**, b. 13 Feb. 1811,
md. **ELIZA ANN LANDON**.
C24. **DAVID J.**, b. c1818, md. 1840
ANN REBE GASQUE.
C25. **VALENTINE**, b. c1820, d. 1902,
md. **MARY COLLINS**.
C26. **STACEY ANN**,
C27. **ELIZABETH**,
C28. **JANE**, b. 24 Nov. 1825, md.
ELISON LANCY.
C29. **SARAH**,
C30. **AGNES**,
C31. **REBECCA**, b. 20 Feb. 1823, md.
ELLY A. COLEMAN.

C15. **VALENTINE ROWELL** [DAVID C3] He was born
about 1820 and died about 1902, age 82 years. He
married **EVA** _____. 1809 in Marion District,
Darlington, S.C.

Children: C32. **KETURAH**, b. 24 Sep. 1813, md.
29 Nov. 1835 **ARCHIBOLD B.
CAMPBELL**.
C33. **NOAH WESLEY**, b. 12 Sep. 1815.
C34. **LENASCA**, b. 17 Oct. 1816.
C35. **JESSE KOLB**, b. 31 July 1818.

APPENDIX

ROWELL FAMILY OF SOUTH CAROLINA

        C36. **TILLMAN**, b. 22 Feb. 1821.
        C37. **JOHN VALENTINE**, b. 17 Sep.
            1823.
        C38. **MARY**, b. 4 Jan. 1826.
        C39. **EDA MARIAH**, b. 22 Apr. 1827.
        C40. **NANCY**, b. 16 Oct. 1829.

C16. **JONAS ROWELL** [DAVID C3] He was born about 1793. He married about 1825 **ISADORA JACKSON**. Res. St. Lukes Parish, Beaufort, S.C.

Children: C41. **JONAS R.**, b. c1847, md. c1911
              IDA EADY MALPHUS at Hampton.
          C42. **ADESSA**, b. 1852.
          C43. **JULIA S.**, b. 1854.
          C44. **HENRY A.**, b. 1856.
          C45. **RICHARD**, ??

C18. **ALFRED ROWELL** [DAVID C3] He married 1st **ELIZA** _____, married 2nd **SARAH** _____. She born about 1830. May have m.3, **ADELINE BUCKNER**. Res. Gillisonville, Beaufort, S.C.

Children by 1st Wife:
          C46. **GEORGIANNA HEYWARD**, b. 20 Oct.
             1840.
By 2nd Wife:
          C47. **CHARLES**, b. 1848.
          C48. **RACHEL A.**, b. 1850.
          C49. **REBECCA**, b. 1851.
          C50. **VALENTINE**, b. 1853.
          C51. **JAMES J.**, b. 1854.
          C52. **ELIZABETH J.**, b. 1858.
          C53. **SUSAN C.**, b. 1859.
          C54. **ALFRED**, b. 1862.
          C55. **SOPHIA LOUELLA**, b. 6 Nov.
             1863.

C20. **WILLIAM BASCOMB ROWELL** [VALENTINE C10] He was born 28 march 1800 and died 22 May 1880. He married first **ELIZABETH AVANT** and married second **MARTHA BRANTLEY**.

APPENDIX

ROWELL FAMILY OF SOUTH CAROLINA

Children by 1st Wife:
   C56. **ANNA ELIZABETH**, md. D.J. TAYLOR
By 2nd Wife:
   C57. **MARTHA ELIZA**, md. CORNELIUS D.
   ROWELL [# 59], Her 1st Cousin.

C21. **CORNELIUS DePRE ROWELL** [DAVID C12] He died
13 March 1831. He married **SUSAN SWEET**, d/o
ANTHONY & MARY SWEET.

Children: C58. **ROBERT W.**,
     C59. **CORNELIUS DuPRE**, b. 1831, d. 2
     May 1887, md. **MARTHA ELIZA**
     ROWELL [#57]. His 1st cousin.

C23. **WILLIAM L. ROWELL** [DAVID C12] He was born
13 Feb. 1811. He married **ELIZA A. LANDON.** Res.
Contenary, Marion District, S.C.

Children: C60. **BENJAMIN**, b. 1835.
     C61. **ANNA**, b. 1839.
     C62. **ELIZABETH**, b. 1841.
     C63. **RICHARD**, b. 1843.
     C64. **MARY JANE**, b. 1845.
     C65. **SARAH**, b. 1849.
     C66. **RACHEL AGNES**, b. 11 Oct. 1854.

C24. **DAVID J. ROWELL** [DAVID C12] He was born
about 1818. He married 1840 **ANN REBE GASQUE.**
Res. Marion District.

Children: C67. **ALBERT**, b. 1851.
     C68. **ANN**, b. Jan. 1848.
     C69. **ELIZABETH L.**, b. Jan. 1851.
     C70. **VALENTINE**, b. 1843.
     C71. **WILLIAM**, b. 1846.
     C72. **JESSE C.**, b. 1 Apr. 1847.
     C73. **EMELINE**, b. 1852.

C25. **VALENTINE ROWELL** [DAVID C12] He was born
about 1820 and died 1902, 82 years. He married
MARY COLLINS.

APPENDIX

ROWELL FAMILY OF SOUTH CAROLINA

Children: C74. WILLIAM.
            C75. DAVID,
            C76. ALEXANDER,
            C77. VALENTINE,
            C78. ROBERT CHARLES,
            C79. JOSEPH, b. c1859, md. SALLIE
                 KEEVER.

            C80. ALICE, d.s.p.

C59. CORNELIUS DuPRE ROWELL Jr. [CORNELIUS C21]
He was born 1831 and died 2 May 1887. He married
MARTHA ELIZA ROWELL [#C57] d/o WILLIAM B. &
MARTHA (BRANTLEY) ROWELL. They were 1st cousins.

Children: C81. W.B.,
            C82. R.D.,
            C83. MELVIN LEANDER, b. 5 Oct. 1857,
                 d. 18 June 1932, m.1, ELLA
                 FOWLER. Had: ALICE, d.y., m.2
                 EVA AGNES RANDELL. 4 children.
            C84. C. THOMAS, d.y.
            C85. PERCIVAL E.,
            C86. MARY A., d.y.
            C87. LENNIE J., md. CAL HOOK, 5 dau.
            C88. MATTIE E., md. _____ CRAWFORD.

C79. JOSEPH ROWELL [VALENTINE C25] He was born
about 1859 and died in 1931. He married SALLIE
KEEVER .

Children: C89. JOSEPH VALENTINE, b. 1885, d.
                 1953, md. ELIZABETH SHELLEY,
                 11 children.
            C90. KEEVER,
            C91. ARCHIE BRUCE,
            C92. GRADY,
            C93. DAVID OSCAR,
            C94. ALICE,
            C95. ELLEN,
            C96. EVA,
            C97. CLARA,

First	Second	Third	Fourth	Fifth	Generation

```
                         PEDIGREE  CHART  ROWELLS
 First      Second      Third        Fourth        Fifth  Generation

                                                   ┌─ 50 Thomas     1702
                                                   ├─ 51 William    1705
                                      ┌─ 21 Valentine ─ 55 Joseph   1710
                          ┌─ 4 Thomas ─┤    1674    └─ 57 Joseph    1724
                          │   1644     │              ┌─ 58 Valentine 1708
                          │            └─ 23 Philip ─┬─ 59 Jacob    1710
                          │               c1678      ├─ 60 Philip   1713
                          ├─ 5 John                  └─ 66 Ichabod  1720
                          │   1645 d.y.              ┌─ 67 Philip   1695
            ┌─ 2 Valentine ─┤        ┌─ 25 Jacob ─┬─ 70 Moses      1699
            │     1622     ├─ 6 Philip ─┤  1671    ├─ 71 Aaron     1701
            │              │   1647   │            ├─ 72 Daniel    1705
            │              │          │            └─ 75 Gideon    1709
            │              └─ 10 John ─┬─ 27 Thomas ─┬─ 76 Thomas   1702
            │                  1655, d.y.  1676      └─ 78 Samuel   1708
            │                          │              ┌─ 87 Abraham 1706
            │                          ├─ 28 Abraham ─┼─ 88 Jacob   1710
            │                          │   1671       └─ 90 Rice    1714
            │                          │              ┌─ 91 Enoch   1716
            │                          │              ├─ 93 Benoni  1720
            │                          ├─ 29 John ───┼─ 94 John     1726
            │                          │   1683       ├─ 97 Eliphelet 1729
 1 Thomas ─┤                          │              └─ 98 Abendigo 1731 d.y
   1594     │                          │              ┌─ 102 Elijah 1710
            │                          ├─ 30 Job ────┼─ 103 John    1713
            │                          │   1685       ├─ 104 Job    1716
            │                          │              └─ 105 Thomas 1718
            │                          └─ 33 Aaron ──── 109 James   1727
            │                              1689        ┌─ 111 Asa    1743
            │                                          ├─ 112 Philip S. 1745
            │                                          - 113 Jacob   1747
            │                            ┌─ 35 Benoni Jr ┤ 115 Isreal 1752
            │                            │   1715       ├─ 116 Leonard 1755
            │                ┌─ 13 Benoni ─┤            ├─ 117 James  1763
            │                │   1691     │             └─ 120 Simon  1768
            │                │            ├─ 36 Josiah ──┬─ 122 Philip 1745
            │                │            │   1717       └─ 123 Josiah Jr.1747
            └─ 3 Jacob ──────┼─ 14 Elihu ─┴─ 38 Samuel ─┬─ 124 Jacob c1748
                             │   1693         1720       └─ 125 William c1749
                             │            ┌─ 40 John ──── 129 Jacob   1774
                             └─ 17 John ──┤   1730       ┌─ 130 Jonathan 1771
                                 1700     │              ├─ 131 Jesse  1777
                                          ├─ 43 Jacob ──┼─ 132 James
                                          │   1732       ├─ 133 Rufus V. 1793
                                          └─ 44 Moses ──┬─ 136 Henry  1799
                                              1735       └─ 139 Hoak   1806
```

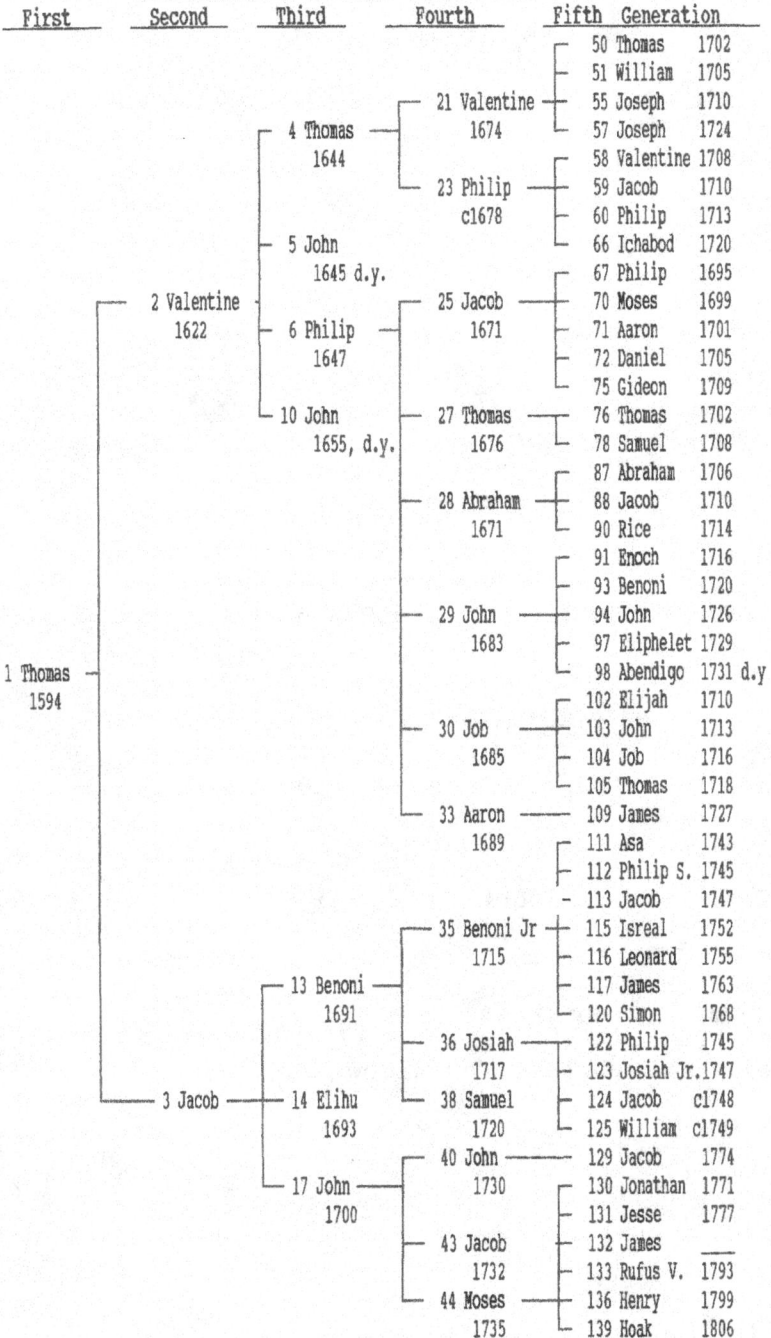

APPENDIX

ABBREVIATIONS

Admin. = Administrator

b.   = born

c   = circa = about

ch.   = children

d.   = died

div.   = divorced

d/o   = daughter of

d.s.p. = died single person

d.y.   = died young

J.P.   = Justice of the Peace

md.   = married

m.1,   = married first

m.2,   = married second, etc.

P.P.   = personal property

Res.   = resident

s/o   = son of

unmd.   = unmarried

w/o   = wife of or widow of

BIBLIOGRAPHY

PRIMARY SOURCES - BOOKS:

1. Melvin Rowell, A Register of Rowells, Northwoods Narrows, N.H., Dec. 1956.

2. Melvin Rowell, The Register of Rowells, Northwoods Narrows, N.H. Sep. 1957.

3. Melvin Rowell, Supplement to the Register of Rowells (1957), Concord, N.H., Mar. 1959.

4. Roland Rowell, Biographical Sketch of Samuel Rowell & Notices of Some of his Descendants with a Genealogy of 7 Generations, Manchester, N.H., 1898.

5. George P. Rowell, Proposed Rowell Genealogy, Stamford, Ct. 1919, Morman Film #1294378.

6. Henry Kent Kilburn, A Genealogy of the Rowell and Allied Families, (1940) Morman Film #0982382.

7. Ezra S. Stearns, Genealogical & Family History of the State of New Hampshire, Lewis Publ. Co., Chicago, 1908, 4 vol., p.646-651.

8. Hoyt, David W., Settlers of Old Families of Salisbury & Amesbury, Mass., 1897

9. Thomas Rowell Family Association, Rowell Family Control Sheets, (1975) Morman Film #0982382.

10. Glenn C. Towle, New Hampshire Genealogical Digest 1623-1900, Baltimore, Heritage Books (1986).

PUBLICATION SOURCES:

1. The Granite Monthly, v.36, p. 90-97, 1904 "A Star In Eclipse."

BIBLIOGRAPHY Cont.

2. Downeast Ancestry, v.3, No.5, Feb. 1980,
   "Jacob Rowell Family of N.H. and Newport,
   Me." by Mrs. Ivan Bohanan. 1 p.

3. Second Boat, v. 10, Mar. 1989, "Jacob Rowell
   Ancestry Questioned," by Priscilla Bohanan.
   1 p.

4. Ashe Tree Echo, v.4, 1969, "Information on
   the Rowell Family," by Even G. Rowell. 2 p.

5. ibid, v.27, Mar. 1992, p.16-28, "Dr. Chester
   H. Rowell & the Fresno Morning Republican,
   Part 1.

6. Shiawasse Steppin Stone, v. 5, June 1976,
   "From the Desk of Avon Rowell Farrow," 1 p.

7. ibid, v.7, June 1978, "Early Rowell
   Marriages," by Avon R. Farrow. 1 p.

8. Gleanings From The Heart of The Corn Belt,
   v. 26, No. 4, winter _____, "Rowell Family,"
   by Kevin G. Hoff. 1 p.

9. NEHGR, v. 138, p. 128-9, 1983, "The English
   Origin of the Rowell Family," by William H.
   Jones.

UNPUBLISHED MANUSCRIPT - SOURCES:

1. Small, Lucile N., Descendants Of Zebedee &
   Judith (Hamblett) Rowell, 3 vol. (1988) Copy
   at New Hampshire Historical Society Library,
   Concord, N.H.

2. Haner, Miriam Elaine Rowell, Meet Your Genes
   (1983) Copy at LDS Libray Salt Lake City,
   Utah Film #1034469.

3. Rowell, Frances Gertrude, The Book of
   Jonathan & Sally (Hoskins) Rowell, (1933)
   Copy at LDS Lirary, Salt Lake City, Utah.
   Film #0982489.

BIBLIOGRAPHY Cont.

4. Newberg, Bessie O., William Rowell Rev.
Soldier & His Descendants, (1938) Copy at
LDS Lirary, Salt Lake City, Utah. Film
#0982489.

5. Rowell, Evan C., Thomas Rowell Family
Control Sheets, (1975) Sandy, Utah. Copy at
LDS Library, Salt lake City, Utah. Film
#0982382.

6. Merrell, Joanne Lee, Lewis Family, (1989),
Copy at LDS Library, Salt Lake City, Utah.
Film #1421498.

OTHER SOURCES:

1. Charles H. Pope, The Pioneers of Maine,
Baltimore, 1965, 393 p.

2. Carlton E. Fisher, Soldiers, Sailers &
Patriots of the Rev. War, Maine, S.A.R.,
Louisville, Ky. 1982.

3. Otis G. Hammond, Some Things About New
Hampshire, Concord, N.H., 1930.

4. George W. Chase, The History of Haverhill,
Mass., Haverhill, 1861.

5. Clarence A. Torrey, New England Marriages,
Prior to 1700, Baltimore, 1985.

6. Rev. Roland D. Sawyer, Bibiliographical
Volume of Kensington (N.H.), Sec. 3, p. 87.

7. John James Currier, History of Newbury,
Mass. 1635-1702, Boston, (1902)

8. Vital Records of Amesbury, Mass., to end
of 1849, Topfield Mass., Historical Society
(1913)

BIBLIOGRAPHY, Cont.

9. Vital Records of Salisbury, Mass.,

10. Probate Records of Essex Co., Mass. 1635-
    1681, The Essex Inst., Salem, Mass. 3 v.,
    (1916-1920)

11. Virgil D. White, Index to War 1812 Pension
    Files, Wayneboro, Tenn. (1989)

12. National Archives, U.S. Census 1850; Maine,
    N.H., Vermont & Mass.

13. Carlton E. Fidor, Soldiers, Sailors &
    Patriots of the Rev. War, Vermont, Camden,
    Me. (1992).

14. John E. Goodrich, Rolls of the Soldiers in
    the Rev. War 1775-1783, 2 vol., Rutland,
    Vt. (1904).

15. N.H. State Papers, Vol. 14 - 17.

16. Military History of N.H. 1623 - 1861,

17. Roster War 1812-14, Vermont,

SOME FINAL THOUGHTS

Regretfully a number of **ROWELL** names were found that could not be associated with early known families. Female marriages were difficult to connect up with their parents.

The list of unknown **ROWELL** names up to 1800 is as follows:

1706 May 15	Son of Nathan Rowle & Mary	born	Marblehead, Mass.
1716 May 13	Hannah, d/o Nathaniel Rowell	born	Chester, N.H.
1718 Dec. 11	Richard Rowell - Leah Stone	md.	Berwick, Me.
1724/5 Mar. 18	Hannah, d/o Philip Rowell & Jemima	born	Kingston, N.H.
1726 June 11	John Rowell - Tabitha Came	md.	York, Me.
1736 June 23	Daniel Rowell - Eunice Brown	md.	Croyden, N.H.
	[d/o Jonathan & Mindwell (Loomis) Brown]		
	they had 5 children bp. 1737 - 1758.		
1739 July 20	John Rowell - Phebe Hunt	md.	Methuen, Mass.
1741 Aug. 4	Son of William Rowell & Mary	born	Marblehead, Mass.
1742	Sarah Rowell - Benjamin Moulton	md.	Hampton Falls, N.H
1745 Mar. 24	Thomas Rowell	died	So. Hampton, N.H.
1747 Mar. 1	John Rowell - Mary Kezar	md.	So. Hampton, N.H.
May _	Daniel Rowell - Anne Fowler	md.	Hampstead, N.H.
1748 June 2	Dorithy Rowell - Abraham Smith	md.	Kingston, N.H.
1751 Dec. 16	Mary Rowell - Edmund Morse	md.	Newbury, Mass.
1752 Aug. 12	Mary Rowell - Isaac Griffin	md.	Kingston, N.H.
1755 Apr. 5	Elizabeth Rowell - Archibald Harper	md.	Marblehead, Mass.
1757 July 26	Thomas Rowell - Mary Barritt	md.	Upton, Mass.
Dec. 5	Jemima Rowell - David Reed	md.	So. Hampton, N.H.
1760 Oct. 19	Sarah, d/o John Rowell & Mary	born	Newbury, Mass.
1762 Feb. 11	Hannah Rowell - Philip Noyes	md.	Salisbury, Mass.
1764 Feb. 1	Hannah Rowell - Charles S. Crouch	md.	Georgetown, Me.
Mar. 25	Anne, d/o Philip Rowell	born	Amesbury, Mass.
Apr. 2	Elizabeth Rowell - Michael Molemer	md.	Salem, Mass.
June 4	Abigail Rowell	born	Danvers, Mass.
1766 Aug. 22	David Rowell - Patrica Greenleaf	md.	Woolwich, Me.
1768 Nov. 10	Ann Rowell - Charles Gussett	md.	Marblehead, Mass.
1769 Jan. 31	Sarah Rowell	born	Nottingham, N.H.
Oct. 8	Orlando Rowell - Ruth Sargent	md.	Amesbury, Mass.
1772 Oct. 6	Sarah Rowell - David Goodham	md.	Ipswich, Mass.
1773 Sep. 12	Betsy Rowell	born	Cambridge, Mass.
1777 Feb. 3	Elizabeth Rowell - Joseph Humphry	md.	Salem, Mass.
1778 Mar. 19	Moses Rowell - Elizabeth Baker	md.	Oxford, Mass.
Sep. 18	Survier (f), d/o Moses Rowell & Elizabeth, b. Charleston, Mass.		
Oct. 4	Miriam Rowell - Ezekiel Keyes	md.	Plymouth, N.H.

ROWELL UNKNOWN NAMES TO 1800

1779 Apr. 8	Martha Rowell - Samuel Farnham	md.	Woolwich, Mass.
1781 Dec. 20	Judith Rowell	died	Dandia, N.H.
1782 Apr. 9	Sarah Rowell - Daniel Gale	md.	Kingston, N.H.
Apr. 11	Meribee, d/o David Rowell & Sally	born	Derryfield, N.H.
1784 July 27	Sally Rowell - Peter Heald Jr.	md.	Temple, N.H.
1785 Dec. 2	Patience (Greenleaf) Rowell, widow of David	m.2, James Hill of Orrington, Me.
1787 Apr. 5	Mary Rowell - Jacob Gale	md.	Belmont, N.H.
1789 Mar. 10	Hannah Rowell - Phineas Gleason	md.	Dublin, N.H.
1791 Apr. 21	John Rowell - Molly Hathorn	md.	Bangor, Me.
Dec. 27	Christopher Rowell - Meriam Lovering	md.	Layden, N.H.
1793 Jan. 22	David Rowell - Martha Walton	md.	Winthrop, Me.
Mar. 4	Polly Rowell - David Currier	md.	Amesbury, Mass.
Aug. 14	Susannah Rowell - Benjamin Colby	md.	New Chester, N.H.
Nov. 21	Polly Rowell - John Knowlton	md.	Dublin, N.H.
1795 Apr. 22	Jenny Rowell - Nathaniel Marston	md.	Deerfield, N.H.
Dec. 24	John Rowell - Sally Upton	md.	Concord, N.H.
1796 Nov. __	Sarah Rowell - Moses Wells	md.	New Chester, N.H.
Dec. 15	Dorothy/Dolly Rowell - James Moses	md.	Epsom, N.H.
1797 June 22	Sally Rowell - Samuel Bernard	md.	So. Hampton, N.H.
1798 Feb. 5	Sally Rowell	died	Bath, N.H.
Apr. 13	Simeon Rowell	died	Bath, N.H.
__ __	David Rowell Jr. - Nancy Grant	md.	Berlington, Me.
Sep. 27	Tabitha Rowell - Hiram Hayes	md.	Berwick, Me.
1799 Aug. 26	Joanna Rowell - Thomas Morland	md.	Danvers, Mass.
Oct. 24	Philip Rowell - Sally Soloway	md.	Salem, N.H.
1800 Oct. 8	Anne Rowell - Adonijah Colby	md.	So. Hampton, N.H.

AUTHOR'S BIOGRAPHY

WILLIAM HASLET JONES, has done extensive English genealogical research in original records at the Public Record Office, London, England and at the County Record Offices of; Cumberland, Devon, Essex, Northamptonshire, Hertfordshire, Lancastershire, Norfolk, Shropshire, Warwickshire and Westmoreland, with additional studies conducted at various English libraries including: Society of Genealogists and St. Catherine's House in London, at the West County Studies library, Exeter, at the Norwich City library, etc.

The results from his English research have been published in PHILIP TOWLE, HAMPTON, N.H. - HIS ENGLISH ORIGIN AND SOME AMERICAN DESCENDANTS, (1995); in the NEHGR REGISTER, and included in two books; John B. Threlfall's ENGLISH ORIGINS OF 50 EARLY NEW ENGLAND FOUNDERS, (1990), and in HISTORY OF THE TOWN OF HAMPTON, N.H. (1989), in connection with their 350th anniversary.

Mr. Jones has conducted North American research at the National Archives and at the Library of Congress in Washington, D.C.; at the State Archives of: Arkansas, Illinois, Kansas, Maine, Missouri, New Hampshire, Tennessee, Vermont and Wisconsin; at State Historical Society Libraries in these States; and at various public and private libraries including the D.A.R. library, Washington, D.C., the Newberry Library, Chicago, Ill., The Southern Baptist Library, Nashville, Tenn., The NEHGS Library, Boston, Mass., the Allen County Library, Ft. Wayne, Ind., the Chattanooga Public library, McGhee-Lawson Library, Knoxville, Tenn., Peabody Library, Memphis, Tenn. and the Family History Center Library. Additional research was conducted at more than 45 County Court Houses in the above named states.

Mr. Jones has served for many years as a volunteer librarian at the Naperville, Illinois branch library of the Family History Center of the Church of Jesus Christ of Later Day Saints.

Key #	NAME	BORN	Key #	NAME	BORN
33	Aaron	1689	87	Abraham	1706
71	Aaron	1701	260	Abraham	c1733
585	Aaron	1767	323	Abraham	1743
580	Aaron	1770	620	Abraham	1761
706	Aaron	1771	770	Abraham	1770
1170	Aaron	1799	745	Abraham	
2273	Aaron	1846	746	Abraham	1776
437	Aaron Holbrook	1828	1238	Abraham	1791
218	Aaron Jr.	1738	1495	Abraham	1803
1385	Aaron Jr.	1803	1500	Abraham	1810
2214	Abbie Elizabeth	1843	3098	Abram/Aaron	1835
2753	Abbie Marie	1830	1456	Abram M.	1813
1596	Abbie Melissa	1853	1503	Achsa	1819
2673	Abbie S.	1849	2921	Acsah	1848
2761	Abby	1837	1562	A. D.	c1838
2789	Abby	1848	6152	Ada	1861
2216	Abby Elizabeth	1843	2870	Ada	1863
5862	Abby M.	1859	3026	Ada May	1871
98	Abednego	1731	1211	Adaline	1823
715	Abel	1765	805	Adaline	1832
2806	Abel W.	1832	1078	Adaline	
910	Abiah	1819	2650	Adaline	c1832
153	Abigail	1733	1347	Adaline J.	1837
156	Abigail	1742	880	Adam	1810
562	Abigail	1764	1361	Adam	1840
704	Abigail	1767	1517	Adda F.	1863
606	Abigail	c1775	1587	Addie C.	1854
856	Abigail	1797	2618	Addie H.	1869
1191	Abigail	1797	5736	Addie M.	1873
661	Abigail	c1801	2424	Addison	1813
1377	Abigail	1801	2653	Addison	c1845
1443	Abigail	1811	2701	Addison	c1850
1083	Abigail	1835	1234	Adelaide E.	1845
2885	Abigail	1836	921	Adelia	
1295	Abigail B.	c1819	1211	Adeline	1823
2234	Abigail F.	1835	2335	Adeline Cordelia	1857
1127	Abigail J.	1821	2400	Adelphus	1843
1056	Abigail M.T.	1798	2603	Adelphus P.	1834
658	Abijah/Elijah	1795	2861	Adniron	1852
1227	Abner	1831	937	Adolphus M.	1855
28	Abraham	1678	800	Adoniran Judson	1822
			2937	Adoniran Judson	

KEY #	NAME	BORN	KEY #	NAME	BORN
5582	Alanson Erastus	1866	940	Almond M.J.	1839
1542	Albert	1828	2782	Almyra	1834
2725	Albert	1841	1177	Alonzo	1822
2309	Albert Abbott	1848	2542	Alonzo	1854
5360	Ablert Chester	1869	2111	Alpheus	1842
1502	Albert Gallatin	1815	5106	Alpheus	___
2875	Albert Kendrick	1830	1096	Alphonso Dwight	1839
5855	Albert Kendrick	1874	5790	Alston	1873
5280	Albert Leonard	1872	5720	Alta Erveme	1899
5369	Albert Lee	1894	2597	Alvah R/B.	1850/1
2710	Albert P.	1848	5885	Alyce Gertrude	1892
871	Albert S.	1820	1370	Amanda	___
446	Albert S/H.	1834	1465	Amanda	1807
5355	Alberta Lucinda	1864	1366	Amassy	1820
5709	Albion K.	1863	2698	Ambrose	1835
1664	Albuntur	1874	326	Amos	1770
417	Alden	1804	589	Amos	1772
2694	Alden Augustus	1846	367	Amos	1773
2619	Aldora J.	1851	687	Amos	1797/8
2372	Alexander	1842	1567	Amos	1827
2784	Alfred	1837	2140	Amos	1837
1601	Alfred	1855	5240	Amos Fremont	1857
5745	Alfred Alphane	1861	1725	Andrew J.	1832
938	Alfred H.	1856	432	Andrew Jackson	1815
5369	Alfred Lee	1894	2672	Angelia M.	1842
64	Alice/Allis	1723	1113	Ann	1810
1516	Alice	1860	1060	Ann	1817
5391	Alice	___	2007	Ann Bray	1841
5840	Alice	___	1418	Ann L.	1798
2871	Alice	1868	1425	Ann M.	c1837
6143	Alice	___	2221	Ann Maria	1844
2366	Alice C.	1868	444	Ann Smith	1829
2506	Alice M.	___	54	Anna	1718
2970	Alice Mabel	1880	158	Anna	1748
3013	Alice Winifred	1883	603	Anna	c1769
2843	Allen	1845	567	Anna	1774
5288	Allen B.	1891	731	Anna	1777
5029	Alma	1889	845	Anna	1794
2829	Almeda	1837	1201	Anna	1802
2401	Almenzer C.	1845	861	Anna	1809
1731	Almira	1848	1141	Anna	1810
2951	Almon Bartlett	1859	1066	Anna	1813
1336	Almond	c1824	1508	Anna/Annie	1817
1551	Almond Bartlet	1838	2241	Anna	1849

INDEX ROWELL NAMES

KEY #	NAME	BORN	KEY #	NAME	BORN
2205	Anna Jackson	1823	595	Avon	1780
2221	Annabel H.	1844			
162	Anne	1738			
511	Anne	1761	5750	Bartha M.	1869
713	Anne	1780	2039	Barton	c1832
530	Anne	1780	870	Bartlett C.	1818
1564	Anne	1843	1146	Belinda	1810
5713	Anne	1882	2169	Belle	——
2768	Anne Marie	1857	2184	Belle	——
5286	Anne Tewksbury	1885	1667	Ben	——
619	Annie/Anna	1794	5570	Ben Irving	——
5115	Annie	——	242	Benjamin	1736
5752	Annie	1881	286	Benjamin	1750
1623	Annie M.	1858	330	Benjamin	1777
6142	Annie Marie	1873	529	Benjamin	1778
2836	Antoinette	1844	748	Benjamin	——
5120	Aretus	1863	1399	Benjamin	1792
423	Arlette/Aralette	1815	1497	Benjamin	1806
1792	Artemus	1796	2831	Benjamin	1841
3112	Artemus Milo	1821	2707	Benjamin	1844
5858	Arthur	1884	2152	Benjamin	1858
5737	Arthur B.	1874	455	Benj./Benning	c1756
5703	Arthur B.	1887	3018	Benjamin F.	1866
5371	Arthur Howard	1877	1622	Benjamin Forh	1846
2621	Arthur J.	1863	1205	Benjamin Franklin	1810
2960	Arthur S.	1876	1463	Benjamin Franklin	1815
5244	Arthur W.	1870	435	Benjamin Franklin	c1820
5020	Arthur William	1870	1405	Benjamin Greeley	1815
5821	Arthurd	1880	2617	Benjamin Greeley	1857
111	Asa	1743	2011	Benjamin H.	c1834
329	Asa	1775	784	Benjamin House	1814
780	Asa	1803	2708	Benjamin Winslow	1845
1005	Asa Tilton	1806	988	Benning/Benj. Jr.	1787
1372	Asabel/Ashel	1793	1723	Benning	1825
5562	Ashley Hill	1886	13	Benoni	1691
2202	Ashley Quintstand	1886	93	Benoni	1720/3
2920	Ashsah J.	1846	35	Benoni Jr.	1715
1012	Asneth/Asanath	1800	2863	Benton	1859
1344	Augusta	1822	2471	Bernice Adaline	1836
1228	Augusta Adelia	1831	5330	Bernice Cynthia	1882
2610	Augustus	c1835	2993	Bernice F.	1884
3117	Austin A.	1833	5782	Bernice L.	1883
2420	Ava	1853	3031	Bertha A.	1887
5349	Avery Edison	1863	2507	Bertha E.	——

KEY #	NAME	BORN	KEY #	NAME	BORN
5580	Bertha M.	1865	793	Caroline Haskell	1829
6039	Bertha Margarite	1917	811	Caroline Jane	1826
5831	Bertram Gustave	1892	2279	Caroline L.	___
1666	Bessie	___	2491	Caroline Luvia	1855
5061	Bessie Lottie	1872	2800	Caroline Prescott	1845
1713	Bethewal	___	2439	Caroline Viola	1860
986	Bethewal C.	c1797	2809	Caroline Wood	1842
623	Betsy	1767	5764	Carolyn	1869
771	Betsey/Bette	1772	6082	Carolyn June	1936
664	Betsy	1780	5242	Carrie	1862
635	Betsey	1782	5583	Carrie	1875
538	Betsy	1788	2444	Carrie Florance	1859
1154	Betsy	1799	5041	Carrie May	1877
1305	Betsy	___	3051	Carroll	1906
1437	Betsy	1811	5043	Cassie Hattie	1882
1470	Betsy	1813	2367	Cate	1867
1269	Betsey	1816	1355	Catherine	___
1729	Betsey	1844	5202	Catherine	1909
1339	Betsy Beard	1809	2255	Catherine E.	1842
852	Betsy L.	1808	2642	Catherine P.	c1833
2612	Betsy J.	c1841	3067	Catherine/Calista O.	1842
1040	Bette	1800	1561	C.C.	c1835
313	Betty	1757	2486	Celia Belinda	1843
701	Betty	1762	5342	Charity Elizabeth	1887
717	Betty	1768	352	Charles	1785
346	Betty	1792	1338	Charles	1807
660	Beulah	c1799	1455	Charles	1811
5470	Beverley E.	___	1465	Charles	1811
5340	Bird	1879	1125	Charles	1817
3036	Blanche	1892	841	Charles	1835
5573	Blanch	___	2165	Charles	___
5781	Blanche Ethel	1878	2246	Charles	1838
5376	Byran Joshua	1881	2222	Charles	1848
2605	Byron	1842	5785	Charles	1873
			3038	Charles	1896
			1584	Charles A.	1859
381	Calib	c1787	971	Charles Abbott	___
1214	Calib	1804	1593	Charles Adam	1843
3012	Calla Ethel	1879	5540	Charles Allen	___
1236	Cardine	___	5860	Charles Augustus	1851
5337	Carlton F.	1885	1367	Charles C.	1824
1720	Caroline	1813	2645	Charles C.	1849
1053	Caroline Elizabeth	1823	2304	Charles Carroll	1836
1225	Caroline H.	1827	5312	Charles Carroll	1869

KEY #	NAME	BORN	KEY #	NAME	BORN
2040	Charles Christopher	1837	873	Charlotte	1824
2755	Charles Dinsmore	1833	911	Chase Hall	1822
2691	Charles E.	1836	5726	Cheney Dexter	1876
2586	Charles Edgar	1851	2308	Chester	1844
2923	Charles Edwin	1852	5305	Chester Harvey	1867
5571	Charles Edwin	1885	3064	Chester Otis	1935
2502	Charles Emory	1849	5788	Chispa	1882
5701	Charles Everett	1871	159	Christopher	1732
1538	Charles F.	1850	502	Christopher	1761
2276	Charles F.	1850	505	Christopher	1769
2592	Charles F.	____	1014	Christopher Clark	1806
2846	Charles Franklin	1855	2077	Christopher Ira	1846
2986	Charles Foster	1873	5087	Clara Alice	1881
6060	Charles Foster Jr.	1900	5866	Clara Ann	1874
2626	Charles Guy	1863	2622	Clara Elizabeth	1846
453	Charles H.	1840	2801	Clara Florance	1848
2365	Charles H.	1864	2562	Clara L.	1858
5351	Charles H.	1865	2503	Clara Lillian	1851
1317	Charles Havrey	1820	973	Clara Louise	____
2498	Charles Henry	1846	2950	Clara Maria	1858
6035	Charles Irving	1914	5768	Clarance Parkman	1868
1423	Charles Lewis	1810	358	Clarisse	
5884	Charles Lewis	1889	1315	Clarissa W.	____
2120	Charles M.	1853	2351	Clark	1840
1535	Charles Nelson	1852	5354	Clark	1861
5362	Charles Paige	1873	2332	Clark	1862
2901	Charles Parker	1828	3050	Claude	1904
2594	Charles Pitt	____	5841	Clayton Fremont	1861
953	Charles Potter	1844	839	Clementine	c1832
2540	Charles S.	1849	2933	Clementine	1881
2916	Charles S.	1857	2931	Clementine Osgood	1872
1099	Charles Sholl	1845	3037	Clifton	1895
829	Chalres T.	____	2321	Clinton	1838
1224	Charles W.	1824	2929	Clinton C.	1867
2783	Charles W.	1835	1488	Comfort	1789
1101	Charles Walter	1850	652	Converse	1798
2201	Charles Walter	1884	1293	Converse Willard	1830
5283	Charles Warren	1877	2357	Cora	1855
2971	Charles Warren	1883	5767	Cora	1877
1321	Charles Wesley	1820	5856	Cora	1877
2245	Charles William	1837	2927	Cora Dell	1861
2560	Charles William	1852	5050	Cora F.	1865
2624	Charlie Hiram	1857	5306	Cora M.	1869
			1179	Cromwell G.	1826

KEY #	NAME	BORN	KEY #	NAME	BORN
550	Ebenezer Eaton	1798	1466	Elbridge	1813
2866	Eda	1859	929	Elbrdige	1830
2852	Edgar Allen	1843	2818	Elbridge	1839
1629	Edgar Witters	1858	2150	Elbridge Brooks	1838
1334	Edith	1795	2151	Elbridge Brooks	1857
2177	Edith	____	1471	Elbridge Jerry	1815
3060	Edith Evelyn	1933	6051	Eleanor Pitkins	1922
5303	Edith Irene	1879	2012	Electra	c1841
6112	Edla/Ella Ingram	1878	298	Eli	1774
1057	Edmund	1803	2112	Elias D.	1844
820	Edmund	1826	14	Elihu/Ellhu	1693
2141	Edmund M.	1842	102	Elijah	1710
2459	Edmund P.	1846	308	Elijah	1741
835	Edmund R.	1814	588	Elijah	1768
351	Edmund Randolph	1783	705	Elijah	1769
5731	Edna	1891	1378	Elijah	1785
5319	Edna Ellen	1879	726	Elijah	1788
2454	Edna Jane	1865	658	Elijah	1795
5432	Edna Mabel	1892	1092	Elijah Gibson	1831
6136	Edna May	____	3025	Eliot	1894
5822	Edson H.	1882	97	Eliphelet	1729
609	Edward	1769	294	Eliphalet	c1753
1195	Edward Jr.	1807	276	Eliphalet	1768
1112	Edward	1808	682	Eliphelet	1782
2541	Edward	____	651	Eliphalet	1796
2723	Edward	1835	1296	Eliphalet	1822
1620	Edward	1844	1348	Elisa N.	1844
1532	Edward	c1855	174	Elisabeth	1757
2499	Edward Alonzo	1848	416	Eliza	1803
2504	Edward Everett	1853	859	Eliza	1804
2451	Edward Everett	1865	1044	Eliza	1804
5495	Edward Everett	1876	1030	Eliza	1806
5492	Edward Everett	1878	804	Eliza	1829
5705	Edward F.	1866	961	Eliza	1844
936	Edward L.	1848	1515	Eliza	1849
5078	Edward Murrey	1868	1255	Eliza D.	1816
825	Edward P.	c1815	553	Eliza Ellen	1810
2006	Edward P.	1839	1408	Eliza Jane	1824
5284	Edward Stevens	1879	918	Eliza Jane	1839
2073	Edward Thomas	1835	2862	Eliza/Lida	1857
5086	Edward Webster	1878	605	Eliza R.	c1773
1308	Edwin	____	881	Eliza R.P.	1811
5100	Edwin Deane	____	11	Elizabeth	1657
1298	Edwin W.	c1835	15	Elizabeth	1695

KEY #	NAME	BORN	KEY #	NAME	BORN
3070	Emma	____	152	Eunice	1731/2
2987	Emma Belle	1880	2973	Eunice Mary	1887
5708	Emma F.	1860	688	Euphana	1800
2644	Emma J.	c1846	2891	Eva	1855
919	Emma M.	1842	3046	Eva	1904
6150	Emma Maria	1852	5430	Eva May	1888
2926	Emma Viola	1859	5105	Evan	____
91	Enoch	1716	5440	Evelyn Elizabeth	1906
273	Enoch	1756	933	Ezekiel P.	1842
642	Enoch	1779			
738	Enoch	1796			
1275	Enoch	1821			
1271	Enoch	1835	1277	Fanna/Fanny	1837
1285	Enoch	1835	418	Fanny	1811
2839	Enoch H.	1839	629	Fanny	____
2455	Enoch John	1886	685	Fanny	1789
5466	Enoch John	1925	798	Fanny	1814
747	Enoch Page	1780	1383	Fanny	____
2706	Enoch P.	1843	1341	Fanny Morgan	1827
1328	Ephraim Kelley	1822	1351	Fanny Ross	1860
2880	Erastus	____	1079	Finatha	____
2613	Erastus B.	1832	2722	Flavis L.	1833
5378	Erastus Chase	1865	1726	Fletcher B.	1835
2606	Erastus N.	1846	5579	Flora A.	1862
5765	Ernest	1858	2858	Flora Estelle	1860
5797	Ernest	1883	5028	Florance	____
5842	Ernest Clinton	c1872	5711	Florance	1876
3027	Erskine Pliny	1877	3076	Florance Belle	
1382	Esther	____	5776	Florance E.	1871
2113	Esther	1846	6090	Florance Mae	1894
411	Esther (Ann)	1809	5180	Ford Owen	
2424	Ethan Allen	1876	2715	Frances Adelaide	1848
5796	Ethel	1881	1607	Frances Elizabeth	1856/7
5883	Ethel	1887	5315	Frances Gertrude	1868
1663	Ethel May	1872	2320	Frances Harriet	1835
5771	Ethelyn	1825	1574	Frances Lavina	1847
1615	Etta M.	1860	877	Frances M.	1836
5792	Etta M.	1867	1727	Francis	1840
2449	Eugene	1848	5040	Francis Elmer	1876
2750	Eugene	1858	5733	Francis Martin	1863
1568	Eugene A.	1848	965	Frank	____
5363	Eugene Clark	1875	976	Frank	____
5728	Eugene Dombar	1885	2985	Frank	____
5335	Eugene May	1870	2654	Frank	1846

KEY #	NAME	BORN	KEY #	NAME	BORN
2748	Frank	1852	2016	Georganna	1855
3077	Frank	___	546	George	1770
5108	Frank	___	989	George	___
6117	Frank	___	1368	George	1826
2360	Frank A.	___	2756	George	1835
966	Frank Abbott	___	2817	George	1837
2402	Frank B.	1847	1728	George	1842
5473	Frank Converse	___	1650	George	1889
1332	Frank D.	1832	1578	George A.	c1847
957	Frank E.	1849	2620	George A.	1858
1655	Frank E.	1867	2952	George A.	___
2322	Frank F.	1850	5392	George A.	1870
2188	Frank Ford	1884	5572	George Amassy	___
2972	Frank Fulton	1885	1460	George B.	1800
5875	Frank Henry	1878	1080	George B.	1830
5725	Frank L.	1877	2341	George B.	1829
2456	Frank Plumby	1888	1230	George B.	1836
1537	Frank Sherburne	1857	1531	George Barker	1842
2601	Frank W.	c1859	2936	George Barker Jr.	1896
2200	Frank Wheaton	1880	2307	George Barney	1842
5201	Frank Wheaton	1907	5353	George Bell, Dr.	1858
832	Franklin B.	1821	1049	George Berkley	1815
1553	Franklin Pierce	1850	1636	George Cyrus	1872
2751	Fred	1860	2125	George Edward	1841
5691	Fred	1869	5867	George Eaton	1876
6141	Fred Abram	1864	2272	George F.	c1831
5581	Fred Nelson	1869	451	George F.	1834
2430	Fred Rice	1856	2243	George F.	c1834
5431	Fred William	1890	1552	George F.	1846
5350	Freddie Grant	1867	5775	George F.	1868
1070	Frederick	c1800	964	George Freeman	1853
1459	Frederick	1801	1513	George H.	c1838
1306	Frederick	1820	5225	George H.	1891
2155	Frederick	1839	5379	George Harvey	1867
5761	Frederick	1857	6151	George Henry	1869
5289	Frederick Bach.	1895	2872	George Henry	1870
3021	Frederick Frank	1873	2226	George H.P.	1842
5204	Frederick Mercer	1922	421	George J.	1811
5832	Frederick William	1894	2213	George Jones	1841
2807	Frederick Jr.	___	2472	George Presbury	1838
			5491	George Presbury	1876
			950	George Pratt	1858
6099	Gail Elaine	1926	972	George Rufus	___
2271	Gardner P.	___	1126	George S.	1819

KEY #	NAME	BORN	KEY #	NAME	BORN
2458	George Smith	1846	5786	Guy Paris	1875
2900	George Silas	1827			
1196	George W.	1809			
1319	George W.	c1817			
930	George W.	1836	1477	Hamilton	____
2736	George W.	1848	9	Hannah	1653
1609	George W.	1860	80	Hannah	1709
2189	George Walsh	1886	81	Hannah	1711
384	George Wash.	1794	53	Hannah	1713
882	George Wash.	1813	95	Hannah	1724
1304	George Wash.	1819	210	Hannah	1724/5
915	George Wash. Jr.	1833	216	Hannah	1730
1098	George Wayland	1843	206	Hannah	1732
5001	George Wilmer	1867	227	Hannah	1737
1590	George Wylie	1838	243	Hannah	1738
2982	George Wylie	1861	163	Hannah	1740
5480	Georgia A.	1876	170	Hannah	1748
5245	Georgie Lena	____	119	Hannah	c1766
5126	Gertrude	1871	602	Hannah	c1767
5200	Gertrude Mercer	1905	517	Hannah	1769
75	Gideon	1709	526	Hannah	1772
857	Gilman	1800	508	Hannah	1776
878	Gilman	____	720	Hannah	1776
1510	Gilman	1837	749	Hannah	1776
6094	Gladys M.	1899	777	Hannah	1785
3045	Gladys	1900	538	Hannah	1788
3034	Glenn Edgar	1888	1155	Hannah	1800
2988	Glenn Ellis	1886	1375	Hannah	1800
5576	Golda	____	1013	Hannah	1802
630	Grace	____	1193	Hannah	1803
5857	Grace	1882	1444	Hannah	____
5585	Grace	1881	1507	Hannah	1813
2925	Grace Ann	1856	1457	Hannah	1815
3040	Grace C.	1902	1472	Hannah	1818
5702	Grace Darling	1876	425	Hannah	1819
5336	Grace F.	1873	970	Hannah Elizabeth	____
2564	Grace L.	____	1262	Hannah Haydon	1836
5434	Grace Matthew	1895	912	Hannah L.	1825
2242	Green L.	c1834	168	Hannah Morse	1765
812	Gridley Bryant	1829	1061	Hannah Morse	1803
1094	Guildford Dudley	1834	167	Hannah Rogers	1762
2180	Guy	____	2837	Harlow Kilgore	____
1204	Guy Carlton	1809	5707	Harlow Wood	1858
1274	Guy Elbridge	1818	5798	Harold	1888

KEY #	NAME	BORN	KEY #	NAME	BORN
3001	Harold Leon	1910	2922	Henry A.	1850
6085	Harold Leon	1935	5070	Henry A.	1850
138	Harriet	1806	3090	Henry C.	1819
1198	Harriet	1815	5079	Henry Durrant	1875
434	Harriet	1819	1661	Henry F.	1868
801	Harriet	1824	963	Henry Frank	1849
2340	Harriet	1827	2581	Henry Gault	____
1570	Harriet	c1844	1478	Henry Geo. Wash.	____
5338	Harriet	1876	5348	Henry Irving	1860
1084	Harriet A.	1838	2566	Henry Irving	1870
810	Harriet Ann	1823	1281	Henry J.	1826
790	Harriet Beck	____	2930	Henry K.	1870
2913	Harriet Ella	1846	2126	Henry Louis	1843
2914	Harriet Ella	____	2769	Henry Leonard	1861
5281	Harriet Frances	1873	1520	Henry Plant	1838
1054	Harriet Louise	1826	2758	Henry S.	1839
2470	Harriet Moore	1834	2404	Henry S.	1853
2320	Harriet Newell	1835	2850	Henry Stevens	1837
2712	Harriet Newhall	1842	2041	Henry Valentine	1838
2596	Harriet Phebe	____	1229	Henry Ward	1834
797	Harriet Z.C.	1837	31	Hepzibah	1687
1006	Harris	1808	85	Hepzibah	1702
2176	Harry H.	____	5710	Herbert	____
5318	Harry Dickinson	1875	5763	Herbert B.	1867
5870	Harry F.	1873	1646	Herbert Edgar	1858
2342	Harvey	1834	2857	Herbert Leslie	1852
2179	Hattie	____	2561	Herbert Sidney	1854
2328	Hattie/Harriet	1844	5793	Herman L.	1870
5766	Hattie	1860	337	Hezekiah	1781
5714	Hattie	____	791	Hezekiah Smith	1824
2337	Hattie Edith	1862	5830	Hilda Marie	1891
2277	Hattie M.	1873	847	Hilliard	1798
5345	Hattie M.	1892	1541	Hilliard	1827
1610	Heber Moses	1869	2942	Hilliard Elmer	1867
5030	Helen	____	385	Hiram	____
2323	Helen Edna	1852	1172	Hiram	1803
934	Helen/Ellen M.	1844	1438	Hiram	1813
5077	Helen Flint	1866	1178	Hiram	1824
5372	Helen Louise	1878	1474	Hiram	1824
794	Helen Maria	1831	2747	Hiram Cheney	1850
2810	Helen S.	____	2766	Hiram Davis	1849
3111	Henderson	1820	1276	Hiram J.	1831
2615	Henrietta A.	1849	2282	Hiram Leonard	1837
136	Henry	1799	2495	Hiram Vandelia	1851

KEY #	NAME	BORN	KEY #	NAME	BORN
5850	Hiram Wallace	1857	2963	Irving William	1885
328	Hitty	1773	754	Isaac	1770
139	Hoak/Hooker	1806	772	Isaac	1774
1476	Horace	1841	1432	Isaac	1800
875	Horace Hill	1830	1451	Isaac	1803
1411	Horace N.	c1824	1421	Isaac	1805
1100	Horace Vincent	1847	1501	Isaac	1813
5584	Howard	1877	1428	Isaac	1814
6061	Howard Herbert	1902	1221	Isaac, Dr.	1818
5846	Hubert N.	____	1343	Isaac Clough	1820
2935	Hugh Grant	1892	2652	Isaac H.	c1840
			806	Isaac Henry	1835
			3091	Isaac Newton	1821
66	Ichabod	1729	2350	Isaac Smith	1838
5339	Ida	1877	5322	Isabell	1890
2855	Ida Frances	1849	383	Isaiah	1792
2149	Ida Lucy	c1846	115	Isreal	1753
2864	Ida M.	1872	335	Isreal	1776
5441	Ida Mabel	1929	5795	Ivan	1877
3014	Ida Madge	1885	2465	Ivy Louise	1875
2431	Ida May	1859			
786	Ignatius Haskell	1812			
2361	Imogene	1866	1563	J. A.	c1841
5343	Imogene	1887	3	Jacob	1656
5044	Ina Ila Isa	1889	25	Jacob	1671/2
5367	Ina Martha	____	59	Jacob	1710
1020	Ira	1797	89	Jacob	1710
555	Ira	1803	200	Jacob	1720
1493	Ira	1807	202	Jacob	1724
1210	Ira	1821	43	Jacob	1732
1710	Ira	____	160	Jacob	1733
2168	Ira	____	226	Jacob	1735
2301	Ira	1831	113	Jacob	1747
3065	Ira	1836	124	Jacob	c1748
1093	Ira Benjamin	1833	767	Jacob	1768
6113	Ira Clarence	1884	566	Jacob	1771
2918	Ira F.	1839	519	Jacob	1773
1625	Ira Hill	1848	129	Jacob	1774
5304	Ira Homer	1885	648	Jacob	1792
2185	Ira Wayland	1878	596	Jacob	1793
2447	Irene B.	1868	1790	Jacob Jr.	1793
6045	Irving Clarke	1911	1110	Jacob	c1794
1554	Irving Greeley	1851/54	1035	Jacob	1796
5282	Irving H.	1875	1039	Jacob	1796

KEY #	NAME	BORN	KEY #	NAME	BORN
402	Jacob	1803	6075	James Hamilton	1924
1786	Jacob	1805	2074	James Harris	1838
1122	Jacob	1809	433	James Harvey	1817
999	Jacob	____	2238	James Henry	1839
2608	Jacob	c1827	2490	James Herbert	1850
2105	Jacob	1829	1199	James M.	1817
5692	Jacob	c1870	2252	James M.	1836
2220	Jacob A.	1840	1017	James Madison	1809
1422	Jacob H.	1807	1606	James Madison	1855
2215	Jacob Ham	1843	2590	James P.	1848
3092	Jacob Rodney	1823	1628	James Perrin	1856
132	James	____	1333	James R.	1833
215	James	1727/8	2616	James Roby	1852
117	James	1763	2643	James R.	c1839
379	James	____	2754	James S.	1831
563	James	1766	1152	Jane	1796
547	James	1772	624	Jane	c1799
568	James	1776	422	Jane	1813
540	James	1791	1433	Jane	1802
684	James	1787	1722	Jane	1823
686	James	1795	1279	Jane	c1831
1417	James	1796	2741	Jane/Jennie	1842
1140	James	1808	887	Jane B.	1824
1342	James	1817	1350	Jane C.	1823
3078	James	____	614	Janet	1781
962	James	1846	987	Jared M.	____
6118	James	____	6036	Jean Elizabeth	1916
2912	James A.	____	5738	Jeanette	____
5042	James Albert	1879	2347	Jeanette Koffran	1833
5062	James Albert	1883	2877	Jefferson	____
2236	James Alfred	1843	1572	Jefferson Washington	1848
2024	James Bartlett	1836	100	Jemima	1705
1302	James Colwell	1813	214	Jemima	1732/3
669	James Colwell	1793	742	Jemima	1766
2235	James Cyrus	1840	2873	Jennie	____
5734	James D.	1865	6110	Jennie/Maybelle	1870
955	James Edwin	1842	5853	Jennie	1874
2591	James Frank	1852	2992	Jennie Lena	1883
2565	James Francis	1868	3044	Jennie	1898
952	James Frederick	1842	5816	Jennie Miranda	1888
5490	James Frederick	1874	131	Jesse	1777
2721	James Green	1831	552	Jesse	1807
1235	James H.	____	1397	Jesse	1805
			2609	Jesse	c1820

INDEX ROWELL NAMES

KEY #	NAME	BORN	KEY #	NAME	BORN
429	Jesse C.	1831	1120	John	1806
2964	Jesse Richard	1890	2166	John	
413	Jesse Shaw	1813	1406	John	1817
5116	Jessie		1396	John	
2995	Jessie Dutton	1888	2104	John	1827
1194	Jinne	1805	2457	John	
6053	Joan Alexander	1929	1576	John	c1843
22	Joanna	c1676	1573	John	1849
2101	Joanna	1819	2219	John	1859
30	Job	1685	5813	John	1871
104	Job	1716	1297	John A.	c1829
307	Job	1738	1016	John Adams	1809
753	Job	1771	2010	John Andrew	1850
708	Job Jr.	1776	2702	John B.	1828
758	Johanna		895	John C.	
5	John	1645	1721	John C.	1819
10	John	1655	1346	John C.	1828
29	John	1683	6097	John Chase	1923
17	John	1700	2368	John Colby	1835
103	John	1713	2025	John Daniel	1836
94	John	1729	2671	John Edwin	1838
40	John	1730	5700	John Edward E.M.	1871
262	John	c1735	2002	John F.	1826
315	John	1737	2231	John F.	1860
311	John	1750	1618	John F.	1869
271	John	1752	6046	John Fulton	1913
638	John		5031	John Hale	
741	John	1764	2815	John Hamblett	1834
586	John	1767	3113	John Harris	1823
564	John	1768	2922	John Henry	1850
506	John	1772	5327	John Henry	1874
631	John	1774	1410	John Hiram	1818
680	John	1778	2974	John Irving	1890
760	John	1778	1090	John Kendrick	1828
985	John	1782	1524	John Kirby	1846
724	John	1783	1327	John Lord	1821
735	John	1787	2614	John M.	1846
1000	John, Capt.	1790	1469	John Miranda	1809
737	John	1793	2121	John N.	1858
1010	John	1796	2781	John Orlando	1831
400	John	1797	1446	John P.	1809
1450	John	1799	670	John Page	1796
543	John	1802	1303	John Page	1816

INDEX ROWELL NAMES

KEY #	NAME	BORN	KEY #	NAME	BORN
1323	John Page	1822	173	Joseph	1754
5563	John Page Stark	1883	571	Joseph	1766
1335	John Parker	1797	523	Joseph	1767
1496	John Pettingill	1805	537	Joseph	___
1043	John R.	1813	681	Joseph	1780
341	John Redington	1790	338	Joseph	1783
1715	John S.	1827	683	Joseph	1784
2856	John S.	1849	340	Joseph	1787
2693	John Sandbourn	1842	727	Joseph	1792
2700	John Shute	1842	1340	Joseph Jr.	1811
5373	John Spaulding	1883	1051	Joseph	1820
2210	John Stewart	1833	2827	Joseph	1835
377	John Sullivan	1779	1525	Joseph	1848
450	John W.	1830	6093	Joseph A.	1897
2730	John W.	1834	803	Joseph Bartlett	1827
2278	John W.	1835	2763	Joseph F.	1841
3017	John W.	1877	1427	Joseph Mason	1817
2941	John Wesley	1864	1441	Joseph Melchoir	1807
1426	John Winslow	1813	3079	Joseph Newell	___
1416	John Jr.	1794	6119	Joseph Newell	___
2183	Johnny	___	1147	Joseph P.	1815
233	Jonathan	1743	2709	Joseph W.	1847
322	Jonathan	1753	289	Josephine	1756
702	Jonathan	1763	5344	Josephine	1890
766	Jonathan	1766	527	Joshua	1774
743	Jonathan	1769	615	Joshua	1784
130	Jonathan	c1771	1216	Joshua	1808
601	Jonathan	c1765	1209	Joshua	1818
610	Jonathan	1771	2353	Joshua	1844
521	Jonathan	1778	36	Josiah	1717
369	Jonathan	1781	123	Josiah Jr.	c1747
541	Jonathan	1793	5472	Joyce Mae	1913
1430	Jonathan	1796	225	Juda/Judith	1733
757	Jonathan	___	32	Judith	1689
2325	Jonathan	1838	61	Judith	1716
932	Jonathan	1839	92	Judith	1718
5321	Jonathan	1887	96	Judith	1726
1200	Jonathan Barney	1800	264	Judith	___
1045	Jonathan Edward	1806	730	Judith	1771
2302	Jonathan Harvey	1833	604	Judith	c1771
52	Joseph	1710	520	Judith	1775
55	Joseph	1724	573	Judith	1777
172	Joseph	1752	522	Judith	1779

KEY #	NAME	BORN	KEY #	NAME	BORN
332	Lois	1781	725	Lydia	1786
1202	Lois	1804	618	Lydia	1792
1217	Lois	1810	597	Lydia	1795
828	Lois	1826	1171	Lydia	1802
2330	Lois	1855	1041	Lydia	1805
5341	Lois	1882	2081	Lydia	1830
2563	Lois Alma	____	838	Lydia	c1830
1512	Loraine M.	1836	2274	Lydia A.	1867
2780	Lorenzo D.	1830	1015	Lydia Abbott	1807
430	Lorenzo Dow	1811	2607	Lydia Ann	1848
2895	Lorinde	1820	1403	Lydia C.	____
1174	Louise	1809	2250	Lydia D.A.	1833
1569	Louise	c1843	2206	Lydia Dean	1825
2022	Louisa Maria	1832	2217	Lydia L.D.	1845
625	Love	____	1218	Lydia M.	1812
863	Lovina	1816	2023	Lydia Williams	1834
2345	Lovina	1830	2786	Lyman	1841
2363	Lovina Mehitable	1850			
5366	Lovina Penelope	1884			
135	Lucinda	1797	2932	Mabel	1879
827	Lucinda	____	5881	Mabel	1883
1289	Lucinda	1820	5882	Mabel	1885
297	Lucy	1768	2423	Mabel Atwood	1865
993	Lucy	____	5080	Mabel Chester	1877
1485	Lucy	1803	2996	Mabel Frances	1890
1059	Lucy	1811	3024	Mabel Louise	1880
2326	Lucy Amanda	1839	2175	Mabel M.	____
884	Lucy Ann	1818	5833	Mable	1897
1585	Lucy A./Lucinda	1845	5834	Mable	1899
2303	Lucy Maria	1835	6038	Malcolm Wilmarth	1914
1097	Lucy Matilda	1841	1402	Manley A.	____
1480	Luddua/Lydia	1790	1497	Manley A.	1807
939	Luella C.	1858	917	Marcellus C.	1837
2981	Luella Vanlora	1860	916	Marcia C.	c1835
5742	Lula Blanche	1877	2108	Marcus	1835
5302	Lula Josephine	1875	321	Marey	1744
2826	Luther	1833	1259	Margaret	1827
1261	Luther Hayden	1834	6076	Margaret Anne	1926
204	Lydia	1728	6063	Margaret Belle	1905
359	Lydia	____	2406	Margaret D.	1858
515	Lydia	1767	12	Margarite	1659
722	Lydia	1779	5739	Margerie	1886
574	Lydia	1779	583	Margery	____
666	Lydia	1785	2990	Marguerite	1874

KEY #	NAME	BORN	KEY #	NAME	BORN
2878	Maria	____	114	Mary	c1750
2186	Maria Blanch	1880	246	Mary	1752
1046	Maria Chase	1808	263	Mary	____
920	Maria F.	1843?	274	Mary	1763
3056	Marian I.	1898	357	Mary	____
1055	Marianne	1811	382	Mary	____
2802	Mariabah Ella	1852	582	Mary	____
2505	Mariette A.	____	751	Mary	1768
5150	Mariette B.	1862	643	Mary/Polly	1780
977	Marina	____	710	Mary	1783
5026	Marion E.	____	668	Mary	1791
5287	Marion Lucretia	1889	744	Mary	____
6081	Marilyn Clare	1935	640	Mary	1794
5739	Marjorie	1886	1791	Mary/Polly	1794
572	Mark	1776	1483	Mary	1798
1711	Mark	1809	401	Mary	1801
2432	Mark Edwin	1863	1156	Mary	1802
3069	Mark Jr.	____	362	Mary/Polly	1806
718	Martha	1771	410	Mary	1807
3093	Martha	1825	1267	Mary	1810
3114	Martha	1825	3110	Mary	1813
3099	Martha A.	1837	883	Mary	1816
2355	Martha E.	1843	1278	Mary	1820
792	Martha Haskell	1826	1129	Mary	1825
1048	Martha Laurence	1812	1444	Mary	1817
3022	Martha May	1876	2595	Mary	____
1081	Martha Payton	1827	3094	Mary	1825
356	Martha Wheeler	1794	2740	Mary	1841
1626	Martin Chase	1851	1185	Mary	c1835
5171	Martin O'Conner	____	3068	Mary	1844
7	Mary	1649/50	2867	Mary	1861
20	Mary	1671/2	5140	Mary	1861
16	Mary	1698	1641	Mary	1869
56	Mary	1704	5577	Mary	____
86	Mary	1704	6096	Mary	1919
83	Mary	c1715	1307	Mary A.	____
37	Mary	1728	1537	Mary A.	c1848
205	Mary	1729/30	2227	Mary An	1843
41	Mary	1730	420	Mary Ann	1809
306	Mary	1736	1055	Mary Ann	1811
157	Mary	1745	799	Mary Ann	1817
222	Mary	1747	1352	Mary Ann	1830
234	Mary	1749	2370	Mary Ann	1835

INDEX ROWELL NAMES

KEY #	NAME	BORN	KEY #	NAME	BORN
2917	Mary Ann	1837	5880	Maud E.	1882
2713	Mary Ann	1845	1660	Maud Elizabeth	1882
2356	Mary Ann	1850	5027	Maurice H.	___
2623	Mary Ann	1854	305	Mehitabel	1734
2233	Mary Augusta	1833	762	Mehitable	1791
2695	Mary Augustus	1848	1420	Mehitable F.	1803
867	Mary C.	___	2488	Melissa Ann	1844
2598	Mary C.	1852	5122	Melvin	___
2075	Mary Clark	1841	5381	Melvin Weston, Col.	1888
796	Mary D.	1835	1161	Mengary	1813
1263	Mary D.	1839	848	Mercy	1800
789	Mary Dorcus	1819	62	Meriam	1718
2496	Mary E.	___	244	Meriam	1740
2500	Mary E.	___	272	Meriam	1753
2407	Mary E.	1856	756	Meribee	1782
2915	Mary E.	___	1453	Meribah	1807
6050	Mary Elizabeth	1921	5780	Merman C.	1876
920	Mary Ellen	1843	454	Merrell	1838
1594	Mary Ellen	1847	5747	Mertle Frances	1879
5861	Mary Ellen	1854	507	Micajah	1774
2208	Mary Esther	1835	1003	Micajah	1802/3
1630	Mary I.C.	1860	5721	Mildred Alice	1904
826	Mary J.	___	5565	Mildred Catherine	1902
2760	Mary J.	1834	1273	Millisen M.	1815
2009	Mary J.	1848	2306	Milo A.	1840
2300	Mary Jane	1829	5316	Milo Loren	1871
5851	Mary Jane	1862	5125	Mina	1868
5317	Mary Jane	1873	5730	Mina	1889
5814	Mary Josephine	1872	1203	Mindwell	1806
1325	Mary L.	___	1287	Minerva J.	1840
2452	Mary L.	1867	5746	Minneola	1864
5735	Mary L.	1868	5110	Minnie	___
3043	Mary Mildred	1920	1638	Minnie Bell	1880
1095	Mary Milton	1836	3080	Minnie E.	1866
1082	Mary P.	1832	2983	Minnie Estelle	1864
2212	Mary Rebecca	1839	5361	Minnie Irene	1871
2207	Mary Stevens	1831	201	Miriam	1722
785	Mary Strickland	1810	228	Miriam	1739
1521	Mary Strickney	1840	608	Miriam	1779
1586	Mary Sophia	1847/8	1371	Miriam	1789
2440	Mary V.	___	1374	Miriam	1796
3019	Matthew Joseph	1867	659	Miriam	c1797
3020	Matthew Joseph	1871	1215	Miriam	1806

INDEX ROWELL NAMES

KEY #	NAME	BORN	KEY #	NAME	BORN
1175	Miriam	1812	1042	Myran P.	c1809
2699	Miriam	c1838	6064	Myrta Gifford	1907
3056	Mirian I.	1898	1617	Myrta Viola	1868
72	Miriam A.	1703	3030	Myrtle E.	1882
1270	Miriam Miranda	1820			
5740	Mirtie F.	___			
312	Molly	1754			
711	Molley	1764	731	Nancy	1777
518	Molly	1771	134	Nancy	1795
776	Molly	1782	1002	Nancy	1800/2
1481	Molly R.	1794	354	Nancy	___
405	Moody	1810	628	Nancy	___
70	Moses	1699	424	Nancy	1817
207	Moses	1733/4	1313	Nancy	___
44	Moses	1735	778	Nancy Ann	1786
285	Moses	1748	6052	Nancy Jane	1925
236	Moses	1752	2765	Nancy Pollard	1847
599	Moses	c1761	1220	Nancy S.	1817
503	Moses	1764	231	Nanny/Nancy	1744
703	Moses	1765	1484	Nathan	1801
587	Moses	1767	2876	Nathan	c1832
716	Moses	1767	2422	Nathan Clifford	1857
189	Moses	1774	1345	Nathan Palmer	1824
590	Moses	1774	309	Nathaniel	1744
719	Moses	1774	723	Nathaniel	1781
773	Moses	1776	5823	Nathaniel H.	1883
575	Moses	1783	2705	Nathaniel J.	1841
736	Moses	1788	2998	Nathaniel Leroy	1898
1001	Moses Jr.	1793	885	Nathaniel Lewis	1820
1145	Moses	1794	1475	Nathaniel P.	1825
1373	Moses	1794	1602	Nathaniel Jr.	1865
551	Moses Jr.	1800	267	Nehemiah	1752
1150	Moses	1805	1237	Nehemiah	1789
376	Moses Duty	1778	2405	Nellie	1856
888	Moses Duty Jr.	1826	5575	Nellie	___
1595	Moses Duty	1849	5770	Nellie	1882
2329	Moses Franklin	1848	5760	Nellie/Ella F.	1854
2013	Moses P.	1845	5377	Nellie Imogene	1886
2228	Moses T.	1845	5032	Nellie Luella	1881
1407	Moses Warren	1821	2445	Nellie M.	1865
5844	Muriel	___	5727	Nellie M.	1878
1434	Myra	1804	2980	Nelly S. (Nora)	1859
2735	Myra	1846	2727	Nelson	1846
5021	Myra Lillian	___	5794	Nettie	1883

KEY #	NAME	BORN	KEY #	NAME	BORN
5060	Nettie May	1868	1358	Permalia	1830
2042	Neva Hunter	____	2473	Persis Ann	1840
5065	Neva Hunter	1882	5479	Persis E.	____
1505	Nicholas	1807	295	Peter	1758
3023	Nicholas M.	1877	872	Peter C.	1822
3035	Nora	1890	2080	Peter C.F.	1828
5690	Nora	____	370	Peter Clements	1794
6068	Norma	1916	1419	Peter T.	1801
5471	Norma Brock	____	212	Phebe	1725
6071	Norma Jean	1929	118	Phebe	c1764
3062	Norma Louis	1926	365	Pheobe	1767
			1487	Phebe	1809
			415	Phebe	1818
5320	Ola Lois	1882	1381	Phebe	____
419	Olive	1808	2110	Pheobe	1839
1324	Olive	1824	2887	Phebe	1840
1675	Olive	____	5368	Phoebe Loretta	1891
2744	Olive	1846	3071	Philadelphia	____
1326	Olive Ann	1833	6	Philip	1647/8
1676	Olive F.	____	23	Philip	1678
3049	Olive Laird	1905	67	Philip	1695
2218	Oliver D.	c1848	60	Philip	1713
443	Oliver Perry	1826	122	Philip	1745
2604	Orange	1840	224	Philip	1755
3097	Orlando	1832	561	Philip	1762
2109	Orinda P.	1837	600	Philip	c1763
2442	Orville	c1847	1111	Philip	1806
1645	Orville E.	1856	5231	Philip L.	1885
1632	Orvis Abbott	1859	787	Philip Redington	1814
2334	Otis Fillmore	1848	112	Philip S.	1745
1064	Otis Robertson	1809	5468	Philip Wayne	1928
			154	Phineas	1735
			556	Phineas Ashley	1807
428	Paris, Rev	1825	5442	Phylis Alberta	1931
287	Patience	1752	769	Polly	c1771
1514	Patricia A.	c1840	626	Polly	1778
6062	Paul	1903	643	Polly	1780
5465	Pauline Esther	1923	1481	Polly	1794
617	Percy/Piercy	1790	1791	Polly	1794
3039	Perley	1899	739	Polly	1800
5787	Perley Acton	1877	362	Polly/Mary	1806
691	Perley Marsh	____	1058	Polly	1809
1366	Perley Marsh	1822	1311	Polly	1809
2001	Perley W.	1823	992	Polly	____

INDEX ROWELL NAMES

KEY #	NAME	BORN	KEY #	NAME	BORN
1785	Polly Clement	1803	1550	Richard S.	1833
1481	Polly R.	1794	6080	Rita May	1933
			6120	Robert	——
65	Rachel	1725/6	3000	Robert Clare	1908
1376	Rachel	1799	1257	Robert D.	1821
653	Rachel	1801	709	Robert Emerson	1779
1354	Rachel	1822	5181	Robert George	——
1491	Rachel Annis	1799	6077	Robert Lee	1931
1379	Ralph	——	3063	Robert Lee	1932
5748	Ralph Harold	1879	712	Roda	1769
3033	Ralph King	1884	1299	Rodney	c1805
2434	Ralph Robert	1880	2497	Rodney	——
1380	Ranson	c1827	5496	Rodney Wallace	1893
3055	Raymond C.	1897	2585	Roland	1849
82	Rebecca	1714	840	Rose E.	——
1398	Rebecca	1789/90	980	Roselind E.	1859
2641	Rebecca	c1828	1793	Roswell	c1800
5076	Rebecca Augusta	1864	5112	Roswell	——
2000	Rebecca E.	1835	862	Roxana	1814
1415	Rebecca G.	1792	1504	Roxana	1823
2848	Rebecca Judith	1842	5884	Rubin Lewis	1889
2076	Rebecca Kimball	1843	2835	Ruel E.	1840
1123	Rebekah	1812	1384	Rufus	c1803
6070	Reginald Lewis	1921	1008	Rufus	1814
5729	Rena L.	1887	133	Rufus Viney	1793
781	Rensclair	c1812	1157	Ruhanan	1804
2100	Reuben P.	1817	68	Ruth	1696
230	Rhoda	1743	208	Ruth	1735
90	Rice	1714	220	Ruth	1742
261	Rice	1734	501	Ruth	1761
637	Rice	1789	639	Ruth	1792
2403	Rice	1852	913	Ruth	——
627	Rice Richardson	1782	1153	Ruth	1797
190	Richard	c1775	1004	Ruth	1804
368	Richard	1770	1258	Ruth Ann	1824
1206	Richard	1812	2142	Ruth Ann	1844
1207	Richard	1814	6037	Ruth Eleanor	1919
2611	Richard	c1839	1062	Ruth Hoyt	1805
1226	Richard C.	1829	6104	Ruth Olive	——
2338	Richard Clark	1865			
616	Richard F.	1788			
866	Richard H.	1821	1159	Sabina	1808
6030	Richard Irving	1899	5085	Sadie Webster	1875
3032	Richard Martin	1892	768	Sally	c1768

INDEX ROWELL NAMES

KEY #	NAME	BORN	KEY #	NAME	BORN
795	Sarah E.	1833	331	Stephen	1779
2703	Sarah E.	1836	1400	Stephen	1794
2433	Sarah Eliza	1871	849	Stephen	1802
788	Sarah Elizabeth	1817	2102	Stephen	1822
807	Sarah Elizabeth	1837	2961	Stephen Franklin	1878
2239	Sarah Ellen	1842	1330	Stephen Sargent	1827
935	Sarah F.	1846	690	Stratton	1791
611	Sarah H.	1773	1360	Stratton	____
1627	Sarah Hill	1854	6072	Sula Jane	1941
2714	Sarah Irene	1847	2842	Sumner	1844
1369	Sarah J.	1828	2822	Sumner	1847
2599	Sarah J.	c1856	436	Susan	____
2757	Sarah Jane	1837	442	Susan	1824
1591	Sarah Jane	1839	2170	Susan	____
2851	Sarah Jane	1841	445	Susan Ann	1838
2940	Sarah Jennie	1861	2020	Susan Frances	1829
1009	Sarah/Sally L.	1817	886	Susan M.	1822
5817	Sarah Lillian	1890	74	Susanna	1707
1294	Sarah M.	c1837	213	Susanna	1725
2733	Sarah M.	1842	403	Susanna	1805
5000	Sarah W.	____	1579	Susanna	1850
2589	Savelle	1842	1197	Susannah	1813
6031	Sayward Franklin	1900	5365	Sybil Ann	1882
2928	Selena May	1864	2354	Sybil Eunice	1848
1288	Sen.	1819	5356	Sybil Eunice	1867
2352	Seneca Paige	1843	2805	Sybil S.	1869
353	Sherburne B.	1788	5357	Sydney	1872
830	Sherburne B.	____	1545	Sylvester	1831
837	Sherburne B. Jr.	1824	1605	Sylvia E.	1854
5586	Sidney Forest	1885			
1490	Silas	1793			
1265	Siloam	1806			
1337	Siloam/Sylvanus	1804	1724	Tameson	1828
325	Simeon	1768	900	Thaddeus M.H.	c1816
782	Simeon	1822	3072	Theodore B.	1872
531	Simmons	1783	3052	Theodore Earl	1882
120	Simon	1768	6135	Theodore H.	____
406	Simon	____	1	Thomas	1594
2745	Simon M.	1847	4	Thomas	1644
2627	Smith A.	1828	27	Thomas	1676
2346	Spaulding	1831	50	Thomas	1702/3
5329	Stanley	1882	76	Thomas	1702/3
2187	Stella Mae	1882	105	Thomas	1718/9
513	Stephen	c1764	217	Thomas	1737

INDEX ROWELL NAMES

KEY #	NAME	BORN	KEY #	NAME	BORN
310	Thomas	1748	6111	Wallie	1873
171	Thomas	1750	1662	Walter	1869
504	Thomas	1767	5390	Walter	____
535	Thomas	____	2767	Walter Aaron	1856
1479	Thomas	1796	2718	Walter Adams	1868
1021	Thomas	1799	814	Walter Belfour	1838
2889	Thomas	1848	1637	Walter Everett	1876
5845	Thomas	____	5285	Walter Gifford	1884
1788	Thomas Asbury	1811	954	Walter Henry	1859
765	Thomas B.	1764	1447	Walter P.	1815
2787	Thomas Barton	1843	974	Walter Perry	____
2021	Thomas Clark	1829	1680	Walter Raymond	1896
6095	Thomas Edgar	1915	3061	Walter Raymond Jr.	1925
1413	Thomas M.	c1830	5561	Walter Stark	1878
2070	Thompson	1826	5712	Walter Wood	1878
2902	Thompson	____	1635	Ward Adams	1868
1142	Timothy	1812	831	Warren	c1819
2240	Timothy Bryant	1845	1583	Warren C.	1876
1050	Timothy Dwight	1817	2275	Warren H.	1844
783	Timothy H.	c1827	1260	Warren Rayburn	1829
1494	Trueworthy	1802	2421	Warren R. Jr.	1856
1292	Tyler M.	1832	5865	Warren Silas	1866
			1436	Washington	1808
			2103	Watey	1824
1518	Urbane F.	1865	5370	Watson Joshua	1873
			6098	Wayne Daniels	1925
			2450	Welma E.	1857
2	Valentine	1622	5383	Wesley Alexander	1873
21	Valentine	1674	956	Wesley D.	1844
58	Valentine	1708	813	Whittemore	1833
150	Valentine	1727/8	2886	Wiear Leavitt	1838
155	Valentine	1738	958	Wilber F.	____
175	Valentine	1760	1600	Wilber Fiske	1842
512	Valentine	1763	5380	Wilber James	1873
5578	Verne	____	5852	Wilber Nathan	1867
2254	Victoria A.	1840	5364	Wilber Spaulding	1880
1280	Viola	c1837	5025	Wilfred Asa	1871
5203	Virginia	1915	2984	Will	____
			1640	Will Marcellus	1859
			1293	Willard Converse	1830
3066	Walden	1839	51	William	1705
6111	Walden Thompson	1873	161	William	1735/6
2190	Wallace Arthur	1888	180	William	1740

KEY #	NAME	BORN	KEY #	NAME	BORN
221	William	1745	1412	William Lyman	1828
125	William	c1749	2251	William Lyman	1834
269	William	1755	5243	William L. Jr.	1864
525	William	1770	2890	William Nathan	1850
536	William	___	6092	William N.	1895
636	William	___	2438	William Owen	1865
644	William	1780	2820	William Parkman	1843
647	William	1791	1530	William R.	1844
1075	William	1797	1522	William Reddington	1842
1431	William	1798	5311	William Sherman	1864
1077	William	___	5358	William Spaulding	1877
1158	William	1805	2770	William Stinson	1863
1063	William	1807	5075	William Tenney	1862
1301	William	1811	2008	William Tilton	1843
554	William	1812	2448	William W.	1852
414	William	1816	2463	William W.	1861
1256	William	1819	1612	William Jr.	1848
1353	William	1820	3081	Willis S./Samuel	c1864
889	William	1826	1616	Wilmot C.	1882
3095	William	1827	3127	Winchester	c1827
2107	William	1833	5246	Winifred	___
2229	William	1847	2716	Winslow H.	1853
2737	William	1853			
2374	William	1842			
5071	William	1860	755	Zebedee	1782
5117	William	___	1462	Zebedee Jr.	1808
5467	William Brown	1926	2808	Zebedee	___
1240	William C.	1812	1266	Zelda	1808
2625	William C.	1857	1272	Zelima	1813
1670	William E.	c1886	2026	Ziba Aretus	1840
2593	William Edwin	1850	1011	Ziba Morse	1798
2305	William Franklin	1838	1264	Zuar	1804
6091	William Grant	1904			
441	William H.	1822			
2602	William H.	1836			
2005	William H.	1837			
1232	William H.	1840			
2724	William Harrison	1838			
1322	William Henry	1822			
1331	William Henry	1828			
2841	William Henry	1842			
2726	William Henry	1843			
1621	William Henry	1845			
2071	William Kimball	1829			

NAME	KEY #	NAME	KEY #
Abbott, Arthur A.	2987	Arnold, Hattie M.	3066
Charity	1205	Joshua	1473
Cynthia	1200	Melville	2735
Daniel E.	2988	Atherton, Alice	2997
Frank	1632	Atkins, Francelia	2613
George Frank	2241	John J.	704
Jabez	505	Atkinson, John Parker	2891
Lydia	505	Atwood, Mary	663
Minnie E.	1632	Sophia	2815
Moses	1200, 1205	Austin, Isabel	2140
Philip	810	Joseph M.	2141
Reta	2988	Avery, Mary	1474, 1475
Mr.	2888	Mary Ann	2346
Able, C.L.	6053	Ayer, Bethel Sarah	1462
Abner, Margaret	6045	Thursey	2886
Adams, Elizabeth	78	Ayers, Mary F.	1458
Harriet A.	1501	Ruth	22
James	1500	Thankful	780
Lucy Ann	376	Thursday	2886
Mr.	1313		
Adler, Lizzie	1635		
Albertson, Margaret	377		
Aldrich, Jane M.	1513	Bacon, Eda	133
Allen, Mrs. Eunice	637	Mrs. Hannah	1450
Frances S.	2540	Jabez	133
Martha	323	Josiah	1449
Mr.	1358	Bailey, Fanny	3117
Ally, Mrs. Sally	637	Mr.	3099
Ambrose, Dorothy	29	Baird, John	2345
Ames, Arvilla	2818	Baker, Mehitable	97
Anderson, Carolyn	5468	Polly	1216
Isabella	1292	Sidney	5766
Andressen, Mr.	5028	Balknap, Sarah	129
Andrews, Charles L.	2274	Ball, Almon	2346
Ella H.	2271	Martha	2346
Frederick L.	5471	Mary Martha	1715
Andrus, Clarence G.	5729	Ballou, Cordelia	1208
Annis, John b.	411	Otis	1208
Appleton, Bolinda	870	Banfield, Abigail	551
Robert	870	George	553
Arnold, Donald S. Jr.	6076	Mary	1214
Eunice T.	1474	Banfill, Rosaline A.	1306

INDEX OTHER NAMES

INDEX OTHER NAMES

NAME	KEY #	NAME	KEY #
Bowker, Maria E.	963	Bryant, Sarah	1142
Bowles, Mr.	289	Buck, Eliza	1396
Boyer, Edward	2406	Bucklin, Elizabeth	637
Bracket, Araxzene I.	1298	Bundy, Margaret	2338
Samuel	1298	Bunker, James	2444
Bradlee, Thomas	2992	Buntin, Mary	5070
Brandige, Olive	1711	Lydia M.	2922
Brandingham, Charles H.	5764	William	5070
Brink, Ellen A.	1510	Bunting, Ann	665
Brennen, Mr.	5060	Burbank, Stephen	762
Brighton, Polly	882	Burch, Georgianna P.	443
Bristol, Avis Collins	2875	Burgess, Hellen A.	3111
Brock, Georgianne	2456	Burke, Mary Ann	1070
Brock, Margaret	1070	Burnham, C. Samuel	862
Viola J.	2961	Burns, Almeda W.	2806
Brooks, Joseph W.	1512	Samuel	2806
Broussean, Elizabeth	5357	Burrell, Harriet	865
Brower, Isabel	1637	Burroughs, Olynthus, Dr.	5300
Brown, Abbie F.	2726	Burtch, Edee	690
Abraham	30	Olive	690
Anna Augusta	1602	Burton, Clyde L.	5340
Bethia	30, 55	David	999
Caroline A.	1412	Bush, Mike	1097
Eleanor Jane	1353	Buswell, Joseph	8
Elizabeth	1237	Butler, Briggs	639
Eliphelet	1237	Butterfield, Mary	1461
Emanuel	1362	Buxton, Anna	202
George	939	James	202
Jacob	70		
Joseph	1412		
Josiah	366	Cadman, William	653
Lettie May	2626	Cady, Jane J.	1600
Martha	929	Caldwell, Clarnece	5345
Mary	180, 366	Joseph	5883
Mary L.	2141	Mr.	2753
Mildred A.	2455	Calif, William	162
Moses	731	Cammet, John, Gen'l	272
Nathaniel	742	Camp, Annis	763
Ruth	590	Campbell, Catherine	269
Samuel	180	Capp, Martha	4, 8
Sewell	929	Carlisle, C.D.	5585
William V/C	1356	Carlock, Lavina	2301
Wilder	1602	Carlton, Hannah	43
Mr.	5203	Jonathan	53

INDEX OTHER NAMES

NAME	KEY #	NAME	KEY #
Daggett, Eda	5706	Dow, Lorenzo	1545
Dahlgren, Arthur L.	5330	Lydia	26
Damon, Merritt	425	Sarah C.	1545
Danforth, Sara	767	Drake, John S.	877
Daniel, Lou	3034	Dressler, Mr.	5200
Persis	1204	Dudley, Trueworthy	611
Darling, Daniel	1531	Dunlap, Ernest R.	5721
Isodore	1531	Dunning, Robert	637, 640
Davis, Eloise R.	6061	Sally	637
Eunice, Mrs.	637	Duntin, Elsie D.	5111
Hannah	36	Durfee, Joseph	1655
John	23, 36	Ruth W.	1655
Joseph	22	Durkee, Eliza H.	1407
Lucy	847	Payne	881
Martha A.	3117	Durrell, Mary	2825
Mary/Polly	352	Naomi	2825
Mary Amanda	1328	Dustin, Abigail, Mrs.	123
Merrill	3118	Benjamin	375
Robert	1326	Hannah	320
Sarah	23	Jonathan	1474, 1475
Day, Sarah	51	Lucinda	1475
Dayley, Mr.	436	Malinda May	1476
Dawin, Lovina	2826	Moses	895
Dean, Isabella	5380	Paul	288
Deggendorf, Emma F.	2872	Sarah	288
Hugo	2872	Duston, Sarah	895
Delano, Ira L.	426	Dutton, Amasa	886
Dennis, Sara Miller	2930	John	884
William	2930	John G.	885
Denton, Minnie L.	5311	Susanna	885
Diamond, Emma Forster, Mrs.	1595	Duty, Hannah	125
Dickinson, Isabell	2305	Moses	125
Dickey, Janette	750	William	114
Dinsmore, Betsy B., Mrs.	753		
Isaac A.	1442		
Frank	2849	Eastman, Benjamin	773
Robert	753	Charlotte Ann	2040
Dolbier, Mary Ann	2749	Charles B.	2503
Donnelly, Catherine	3033	Elizabeth	323
Dorman, Susannah	2008	Jamieson	773
Dorn, Martha	2837	Jonathan	323
Dow, Andrew J.P.	2854	Lucretia Abigail	2901
George Washington	2855	Philatus H.	2486
Kate Isabel	2857	Sally	726

INDEX OTHER NAMES

NAME	KEY #	NAME	KEY #
Kittridge, Mary S.	1345	LeGro, David	2251
Klein, August	2872	Martha A.	2251
Knapp, Robert	3040	Leighton, Joseph	1198
Knight, Dorothy	27	Lemfest, Mary Ann	2070
Mary	2832	Thomas	2070
Knowlton, Frank B.	2562	Lemmon, Joseph	15
Knox, Cynthia	1606	Lenox, Belle	2278
Kostowlatsky, Lily	5841	Leslie, Mina Belle	2749
Zuelema	5841	Robert	2670
		Samuel C.	2749
		Lewis, Susan H.	2708
		Libby, Mabel Olive	6060
Labodie, Francis	2596	Lingle, Myrtle M.	5305
Ladd, Adelia	384	Linscott, Susannah	131
Daniel	630	Little, Arthur S. Jr.	5470
Laird, Eva	1636	William Coffin	157
Lake, Esther	1000	Littlefield, Phebe	513
John	1004	Littleford, Martha Jane	1458
Lane, Gilbert E.	5242	Susan	132
Lancaster, Daniel	26	Locke, Edwin	1048
Langchamp, Jeanne	5381	Lodbell, Eunice	1473
Langley, Milton	2720	Long, Stephen	225, 227
Langmaid, Jennie	1633	Loomer, Maude	5779
Frank	1633	Loomis, Warren	2845
LaRue, Jacob S.	2023	Lord, Abram L.	2742
Lathrop, Amanda F.	783	Abram Tapley	794
Elizabeth C.	2240	James	668
Latimore, Edward	7	John, Rev.	668
Laverly, Eva L.	5316	Rachel	4
Lazenby, Lavina	1359	Weston P.	2962
Lear, John	859	Mr.	2543
Joseph	855	Lougee, Mary A.	900
Mary	855	Robert	900
Leathe, Sophia	658	Loverin, Ebenezer Jr.	845
Leavitt, Anne	1483	Lovering, Dolly	366
Caroline	1275	Lovett, George F.	5727
Dolly/Dorothy	311	Lowe, Bessie Mae	3052
John	1481	Sylvanus	3052
Jonathan	503	Lowell, Dennis	2741
Lydia	1481	Hannah	218
Margaret	2342	Lowis, Hannah D.	3113
Nancy	503	Lyford, Elijah W.	2337
Nathaniel	1275	Lyman, Frances C.	1601
Sally	647	Jasper	1601

INDEX OTHER NAMES

NAME	KEY #	NAME	KEY #
Millett, Alma	5763	Munro, Widow Margaret	5357
Mitchell, David	2781	Murch, Etta S.	3021
Jane (Jennie)	2781	George F.	3024
Nathaniel	5731	Murrey, May	171
Montgomery, Rachel	1432		
Robert	1432		
Mr.	119		
Wealthy	1625	Nash, Mary	1240
Moon, Jane	1455	Narbonee, Maud	5490
Moore, Bradford	2986	Neal, James, Capt.	545
Hiram	654	Lydia J.	1124
Margaret Bradford	2986	Nancy	545
Mary	649	Newell, Ella G.	2434
Sally	985	William G.	5339
Mr.	1307	Mr.	290
Moray, Polly	333	Newhall, Henry Willard	2708
Morden, Samuel	1467	Susan Augusta	2708
Morell/Morrell - see Morrill		Newman, Hannah	322
Morgan, Deborah	38	Newton, Sarah A.	954
Morrill, Abraham	6	Nichols, Hannah	668
Andrew	105	Sarah	50
Daniel	75	Noble, James K. Jr.	6071
Elinor	75	Norcross, Roxanne F.	1275
Jacob	105	Mr.	630
Lydia	914	Northfield, Abigail	1237
Nathaniel	749	Norton, Caleb	7
Polly	547	Eleanor	2745
Sally	888	Noyes, Alexander N.	792
Sarah	6, 105	James Solon	1606
Morse, Benjamin	159, 161	Lizzie	1606
Edward	65		
Hannah	161		
Judith	309		
Maria	936	Ober, Betsy P.	1489
Ruth	159	Olney, Albert C.	5306
Moses, Benjamin	633	Olson, Minnie	5363
Thomas	267	Ordway, Esther	580
Moulton, Abigail S.	1005	Mary H.	872
Jacob	1005	Mr.	362
Mary Keller	24	Osburn, Eliza	1093
Moxley, Abigail	885	Osgood, Benjamin	216
Thomas K.	1585	Christopher	1
Muchmore, James	268	Clementine	787
Mullickin, Robert	24	Margaret (Fowler)	1

NAME	KEY #	NAME	KEY #
Smith, Elisha	276	Steeves, Mr.	5391
Ellen Frances	1296	Stetson, Alice	5842
Elmer L.	6142	Mary Florance	2430
Etta	2736	Stevens, Abigail	50
Francis	5328	Bertha	5586
Fuller	1371	Elizabeth	105
George W.	2936	Hannah 26, 75,	1440
Marion C.	2936	Henry	2357
Mary	1436	Hepzibah	505
Mary, Mrs.	669	Hiram	1113
Mehitable	336, 612	Judith	73
Reuben, G.	2940	Lula J.	5709
Sade	1727	Martha Lord	1426
Samuel, Capt.	1296	Mary	1150
Stanley B.	5322	Nathaniel	1426
Sula A.	1602	Polly	1110
Tiphona	1595	Roger	50
William	7, 852	Sarah	1426
Snell, John	382	Sarah M.	1550
Snow, Alice May	2432	William, Capt.	1150
Mary	2843	Stewart, Sarah M.	1120
Samuel B.	2432	Stickland, Mary	337
Snyder, Angeline	1723	Stickney, Mary	2071
Southmaid, Elinuyer	1730	Stockton, George	3014
Southwick, Edward	562	Stone, John M. Jr.	2993
Mary	5852	Lizzie M.	2008
Soule, Zetta E.	2737	Simon	2008
Sowards, Mr.	2500	Storer, Arville	1337
Spaulding, Alice O.	5020	Stover, Mary Ann	1150
John F.	1228	William, Capt.	1150
Mary S.	1290	Stow, Dorothy	59
Phineas	1216	Stratton, Enoch	1352
Rufus	1215	Straw, Dorothy	59
Sarah	750	William	59
Sybil Eunice	1216	Strong, John	1354
William	750	Mr.	772
Speer, Mildred P.	5062	Sullivan, Elizabeth	3033
Spencer, William F.	5341	Shirley Ann	3064
Spinney, Sarah	627	Thomas	3033
Spooner, Martha	2401	Sutherland, John E.	5044
Stanbus, J. Louis	2327	Minnie B.	5040
Starbird, Rose Ann	2783	Swallow, Betsy	1792
Starke, Mary E.	2560	Mina	2625
Steenberg, Alma	2865	Swasey, Henry	1415

www.ingramcontent.com/pod-product-compliance
Lightning Source LLC
Chambersburg PA
CBHW070551270326
41926CB00013B/2279

* 9 7 8 0 7 8 8 4 0 4 2 1 4 *